The
Disordered
Body

SUNY series in Medical Anthropology
Setha Low, editor

The Disordered Body

Epidemic Disease and Cultural Transformation

Suzanne E. Hatty
and James Hatty

State University of New York Press

CBB 7014

Published by
State University of New York Press, Albany

For information, address State University of New York
Press, State University Plaza, Albany, N.Y., 12246

Production by Diane Ganeles
Marketing by Dana Yanulavich

Library of Congress Cataloging-in-Publication Data

Hatty, Suzanne.
    The disordered body : epidemic disease and cultural transformation
/ Suzanne E. Hatty and James Hatty.
        p.   cm. — (SUNY series in medical anthropology)
    Includes bibliographical references and index.
    ISBN 0-7914-4365-5 (hardcover : alk. paper). — ISBN 0-7914-4366-3
(pbk. : alk. paper)
    1. Epidemics—History. 2. Epidemics—Social aspects. 3. Medical
anthropology. 4. Body, Human. I. Hatty, James.
II. Title. III. Series.
RA649.H28 1999
614.4'9—dc21   99-17302
                                                                CIP

10 9 8 7 6 5 4 3 2 1

Contents

Part I. The Body: Constructs and Constraints

Chapter 1.   Imaging the Body   3

Chapter 2.   Banishing the "Unclean" Body   31

Part II. Apocalyptic Angst

Chapter 3.   Florence: A "City of the Wicked"   61

Chapter 4.   Disordered Bodies in Abundance   81

Chapter 5.   Castigating the Flesh   101

Chapter 6.   Regulating the Bodies of Citizens   129

Chapter 7.   The Diseased Body Confronts Medicine   163

Part III. *Fin-de-siècle* Forebodings

Chapter 8.   The Danger of Touch:
              The Body and Social Distance   193

Chapter 9.   Corporeal Catastrophe:
              Bodies "Crash" and Disappear   233

Notes   257

Works Cited   319

Index   345

The Body: Constructs and Constraints

[A man's] soul is a helpless prisoner chained hand
and foot in the body, compelled to view reality not
directly but only through its prison bars . . .

—Socrates[1]

I *live* my body. . . . The body is what I immediately
am . . . I *am* my body to the extent that I *am*.

—Jean-Paul Sartre [2]

❧ CHAPTER 1

Imaging the Body

. . . [work] on the history of the human body, and images
of the body, has exerted an important influence on sociological research . . . it has proved an invaluable resource
for sociologists by demonstrating that human bodies have
been invested with a wide range of shifting and unstable
meanings.[1]

It is not simply that the body is represented in a variety
of ways according to historical, social, and cultural exi-
gencies while it remains basically the same; these factors
actively produce the body as a body of determinate type.[2]

The celebrated pronouncement of Descartes—"I think, therefore I am"—marked a major turning point in the history of the
body.[3] In an elaboration of his thesis, he claimed that human beings
are composites of two kinds of substance: mind and body. He
accorded primacy to the mind, or "rational soul," and proposed that
the body be considered "as a machine."[4] Further, he declared that
minds are indivisible whereas bodies are infinitely divisible. This
ran counter to the view of the soul/body relationship that had prevailed in western Europe throughout the Middle Ages. Religious
and community discourses had been predicated on the belief that
the soul and the body were inextricably linked—they were indivisible.[5] However, this conviction was undermined to some extent by
events that occurred during the late fifteenth and the sixteenth
centuries.[6]

It remained for Descartes to enunciate this revolutionary view
of the human body: ". . . I consider man's body as being a machine,

3

so built and composed of bones, nerves, muscles, veins, blood and skin. . . ."[7] For the first time, the human body was defined as an object. For the first time, it was implied that it could be adjusted and manipulated as if it were a device such as a clock. And, to a great extent, this perception of the body remained inherent in philosophical, scientific, and medical discourses until the latter part of the twentieth century.

It is only in the last few decades that there has been a reappraisal of the place of the body in social theory. Amongst the many issues now being canvassed are the ways in which society shapes ideas about socially-appropriate bodies, the construction of the gendered body, the control mechanisms deployed by society for the management of citizens' bodies, and the relationship between the body and identity. In this chapter we examine some of these issues against the background of contemporary developments in the theory of the body, and the emergence of the "modern body." We also include an overview of the issues canvassed in the chapters which follow. In addition, we identify our objectives for the overall work, and outline the way in which we apply current social theory to reach our conclusions.

Rediscovering the Body

For much of the twentieth century, the human mind was accorded primacy over the body. As a consequence, it was generally accepted that the human intellect could be relied upon to create genuine progress for the whole community. And through science and technology, human ingenuity would elevate society to a utopian milieu free from human ills and miseries. This dismissal of the importance of the lived body reached its most absurd level when *Time* magazine nominated a machine as man of the year for 1982.[8]

From the 1970s onward, people began to recognize the limits of the promise that human ingenuity could solve all problems. There was an acknowledgment that this promise had not been, and was not likely to be, fulfilled. This was evident from the fact that although science and technology had created technical solutions to many problems, it was unable to resolve many others. Space travel and sophisticated electronic devices were the stuff of headlines, but many of the problems associated with everyday lived experience persisted. In particular, public confidence in medical science was shaken by the obvious inability of research scientists and medical practitioners to produce cures or adequate treatment for many new and old diseases. It was realized, finally, that conventional medicine could no longer be relied upon for "magic bullet" cures for all diseases. This created a heightened sense of the vulnerability of the body, and a degree of alienation from medical orthodoxy amongst many in the community. It also raised the prospect that there may be no means of coping with infections such as HIV/AIDS, and that the spread of these diseases may even threaten whole nations in some areas.[9] Such threats challenged the pattern established in the 1960s of sexual openness and freedom, and caused a dramatic rethinking of what could be considered "safe" bodily practices.

With this perception of the increased vulnerability of the individual to illness and death, many within the general community began to take a greater interest in their own bodies.[10] Maintaining a healthy life-style by watching diet and by physical exercise were elevated to new heights. The body became a project as people sought to preserve good health and to enshrine this in a perfectly presented body shape. To ward off disease, an increasing number of people turned to holistic medicine, to preventative medical treatment regimes, and to so-called natural medicine, a practice no longer considered the exclusive domain of "alternative lifestylers." Today, such revolutionary approaches to health and medicine are being adopted by many in mainstream society who consider such treatments as complementary to conventional medical therapies. Even amongst medical practitioners, there is a growing minority who practice both types of medicine, accepting that the lived body of the patient should be "listened to."

At much the same time, a new and expanding focus emerged within sociology on the body and bodily practices. Two important early works in this new genre were Brian Turner's *The Body and Society*, and the three volume work entitled *Fragments for A History of the Human Body*, edited by Michel Feher, Ramona Naddaff, and Nadia Tazi.[11] Turner proposed a systematic theory of the body while Feher et al. provided a collection of historical and cross-cultural essays on perceptions of the body. In a later work, Turner commented on the fact that it was only latterly that social theorists had become interested in the body.[12] He pointed out that, in contrast to this lack of interest in the human body within sociology in the past, it "has been accorded a place of central importance in anthropology since the nineteenth century." As a result, the new genre of the sociology of the body was able to draw upon some fundamental contributions from anthropology.[13] The first, according to Turner, was that "human embodiment creates a set of constraints," but at the same time, has a potential which can be realized through "sociocultural development." The second proposition was that there are conflicts and contradictions in issues relating to human sexuality and sociocultural demands. And, finally, these factors impact unevenly according to gender. It was important, therefore, to seek a revaluation of the place of the body in society, taking account of class, culture, and gender.[14] Others believed that there was an even more pressing reason for bringing the body back into serious consideration. O'Neill, for example, foresaw the possibility of a collapse of civilization, and even a real threat to the survival of the human species, unless we "rethink the human body," and "give to history and society a living human shape."[15] He called for a study of the human condition that is designed "to rewrite the human body, [and] to re-inscribe its mind and emotions."[16]

Contemporary Theories of the Body

It was Arthur Frank who noted that although there had been some earlier accounts of the body in social theory, the level of interest and research on the body intensified in the 1980s.[17] He identified three influences which he believed had been instrumental in fostering further research on the body. These he listed as feminism, the pervasive influence of Foucault, and the contradictory impulses of modernity.[18] While still acknowledging the strong influence of Foucault, Frank later reshaped his ideas on the circumstances that had brought the body into greater focus in sociology. Feminism and modernism were still seen as instrumental in promoting the current reconsideration of the body, but the influence of postmodernism was added to Frank's list.[19]

Modernism, according to Arthur Frank, involved two contrasting concepts. First, it drew on ideas of post-Enlightenment positivism, in which the body was viewed as knowable, as something capable of definition in Cartesian terms. The twentieth century, however, introduced a sense of uncertainty about what could be known about the body. Perceptions of the body became much more fluid. In this context, he concludes that the impact of modernism is that it "provides an impetus to study the body, which is the need for some constant in a world of flux, and a problematic of the body: far from becoming a constant, it was subsumed into the flux."[20]

Postmodernism inherited this modernist conflict between the body as a constant in an atmosphere of constant change, and the body as a central element of that flux. Its influence on the burgeoning interest in a sociology of the body produced two distinctly different outcomes: highly theoretical postmodernist theories of the body, and works based on an empirical, minimalist approach to the subject.[21] Clearly, such diversity in approach has produced a very rich body of work on the topic. We do not propose to canvass the full range of theoretical positions stemming from this diversity of approach, but will limit our commentary to the most commonly espoused constructions of the body in current theories of the body.

One of the overarching concepts that informs most recent writing, and which is central to our argument, is that of the relationship between the body and society. This proposes that the body is a sociocultural construct which extends beyond the limits implied by biologism or esentialism. In this context, the body is not only the agency through which the social environment is created, but it is also the surface (or text) upon which is inscribed the range of historical, social, and cultural discourses which prevail in society. As a consequence, human bodies have been invested with a wide range of shifting, and at times, conflicting meanings over time. Concepts of gender and sexuality, concepts of Otherness, and, in turn, definitions of difference, emerge from the sociocultural values which have been dominant in any particular period in history. Similarly, perceptions of the body in general, and the definition of socially appropriate bodily practices, stem from the same shifting sociocultural criteria. Since these issues are relevant to the development of our argument, we offer an overview of some of the most significant perceptions of the body that have evolved through this process.

The Gendered Body

In conventional readings, the basis for gender identity is established at birth, with each child being assigned to the male or female gender on the evidence of bodily differences—his or her genitalia. This decision—so fundamental to modern Western society that it passes as "natural"—is assumed to have a profound influence on the future development and lifestyle of the infant.

Western society has been shaped by the longstanding tradition of dualism on issues of gender, with the categories of male and female being viewed as polarized, as belonging to opposite and unequal categories. At various times this has been projected into a series of binary oppositions such as: masculine/feminine, superior/inferior, rational/irrational, reliable/unpredictable, stronger/weaker, assertive/gentle, and serious/frivolous. These contrasting pairs represent only a few examples of the large set of interrelated and mutually reinforcing dualisms which are diffused throughout Western culture. According to Plumwood, these dualisms form "a fault-line which runs through its entire conceptual system," and reflect the mechanisms of oppression in Western culture.[22] This well-entrenched pattern had its origins in ancient creation myths and the integration of some of these into the traditions of Graeco-Roman and Judeo-Christian cultures. A plethora of religious, medical, and community discourses based on this polarization of gender have been used to legitimate gendered institutions and practices. This has ensured that males have retained a dominant position in the power structures of most Western societies.

It is well-known that the religious discourse of the Christian Church draws on the creation myth of Genesis wherein the woman, Eve, was an afterthought created from Adam. She was also created for him, to dispel his loneliness and be his helper. It followed, according to Christian theologians, that the man was the superior being and the one who should rule. And since, in the same account, it was Eve who led Adam into temptation, man must also be morally superior to the woman. All of this was further consolidated by constructs associated with other figures central to Judeo-Christian beliefs. Anthony Synnott has pointed out that the "gender ideology of Genesis was reinforced in both the Jewish and Christian traditions by the masculinity of the Lord God."[23] Further, all the dominant figures of Jewish history were male, as was the Messiah of the Christian tradition.

Dualism in considerations of gender was also central to the work of many early Greek philosophers. It was the philosophical position of Aristotle, however, which coincided almost precisely with Christian traditions on the gender roles of men and women. Aristotle held that men were stronger, women weaker; men courageous, women cautious; and where women might serve to nurture children, it was the role of man to educate them.[24] Further, he claimed that "the woman is as it were an impotent male," and that the female character should be viewed "as being a sort of natural deficiency." In effect, a woman was a "defective" man. Because the views of Aristotle on women coincided closely with the underlying patriarchal and misogynist stance of Christian theologians of the

Middle Ages, his influence was very great. It underpinned much of the religious discourse which prevailed in the late medieval and early Modern eras, and, in many instances, still informs religious dogma in the twentieth century.

However, it was not only philosophical and religious discourses which defined the inferiority of the female sex. Medical discourse also provided support for such an argument. For many centuries, medical theorists, almost always male, insisted that it was the innate biological weaknesses of women which were responsible for their flawed natures. Women were perceived as ruled by their internal, particularly their sexual organs, with little control over their minds or emotions.[25] This approach focused almost exclusively on what was seen as women's primary role—that of procreation. In this they were seen as subservient to men since they could not conceive without the agency of men. Until the Enlightenment era, this argument had less to do with sexuality than with gender roles.

It has been claimed that from ancient times until the seventeenth century, medical theory was informed by the one-sex model.[26] This model viewed the male body as the basis for all anatomical considerations. In terms of sexual characteristics, this enduring discourse held that while the genitals were external to the body and visible in the case of the male, they were internal and hidden for females. However, it also held that they were simply mirror images of each other. As Avicenna put it, ". . . the instrument of generation in woman is the womb and that was created to resemble the instrument of generation in man, namely, the penis and its accompanying parts."[27] This is but one example of the way in which medical theorists considered the genital and reproductive organs of both men and women to be identical in both form and function. Even with blood, semen, milk and other fluids of the body in the one-sex model, precise parallels were drawn as to their functions in male and female bodies.[28] The one-sex model also envisaged that both men and women could gain pleasure from sexual relations, and postulated that there was a causal association between orgasm and conception. The propensity to view the female body as simply a variation of the male body extended further into the realms of medical vocabulary. Laqueur pointed out that, in fact, there was no precise medical nomenclature for the female genitals, or reproductive system generally, until after the Renaissance.

Until the Enlightenment, considerations of gender were more important than those which involved the reproductive system. Gender assignment, with all its social implications, was determined at birth solely on the basis of the external genitalia. That process established, for the lifetime of the infant, whether he was to enjoy the more privileged lifestyle of those of the masculine gender, or whether she was to be relegated to the lesser roles defined within society for those of the feminine gender. In effect the boundaries between male and female were primarily social and political. They served to define social status, and to entrench male supremacy. And in the public sphere, where men expected to dominate, the one-sex model based on the male as standard reinforced the perception "that man is the measure of all things, and woman does not exist as an ontologically distinct category."[29] This gender division still shapes many concepts of space, place, and the division between public and private domains.[30]

According to Laqueur, the one-sex model was gradually displaced in medical theory from the time of the Enlightenment. It lingered on to some extent in community discourse for a longer period. The discovery that there were two categories of sex stemmed from more attention being paid to anatomical differences actually observed rather than those described in traditional works on anatomy. Once the pattern was broken, medical theorists hastened to use the new information to reinforce religious and community discourses which classed women as weak and inferior. At this point, the principles of biologism and essentialism began to define gender roles for women. In the process, medical discourse rejected any causal association between orgasm and conception, and opened the way for the notion of female passivity, and passionless sex. One remarkable consequence of this development was the inversion of gender roles which had previously dominated western European culture. For centuries, women had been depicted as sexually voracious, and as seducers of men who would otherwise have led sober and chaste lives. Within the two-sex model, women were perceived as having little interest in sex, and being more interested in an overall relationship and their family responsibilities. In this construct, women respond to sexual advances, they do not initiate them. Men on the other hand, were portrayed as predators whose sexual needs could barely be restrained—for them, it was claimed, sex was a biological necessity. This new gender identity for men provided a plausible justification for rape which still has currency in some quarters. It also established the notion of men's "natural" promiscuity, which needed to find outlets in extramarital relationships, or in prostitution.

By the nineteenth century, the two-sex model was being

employed, to devastating effect, within medical and scientific spheres in defining gender roles for women in Western society. Some scientists, for example, claimed that women were less evolved than men, and that their reproductive functions drew vital energy from their brains to the detriment of their intellectual develop-ment.[31] Medical writers warned women of the penalties they may pay for using contraceptive techniques to negate their procreative role, or if they engaged in higher education. These consequences, they declared, could include "death or severe illness . . . cancer, mania leading to suicide, and repulsive nymphomania." This type of "scientific" evidence appears to have supported much of the anti-female suffrage movement in the early part of this century. It also fostered the emergence of "women's diseases"—based largely on what Foucault saw as a process of hysterization of the female body.[32]

Dualism continued to inform medical and community dis-courses, and remained central to the pronouncements of social the-orists, well into the twentieth century. The traditional, stereotypi-cal gender identities defined for men and women persisted. The comments of Carl Jung graphically illustrate the point:

> The conscious attitude of women is in general far more exclusively personal than that of man. Her world is made up of fathers and mothers, brothers and sisters, husbands and children. . . . The man's world is the nation, the state, business concerns etc. His family is simply a means to an end, one of the foundations of the state, and his wife is not necessarily *the* woman for him (at any rate not as the woman means it when she says 'my man'). The general means more to him than the personal; his world consists of a multitude of co-ordinated factors, whereas her world, out-side her husband, terminates in a sort of cosmic mist.[33]

The dualism of the masculine/feminine gender has been compli-cated by a further polarization of gender identities—that which defines two types of women. One is represented by the conforming docile body of the "good" woman, the other by the dangerous, sexu-alized body of the "bad" woman. There is nothing particularly novel in this dichotomy. It carries all the hallmarks of the Christian tra-dition encompassing the virgin/whore dichotomy.

Of course, feminists theorists rejected the imposition of dif-ferences implicit in sex/gender divide. Feminists challenged the notion that there were two distinct and separate biological categories, the basis for the biological essentialism underpinning traditional perceptions of the feminine gender. Some writers drew attention to that fact there were more similarities than differences between the two sexes, for example, in terms of biology, males and females are ninety-eight percent chromosomally identical.[34] They also argued that males and females have the same sex hormones in their bodies, the only variation being in the quantities present in each body, and that there is a great variation in physical characteristics within each of the male and female categories—not just in a male/female comparison. Some feminists argued that the gender categories male and female should be viewed as being at "opposing ends of a continuum, with considerable overlapping in the middle."[35] This concept accommodates the blurring of gender identities heightened by the emergence of groups representing the views of the lesbian and gay movements. It also goes some way toward the practices of cross-dressing and, also, gender transformation.[36]

The conclusion reached by many writers on social theory is that, far from biological considerations being the sole determinants of gender identities, "gender inequality is socially constructed."[37] Chris Shilling concluded that gender identities are based on the suppression of bodily similarities and the exaggeration of bodily differences.[38] This is a distortion of the biological evidence, used to perpetuate the stereotypical images of masculinity and femininity. Overall, however, Shilling believed that both biological and social factors interact to produce gender identities.[39] The innate biological characteristics enable each individual to develop through a learning process—typically the "civilizing" process charted by Elias.[40] In this way he or she is able to interact with society, and, in turn, to be shaped by the constraints of society. As Shilling concluded:

> Gendered categories and practices operate as material forces which help to shape and form women's and men's bodies in ways that reinforce particular images of femininity and masculinity. The mind's conceptualization of bodies is closely related to people's experiences of bodies.[41]

The Sexualized Body

Human sexuality is often perceived as a powerful and disruptive force which would pose a threat to social stability if people were allowed complete sexual freedom. From ancient times to the twentieth century, communities have employed various combinations of religion, law, and medical injunctions to constrain sexual activities. This has been most evident in Western communities.

Contemporary works on social theory generally recognize the crucial importance of the sexualized body to the development of a theory of the body. One writer even argues that sexuality has become the ultimate postmodern discourse.[42] It is, however, the ground breaking work of Foucault that resonates through current theories which stress the relationship between power and sexuality.[43] In particular, there is considerable emphasis on the inequality in this relationship. This was clearly expressed by Turner: "The sociology of the body turns out to be crucially a sociological study of the control of sexuality, specifically female sexuality by men exercising patriarchal power."[44] Shilling also acknowledged the same disparity in considerations of the sexualized body, and the long history of patriarchal institutions attempting to channel female sexuality into avenues which served the interests of a male dominated society.[45] Throughout the Middle Ages and the Renaissance, the dominant discourse on sexuality was that of the church which focused on people's physical expression of their sexuality. During the period of the Reformation and the Counter-Reformation, early in the seventeenth century, the emphasis shifted to people's intentions, so that the locus of sexuality shifted from the body to the mind. And in addition to its importance in the religious discourse of that era, sexuality became a significant element of discourses in other fields—politics, law, philosophy, science, and medicine. All provided significant contributions to the formulation of an increasingly repressive attitude towards human sexuality which evolved during this period.

During the eighteenth and nineteenth centuries, according to Shilling, governments became increasingly involved with all sexual practices within the community. Discourse on sexual practices shifted from that involving only the individual to that embracing the population as a whole, in particular, issues of fertility and management of the population base. Shilling identified four major discursive figures associated with this process:

> the 'hysterical woman' (limited and defined by her sexuality); the 'masturbating child' (prone to engage in immoral behaviour which, through the depletion of vital energies, posed dangers to the future health of the race); the 'Malthu-

sian couple' (socialized into bearing children according to the needs of society); and the 'perverse adult' (whose sexual instincts deviated from the legitimate norm).[46]

In this context, the "legitimate norm" was represented by a heterosexual couple, and all other categories were deemed to be deviant. The issue of paramount importance here was the reproductive fitness of the sexualized body to serve the requirements of society.

By the twentieth century, the state had extended its coverage of, and right to intervene in, most fields which had even the most tenuous of links to human sexuality. A new term has been coined to describe this all-encompassing administrative intervention—"bio-politics." O'Neill posited that this is represented by a continuum ranging from an "anatomo-politics of the human body" to a "bio-politics" of the population.[47] He argued that the first form of intervention works through institutions such as educational establishments, prisons, and factories, where the power involved is that of *discipline* and *punishment*. In the second category, power functions through *regulatory controls* on the bodies of citizens. It impacts upon procreation, births, deaths, and physical and mental health. O'Neill concluded that the sexualized body is well suited to be the target of these two strategies of power. He cites Foucault's comment that: "Broadly speaking, at the juncture of the 'body' and the 'population', sex became a crucial target of power organized around the management of life. . . ."[48]

A combination of circumstances which have emerged in the latter part of the twentieth century has ensured a spirited debate on the whole conceptual basis of the sexualized body. Demands for change from the women's movement spearheaded the attack on the status quo. To these were added claims for recognition from lobby groups representing lesbian and gay movements. And, to further blur the boundaries of sexual identity, spokespersons for bisexual groups insist on acceptance of their position in the continuum between male and female sexual identities. Social theorists are also debating these issues. A recent collection of papers, written from a feminist perspective, set out to examine the various ways in which sexual bodies and practices are produced.[49] It focused particularly on the production of lesbian, bisexual, and heterosexual bodies. There are, however, more problematic circumstances that demand a reshaping of ideas about the sexualized body, and the deployment of human sexuality. These include recent innovations in the field of reproductive techniques—reliable methods of contraception, in vitro fertilization, artificial insemination, and highly reliable ways of determining the sex of a child during pregnancy. In addition, with the arrival of HIV/AIDS, the sexualized body has become a lethal object, carrying the threat of endangering not only individuals, but a significant number within any community. And while these are issues for individual and collective concepts of sexuality, they are also central to the construction of the body trope of the "medicalized body."

The Medicalized Body

The medicalized body is an important construct in contemporary theories of the body. In Foucault's terminology, it is the specific object of the "medical gaze." In addition, it is the primary site for the realization of the "power/knowledge" nexus which is central to the role and function of the medical practitioner. The medicalized body can also be viewed as an outcome of the process which has seen a progressive medicalization of the illness experience.[50]

Contemporary social theorists generally acknowledge the importance of the concept of the medicalized body as representing the way in which the medical profession now exercises a largely unchallenged control over the bodies of patients. As self-legitimating professionals, they define the medical norms against which an individual may be compared and classified. And through the hospital system, they mount a process of surveillance that corresponds to Foucauldian "panopticism." Overall, the medical profession exercises considerable influence in the shaping of the socially constructed body. O'Neill claimed that: "the medicalization of the body is a dramatic part of the pervasive industrialization of the body . . . ," and through this, "we are socialized into bringing every stage of the life style—conception, birth, nurturing, sexual conduct, illness, pain, aging, dying—into the administration of bureaucratized centers of professional care. . . ."[51]

During the nineteenth century, the medical profession finally established for itself a position of great power and influence in society. It achieved this by portraying itself as the custodian of specialized and privileged information which could be used to conquer disease. In this same period, new forms of knowledge and power became available in the practice of medicine. Clinical medicine and psychiatry, for example, delivered new technologies of intervention, new policies, and new targets.[52] Medicine also tended to individualize bodies, diseases, symptoms, and all aspects of living and dying.[53]

According to Turner, this produced a "'crisis' in nervous illnesses during the late nineteenth century," with an emphasis on complaints such as "anorexia, agoraphobia, anorexic hysteria, and virgin's disease."[54] These were among the ailments attributable to women's weaker constitutions—the stereotypical "women's" complaints. Medical categorization of this kind reinforced the dominant Victorian era perception that women possessed fragile bodies, a concept which one writer has claimed was internalized by the middle class women of the time.[55] She noted that these women took to their beds regularly, swooned, and perceived themselves as unable to eat, so confirming the medical stereotype of "delicate" females. This situation was exacerbated by the widespread prescription of opiates for women by medical practitioners.[56]

In his seminal work on the power and influence of the medical profession, Turner drew attention to the importance of medical categorization, resulting as it can, in stigmatization and exclusion.[57] He also highlighted the proliferation within medical discourse of "women's" complaints and the accent on hysteria in the nineteenth century. He noted that hysteria was considered as being caused by a malfunctioning of the womb, and hence a condition peculiar to women.[58] One way of dealing with this problem in the nineteenth century was to perform a hysterectomy. Even the natural functions of menstruation and pregnancy were treated as conditions requiring medical attention.[59] The medicalized body of the female became, and remains, the target for intensive investigation and surveillance by the medical profession.

There is ample evidence that medical practitioners in the twentieth century still perceive women to be psychologically and socially vulnerable and to need their specialized attention. Turner suggests that there is even a difference in the "vocabulary of illness" which is applied to women and men.[60] In the medical ideology of the late twentieth century, women's disorders are still widely categorized as being psychogenic in character and related to their neurotic behaviors and reproductive functions. Yet, Synnott cites the results of recent surveys of women which show that their views about their own bodies and their natural functions are at odds with those articulated in medical texts and medical practice.[61] He argues that these results show that medical science is not gender-neutral, is not always objective, and is inclined to be oppressive toward women, with significant negative social consequences.

The medicalized body has become even more problematic as we approach the end of the twentieth century. An ever increasing number of high technology developments such as nuclear medicine, CAT scans, artificial insemination, organ transplants, and new pharmaceutical products, widens the scope for more diagnostic and surgical interventions and treatment regimes. The shadow of unnecessary surgical procedures, and excessive intervention to prolong life simply because the technology is available, hangs over the medicalized body of the late twentieth century. With the increasingly successful application of organ transplant techniques, the question of the ownership of the body under treatment must arise. Perceptions of the medicalized body have become exceedingly complex.

The Cartesian Body

The image described by Foucault as "Man-the-Machine" is essentially the Cartesian body.[62] The paramount examples of the deployment of this construct in the twentieth century are to be found in medicine and science. The medicalized body is viewed by the medical "gaze" as an intricate machine rather than as a social entity. It is capable of being adjusted, repaired, or reconditioned with spare parts, employing a variety of physical forces—electrical, chemical, and mechanical. Cartesian principles predetermine the way in which a person is to be educated in order to become a scientist, a medical researcher, or a medical practitioner. For these people, the primary emphasis is on an ability to understand and apply technological solutions. Drew Leder concluded that this gave rise to a process which he labelled "medical dehumanization."[63] It leads to reductionist modes of treatments in which treatment of the symptoms becomes more important than attending to the person. Where the patient is viewed principally as a machine needing repairs or adjustments, his or her personal feelings—fears, wishes, or suffering—tend to be viewed as secondary to the medical procedures in hand.

Cartesianism has remained the dominant influence in biomedicine in the twentieth century because rapid advances in medical science seemed to confirm the efficacy of the "scientific" concentration on the mechanics of the body to the exclusion of any other inputs. It fostered the perception that the body could be abused and then cured. As Synnott expressed the idea, people became fixated on the idea that "magic bullets work better and quicker than prayer."[64] The principles of dualism, which presupposed no interaction between the body to the mind, also informed the social sciences in the earlier part of this century.[65] This position prevailed in spite of the fact that Descartes himself believed that there was an interaction between mind and body, and that disease was the result of a disturbance to this situation.

The body-as-machine construct enjoys parallels with the mechanization of society in this century. The term "body mainte-nance" is a clear indication of the popular acceptance of the machine metaphor for the body.[66] Just as cars, and our extensive array of household appliances, need repairs and maintenance, so the body requires servicing, regular care and attention to ensure that it performs efficiently. As we approach the end of the century, the popular dedication to ways of ensuring health and good looks has turned care and maintenance of the body into a series of body projects.[67]

The fascination with Cartesianism has been extended from considerations of the body-as-machine to children and to workers. Synnott quotes from a book on child care to emphasize this con-struction: "It is quite possible to train the baby to be an *efficient lit-tle machine,* and the more nearly perfect we make *the running of this machine,* the more wonderful will be the results achieved, and the less trouble it will be for the mother."[68] Workers were viewed in a similar fashion. In the mechanized factories of the western world, they became ancillary parts of the machinery of production. They were studied "scientifically," and subjected to such regimes as time and motion studies so that their efficiency could be planned and managed. The medical profession ensured that the body was main-tained in good health while the factory management ensured that the body was used effectively to economic advantage.

There have been an increasing number of challenges to the concepts of Cartesianism. Contemporary theories of the body insist that it must be challenged and that the "lived body" should replace the Cartesian body in social theory and practice. Leder points out that, despite the triumphs of therapeutic medicine inspired by Cartesian principles, there have been many distortions introduced to medical practice by the neglect of psychosocial factors.[69] He argues for a rehumanizing of medical practice by the introduction of concepts of holistic medicine which take account of sociocultural factors.

Despite the near unanimity of contemporary social theorists on the centrality of the "lived body" to the human condition, Carte-sianism appears to have become even more firmly entrenched in medicine as a result of the latest technological possibilities. Gene therapy has opened a veritable Pandora's box of possibilities in the manipulation of the body. And now the distinction between life and death has become blurred. The Cartesian body can be plugged into or disconnected from a life support system at the behest of the medical practitioner. It is even possible now, by such means, to maintain indefinitely the physical signs of life in a body which is brain-dead.

The Grotesque Body

Cartesianism was not the only development of the seventeenth century to introduce a critical change in the way the body was perceived. During the same period, shifts in perception became evident in community discourses on the body. These, at least initially, had a wider impact than the concepts of Cartesian dualism which were largely of interest to those associated with philosophy, science, and medicine. From early in the seventeenth century, the body began to be repressed and marginalized in Western society. This process was a reflection of changes which were taking place in society generally—new rituals and rules, and boundaries concerning body behavior became the norm. Amongst these were new concepts about what was polluting or contaminating, and the ways in which bodily activities might be restrained to avoid these outcomes.[70] As a result, the body was progressively redefined and "privatized," and a veil of modesty was drawn over the body and its management. Natural functions, previously of no great concern, became shameful and coarse. The body's sexual needs and other appetites were denied. The naked body became taboo. Undressing for bed, for example, called for care that one's body was not exposed to another's gaze. Even alone, one should avoid disrobing in a way that exposed the body, particularly one's intimate parts, fully.

Much of this formed part of the civilizing process of the seventeenth century which has been charted in detail by Norbert Elias. The presentation and management of the body was increasingly subjected to repressive and limiting societal rules and rituals. A new ideal body emerged, one which has been called the "classical body" by Bakhtin, and the "positive body" by Barker.[71] This ideal body was similar to a classical statue—without orifices and devoid of any coarse bodily functions. The inverse of this body image, one which flaunted its appetites and desires, and was possessed of orifices, genitals, and other features of the normal human body, was labelled the "grotesque body" by Bakhtin.

An important characteristic of the "grotesque body" is its lack of closure, overwhelmingly viewed as an innate condition of the female body.[72] Inevitably, the normal female body, with its "open" periods of birth and menstruation, became identified with the "grotesque body" and its potential to pollute. And because women are held to be intrinsically uncontained, they are frequently subjected to more constraint in their activities in the public sphere than are men. It is as if "they threaten to 'spill over' into social space, breaching its order—in particular, the basic distinction between inside and outside, person and world."[73] Mary Russo concluded that "women and their bodies, certain bodies, in certain public framings, in certain public spaces, are always already transgressive—dangerous and in danger."[74]

Two particular attributes of the female body have led to its categorization as a "grotesque" body. First, as discussed above, there is the perception that it lacks "closure," that it has an excess of orifices, and that it threatens to spill over into the public domain. The second factor leading to the perception of the female body as "grotesque," is its unique reproductive capability, which, from ancient times, has mystified men and, accordingly, appeared threatening to them. It is this combination of factors, which accent the differences from the male body—this sense of Otherness—which leads men to view the female body as "grotesque."[75] Janet Wolff discusses men's fear responses to the female "grotesque" body, or as she labels it, the "monstrous-feminine."[76] She cites arguments for the proposition that there is a widespread horror of the maternal body, stemming from a fear of becoming reincorporated into the mother, and a fear of the mother's generative powers. It is also claimed that it is the male child, in particular, who retains into adult life this fear of reincorporation and hence a loss of masculinity and self. The observations of Jean-Paul Sartre are illuminating in this regard:

> The obscenity of the feminine sex is that of everything which 'gapes open'. It is an *appeal to being* as all holes are. . . . Beyond any doubt her sex is a mouth and a voracious mouth which devours the penis—a fact that can easily lead to the idea of castration. The amorous act is the castration of the man; but this is above all because sex is a hole.[77]

Disguised behind a mask of contempt, these comments still make patently clear the underlying fear of the female body and its "orifices," and the horror of emasculation many men harbor. As a consequence, perhaps, of the perceived threat of the "grotesque," the female body is the perpetual target of the male gaze. Men expect women to conform to their preconceived ideas of the ideal of body shape for women, and what constitutes "feminine" behavior. Anything that deviates from this is deemed to be "unsightly." Women adapt to this "panopticism" in males, and sometimes collude in their own oppression by attempting to conform to male ideals.[78] Women diet, dress for effect, and monitor their movements and gestures in a manner which is effectively an exercise in self-surveillance. Girls learn early to avoid "making a spectacle out of oneself," or transgressing the boundaries of socially acceptable behavior.[79] Susan Bordo claims that this acculturation has entrenched a perception of imperfection in relation to women's self-assessment of their bodies.[80] It has produced the "Body Image Distortion Syndrome," and a great increase in eating disorders among women.

Clearly, the concepts associated with the female/grotesque body still inform many perceptions of the body in the late twentieth century. There is, however, a conflation of these concepts with ideas that formed the basis of the "classical" or "positive" body. Together, these various concepts form the construct which we now identity as the "modern" body.

The Modern Body

Early Modern Europe was the setting for the rise of individualism as well as the privatization of the body. Contemporary social theorists generally recognize the process of individuation as one of great significance for the construction of the "modern" body. With its impact on such factors as manners, modes of dress, and bodily practices generally, it prompted the creation of previously unparalleled boundaries around the self. This process has continued apace well into the twentieth century, becoming captive to the ideologies of corporate capitalism.[81] As a French sociologist described this situation: "We are truly entering into a new society, more individualistic and in which the pursuit of liberty and personal and satisfaction are at a premium."[82] This captures the essentials of modernism with its preoccupation with self-realization, a self-conscious cultivation of style, and an aversion to anything suggestive of self-denial.

Yet, it has been claimed that in the late twentieth century, the body has increasingly become the focal point of an individual's self identity.[83] Shilling believes that it is the gradual desacralization of social life, and a loss of faith in political institutions which are encouraging the individual to turn inwards and reconstitute the self through his or her corporeality. In a period when a premium is set on the "youthful, trim and sensual body," it is through the *surface* of the body that this is often expressed.[84] Shilling concludes that, due to the ambiguities prevailing in the late twentieth century, the "modern" body could also be described as the "uncertain body":

> We now have the means to exert an unprecedented degree of control over bodies, yet we are also living in an age which has thrown into radical doubt our knowledge of what bodies are and how we should control them.[85]

He points to the fact that there are so many developments in the fields of biological reproduction, genetic engineering, plastic surgery, and sports medicine, that the body is becoming increasingly determined by a range of options and choices. In effect, the possibilities for controlling the body have been significantly increased, both for oneself and for others. However, the potential for deployment of the body is still circumscribed by uncertainties. The availability of this wide range of scientific interventions now destabilizes preconceived ideas as to what the body represents and creates misgivings as to how far we should go in permitting such efforts to remodel or restore the body.

One of the important outcomes of this extraordinary focus on the body is, according to Baudrilllard, a new way of viewing one's body. He concluded that:

> It [the body] is the only object on which everyone is made to concentrate, not as a source of pleasure, but as an object of frantic concern, in the obsessive fear of failure or substandard performance, a sign and anticipation of death, that death to which no one can any longer give a meaning, but which everyone knows has at all times to be prevented.[86]

Baudrillard also noted that this cult of the "self" was an expression of contemporary hedonism, the urge to be "into" things. He declared that it was no longer sufficient "to *have* a body, but to be into your own body." Baudrillard expanded on this notion, asserting that it was now necessary to be:

Into your sexuality, into your own desire. Into your own functions, as if they were energy differentials or video screens. The hedonism of the 'into': the body is a scenario and the curious hygienist threnody devoted to it runs through the innumerable fitness centres, body-building gyms, stimulation and simulation studios that stretch from Venice to Tupanga Canyon, bearing witness to a collective asexual obsession.[87]

The modern body is also held captive to the consumer culture. Here the body is offered as a vehicle for the satisfaction of the desires of its owner. Consumption of food, for example, has assumed an important sociocultural significance.[88] It is no longer simply a process by which the individual sustains life. It now is a vehicle for hedonistic pleasures. It is also carefully directed at the production of shapely and healthy bodies. This becomes a daily imperative in the consumer society, with the constant portrayal of the idealized images of youth, health, fitness, and beauty. The following passage encapsulates the insistent message of the consumer culture:

Ours is an age obsessed with youth, health and physical beauty. Television and motion pictures, the dominant visual media, churn out persistent reminders that the lithe and graceful body, the dimpled smile set in an attractive face, are the keys to happiness, perhaps even its essence.[89]

While most writers interpret this desire to conform to the dictates of the consumer culture as an expression of a person's individualism, one writer has a diametrically opposed view of responses to these persuasive influences.[90] Maffesoli argues that it actually reflects a decline in individualism because it represents a form of social collectivity. He suggests that we live in a period marked by "tribal" responses.

However, in the main, it is women who are inexorably ensnared in this world of false body images. Much of the consumer culture promotion material is directed at them, urging them to diet, improve hair styles, and present their bodies according to the male stereotype of femininity. Therein lies the triumph of the thin woman over the fat woman. The success of such disinformation is evident all too frequently in instances of anorexia nervosa, bulimia, and in recourse to cosmetic surgery.[91]

Modernity has delivered control and management of the body

to a wide range of institutions. It has enhanced the power of many arms of governments to intervene in the lives of citizens to regulate almost all bodily activities. And while it has decreased the role of religious authorities in defining and regulating the body, modernity has transferred this power to other entities. The state and the medical profession are notable beneficiaries of this devolvement. However, some writers see new relationships emerging between the world of religious and moral sentiments and the world of the body. Mellor and Shilling, for instance, argue that in contemporary society the apparent collapse of morality, as defined by formal religious constraints, is being replaced by an upsurge in individual and collective moral consciousness.[92] This, they believe, is changing people's self-perception and their ways of relating to the world around them. In an overall sense, however, it could be argued that the medical profession now has a far greater degree of control over the modern body and the mind than was ever available in the past to religious institutions.

Many of the concepts that define the modern body can be traced to changes in perception, which emerged during the late medieval and early Renaissance periods. Some of the more significant of these were further reinforced during the late sixteenth and seventeenth centuries, a period notable for intense religious conflict and vigorous scientific debate. Cultural readings of the body changed markedly in response to changing perceptions of nakedness, sexual desire, and death. In particular, women's bodies began to be configured differently as they became even more closely linked with notions of sex, sin and decay. The advent of Cartesianism prompted further fundamental changes to perceptions of the human body. Apart from the well-known "body-as-machine" image, the fundamental binary oppositions implicit in Cartesiansim were reason/nature and its related dualism mind/body (nature). As women have traditionally been linked with the creative elements of nature, these oppositions represent, according to Susan Bordo, a "flight from the feminine."[93] Bordo also argues that this was accompanied, in the seventeenth century, by a "masculinization of thought" which had a major impact on the dominant intellectual culture.[94]

Bordo poses the question: "Why did the dominant intellectual culture take this decisive turn in the seventeenth century?"[95] She suggests that the answer lies in the rejection by men of all values associated with the maternal world. Bordo believes that this rejection was, to a considerable degree, due to the dissolution of medieval belief systems following experiences of famines, violent wars, plague, and devastating poverty in the sixteenth and seventeenth centuries.[96] The outcome, according to Bordo, was a loss of a sense of unity, of "oneness" with the surrounding world. In response, men retreated into a world of masculinity and rejected the "otherness" of the female.

We argue, in this work, that the masculinization of Western society emerged much earlier, and was due, more importantly, to other factors. Our analysis of medieval and early Renaissance period responses to epidemic diseases provides the basis for the conclusion that major societal changes stemmed, to a major degree, from the intersection of two volatile categories of disorder—bodily disorders resulting from constructs of femaleness and epidemic diseases, and those based on perceptions of the contagious, sexualized body of "woman."

The Present Work: Disorder and Apocalyptic Anxieties

We *are* the imposition of order on the brute raw material of humanity. Order is reason, and Reason is *ourselves*: disorder is the other, the Alien, whose intrusion diminishes us.[97]

There are two issues which resonate throughout the present work—concepts of disorder, and fear of the calamitous events which might accompany the Apocalypse.

In this work, we trace the development of various categories of disorder, particularly bodily disorders, and the perceptions of "otherness" which followed, in the wake of three major epidemics during the medieval and early Renaissance period in western Europe. We also trace the way in which these categories of disorder intersected with gender and class.

This work focuses on several particular themes within specific historical settings: the role of epidemic disease in shaping and altering constructions of the human body over time; the impact of epidemic disease, and the changing perceptions of the human body, upon institutions such as the State and upon the rise of professions such as medicine; and the consequences of such changes for the production of gendered and privatized bodies.

We argue that there has always been a strong connection, largely unrecognized, between epidemics, and body images. We aim to establish the validity of this nexus by reference to the impact of three major epidemics of the late medieval and early Modern periods in Europe: leprosy, plague, and syphilis. These epidemics swept through western Europe between the tenth and the sixteenth centuries with devastating effects on countless millions of the population. Plague appeared just as leprosy was in decline, and remained endemic in western Europe for several centuries. And outbreaks of plague were still causing havoc in many European communities when syphilis first appeared.

Our primary objective is to undertake an in-depth examination of the sociocultural changes attributable to the effects of these major epidemics.[98] Drawing extensively on primary source material from the periods under review, we identify the factors encountered during these epidemics that instigated shifts in perceptions of the body, and, in particular, the "disordered" or diseased body. Significant cultural transformations can also be attributed to these perceptual changes. We aim to demonstrate that many of these changes, in fact, marked major turning points in history in several important areas of social life. On the basis of the evidence presented, we contend that it was the epidemics of that era which shaped societal perceptions of the body and norms for the management and presentation of the body that still inform many twentieth century attitudes. The advent of these diseases also provided the basis for a wide range of enduring regulatory measures which are largely still in place.

Because there are fewer, readily accessible, sources available for an examination of European experiences of leprosy, this section of our work is less detailed than later sections. There is, however, ample evidence to enable us to establish the important perceptions of the body, the diseased or "disordered" body, and the body management practices which resulted from the leprosy epidemic. For the remainder of our research, we have centered our examination of late medieval and early Modern experiences of "disordered" bodies on one specific area: the Italian city of Florence. There are several important reasons for this choice. Florence was, at that time, one of the few large cities of Europe and one of the cities most adversely affected by plague. It was the power house of the Italian Renaissance in the period being reviewed, but still reflected all the traditional beliefs and social values of a major community in the late medieval and Early Modern periods. From our point of view, Florence also offers a rich collection of primary source material—chronicles, diaries, letters, and archival material—from which to identify the nature of individual and collective responses to the epidemics.[99]

This material has enabled us to chart the way in which controls first introduced during the epidemic of leprosy were subsequently employed in efforts to control the spread of plague. Progressively, however, the health measures aimed at controlling the "disordered" bodies of plague victims became instruments of social control directed against disadvantaged and marginalized groups within the community. We show that amongst a range of plague responses, the sexualized bodies of women featured prominently in the "disordered" category, as did the bodies of homosexual men. In addition, legislative measures aimed at controlling or limiting most expressions of human sexuality were intensified.

It is our view that the advent of syphilis reinforced perceptions that the "disordered" body was polluting, and that the sexualized body was a disruptive force in society. We argue that these responses ushered in the era of "social" diseases. We also assert that plague and syphilis greatly strengthened the position of the medical profession and led to the medicalization and institutionalization of the body at the hands of a new and privileged class of self-proclaimed experts. On the evidence we offer, we are convinced that the syphilis epidemic also made a significant contribution to the process of civilizing the body and the establishment of new regimes for the management and presentation of the body.

We extend the interpretation of our research into community responses to the three epidemics by referring to the opinions and conclusions reached by others who have written on generally related topics. On a number of issues, however, we challenge the validity of some of this material. As possible explanations for this divergence of views, we suggest that some other writers have either ignored or been unaware of the historical significance of the available evidence. To support our contentions on these issues, we present persuasive evidence that leads us to conclude that the conclusions reached by some social theorists are invalid.

The present work is located within the framework of contemporary theories of the body, and draws on the fields of historical sociology, cultural studies, and gender studies. The whole work is premised on the assumption that perceptions of the human body are historically and culturally contingent. As a consequence, a multitude of sociocultural factors have invested human bodies with a wide range of shifting, and at times, conflicting meanings over time. We contend that this has always had important ramifications for every community group. In particular, perceptions of the body have always been powerful agents in the process of defining socially acceptable norms for the body and for its management. We aim to investigate particular aspects of this defining process, such as the way in which shifting sociocultural values have shaped concepts of gender, concepts of Otherness, and, in turn, definitions of difference. Our research will show that these factors have increasingly been used to legitimate the intrusion of governments into the lives of citizens.

The second important factor shaping responses to these epidemics was the apocalyptic tradition which is shared by many cultures. For the Christian West, the Apocalypse, as foretold in the Book of Revelation, represented a future reality, something to be greatly feared. It shaped responses to many things, particularly to natural disasters which were interpreted as warnings that the Apocalypse was close at hand. The apocalyptic tradition was no less real to people living in much later periods. It still influences the responses of some in the twentieth century. Even when not interpreted literally, apocalyptic scenarios are frequently linked with many societal concerns in the late twentieth century.[100]

We claim that there are clear parallels between the atmosphere of apocalyptic foreboding which characterized the late medieval and early Modern periods in western Europe, and societal attitudes which have emerged recently. It would seem that the Four Horsemen of the Apocalypse, representing death, war, famine, and pestilence are, metaphorically, already in our midst We point to the resurgence of a sense of imminent disaster, fostered by the media, which is prompted by the apparent inability of medical science to confront a spate of new diseases, and the reappearance, in more virulent form, of epidemics thought to have been vanquished. There is also some evidence of heightened levels of anxiety within the community on many other social issues, as we move from one century into another, and, indeed, from one millennium into another. And, despite the emergence of "rational" and "scientific" constructions of the body, and the "disordered" or diseased body, over the intervening centuries, many previous sociocultural constructs which we identify through our research have resurfaced during the twentieth century.

We suggest that this can be seen where terms such as "plague" and "epidemic" are now applied to diverse social phenomena such as HIV/AIDS, tuberculosis, illicit drugs, and violence. Linda Singer argued that, in effect, the late twentieth century has become the "Age of the Epidemic," in which the fear of contagion shapes social interaction, and in which the panic associated with the communicability of disadvantage and disorder has inspired an intensification of regulatory regimes.[101] Singer notes that the term "epidemic" is now widely applied to phenomena quite outside the sphere of disease; there are now warnings of "'epidemics' of teenage pregnancy, child molestation, abortion, pornography, and divorce." Indeed, Singer argues convincingly that the "epidemic condition" has become the paradigmatic expression of power in contemporary society, and that bodies (and their disorders and pleasures) are now caught within a disciplinary matrix produced by "the logic of contagion."

We conclude this work by discussing the connections between our findings and twentieth century constructions of the "modern" body and the "postmodern" body, and contemporary techniques for the presentation and management of the human body. We suggest that perceptions of Otherness remain largely as they were defined in the period we have reviewed. If anything, the societal distinctions between "inclusion" and "exclusion" have become even more firmly entrenched. It is also evident that the sexualized body still remains at least as problematic for governments now, as it was in the early Modern period. Finally, we explore briefly the factors that are reshaping perceptions of the body in the postmodern era, and the process of deconstruction of the corporeal which is redefining concepts of human embodiment in the cyber age.

CHAPTER 2

Banishing the "Unclean" Body

The sexual act itself is diseased, for it cannot be performed without disorder.

—St. Bonaventure[1]

And the leper in whom plague is, his clothes shall be rent, and his head bare, and he shall put a covering upon his upper lip, and shall cry, Unclean, unclean.

—Leviticus 13:45

To many people, perhaps even to most people, the expression "disordered body" suggests bodies disabled in some way by illness or disease. While this is undoubtedly correct in a general sense, there is a more fundamental difference between ordered and disordered bodies—one which is of critical importance to our review. Before all else, the definition of a "disordered" body springs from the perceived differences between the male and the female body. Consequently, it is shaped by considerations of gender. For this reason it is a construction which transcends considerations of illness and disease. Moreover, defining "disorder" on the basis of gender has ensured that throughout history those whose bodies are classed as being disordered have always been disadvantaged by ruling elites, who are almost always male.

Whenever men have encountered situations which have posed threats to their hegemony, they have always sought to regain control. They have endeavored to restore order out of chaos; they have attempted to control the forces of nature. From prehistoric times onward, the sense of "disorder" associated with women's bodies represented a profound challenge to men's authority. Under such a threat, men in authority frequently turned to religious, philosophical, and medical arguments to defend their dominant role in society. This is well illustrated by the absolute conviction within Graeco-Roman medical and philosophical constructs of the female body that it was inherently inferior because of its "inverted" and "incomplete" nature. This was seen as proof of the "natural" supremacy of the male in all matters—order should take precedence over disorder. But above all, the reproductive capability of the female body represented something unknown, unpredictable, and to a large extent, beyond the control of men. Hence, the female body, already characterized as "disordered" on account of its anatomical "deficiencies," also carried connotations of chaos and challenges to men's notions of social order and control. As a consequence, men have always attempted to gain some control over the bodies and bodily functions of women—restoring order where "disorder" prevailed.

In this chapter, we trace the ways in which the gender divide has become entrenched in Western cultural traditions and how this process has reinforced perceptions of the "disordered" nature of women's bodies. We also examine the evolution of major discourses on disease causation, and the accompanying shifts in treatment regimes, from the Graeco-Roman period to the latter part of the Middle Ages. This chapter also investigates responses to the major epidemic of leprosy which arrived in western Europe in the sixth century. This epidemic posed significant challenges to then current ideas on disease causation and produced radically new approaches to the regulation of the disordered body.

Sexing the Body

Descriptions of human anatomy in the writings of early Greek medical theorists and philosophers underpinned the perceptions of the body which permeated Western culture from the time of the Roman Empire to the latter part of the Middle Ages.[2] This situation arose from the introduction into Roman medicine of the diagnostic techniques and treatment regimes which had evolved in the classical Greek period. Founded, in general, on the concepts enunciated by Hippocrates, and those of the Hippocratic school, these precepts and practices became readily available to practitioners in the West. The agency for this was a substantial corpus of work on medicine complied by Galen (c.130 to 200 A.D.). Galen provided a commentary on the work of Hippocrates and added observations based on his own experiences as a medical practitioner. In particular, he recorded detailed accounts of his convictions about human anatomy. Galen's work came to be accepted in the West as the definitive authority on the structure and function of the human body and its various organs. So well regarded was this work that it underpinned all considerations of human anatomy for a millennium. In fact, it remained largely unchallenged until the early Modern period in western Europe. However, his other pronouncements on diagnosis and treatment of bodily disorders were largely forgotten in the West from the fall of the Roman Empire until late in the Middle Ages. They were then rediscovered through the agency of Arabic medical theory and practice which drew substantially upon the theories and commentaries of Galen. We will discuss the importance of the rediscovery of Galen's medical writings in later chapters.

Galen, like most of his predecessors and many of those who followed him over the next thousand years or so, had little or no direct knowledge of the internal structure of the human body. He had gained his knowledge of anatomy solely from dissecting apes and pigs, and assumed common ground between the anatomies of these animals and those of humans. Nevertheless, this did not prevent him from describing in some detail his hypotheses as to the structure and function of the various organs of the body. One of his most pivotal and unequivocal pronouncements was that male and female bodies were identical as to the functions of their generative organs. He argued that the organs of the female really only differed from the male in their disposition. He asserted that each had organs which performed exactly the same functions and only the placement in each of the bodies was different. This conclusion provided the basis for the one-sex model of human anatomy which prevailed unchallenged for many centuries in western Europe.[3] Galen provided a range of examples, comparing each organ associated with the genitalia of male and female bodies, and "proving," to his satisfaction, that they were identical. He considered that the differences were of no great consequence—in the case of the male, the generative organs were external to the body, while those of the female were simply internal and hidden—one set was the mirror-image of the other. The combination of vagina and cervix, for instance, was simply a penis turned inward, and in the same manner, the uterus was portrayed as an internally positioned scrotum.

So certain was Galen of the interchangeability of these and other related organs that he declared "you could not find a single male part left over that had not simply changed its position."[4] He projected his convictions even further, suggesting that under some undefined conditions, the female generative organs could be turned outward and projecting so that "the neck [cervix and vagina], hitherto concealed inside the perineum, but now pendant, [would] be made into the male member."[5]

Instead of these physical facts indicating a division between the sexes, Galen saw this as proof that the male body was the ideal and the female body an inverted, and therefore less perfect example, of the species. Woman was seen as a "failed" man—one who had not realized the full potential of the male body.[6] As Laqueur interpreted Galen's proposition: "They [women] have exactly the same organs but in exactly the wrong places."[7] He also argued that Galen, in common with other theorists of the time, had used these concepts of biology to express what they were all convinced was a higher truth—that in the grand order of the universe women were, in fact, inferior beings with imperfect bodies.

When it came to declarations about the human body and the way in which it functioned, these invariably emanated from men. Men knew their own bodies but viewed the body of a woman as unknown and mysterious territory. As a result, all their considerations were based first on the male body as the prototype for human beings, and the female body as an imperfect version of their own bodies. What they did not know about women's bodies they imagined, inevitably colored by their perceptions of the ideal nature of man. They portrayed the anatomy of the female body in a way which was consistent with their own preconceived ideas—the female was an incompletely evolved, and hence disordered, version of the male body.

Laqueur concluded that most of the debates about the boundaries of sex in the one-sex model were not about bodies at all. They were, he claimed, "about power, legitimacy, and fatherhood," about "preserving the Father, he who stands not only for order but for the very existence of civilization itself."[8] A disordered female body could then be seen as posing a threat to the male power structure—and constructions of the imagined female body could be viewed as a means of reinscribing the authority of "the Father." Turner expressed a similar view about the meaning accorded to the body when he asserted that the "body is primarily a metaphor of social equilibrium and order."[9]

The very language in which men and women, and their anatomies were discussed powerfully reinforced the perceptions inherent in the gender divide. The Latin word for man (*vir*) is derived from *vis*, meaning strength, force and vigor, whereas woman (*mulier*) is etymologically related to *mollitia*, denoting characteristics of pliability and softness. It also has figurative connotations of weakness, irresolution, voluptuousness, and even wantonness. Clearly, from an early time, language provided a formidable tool for constantly asserting that man was the complete being, superior in all ways, and woman was weak, subject to man's will, and sexually voracious.

Much the same pattern of etymological support for preconceived ideas, predominantly those of men, is apparent in the terminology adopted for descriptions of human anatomy. The genital area was frequently referred to as the *pudenda*, because those parts were viewed as being "shameful." More formally, the generative organs were referred to as the *genitalia,* linguistically linked to *genitor* which denotes "father, creator, sire, parent or begetter." And further revealing the true nature of the gender divide, the female genitals were known as *turpitudo feminarum*, which can be translated as "the repulsiveness, foulness or deformity of females."[10]

A further example of the intersection of anatomical terminology with preconceptions of function or characteristics appears in the work of Jacquart and Thomasset on sexuality and medicine in the Middle Ages.[11] They cite the work of a ninth century writer positing linguistic links with the term "menses." It was claimed that the Latin form, *menstrua*, was linked to the Greek word for "moon." The following gloss was then added: "It is not allowed to approach menstruating women nor to have intercourse with them, because a Catholic man is not allowed to have anything to do with the idolatry of pagans or the heresy of heretics."[12] Here the writer draws on the perception that the moon is associated with pre-Christian religious rites, clearly anathema to a good follower of the church, and longheld convictions that menstrual blood threatens men with physical danger and defilement.[13] His conflation of such ideas, evokes "the sacred horror that accompanies the transgression of taboos."[14]

The one-sex model of human anatomy reinforced long-held views that women's bodies were defective, a concept whose origins reached back into antiquity. It also gave support to perceptions which created the unbalanced nature of the gender divide—that women were inherently inferior to men, both physically and intellectually. And after the collapse of the Roman Empire, these views were expressed even more stridently.

The Disordered Bodies of Women

Women's bodies, as signifiers of difference, inspire both fear and awe. Fear of women's bodies is anchored in antiquity. For example, within the traditions of some tribal communities, menstruation was associated with defilement, and became one of the first rituals of taboo. The menstruating woman was viewed as being infected with an evil spirit and so represented a great danger to men. One writer has reported that, in response to this threat, "the men of the tribe would be compelled to protect themselves by segregating the dangerous female, and in this way protect themselves from the devastating effect of their own sexuality."[15] This reaction suggests that men have acted in this fashion since time immemorial—transferring fears of their own sexuality and weaknesses onto women. Fear of menstruating women is evident also in Judaic and Christian traditions. There is a requirement in the Old Testament that a man should not "come near a menstruous woman" (Ezek. 18:6). In addition, it prescribes rituals for the cleansing of persons, clothing and other articles which have been contaminated by women's blood (Lev. 15:19–31). The early Christian Church extended this concept of ritual defilement to include sexual intercourse and childbirth. It excluded from participation in religious ceremonies those perceived as defiled in this manner. In a conflation of superstition and religious ritual, there was, according to McLaughlin, a "demonizing of sex."[16]

Early in the fourth century, the Roman Emperor Constantine decreed that Christianity should become the official state religion. From that point, the Christian Church began to impose its views of the human body and bodily practices upon Western societies. Although initially marked by conflicting interpretations of biblical injunctions, Christian perceptions of the body soon reflected a horror of the body, and particularly its sexuality. This marked what Jacques Le Goff has identified as *la déroute du corporel*, the "rout of the body," central to emerging Christian discourse on the human body.[17] While both men and women were exhorted to accept this renunciation of the physical implications of human embodiment, the main focus of attention became the bodies of women. This reflected the moral condemnation of all women expressed by the church, based on Eve's role in the Fall, and the conviction that women were sexual predators plotting the downfall of men. Theologians also drew upon the notions of women's "disordered" bodies promoted by the one-sex model of human anatomy, and age-old fears of the contaminating effects inherent in the female body.[18] They bolstered these arguments with recourse to traditional fears that sexual intercourse could be morally and physically damaging to men. Soranus, writing in the early part of the Middle Ages, claimed that: "Men who remain chaste are stronger and better than others and pass their lives in better health."[19]

These various factors, taken together, proved immensely powerful in denigrating women and relegating them to an inferior position in community and religious affairs.[20] They also legitimated the regulation of women's bodies and the imposition of controls on their sexuality. There was, however, an ambivalence apparent in the patristic doctrines about women and their bodies. At the same time as a renunciation of the body and a horror of sex became manifest in an avowed loathing of women, theologians elevated virginity to a level almost equivalent to that to which a devout, celibate man might aspire. This twofold definition of Woman focused on her corporeality, and posited her as a "submissive body in the order of nature and 'revolting' body in the disorder of sin."[21] Woman was viewed as the symbol of "body," of the "animal-like" characteristics of human behavior, while Man was symbolic of matters of a higher order. He represented "mind" and "soul." Theologians claimed the truth of this contention on the basis of biblical exegesis. Centuries earlier, when commenting on the respective contributions made by men and women to their offspring, Aristotle had posited that "while the body is from the female, it is the soul that is from the male."[22] Beyond all of these issues, Woman was perceived as the archetypal "disordered" body.

Beware: Dangerous Bodies!

Men have long felt the need to preserve themselves from physical dangers they believed were inherent in the bodies of women. They have been apprehensive about effects on their bodies arising from sexual intercourse, about perceptions that it has a debilitating effect. They have seen women's sexuality as having the ability to undermine their power and influence, and to exploit their own weaknesses. The danger which men felt they faced in their dealings with women is patently clear from the frequent use made of the "serpent" metaphor in their vilification of women.

It was, of course, a serpent which persuaded Eve to partake of the forbidden fruit. As the story is written, Eve then overcame the scruples of Adam and led him into temptation, and it was her actions which led to their banishment from the Garden of Eden. This account of the Fall underpins the doctrine of Original Sin which thereafter heaped opprobrium on the heads of all women. Medieval religious figures drew heavily on the Eve/serpent and sin/sexuality associations as a few examples will illustrate. Marbode of Rennes declared that "Woman was . . . a serpent, . . . a poison," Peter Damian described women as "furious vipers," and Geoffroy of Vendôme asserted that ". . . the [female] sex poisoned our first ancestor. . . ."[23] And, according to Thomasset, "the womb . . . was likened to the serpent. . . ."[24]

The same metaphor, with all its connotations of physical injury from poisonous substances, was applied to women's sexuality.[25] Even eye contact with a woman was reputed to be capable of poisoning a bystander. The Hebrew Testament of Reuben, from the Testaments of the Twelve Patriarchs, also raises this possibility, although, perhaps, figuratively : ". . . and by a glance of the eye [they] instil the poison. . . ."[26] Arguably, one of the most enduring of the legends which associates women with poisons which cause the demise of men is the myth of the Poison-Damsel.

The origins of this fable can be traced back to early Sanscrit and Indian legends.[27] It was introduced into western Europe in the twelfth century in a manuscript written in Latin and entitled *Secretum Secretorum* (The Secret of Secrets). It purported to be a collection of letters of advice written by Aristotle to Alexander the Great after Aristotle had become too old to continue his role of tutor and adviser to the king.[28]

There are several versions of this story, but the essential elements remain the same regardless of how the story has been retold. A sixteenth century version of the story holds that a certain king learned from a soothsayer that a newly-born child named Alexander would one day be his downfall. Disconcerted by this news, the king plotted ways of thwarting destiny, giving orders that several infant girls be nourished with a deadly poison, administered in small but ever increasing doses. Some of the children died but one survived and became a beautiful young woman possessed of deadly powers. She was so poisonous that her breath polluted the atmosphere, and just to approach animals caused them to die very quickly. To see if his plan would work, the king sent the girl into the camp of a hostile army surrounding his city. The enemy king was smitten by her beauty and invited her to his tent. As soon as he kissed her, he fell down dead as did others of his followers who tried to embrace the girl. With their leaders so easily overcome the demoralized army retreated.[29]

Encouraged by his success, the king despatched the poison damsel—together with other girls who lacked her fatal potential—to the court of Alexander, who had grown to manhood. Greatly attracted by the beauty of the poison damsel, Alexander hastened to embrace her. But Aristotle, Alexander's tutor, sensed the poisonous nature of the girl, and restrained the king from approaching her. Socrates, the master of Aristotle, supported this advice. He proceeded to conduct an experiment to prove the danger. He ordered two slaves to kiss the girl and they died immediately. He also made the girl touch animals and they too fell down dead at the first touch. Alexander then had the girl beheaded, and her body burned.[30]

The myth of the Poison-Damsel became extremely popular when reintroduced into the West in the latter part of the Middle Ages. It reinforced all traditional perceptions of the dangers inherent in sexual relations with a woman, and discourses that posited that women's bodies were capable of producing poisonous materials. Of the latter, the most widely held was that concerned with the dangers inherent in menstrual blood. Early treatises which contained the beliefs of a number of philosophers and scholars, such as Pliny, contained dire warnings about the evil effects of menstrual blood. These were supported by the medical theories of the Classical Greek period. All of these male fantasies were gathered together by the encylopedists of the early Middle Ages, such as Isidore of Seville, for the information of a wider readership than those working within the field of medicine.

Thomasset listed many of these beliefs about the nefarious effects of menstrual blood.[31] One commonly held belief was that a child conceived during menstruation would be born with red hair. Another was that a child may develop measles or smallpox, diseases caused by the absorption of menstrual blood. Aristotle, whose pronouncements were taken very seriously during the Middle Ages, declared that the gaze of a menstruating woman could darken a mirror. Albertus Magnus asserted that after menopause women were no longer able to purge their systems through menstruation, and the dangerous vapors which accumulated had to be exited through the eyes. For this reason, he stated, old women could poison infants by staring at them in their cradles. Menstrual blood was believed to have other effects of a damaging nature. It was blamed for preventing seeds from germinating, for causing trees to shed their leaves, for rusting iron and blackening brass, and causing dogs to develop rabies. Many other deleterious effects were attributed to menstrual blood throughout the Middle Ages and into the early Modern period. For this reason the issue will be further canvassed in later chapters.

Beyond the specific categorization of women's bodies as disordered and dangerous, there were other categories of disordered body, the principal one of which is the body disabled by disease or illness. We turn our attention now to the way in which various communities have responded to outbreaks of disease or illness in their midst. We will explore the most important theories of disease causation which emerged, and the way in which these discourses shaped responses to outbreaks of epidemic disease within western European communities from the Middle Ages onward.

Disease and the Disordered Body

In every part of the world, and in every age, every societal group—tribe, clan or nation-state—has generated its own ideas about the human body. These groups also establish canons for the management and presentation of the body.

Even pre-literate communities accepted that the human body was central to the normal day-to-day enterprise of the whole group—a healthy body was a productive body. Equally important was the role of the body in ensuring the survival and continuity of the community. Until relatively recently, all western European communities had to contend with high infant mortality, and a high death rate among those who managed to survive childhood. In the second century A.D., for instance, only four percent of men, and even fewer women, remained alive beyond the age of fifty years.[32] In fact, the average life expectancy was less than twenty-five years. In the words of St. John Chrysostom (c. 347–407), it was a population "grazed by death."[33] And to even maintain population levels in the period of the late Roman Empire, one writer has estimated that each woman would have had to produce an average of four children.[34]

This pattern differed little, if at all, from the problems every western European community faced, both before and after the period of the Roman Empire. Hence, throughout the ages every cohesive social group has viewed the health of its members as a matter of primary concern. The bodies of citizens needed to be healthy, productive, and fertile to ensure the survival of the community group. For this reason, seeking explanations for bodily disorders, and devising remedial strategies for bodies so affected, have always ranked high in societal considerations. For most early societies, this meant looking to supernatural rather than natural forces for both cause and remedy. A variety of rituals and treatment regimes emerged from these considerations of the disordered body. And those who were perceived as possessing the esoteric knowledge required to minister to the disordered body were, and continue to be, accorded a privileged position within the social group. One could argue that, in fact, the witch doctor or medicine man and today's medical specialist simply lie at opposite ends of a continuum of practitioners of the healing arts. Their function is similar—to care for the disordered body—but their respective interventions were, and are, based on markedly different discourses of disease causation.

The Disordered Body: Discourses of Causation

Western perceptions of the disordered body have drawn upon many pre-existing discourses on the body and its susceptibility to becoming disordered. Some concepts have been incorporated into Western discourse, although sometimes in a modified form, while others have been discarded in favor of ideas more consistent with the prevailing belief systems of the receiving communities. One particularly significant concept, which was common in many early societies, became firmly entrenched in Western discourse of the disordered body. This was the perception that body fluids and excretions, and elements of the body such as hair and nail parings, were damaging to the health.[35] Previously associated with ancient taboos, and notions of harmful physical consequences from contact with unclean substances, these notions provided the basis for a nexus between pollution and disease. They also provided an argument for extending the definition of a disordered body from that affected only by illness or disease to one perceived as capable of contaminating others.

From antiquity to the late Middle Ages, four main theories relating to causation of illness and disease enjoyed varying degrees of support. Two of these posited that disorders of the body stemmed from supernatural causes, that is, occult influences outside the natural world—the malevolence of evil spirits; or the wrath of some deity. The other discourses did not attribute illness or disease to the intervention of supernatural entities. One of these theories looked to natural events on earth, that is, to disturbances in the ambient conditions in which men and women lived; the other to an unfavorable conjunction of the stars and planets.

Magico-Religious Discourse

The first of the theories on causation, probably the earliest, and certainly one of the most enduring, saw disease as due to spells or curses invoked against a living being by spirits or demons, or by some other supernatural entity acting with malice. It was held that some humans also had the power to cause disease and death by engaging these spirits to harm an enemy. These beliefs formed part of the broader religious philosophy of animism, which Garrison suggested was the "common point of convergence of all medical folk-lore, [that is] the notion that the world swarms with invisible spirits which are the efficient causes of disease and death."[36] In the context of western European communities, however, these ideas were frequently associated with agrarian-based religions which were never completely displaced by the dominant discourse of the church. As a result, many communities continued to place reliance on "magic"—incantations, mystic ceremonies, charms and amulets—to combat disease. And those who had the power to effect cures were the precursors of the medical practitioners of later societies. The resilience of such beliefs is demonstrated by the fact that there are many folkloric traditions still in existence in Western society that retain elements of magic symbolism and ritual.[37]

Divine Punishment Discourse

The second important discourse of disease causation held that disorders of the body represented punishment inflicted by a deity offended by the actions of mortal beings. This became a widely held view in communities with pantheistic and monotheistic religious belief systems. The early Greek pantheistic religion was notable for its belief in the swift and terrible revenge that gods and goddesses visited upon humans who had offended them.[38] The most prominent of the monotheistic religious systems were, of course, those based on Judeo-Christian traditions. These established a nexus between human transgressions and divine punishment, and the perceived relationship between sin and sickness was central to medieval responses to disease which were based on Christian beliefs.[39] Discourses of causation that linked disease with divine punishment also looked to divine intervention to alleviate the discomforts associated with illness. The Christian God not only inflicted disease and illness as punishment, or as a salutary lesson, but He also had the power to suspend or deflect such scourges. It is of interest to note that there were significant similarities between the two theories of disease causation which were based on supernatural influences. Both accepted that demons could cause bodily disorders, and both relied on countering the demonic influence to relief distress; for example, a great part of New Testament healing relied on exorcising demons to achieve this end.

Natural Events / Natural Conditions Discourse

Opposed to these theories of disease causation was a third important discourse, one which rejected supernatural causes or cures. It saw disease as arising from natural events which could be explained if one knew all the factors involved. Similarly, this discourse looked to natural remedies, often the "contraries" of the causative elements, to effect cures. In very broad terms, this discourse viewed the human body as a system in which good health depended on the maintenance of a harmonious balance of inner humours. This was not unlike that envisaged in other belief systems in which the body needed to be in tune with the universe. In another parallel, the theory of natural causes saw disturbances to the ambient conditions in which humans lived as elements with the potential to produce an imbalance which resulted in illness. The main causes of these imbalances, according to this discourse, were external influences such as changes in the atmosphere, and by extension, the effects of seasonal changes. A pestilential atmosphere, a "miasma," could develop from polluting influences such as "a multitude of dead bodies which have not been burned, . . . or an exhalation from swamps or stagnant water in the summer time. . . ."[40]

Astral Influence Discourse

The study of astrology, and the belief that astral bodies influenced human activities, can be traced to ancient times. Evidence of this can be found in the Sumerian period of 1185 B.C.; and it was also central to Chaldean medicine.[41] In fact, the association between medicine and astrology continued through the Muslim and Aztec cultures, and ultimately formed an element of Hellenic and Arabic medicine. However, it had little influence on Western medicine until the late Middle Ages. It was then widely adopted in medical theory and practice although treated with great suspicion by many prominent philosophers and writers.[42] Its acceptance within the field of medicine was facilitated by the harmonizing of the astral influence discourse of disease causation with Christian religious discourse. This was effected by asserting that God was the central and omnipotent being in the universe, the ultimate First Cause of the motion of the planetary system, and the controller of life on earth.

These theories of disease causation had a major impact on Western medicine through to the early Modern period. Their reception in the West occurred in two distinct phases: the first during the period of the Roman Empire and the second toward the close of the Middle Ages. Graeco-Roman medicine was the outcome of combining Greek and Roman ideas on medical practice in the late Empire period. From early in the Middle Ages, this was largely supplanted by a new form of medicine based on discourses on the body espoused by the Christian Church. Then, toward the latter part of the Middle Ages, Greek medicine was reintroduced into western Europe, in association with Arabian medical knowledge. The outcome was that the social construction of Western medicine evolved slowly as new knowledge, drawn from many sources, became available between the period of the Roman Empire and the end of the Middle Ages.[43]

Graeco-Roman Medicine

While there was, initially, some element of divine causation implicit in early Greek medicine, it began to disappear about the time of Hippocrates (460–350 B.C.), undoubtedly the towering figure of Greek medicine. His work on disorders of the body, on diagnostic techniques, and treatment regimes was supplemented by many other writers who are generally grouped together under the label of the Hippocratic tradition. There were, in fact, two conflicting discourses within the Hippocratic tradition: "dogmatism," which relied on *diagnosis*, or causal reasoning to determine the proximate causes of external symptoms, and "empiricism," in which *semiosis*, or historico-circumstantial reasoning was central.[44] From the time of Galen (130–200 A.D.), the main exponent of classical Greek medicine, there was a degree of blending of these two discourses. Further, there was no trace of supernatural causation of disease in his work.

From the outset, the Hippocratic tradition was based on the concept of disease or other malfunctions of the body as due to an imbalance within the body system. It was the role of the medical practitioner to identify the factors which caused the imbalance and prescribe measures that would assist the body to recover its equilibrium through its own natural curative forces. To be adept at diagnosis and treatment, a medical practitioner was required to have knowledge of the organs of the body and their functions. Early Greek medicine sought to establish this through an accumulation of information in casebooks, records of epidemic outbreaks, and close observation of illness experiences. This was supplemented to a limited extent by some early dissections performed in the third century B.C. Two Alexandrian practitioners, Herophilus and Erastistratus, dissected human cadavers and performed vivisections on condemned criminals.[45] This resulted in the identification of the brain as the center of the nervous system, and the establishment of the rate, pattern, and pressure of the pulse. Despite this early interest in the contents of the "body envelope," the practice of human dissection was not common, and much of the early knowledge of anatomy was gained from the dissection of animals. As we noted earlier, even when Galen studied at Alexandria, his knowledge of anatomy was confined to observation of skeletal remains and the dissection of apes and pigs.

Early Greek medicine established regimes for the body which were remarkably persistent, despite the later emergence of different theories on the causation of illness and disease. Even in the third century B.C., diet and exercise were classed as important elements in regimes for the maintenance of health. And efforts to restore the balance of the bodily systems affected by disease or illness involved recommendations on these issues, together with advice on the avoidance of particular activities. Recommendations included advice on eating, sleeping, drinking, and bathing, when to induce vomiting or purging, and when to let blood. Another issue addressed within Greek medicine was that of sexual activity. Those who wished to remain healthy were counselled to exercise restraint, or to avoid sexual relations at certain specified times to ensure that the equilibrium of the body was not disturbed. Many of the treatments prescribed relied on the administration of pills or potions derived from herbal and mineral materials. And, as a rule, these mixtures were based on the *Greek Herbal*. This was an elaborate encyclopedia, compiled by Dioscorides in the first century A.D., describing the medicinal properties of "herbs, oils, ointments, trees, animals, fish, reptiles, insects, human effluences and excreta, cereals, roots, juices, saps, vines, wines" and many other materials such as mineral ores and stones.[46]

Greek medicine reached its most complete development with Galen in the second century A.D. As we have already noted, this was absorbed into medical practice in the western Roman Empire. Medical practitioners of the Empire were frequently Greek slaves or freedmen. However, there were others whose intellectual standing was such that they could read the medical, scientific, and philosophical texts in the original Greek.[47] There were also writers of Latin treatises on medicine who drew from Greek medical texts. Yet the information which had been translated from Greek to Latin represented only a small fraction of the available literature on Greek medicine. Nevertheless, there was sufficient information available to ensure that the *secular* medicine, which was widely practiced in the Roman Empire, was based on the Galenic interpretation of the Hippocratic tradition, with its accompanying use of the Greek herbal remedies.

The essentially urban character of the Roman Empire favored the rapid dissemination of medical knowledge gathered from Greek medicine, and the expansion of secular medical practice. However, from the third to the fourth century A.D., internal revolt and attacks by marauding bands of invaders triggered the disintegration of the Empire. And in the fifth century, Rome was sacked by the Vandals and the western Roman Empire finally collapsed. As a result, urban populations were dispersed and cities declined in importance.[48] At about the same time, the practice of secular medicine also suffered an eclipse. This was due in part to the disintegration of the cities but also to new perceptions of the body and disease promoted by the rapidly spreading doctrine of Christianity. The process of change was relatively slow at first, and even in the longer term the practice of secular medicine continued in some form throughout the Middle Ages. Nevertheless, there is little record of its existence during the main part of the medieval period, and most of that evidence is of an indirect nature. Consequently, those who practiced Graeco-Roman secular medicine became part of the unseen and voiceless majority in medieval society. They came to occupy much the same position as that of others who treated ailments in every community. The latter were the community healers and "wise women" who served neighborhood groups unused to consulting established practitioners. Their treatment regimes relied on traditional information transmitted orally from one generation to the next, and on knowledge of Greek medicine and herbal remedies gleaned from other practitioners. However, both community healers and secular medical practitioners soon found that a new group began to tend the disordered bodies of the community. These were the monks who belonged to the new Monastic Orders of the church, and whose "monastic medicine" was based on the doctrines of the Christian Church.

Imposing the Christian View of the Body on Medicine

During the fourth century, Christianity became the official state religion of the Roman empire, and its influence on the way in which the body, illness, and disease were viewed was profound. The centrality of Christian beliefs in divine intervention as both cause of and cure for illness diverged markedly from the rational and systematic investigation of nature which informed Greek scientific, medical, and philosophical theories on human existence. As a consequence, there was less demand for translations into Latin of Greek medical works, and greater emphasis on biblical exegesis and patristic interpretations of the body and its disorders. Secular medical practice did not disappear, but it was progressively overshadowed by healing practices which turned increasingly to appeals to the Virgin, to the saints, and to holy martyrs for cures since illness and disease were perceived by the Christian Church as God's punishment for sin. This nexus between sin and punishment, accepted within Christianity, was seen to have its origins in the Fall of Man. Subsequently, illness and disease entered the world as retribution for sinful human activity. St. Augustine focused on this relationship when he stated :

> This life of ours—if a life so full of such great ills can properly be called a life—bears witness to the fact that, from its very start, the race of mortal men has been a race condemned. . . . Turn, now, to the maladies that affect our bodies. Not even medical libraries have catalogued all the diseases; in most cases, it takes pain to drive out pain, so that medical care and cures can be as cruel as the complaints themselves. . . . From this all but hell of unhappiness here on earth, nothing can save us but the grace of Jesus Christ. . . .[49]

For all Christian theologians it was essential that curing the soul must take precedence over curing the physical body, and unless that were done, the likelihood that a person might be returned to good health was greatly diminished. They also envisaged that disease or illness could be sent by God as a salutary lesson, or as a test of faith rather than as a punishment. In these circumstances, the sufferer should accept the disability patiently, in the expectation that he or she would be rewarded spiritually.

With the disintegration of the western Roman Empire, the church was almost alone in having a formal structure which could extend its authority across Europe. As cities declined and populations were dispersed, many bishops assumed temporal as well as spiritual leadership roles. In the process, the church reinforced its authority in the medical field because of the perceived link between spiritual well-being and good physical health. This required a reversal of the orientation of Graeco-Roman medicine, and ensured that perceptions of illness and disease in the Middle Ages focused on divine intervention as the instrument of causation and relief, the views propounded by the Christian Church. It was the era of fervent belief in miracle cures obtained through visiting shrines where the relics of saints, martyrs, or other revered religious figures were held. Gregory of Tours, a Frankish historian of the sixth century, provided extensive evidence of this phenomenon. He claimed that his own recovery from serious illness was due to his pilgrimage to the tomb of St. Martin of Tours. This led him to devote his life to the church, and his election as Bishop of Tours in 573. But he is remembered more for *The History of the Franks* than for his personal life. This chronicle is liberally sprinkled with reports of miracle cures, some through holy relics, others through the agency of an especially devout monk. According to Gregory, for one such monk "it was a simple thing to cure those possessed of the devil, to restore their sight to the blind and to heal all other infirmities by calling on the name of our Lord or by making the sign of the Holy Cross. . . . Often he would relieve quartan fevers and other such diseases by prayer."[50]

The chronicle of Gregory of Tours is revealing of other circumstances associated with illness and disease in the early part of the Middle Ages. In another account of miracles performed at the tomb of St. Martin of Tours, Gregory gave direct evidence of the continuing presence of secular medical practitioners. And, incidentally, he revealed the tension which existed between those who were ardent supporters of miraculous religious cures and those who still favored the treatment offered by secular practitioners. Gregory told of an archdeacon who consulted "a number of doctors" when cataracts caused him to lose his sight. With no improvement from such treatments he undertook three months of prayer and fasting at the tomb of St. Martin after which his "eyes cleared and he began to see."[51] However, seeking even further improvement, the man consulted and was bled by a Jewish medical practitioner. The outcome, according to Gregory, was that the man became as blind as he had been originally. And to underscore his belief in the superiority of divine over earthly intervention he added: "Let this story be a warning to every Christian man, that when it has been granted to him to receive a cure from Heaven, he should not then seek earthly remedies."

The church also became more involved in medieval medicine at a more practical level. With the decline in secular medical practice, monasteries throughout Europe became the centers in which medical knowledge was preserved and where care for the sick was available. Initially, monastic involvement in medical care arose from the need to attend to those of their own Order who became ill or contracted some disease. This was soon extended to caring for the people living around the monastery, through a conviction that it was their Christian duty to offer such services. Some monks had particular skills in this area, others gained a modicum of medical knowledge from copying the many manuscripts which were safely preserved in monasteries during the Middle Ages. Monks also cultivated medicinal and culinary herbs in the monastery gardens and became skilled at prescribing and preparing herbal remedies. In this sense, their work overlapped with the community healers who used many of these remedies which had become traditional within most communities. There was, however, a difference in conceptual orientation between monastic medicine and that practiced by secular practitioners. Where the latter aimed to provide cures, as well as to relieve suffering, monastic medicine was focused on care rather than cure. Instead of attempting to deal with the disease, monastic medicine became an expression of comfort and support, coupled with efforts to relieve the effects of the disorder. This simply reflected their acceptance of the nexus between sin and divine punishment in the form of sickness, and the belief that a punishment should be endured for its spiritual benefits. Further, there were some reservations as to whether there should be any human intervention since this might be construed as thwarting God's will. Overall, monastic medicine was based on the conviction that caring for the soul took precedence over caring for the body.

This focus on a perceived nexus between spiritual and corporeal "disorders" was of profound significance in the shaping of responses to outbreaks of disease during the Middle Ages. It was most apparent in the religious, medical, and community reactions to the disfiguring and disabling disease of leprosy that appeared in the West about midway through the Middle Ages, and spread throughout Europe. The new epidemic introduced a totally new concept into community discourse on the body—that of the "unclean" body, which posed a threat to the rest of the population.

The Leprous "Unclean" Body

Leprosy appeared in western Europe in the sixth century. It demanded a reassessment of theories of disease causation, new treatment regimes, and a radically different societal approach to the regulation of the disordered body. Leprosy was also a disease which saw a conflation of ideas on sin, sexuality, and divine punishment. As a consequence of this construct, leprosy was perceived as God's punishment for sexual excesses.

Although, in the early phase of the epidemic this accusation was directed at all victims, it was soon focused, to a greater extent, on women. And since women had long been viewed as having insatiable sexual appetites, it was a short step to blaming them for the spread of leprosy. In effect, there was a conflation of ideas about the perceived dangers inherent in women's bodies. Their bodies, already seen as fundamentally "disordered," constituted a further threat to men from their sexuality and their "disorderly" deployment of such sexuality. Finally, fears of women's sexuality were compounded by fears that they could be the means of transmitting leprosy to men.

Leprosy, in one form or another, has been known since ancient times. However, it is more than likely that many of the conditions diagnosed as leprosy in earlier periods were instances of other types of skin complaints. During the sixth and seventh centuries, a disfiguring disease diagnosed as leprosy began to spread across western Europe. The intensity of this outbreak gradually increased until it was of epidemic proportions. Its most active period was reached between the tenth and the thirteenth centuries. After that, it declined in intensity in the Mediterranean area, where it had largely disappeared by the beginning of the fourteenth century.

Nevertheless, leprosy continued to take its toll in other parts of Europe for another two centuries or so.[52]

It is considered doubtful that the epidemic of leprosy, which spread across Europe during the Middle Ages, was of the same type as that described in the Bible. And, given the medieval propensity to diagnose a wide range of skin eruptions as leprosy, the extent of the outbreak may have been less severe than it appears from accounts of that period.[53] Nevertheless, the evidence is sufficiently strong to accept that a form of leprosy which physically disabled many people did sweep across Europe in that period. In any case, the general conviction within communities in western Europe was that they were witnessing an outbreak of the dreaded disease of leprosy. And for medieval Western communities, steeped in the teachings of the church, any condition diagnosed as leprosy was invariably associated with biblical accounts of that disease, and the perceptions of uncleanness and moral opprobrium associated with it.

Unable to establish the source of the infection, medieval authorities fell back on an old theory that diseases, particularly those associated with skin disorders, could be transmitted through sexual intercourse.[54] One writer, for example, asserted that if a leprous man had sexual intercourse with a woman, "not she but the next man who slept with her would come down with the disease."[55] With a bizarre twist, this writer drew a parallel with the dangers spelt out in the myth of the Poison-Damsel, although with leprosy, sexual encounters would appear to entail the risk of a lingering, rather than an immediate death. Nevertheless, once again this hypothesis raised the spectre of lethal sexual encounters.

In fact, there was no way in which the source of the infection or the means of transmission could have been established during the Middle Ages.[56] Medieval living conditions were frequently crowded and unhygienic by later standards, so fostering the spread of a wide range of diseases affecting the skin.[57] Some early writers blamed returning Crusaders for carrying the disease to the West. They may have assisted to spread the infection during its late phase, but such a hypothesis would not explain the outbreak of leprosy in the early part of the Middle Ages. Further, the disease has a fairly lengthy incubation period so that causal links would be difficult to establish.

Overall, leprosy became inextricably linked with notions of sexual depravity. This took two forms. Sexual excesses were linked to perceptions of disease causation where leprosy was involved, and there was a widely-held belief that all lepers were beset by a fren-

zied and uncontrollable desire for sex. Leprosy became the archetypal sexualized disease and has remained so in popular discourse
until recent times, despite the fact that there is no credible evidence to support such a proposition.

All medieval explanations or theories concerned with leprosy
were invariably couched in similar terms. This is not surprising
since the church dominated all areas of community life in the Middle Ages. As a consequence, the dictates of the church on moral
issues became an integral part of both religious and medical discourses on leprosy. This stemmed, in part, from the authority
claimed by the church to be the sole arbiter on matters of biblical
exegesis, and hence, in defining moral standards. Equally important, however, was the fact that debate on medical theory, and the
practice of medicine, was largely in the hands of the church for
most of the Middle Ages.[58] Although secular medicine was still practiced throughout the period, it was on a much reduced scale and
largely invisible, as far as records are concerned. Those who tended
the sick were more likely to be men in holy orders, although not
necessarily monks or priests.

Christian doctrine insisted that bodily disorders were causally
linked to an individual's moral lapses. Illness and disease were perceived as God's punishment for sinful behavior, and treating the
disease, other than providing palliative care, was seen as problematic. Such an intervention, it was held, might be seen as thwarting
God's intentions. Accordingly, the church placed its main emphasis
on ensuring that the patient sought forgiveness for his or her sins.
Inevitably, this meant that during the Middle Ages the priest took
primary responsibility for attending to the disordered body. He
cured the soul so that the body might be restored to physical health.
Nowhere was this pattern more apparent than in dealing with victims of the epidemic of leprosy in the Middle Ages. And, arguably,
at no other time have biblical prescriptions for dealing with the disordered body been more rigidly observed.

Targeting the "Unclean" Body

Leprosy gained its association with "uncleanness" from biblical pronouncements. In the Middle Ages, this provided the incentive for the segregation of lepers, and the categorization of their
"unclean" bodies as "disordered." The "clean" and "ordered" bodies
of the unaffected within medieval society distanced themselves
from those suffering from leprosy.

To many observers, the body of the leper becomes increasingly repugnant as the disease progresses. The onset of the disease is characterized by neurological changes—a loss of feeling which may lead to the victim inadvertently suffering injuries to parts of the body. This may even result in the loss of fingers, toes, or other limbs. Visually, the early indications may be a thickening of the skin, which also exhibits patches of darker pigmentation. There may also be a loss of hair. Depending on the form of leprosy, the disease may progress to a stage where large nodules appear over the face and body, and the mucous membranes of the eyes, nose, and throat become affected. In extreme cases, the voice may change completely, blindness may occur, or a person's nose may be destroyed. Edema of the extremities may occur and produce deformities of the hands and feet.[59]

As with other diseases which indicate their presence on the exterior of the body, a diagnosis of leprosy was always possible when the above symptoms were present, even though some of the signs may also indicate conditions other than leprosy. That, of course, was the pattern of diagnosis in the Middle Ages. After communities had become aware of the possibility that leprosy was in their midst, there was a bias toward such a diagnosis whenever any doubt existed. While the law required those who had contracted leprosy to submit themselves for examination, it is more likely that public denunciation by others in the community led to action being taken.[60] And, in accordance with the injunctions in Leviticus (13:2), the priest was the final arbiter. In some communities, panels of individuals chosen for the purpose debated the diagnosis, but they also relied on advice from a priest and generally followed the requirements laid down in Leviticus, 13:3:

> And the priest shall look on the plague in the skin of the flesh, and when the hair in the plague is turned white, and the plague in sight be deeper than the skin of his flesh, it is a plague of leprosy; and the priest shall look on him, and pronounce him unclean.

The examination of someone suspected of having leprosy could produce alternative conclusions. The person may be declared "clean" and free of the disease. However, if his or her sinful life-style may ultimately attract God's punishment in the form of leprosy, such persons were admonished to mend their ways. If, on the other hand, a skin disease which could not be diagnosed as leprosy was present, the person was kept under observation and confined to his or her own home for seven days and then re-examined. If a diagnosis of leprosy was confirmed, the person concerned was banished from the community.

Banishing the "Unclean" Body

The moral and civic status of a person diagnosed as having leprosy changed completely. According to the Scriptures, when there was clear evidence of reddish sores, whitened hair, or other indications of the disease, a declaration was to be made: "He is a leprous man, he is unclean; and the priest shall pronounce him utterly unclean . . ." (Lev.13:44). And after being stigmatized by having his clothes rent, his head bared, and being required to cover the upper lip and go about crying "unclean, unclean," he was to be banished from the community—"without the camp shall his habitation be" (Lev. 13:46). These injunctions shaped all responses to the medieval epidemic of leprosy. All communities were seized with the need to segregate lepers from the majority who were healthy. The general perception was that even being close to an infected person could expose one to contracting the disease. There was another factor shaping responses. The incapacitating nature of the disease, and its resistance to any known treatments, convinced people that the sin for which leprosy was the punishment must have been equally loathsome and abhorrent. It followed that the leper represented both a moral and a physical danger to God-fearing, law-abiding citizens.

Banishment or segregation could involve being forced to live outside the town in a hut built in the open fields, or for a wealthy citizen, being confined within one's own house while any signs of the disease were present. For the majority, banishment from the community meant being confined within a leper asylum—variously known as a leprosarium, lazaretto, or lazar house. The church began to assume responsibility for lepers, and to establish these places of confinement for them, during the sixth century. As the numbers of lepers escalated, an increasing number of asylums had to be established throughout Europe. Later in the Middle Ages, secular authorities also became involved in the establishment and control of leper houses. The disciplinary regime within these establishments was severe, reflecting the view of both church and secular society that the leper was both a moral and a physical outcast. The rules for inmates in one such establishment are a reflection of this condemnation:

Amongst all infirmities, the disease of leprosy may be considered the most loathsome, and those who are smitten with it ought at all times, and in all places, as well in their conduct as in their dress, to bear themselves as more to be despised and as more humble than all other men.[61]

The process of degradation and stigmatization of the leper was completed by rituals associated with his or her banishment from society. The decree issued in 1179, by the Third Lateral Council, established a format for such ceremonies that differed little from the Offices for the Dead.[62] The edicts of the council also stipulated that lepers must wear distinctive clothing, enabling them to be readily identified, and avoided by others in the community.[63] This gave visible proof of the "otherness" of lepers. It also facilitated the process of surveillance which was necessary to ensure their exclusion from the rest of society. While distinguishing signs varied from community to community across Europe, the essential characteristics remained much the same. Every leper was required to wear the prescribed leper's costume, and to carry something which would indicate his or her approach to a healthy person. Sometimes, the warning device was a bell, either carried or worn on the shoes, in other communities the leper carried and used a clapper or rattle. The leper also carried a bowl with which to seek alms.

Along with their banishment from the community and being classed as spiritual outcasts, lepers lost all legal and civil rights. They became "non-persons" and frequently had all their goods confiscated by the secular authorities. And from the twelfth century onward, lepers became the victims of increasingly harsh and oppressive measures implemented by various western European States.

New Regimes for the "Disordered" Body

Fundamentally, medieval responses to leprosy were founded on precepts and principles defined in the Scriptures, and central to doctrines espoused by the church. They shaped community perceptions of the disease, and of the leper, which became indelibly imprinted in community consciousness. Hence, the leper was forever categorized as morally decadent as well as posing a threat to the health of others in the community. This conflation of ideas reinforced the perception of lepers as "dangerous others." As Mary Dou-

glas pointed out, as soon as immorality is associated with "accusations of causing insidious harm," the "syndrome of social exclusion"
is heavily reinforced.[64] Secular authorities in western Europe,
always alert to the threats posed by "dangerous others," responded
vigorously. In the process, two marginalized groups, lepers and
Jews, were vilified and frequently accused of acting together
against the interests of the state.

France, in particular, was an area in which these groups were
ruthlessly pursued. In the early fourteenth century, lepers in
France were accused of trying to kill the entire population. There
are several versions of this supposed plot, but all contain the same
fundamental accusation—that the lepers placed poisonous powders
in the fountains, wells, and rivers so that the healthy would become
infected and die from leprosy.[65] The motive, it was claimed, was to
gain power over the towns and countryside. In response, the King
of France issued an edict in 1321 for the extermination or confinement of all lepers for their crimes against the state. In some
accounts of these events, lepers and Jews were said to have acted
together. In this version, the Jews, desirous of destroying Christianity, enlisted the aid of lepers to carry out the poisoning.[66] Many
lepers were burnt at the stake.[67] A later modification of this edict
reduced the numbers of those put to death, but demanded that all
lepers be confined. As Ginsburg noted, this was "the first time in
the history of Europe that such a large programme of segregation
was undertaken."[68] The ritual banishment, or confinement in a hos-
pital-like institution administered by religious orders, was replaced
by incarceration for life.

The confinement and segregation from society of lepers constituted the final element of a new regime for regulating and controlling the disordered body. It was accompanied by a process of
stigmatization of lepers which followed the patterns of stigma identified Goffman.[69] First, their disordered bodies represented "abomi-
nations of the body," the perceptions that they indulged in grossly
sinful behavior represented "blemishes of individual character,"
and finally, they were perceived as having a "tribal stigma,"
reflected in their total rejection as a group, by the rest of society.
One outcome of this process of stigmatization is that leprosy has
forever been associated with perceptions of moral turpitude, mainly
of a sexual nature. And, in the twentieth century the term "leper"
is more likely to call up an image of a "social outcast" rather than
one suffering from the disease.

Leprosy was the first major epidemic disease to be closely

identified with human sexuality. It established a perception which has endured for centuries, that there is a nexus between sexuality, sin, and disease. Even the twentieth century has witnessed a resurgence of this idea in some sections of Western society. The epidemic of leprosy also focused further attention on the perceived dangers associated with women's bodies and their sexuality. Experiences with the epidemic of leprosy also left another legacy—the perception that women's bodies should be viewed as potential vectors of disease transmission.

There was another significant outcome from the epidemic of leprosy—a range of measures introduced to control and regulate lepers. Not only did these measures establish a new regime for the regulation of the disordered body, but they also provided the framework for the subsequent regulatory apparatus of the carceral state, as defined by Foucault.[70] In addition, the techniques involved in the examination, classification, surveillance, and segregation of lepers provided a powerful tool, already proven, for western European communities threatened with other epidemics.

We turn our attention now to the next major epidemic, which arrived in western Europe just as the impact of leprosy was beginning to diminish. Unlike leprosy, the new scourge was not directly associated with sexuality. Nevertheless, it was responsible for a wide range of significant cultural transformations in Western society. The new epidemic also exercised a profound influence on societal perceptions of the body, of bodily disorders and of bodily practices.

This new epidemic was a calamity of such immense proportions that it produced a reign of terror throughout the West. Steeped in the teachings of the Christian Church, and the semiotics of disaster, all communities became convinced that the Fourth Horseman of the Apocalypse—Pestilence—was about to descend upon them.[71]

Apocalyptic Angst

These words, of gloomy color I saw
Inscribed above a gateway . . .
THROUGH ME IS THE WAY TO THE CITY OF DESPAIR,
THROUGH ME IS THE WAY TO PERPETUAL ANGUISH,
THROUGH ME IS THE WAY TO THE PLACE OF THE DAMNED,
. . .
ABANDON HOPE ALL YOU WHO ENTER HERE.

—Dante, Inferno (Hell), Canto III[1]

Florence: A "City of the Wicked"

... yet are there but two sorts of men that do properly make the two cities we speak of; the one is of men that live according to the flesh, and the other of those that live according to the spirit, ... For in the city of the wicked, where God does not govern and men do not obey ... and consequently where the soul does not rule the body, nor reason passion, there is generally found wanting the virtue of true justice.

—Saint Augustine[1]

If *men* could see beneath the skin, the sight of *women* would make them nauseous. . . . Since we are loath to touch spittle or dung even with our fingertips, how can we desire to embrace such a sack of dung?

—Odo of Cluny[2]

O fellow humans, how full you are of vanity and self-love. You can see what is going on all around you, yet you remain blind to the realities of life! You rejoice in earthly riches, in the fame and honour that the world can bestow, and in fulfilling the desires of the flesh, ... and these sins are truly your death, because they earn for you severe and everlasting punishment in the next world.

—Bono Giamboni[3]

Late medieval Florence, in the eyes of its citizens, was a "city of the wicked." Torn by political feuding, and under strain from the problems of rapid growth and urbanization, Florentines were troubled by a conviction that vice was rife in their city. From their own observations and the denunciations of their behavior from the pulpit, the citizens of Florence came to believe that they lived in a hotbed of sin. Preachers of the period constantly harangued them about the perils of envy, greed, violence, avarice, and lust. But above all else, it was the sexuality of the body, and in particular, the dangers inherent in the female body, which became the main targets of clerical attack. Secular literature frequently mirrored these concerns. Doubtless, there were people who did not fully share these sexually repressive views, but the medieval church so dominated community perceptions and practices that it was the voice of the church which prevailed. And it is this voice that is revealed when we peruse public and personal records of the late Middle Ages.[4]

The chronicles of Giovanni Villani, an influential merchant of Florence, provide a wealth of information on contemporary beliefs and perceptions within the community.[5] Villani was proud of his city and its achievements. However, he was also greatly concerned about the inherent wickedness of his fellow citizens. He feared that this would prevent Florence from fulfilling her destiny as "the daughter and creature of Rome."[6] In his chronicles, Villani devoted a whole chapter to a review of Florence in 1338. He entitled this "On the Greatness and State and Magnificence of the Commune of Florence."[7] In this he gathered a great deal of information on the size of the city, how it compared with other cities of northern Italy, and its position in international banking and commerce. In the main, he allowed the figures to tell the story of the importance of the city, but toward the end of the chapter his patriotic pride overcame any tendency toward modesty. He wrote glowingly of the city's beauty and magnificence, and the numerous palaces, churches, and other public buildings which were clear signs of the great wealth of Florence and its citizens. Even those with no particular reason to praise the accomplishments of Florence echoed the same sentiments. Benzo d'Alessandria, a resident of Milan wrote of Florence: "Indeed this magnificent city flourishes to such an extent that it may be called the most opulent, populous and rich of the cities of the world."[8]

A Vibrant City—Late Medieval Florence

Florence was a vibrant city and an important international center by the early fourteenth century. It had expanded rapidly toward the end of the Middle Ages. Estimates of the population suggest that it grew from 10,000 to 30,000 in the one hundred years before 1300, and then from 30,000 to between 100,000 and 120,000 by 1345.[9] While four cities in northern Italy—Florence, Milan, Venice, and Genoa—were of similar size, only Paris in the north of Europe approached this size.[10] London, for example, had a population of not more than 50,000 inhabitants. Even amongst the Italian cities of the early fourteenth century, however, Florence was unique. Its prominent position was derived from its extensive international banking, commercial, and manufacturing activities which produced considerable wealth and attracted people from other centers. To accommodate this physical growth, a third circle of city walls had to be constructed in the late thirteenth and early fourteenth centuries.

Walled towns and cities were a feature of the Middle Ages. The fortified walls and their observation towers provided a means of defense against attack by foreign armies, whether these were from neighboring cities or from much further afield. They also enabled the city authorities to enforce bans on entry by individuals or groups considered a danger to the community. In effect, the walls created the boundaries of inclusion-exclusion which were important societal concepts in the Middle Ages, and even in later periods. They also gave the inhabitants a sense of community identity, of "belonging" to the group. The encircling walls also reinforced the concept that one's identity was inextricably associated with that of the commune, and the other corporate structures within the city— the guilds, kinship groups, and the parish or neighborhood societies. Furthermore, the enclosed space, and the corporate sense which it gave to the community, reinforced the concept that imprudent actions by an individual or by a group of people could have dire consequences for the whole community.

Life within the walls of a crowded city such as Florence provided little opportunity to escape the curious eyes of neighbors. There were few thoroughfares, those which did exist usually provided access from the city gates to the main square or the principal church. All other streets were narrow, and were lined with buildings which served both as domestic quarters and shops or workshops. Whatever the purpose, all going and coming was easily observed. And any activities deemed to be contrary to the community good—as detrimental to the cohesiveness of the community— could not be readily concealed. It was the ease of observation that enabled many informants to offer the evidence which was required to support charges laid against another person. This was particularly the case for offenses involving moral lapses. What neighbors saw, or thought they saw, would be evidence enough to prove adultery, the practice of prostitution, or homosexual behavior, in court. Only the very wealthy could afford the luxury of some separation from the crowd, and even they often carried on their business activities in a section of the same building which served as the family residence. At the other end of the social scale, the indigent always lived in over-crowded quarters, having to accept that being constantly exposed to public gaze was their lot in life.

Despite being enclosed by typically medieval city walls, Florence was not like many other medieval cities. It did not reflect some of the medieval characteristics commonly found in northern European communities. A similar pattern prevailed in other northern Italian cities. Essentially, they had never fully lost touch with the concepts associated with the urbanized culture of classical Roman times. One of the important elements of the latter was the conviction that the city ruled the surrounding countryside. Consequently, there was considerable conflict between the city and the rural nobility as the Imperial power exercised from northern Europe weakened in the eleventh and twelfth centuries. This was exacerbated as the communes, or city-states, of northern Italy emerged.

Politics and Power

The city-states gradually evolved their own community power structures. These emerged as various local groups vied with each other for supremacy in communal affairs. One of the older groups, the rural magnates, had always been influential in the urban affairs of Florence and similar northern Italian cities. And in confirmation of their involvement, most maintained houses in both the city and the country. This differed markedly from the patterns that prevailed in northern Europe. As the Franciscan chronicler, Salimbene de Adam, noted: "in France only the bourgeoisie live in the cities while the knights and their noble ladies live in villas on their estates."[11] In Florence, the magnates from the surrounding countryside made common cause with their city counterparts as jointly they sought to retain administrative control of the commune. However, the emerging merchant and professional classes, as well as the master tradesmen who provided much of the employment, rejected this position. By the middle of the thirteenth century, the latter groups gained control of the commune, and extended communal control over the magnate and clerical landlords of the countryside. From 1282, the power of the city magnates was curtailed and only those who were members of the guilds—bankers, merchants, manufacturers, skilled tradesmen, and the like—were eligible to hold civic office. In effect, by the end of the thirteenth century only those who actually created the wealth of the city through their daily activities could participate in the government of the commune.

To consolidate their position, these groups established a new constitution providing for elections to fill the ranks of the ruling councils, and to specific civic office in Florence. It also defined a fairly short period during which any person could occupy these positions, after which new elections had to be called. While this system appears to have opened up opportunities for sharing administrative responsibilities in Florence, the list of those eligible for election was fairly limited and represented, for the most part, well-entrenched interests. Consequently, feuding between powerful groups continued into the fourteenth century. Many members of Florentine ruling families spent part of their lives in exile awaiting the return to power of their group, and plotting the overthrow of the incumbent ruling party was common. Despite these administrative interruptions, there was a marked continuity in the range of legislation enacted. To some extent, this was due to the all-pervasive influence of the dominant religious discourse on the definition of community norms. In addition, however, it also reflected the fact that all the ruling groups belonged to a similar level in Florentine society and sought to achieve similar goals. In practical terms, it was only the beneficiaries of legislation who changed places.

This apparent continuity in legislative activity owed much to the pattern of Florentine society in the late-thirteenth and early-fourteenth centuries. As we have already noted, those who exercised the power of government in Florence were drawn from a relatively small percentage of the city's population. In theory, many more were eligible to vote, and to participate, because of their membership of one of the trade guilds of Florence. In practice, however, the electoral system was weighted heavily in favor of the professional, manufacturing, and merchant guilds. These guilds, to which all had to belong if they wished to practice their trade or profession in Florence, were particular examples of the fact that this was still the era of the corporation, and not the individual. Other important corporate bodies in Florence at that time include neighborhood and parish groups, local militia units, clan groups, extended family groups, and lay confraternities.[12] These corporate groups provided a complex network of inter-relationships which instilled loyalty to the group amongst members, and provided an immensely powerful sense of social cohesion in the community. All employed unifying symbols to reinforce the sense of brotherhood or association— patron saints, cult objects and relics, banners and emblems, ritual assemblies, and distinctive ceremonial clothing. Reflecting the all-pervasive influence of the church, most corporate entities maintained close ties with one of the many religious bodies in the city and included regular religious observances in their corporate practices. Accordingly, they became important channels through which the community concepts of moral boundaries and deviance were disseminated. In effect, they acted as instruments of social regulation at the same time as they provided opportunities for social contact, and supplied social support services for their members or adherents.

The Evolution of Secular Law

More direct measures aimed at social regulation were embodied in constraints imposed by both ecclesiastical and secular laws which had been in varying degrees of conflict throughout the Middle Ages. In the twentieth century it is easy to overlook the fact that the law of the church was very powerful in medieval times, and that canon law was applicable to the whole community not simply to the clergy.[13] Predictably, the church claimed jurisdiction over all matters pertaining to its own organization and administration. Even this area of jurisdiction was often disputed by secular governments, particularly in matters relating to property and hence, liability for taxes. The church also claimed to rule on matters which were linked to the sacraments—marriage and family relationships, wills, vows and pledges, and any contracts which relied on the good faith of the parties. It also claimed a primary role in dealing with matters arising from sin, and with many crimes which were the public manifestation of sin. In general, the latter included false doctrine, heresy, perjury and usury, and most sexual offenses. Punishments imposed by church courts ranged from simple forms of penance, to sentences of death. When it came to carrying out the death penalty, however, the church courts were happy for secular authorities to play a part in legal matters. As Bullough has phrased it: "The pious hypocrisy of allowing the state to execute the condemned kept the Church officially from shedding blood or executing anyone."[14]

Secular authorities in the late Middle Ages also enacted a good deal of legislation for the regulation of daily life. Apart from developing a criminal code, Florence enacted a considerable body of sanitary legislation, mostly originating in the thirteenth century. Generally, this legislation aimed at establishing preventative health measures. In their practical application, such Florentine regulations applied to the cleaning of streets, drains and sewers, and the storage and sale of meat, fish, and fruits.[15] Progressively, Florence also enacted laws which covered issues previously claimed by the church to be its province. In following this practice, however, most issues concerned with moral deviance were simply transferred from ecclesiastical to civil laws, retaining the condemnation of sinful behavior contained in canon law.

The Sinful Community

It is not surprising that the citizens of Florence were overwhelmed by a sense of guilt. They were constantly harangued about their moral shortcomings from the pulpit. The sermons of Giordano da Rivalto-Moreni (Pisa), a prominent and influential Dominican friar, reveal the pattern of these denunciations. Preaching in Florence in 1302, his exhortations were replete with images about the sinfulness of the community.[16] In blunt and picturesque language, he berated his listeners for their moral failures and urged them to repent before it was too late. Giordano focused his attention on the three categories of sin, defined previously by John the Evangelist— "the lust of the flesh, the lust of the eyes, and the pride of life."[17] He explained these categories of sin in everyday terms indicating that they represented lascivious behavior, avarice, and arrogant pride. Giordano also asserted that: "These three main vices are the initiators and the root of all vices, sins and evils which are committed and that are possible to commit in the world."[18]

Of the three types of sin, the one which became a frequent theme in Giordano's sermons was lust of the flesh. He exhorted his listeners to constantly battle against the attractions of carnal pleasures. During one of his sermons, Giordano asserted that everyone must strive to resist the temptations of sex. They must constantly try to break the chains of lasciviousness which bound all humans to earthly things.[19] Furthermore, he likened this never-ending battle

against the desires of the body to the action of a heavy grinding mill
bearing down relentlessly on the soul.[20]

In a sermon delivered in Florence in 1304, Giordano launched
a fiery attack on what he saw as widespread wickedness among the
young people of the city, reserving his strongest condemnation for
their grave sexual transgressions. He laid the blame for this state
of affairs on parents, accusing them of acting irresponsibly by doing
nothing to chastise and correct their sons. By neglecting their duty
in this way, he declared, parents could only expect their offspring
to become even more depraved in later years. Giordano was convinced that the moral standards of the community had reached
such a low point that:

> . . . this city is much corrupted by youths who indulge in the
> worst habits in the world, who are taken up with carnal
> pleasures, and with foul and barbarous sins . . . the fault of
> their fathers and mothers who do not chastise them. . . . But
> amongst all kinds of vices, they [the parents] will see them
> participating in acts of sodomy and other wicked vices
> every day, and they say nothing to their sons. . . .[21]

It is not surprising that Giordano considered sodomy to be a singularly evil sin. Sodomy had become a matter of grave concern to both
church and state authorities in Florence by the fourteenth century.
It was believed to be widely practiced by males of all classes in the
city. It was also believed to have the potential to undermine the
social fabric of the community.[22]

The term "sodomy" lacked precise definition during the Middle Ages, and even in later periods. Many of the clergy used the
term "sodomy" in a very broad sense to include all non-procreative
sexual activity, regardless of the sex of the participants.[23] Others
avoided the use of the term, preferring to include homosexual
behavior among a broad range of sexual activities described generally as "sins against nature." The term could mean different things
to different preachers, depending on the degree of fear and repugnance each harbored for human sexuality. But there is little ambi-
guity in Giordano's denunciations. Without doubt, he was targeting
male homosexual activity, a practice deemed particularly abhorrent in late medieval religious discourse.

This condemnation reflected a marked hardening of attitudes
toward all sexual activities, but especially toward homosexual
activity. This influenced the attitudes of the entire community.

Boswell concluded that "from 1150 to 1350, homosexual behavior appears to have changed, in the eyes of the public, from the personal preference of a prosperous minority, . . . to a dangerous, anti-social, and severely sinful aberration."[24] In addition, it "passed from being completely legal in most of Europe to incurring the death penalty in all but a few contemporary legal compilations." By 1325, for example, Florence had enacted penalties for homosexual activities ranging from fines to being burned at the stake.[25] Although severe penalties were inflicted only rarely, the regulations clearly reflect the moral position of the Florentine community toward the middle of the fourteenth century.

Giordano was not a lone voice thundering against the wickedness of the community. Similar denunciations of sinful behavior were delivered by the clergy of the parish churches, and particularly by the mendicant friars of the Dominican and Franciscan Orders.[26] Locating themselves in urban communities, the mendicants established close contact with the citizens on whom they relied for the necessities of life. Many developed great reputations as preachers, attracting large and receptive audiences, even though their sermons concentrated on the shortcomings of their listeners. The themes of these sermons remained essentially the same. Only the oratorical skills and personal emphases varied from one friar to another. For Florentines these sermons were a persistent call to mend their wicked ways. However, with so many behaviors classed as sinful it must have been rather perplexing for a listener to decide which human activities would not incur God's wrath in some way or another.

Changing Concepts of Sin

Many writers and preachers were strident and emphatic in their denunciations of sinful behavior. In particular, they displayed a near obsession with the evils associated with the human body, perceived by many as a disgusting and degrading element of earthly existence. To support their stance, they could turn to biblical sources which expressed repugnance for the body and its functions. They could draw on declarations that the true path lay in ". . . putting away the filth of the flesh," that one should "abstain from fleshly lusts, which war against the soul . . ." (I Peter 2:11, and 3:21).[27]

Nowhere was the support for renunciation of the body and its sexuality clearer than in Paul's advice that "it is better for a man not to touch a woman" (I Cor. 7:1). And nothing could better illustrate the way in which thirteenth-century literature promoted this precept than the work of Jacopone da Todi. Jacopone was a notary who became a lay friar within the Franciscan Order and wrote on many topics related to the religious life. However, when he wrote of the body, his abhorrence of it was abundantly clear. He was certain that renunciation of the flesh in all its aspects and the adoption of an ascetic way of life provided the only path to salvation. To Jacopone the visible manifestation of human life was a "filthy, evil body—lascivious and gluttonous."[28]

This extreme position was not shared by all. Even among clerics, there were many who accepted that the human body was not intrinsically repulsive. Nevertheless, they also subscribed to the view that the origins of sinful behavior often lay in giving free rein to carnal desires. These two viewpoints represent the divergence that existed in the perceptions of sinful behavior toward the end of the Middle Ages. But these competing religious discourses were the outcomes of an extensive theological debate during the Middle Ages, often erroneously portrayed as a period of intellectual and social stagnation. In fact, there was a great deal of consideration given to the fundamentals of Christian dogma during that period. There were also fundamental shifts in both ecclesiastical and secular power structures and relationships, and changes in social conditions. Perceptions of sin also responded to these changes, and new definitions of moral boundaries emerged. It would be useful for us to briefly review these shifts in order to chart the evolution of community discourse on sin and the body that prevailed in Florence in the early fourteenth century.

The importance of the seven cardinal sins in the Middle Ages started in the fifth century with the work of Cassian.[29] He concluded that even though pride was the worst of all sins, carnal sins were the most difficult to eradicate. Initially, discourses on sin focused principally on the temptations faced by young men entering the monastic life—gluttony, lust, and lack of spiritual commitment (*gula, fornicatio,* and *accidia*).[30] Over time, the same strictures formed the basis of rules that were recommended to the lay world. This process of broadening the application of the cardinal sins to become part of the general dogma that guided the church was completed by Gregory the Great in the seventh century. From that point the list of cardinal sins did not change significantly, although its order was occasionally rearranged. It comprised pride, anger, envy, avarice, lack of spiritual commitment, gluttony, and lust (*superbia, ira, invidia, avaritia, accidia, gula,* and *luxuria).* Toward the end of the medieval period, as we have already seen, there was a marked increase in the amount of attention paid to carnal sins. In effect, there was a return to the preoccupation with sins of the flesh displayed by the Desert Fathers such as Cassian. There is little doubt that this resurgence of interest was stimulated by the strong stand taken by Jerome, Ambrose, Augustine, and Aquinas on resisting the evils of lust. In addition to their authoritative pronouncements, theological debate in the late medieval period gave rise to a vast body of canon law that codified a range of behaviors, which was considered reprehensible. These laws, which provided the basis for the conduct of ecclesiastical courts, and set precedents for emerging civil laws, placed considerable emphasis on the regulation of sexual behavior, both within and outside of marriage. This codification also led to a great preoccupation with sexual sin by the clergy and moralists of the late-thirteenth-century. The pervasiveness of lechery, even among the faithful, appears to have been their favored topic.[31]

The intensive speculation on theological issues, which was characteristic of the eleventh to the thirteenth centuries, also produced some new doctrines which related to ways of purging sins, and to perceptions of the body and its sexuality. Some of the doctrinal innovations had a direct bearing on the matters that we are investigating. The first of these related to the ways in which sins could be purged. While formal confession of sins had been long recognized as an element of church ritual, it was not until the Fourth Lateran Council (1215–16) that it was made obligatory for all adherents. This increased the demand for the services of confessors, and to assist them in the execution of their duties, the so-called penitentials, handbooks specially prepared for their guidance, proliferated. This new genre of moral literature focused sharply on the evils of the flesh, and was very influential in shaping Western Christian doctrine on sexual matters. So intense was the preoccupation with the body and its functions that sexual offenses constituted the largest single category of deviant behavior that the penitentials listed.[32] These handbooks of moral behavior also encouraged the conflation of the terms "cardinal sins" and "deadly sins" as this provided the simplest way of illustrating the types of sin which would incur eternal punishment in Hell, the "sins unto death" referred to by John the Evangelist (I John, 5:16).[33]

In the early years of the Middle Ages, Christian doctrine allowed only limited possibilities in the afterlife for the sinner.

Those who did not purge their sins before death could expect that bodily death also signified death of the soul and eternal damnation. However, another possibility for the redemption of the soul emerged in the latter part of the Middle Ages, the concept of Purgatory. Now those who had repented of their sins on earth, perhaps with a death bed confession, but had not had time to purge the stain of sin, had the opportunity to complete the process before being welcomed into Paradise. The final cleansing of the stain of sin was to be undertaken during a period in Purgatory. On the other hand, those who failed to repent during their lifetime, whether through neglect or through meeting an untimely end, had to suffer eternal punishment in Hell. However, the new concept of Purgatory provided added ways of purging one's sins, and allowed scope for the living to offer prayers for a speedy passage through Purgatory for the departed. Some of these innovations in church dogma were to have an important place in community responses during the fourteenth and later centuries, issues which we investigate in detail.

Two other extensions to Western Christian dogma added new elements to religious discourse on the body. The first of these is contained in the concept of the *Imitatio Christi* (Imitation of Christ). This inspired a desire to replicate the suffering of Christ, not in terms of the Crucifixion, but through inflicting bodily pain on oneself as a means of gaining divine patronage, or in expiation of one's sins. The development of this concept led to a great expansion in penitential self-scourging, a practice previously limited to small groups of ascetics living in religious communities dedicated to extremes of pious observance. The wider application of this practice within religious communities and its extension to some groups within the lay population suggests an increasing acceptance of an image of the body as a vile and degrading element of human existence. Such a conclusion is encouraged by the results of self-flagellation. It was common for the practice to produce extensive lacerations to the body, and a flow of blood from the self-inflicted wounds.

The second of the new doctrinal elements that changed religious and community discourses on the body and sin was the Cult of the Virgin Mary. This focused attention on Mary as the supreme example of ideal womanhood. Although a mother, she was seen as without the blemish associated with carnal relations, and free of all sin. She became revered as the most powerful of the saints who could be asked to intercede on behalf of an individual or a community in times of crisis. As a consequence, images of the Madonna proliferated, and became central to religious rituals which sought deliverance from disease and disaster. This innovation further emphasized the sexualization of the body, making a sharp distinction between the woman who entered into normal human sexual activities and the one who renounced this participation in favor of pursuit of the spiritual. The only possible conclusion to be drawn from this perception was that women who renounced sex were superior to all other women, and almost attained the status of a celibate male. And with such a conclusion, the dichotomy between the virgin saint and the evil whore was established. The new cult also perpetuated and reinforced existing gender stereotypes, emphasizing the dangers attached to any association with women. It captured precisely the misogynist stance of most of the early Church Fathers, and the essence of the following vitriolic denunciation of women:

> And I find it more bitter than death the woman, whose heart is snares and nets, and her hands as bonds; whoso pleased God shall escape from her; but the sinner shall be taken by her. (Eccl. 7:26)

Spreading the Message on Sin: From Image to Word

It was not the written word that was the main vehicle for setting the moral tone in communities such as Florence in the thirteenth century. The majority of Florentines were unable to read, and in this period before the introduction of printing, it was only the privileged minority which had access to the manuscripts that preceded printed books. Nevertheless, the numbers of those who could read were increasing during the thirteenth and early-fourteenth centuries, as was the supply of works written in the vernacular by clerical and lay writers. Most of these reflected the values of late Medieval Church doctrine with its nexus between sin and divine retribution. Many also mirrored the repressive stance of the church on human sexuality.

The work of the thirteenth-century lay writer, Bono Giambono, *Il libro de' vizi e delle virtudi* (The Book of Vices and Virtues), is an example of works of this genre. Arguably, the most prominent work of this type is *La Divina Commedia* (The Divine Comedy) of Dante Alighieri, begun in 1308.[34] This great allegory explores the catalogue of sins which, in accordance with medieval

Christian doctrine, would earn eternal damnation. It frequently refers to Florence as a city corrupted by moral decadence, and depicts several of its former citizens in perpetual torment in Hell for their sins. However, despite their growing readership, vernacular treatises of this nature only influenced the majority of Florentines indirectly. Their influence was through the educated elite with the power to define moral boundaries for the whole community—the lawmakers of Florence.

Consequently, it was from religious art and sermons, and not from pious tracts, that the majority of people in Florence gained their understanding in the thirteenth and fourteenth centuries of moral limits. Throughout the Middle Ages, the church had relied on its message being conveyed to the people by means of the spoken word, and through religious paintings, murals, and sculpture. However, preaching was abandoned to a great extent during the High Middle Ages by the older monastic orders, and many amongst the secular clergy of the parishes lacked the education and the communication skills necessary to be effective in this field. Until the twelfth century at least, there was, by default, a considerable reliance on religious art, the only form of art in the Middle Ages, to spread the message. This task was accomplished by providing visual representations of the principal figures and events on which the Christian faith rests. To many clerics, this was sufficient to convey the whole Christian message. All that the laity needed to know could be gained from contemplating religious images, in particular, by concentrating their attention on images of the Crucifixion. As the Dominican friar Domenico Cavalca asserted:

> Because Christ Crucified demonstrates and teaches all virtues and all useful knowledge, we can truly say that he is the book of life in which every ignorant commoner and others of different condition can read and see before them the whole of the Christian doctrine in abbreviated form.[35]

In essence, the frescoes that covered the walls of Western Christian churches were "the poor man's Bible."[36]

This situation began to change markedly in the early part of the thirteenth century when the two Orders of mendicant friars, the Dominicans and the Franciscans, were created. They differed markedly from the previously established monastic Orders. The latter were primarily contemplative orders operating in rural monasteries, somewhat aloof from the daily life which surrounded them. The friars on the other hand belonged to an environment which hardly existed even a century previously—that of the expanding cities and towns, and of the universities. Both of the new Orders located their convents within and as close as possible to the centers of cities such as Florence, where the focus was on manufacturing, trade, and finance rather than on agricultural activities. The friars rapidly established strong links within any community for two reasons. First, as mendicants, they needed this degree of contact since they depended for their sustenance on the inhabitants of urban communities such as Florence. Second, they met a rising demand for greater participation by the laity in religious exercises.

The Dominican Order was established as an Order of Preachers, with the important objective of identifying and stamping out heresy. While the Franciscans had a less focused objective initially, they soon became just as active in the area of preaching. Both Orders expanded rapidly and received considerable support from many city authorities and citizen benefactors in establishing their churches. Generally, in the past, the message of the church had been disseminated through its system of parish churches which were usually quite small. By comparison, the churches built by or for the mendicant friars were often immense, capable of attracting large congregations to hear the preacher. The two most important of these in Florence, the Church of Santa Croce (Franciscan) and the Church of Santa Maria Novella (Dominican) were begun in this period. Even by the standards of today, both are very large. The cathedral of Florence and several other churches capable of holding large congregations were also started or rebuilt in the thirteenth century. As a result, the friars were able to reach much larger audiences with their denunciations of sinful behavior, and their exhortations to repentance.[37] Not only did they have an advantage over the parish clergy in the capacity of their churches, but they made a much more direct impact because they delivered their message in the vernacular instead of the formal Latin used in the parish churches.[38]

The friars always delivered their sermons in colorful, often earthy and abrasive language, emphasizing their message with vivid images readily understood by their listeners. Preachers from the mendicant orders became very popular and the most eloquent of these were invited to various cities to preach, particularly during the Lenten season. The chronicles of the Franciscan Salimbene de Adam contain frequent references to the preaching skills and popularity of friars from both Orders. One particular preacher was described thus by Salimbene:

> He was one of the greatest scholars in the world and a fine
> preacher, pleasing to the learned and the unlearned
> alike. . . . His tongue was most eloquent and his voice like
> a trumpet or thunder, like the sounds of many waters rush-
> ing through a gulf. His eloquence was always flowing and
> never hesitated. . . . He told marvellous things of the king-
> dom of heaven, that is, the glories of paradise, and terrible
> things of the pains of hell.[39]

Perhaps Salimbene was a little effusive in his praise, but this passage gives us some indication of the impression this preacher's message must have made on his listeners.

The inhabitants of Florence welcomed the friars and listened
attentively to their message. They were profoundly influenced by
the trenchant criticism of sinful behavior which was central to the
messages delivered by the mendicant friars. Inevitably, sin and its
consequences, and the need for repentance, were elevated to
greater prominence in the prevailing religious discourse. Furthermore, the whole community became fearful of the consequences for
Florence, and for individuals, of failing to heed the message and
turn away from their evil ways.

No new categories of sinful behavior were formulated by the
friars. What did change, however, was the emphasis which was
placed on various types of sin. As we have already observed,
increasing attention was focused on the body and its contribution
to deviant behavior. To a very large extent, there was a sexualization of sin, and a declaration that much of human sexual behavior
was "against nature." The concept that some sexual activities were
"against nature" was progressively reinterpreted and widened during the theological debates of the Middle Ages so that ultimately
"sins against nature" became "crimes against nature."[40] This conflation of moral and criminal definitions of sexual activities is
reflected in the fact that by the end of the twelfth century, sexual
offenses "constituted a major part of the case load of the ecclesiastical courts," and in the following century, there was an increased
concentration on enforcing the canon laws relating to sexual matters.[41]

Clearly, it would be simplistic to attribute this societal change
solely to the work of the friars, but it could be argued that if they
had not been so active in preaching in cities such as Florence, community moral standards may well have taken a different form. Furthermore, it has to be recognized that the development of new reli-

gious concepts was largely fostered by the friars at the leading universities of Europe.[42] In this context, all the leading theologians of the thirteenth and fourteenth centuries belonged to either the Dominican or the Franciscan Orders. Of these, the Dominican Thomas Aquinas was undoubtedly the most influential figure in the formulation of church doctrine at that time, and for some centuries afterwards. However, at the level which involved the inhabitants of Florence and similar cities, the changed attitude toward the body which had emerged in late medieval religious discourse was translated into sermons on the dangers of surrendering to the desires of the flesh. Even marriage was seen as a "kind of preventive medicine given by God to save man from immorality."[43] And within that institution, demonstrations of affection were viewed with disfavor by some preachers, as in the following example: "Married couples must not touch each other, neither seductively nor playfully, because this puts the fire of lust into their flesh."[44] Vehement denunciations of the body in all but procreative sex—and then only with reservations such as we have just noted—became a hallmark of the period.

Community Perceptions of Sin

There is ample evidence that thirteenth-century communities were convinced that their sins were many, and that God sent warnings and punishments by inflicting disasters on individuals or on the whole city. People were always alert to the possibility that some unusual event might be a sign of divine displeasure at their sinful ways. Salimbene de Adam recorded reactions to just such an event, a total eclipse of the sun in 1239. According to Salimbene, this caused men and women to go about "in the grip of fear and panic" and to placate God, "they hastened to confession and did penance for their sins."[45] With this evidence of community attitudes in the thirteenth century to sinful behavior and the inevitability of divine retribution, we might ask whether the same sense of guilt and fear was carried forward into the next century. Were the citizens of Florence still convinced that they were inherently sinful by nature and in constant danger of provoking God's wrath? Evidence from contemporary documents confirms that, if anything, they were even more certain that they were essentially flawed, and they remained fearful of the dire consequences of sin both during their earthly existence and in the afterlife. Records of the times often contained references to the inevitability of divine retribution, to "God's

vendettas" against sinful behavior.[46] One chronicler of the period
noted a constant concern of Florentines with the threat of retribution for their sins, asserting that they were "terrified of God's
vendettas."[47]

It is not surprising that this sense of guilt and impending
retribution was so prevalent. During the early part of the fourteenth century the mendicant friars continued to play a major role
in the religious life of Florence, convincing the inhabitants that
their behavior was an affront to God. And there is ample evidence
in the chronicles of the Florentine Giovanni Villani to confirm that
community perceptions on moral issues reflected these teachings
of the friars. Villani was not a member of the clergy nor was he a
literary philosopher, but his views on the sins of Florence were
similar to those expressed by Giordano da Rivalto-Moreni and
other preachers of the period. He was an astute merchant with
experience in international banking, a participant in civic government, and a keen observer of the social and political life around
him. For these reasons, the chronicles in which Villani recorded
the important events of Florentine history and those of his own
lifetime, are a valuable source of evidence on community attitudes.

Throughout the chronicles there are references to the sinful
behavior that prevailed in Florence, and which, in Villani's judgement, had been responsible for various calamities visited upon the
city as divine punishment. However, according to Villani, disasters
could also be divine warnings. Accordingly, Villani urged his fellow
citizens to heed any warnings given by calamities and repent before
anything worse happened.[48] To emphasize the truth of his asser-
tions Villani drew up a catalogue of a succession of disasters which
had befallen Florence. He drew attention to the wars, famines,
fires, earthquakes, floods, and pestilence that had been experienced
in Florence, and he declared his belief that they all were due to the
sinful behavior of the city's inhabitants. He entreated his fellow citizens to turn to "penance and communion . . . to appease the wrath
of God." Villani then proceeded to list the range of sinful behavior
to be found in Florence. Such moral failures, he was convinced,
were certain to attract divine punishment to the detriment of the
whole community. In his view, the vices of the Florentines included
pride; avarice; fraudulent dealings in trading and in usury; envy of
one's neighbors; gluttony and excessive drinking; ingratitude
toward God for His many blessings; women's vanity, extravagance,
immodest dress and ornamentation, and "unbridled lust amongst
men and women."

While Villani's list directly reflected the orthodox view of the seven sins, he placed his own emphasis on the behavior of women which, in the conventional wisdom of the times, was the prime factor which led men into sexual weakness. His comments on excessive drinking also reflected the current conviction that overindulgence in food and drink inevitably led to sexual sins. Villani's concern for intemperate drinking and the danger this entailed is apparent in his assertion that the customers in any one tavern in the city then drank as much as was consumed in the whole city in ancient times. Clearly, the message of the friars that any form of bodily indulgence led to sexual transgressions and, inevitably, to some form of divine retribution, had been firmly implanted in community religious discourse within the Florentine community.

The deep concern felt by Florentines that their inherent sinfulness would attract divine retribution upon the city was translated into legislative measures. Any activities perceived as incurring divine wrath were subject to prohibition or other limitations so that the city may be spared. Particular attention was paid to activities that could be described in moral terms as "sins of the flesh." Whenever Florence faced a crisis in the early-fourteenth century, prostitutes and homosexuals were ejected from the city, gambling restrictions were policed more strictly, and taverns were closed. In effect, any form of bodily indulgence was perceived as likely to provoke divine wrath and bring outbreaks of pestilence or other disasters to the city, with or without warning.

The citizens of Florence set great store by the semiotics of disasters. Comets, floods, earthquakes, eclipses, and the birth of deformed children or animals were among the portents of disaster. Nobody knew what form the disaster would take, but no one denied that some type of calamity would strike the city. A major flood in 1333, and unusually severe thunderstorms in 1339 were followed in the same year by a very poor harvest. The dismal chain of events continued in Florence. In the early 1340s, two of the major banks collapsed due to the inability of European monarchs to repay their debts, and in the following year another epidemic outbreak accounted for the deaths of some four thousand citizens.[49] Then even more severe famine conditions reappeared in 1346. All of this constituted the prelude to a disaster of such proportions that it has no equal even in modern times. It is to this disaster, the Black Death, that we now turn our attention.

CHAPTER 4

Disordered Bodies in Abundance

> ... and we have clear and reliable reports that in the countries of [the Far East] a great fire issued from underground or descended from the skies, consuming men, beasts, houses, trees, rocks, and the earth itself. Of those who did not flee every creature and inhabitant was consumed. Those men and women who did escape from the fire died of pestilence ... and in all of those countries only one in five escaped death from the outbreak of pestilence ...
>
> And from letters from some of our trustworthy citizens who were in those countries, [we learn that]a great quantity of large, eight-legged black, serpent-like creatures, both alive and dead, rained down over the whole countryside and created a great stench everywhere. They were terrifying to look at, and when punctured gave off a vile matter like poison.
>
> —Giovanni Villani[1]

Just travellers' tales from afar. So thought Villani when he noted these reports in his chronicles. He could not have anticipated the disaster this pestilence would soon bring to Europe. He could not have known that, before long, his native Florence would also face the same disaster. Without realizing it, Villani was recording the origins of the Black Death. This was the pandemic that was to sweep across most of Asia and Europe bringing death and misery to countless millions. In its wake it would leave many institutions and community beliefs and practices changed forever. In western Europe, it marked a major turning point in history. It initiated or accelerated changes to the structure of society, to perceptions of disease and death, and to new images of the body which laid the foun-

dations for concepts which define the "modern body." We identify
the evolution of these significant shifts in perceptions and practices
by reference to the responses of the citizens of Florence.

We would now see Villani's accounts of events in the Far East
as extremely fanciful, but they were not so to him or his fellow citizens. The citizens of Florence were accustomed to interpret any
unusual events as portents of disaster, particularly when astrological predictions appeared to support such explanations. Whether
the strange events occurred locally or in distant lands, the interpretation was the same—some catastrophe would follow.

Tales of this terrible outbreak of disease which was causing
countless deaths in China began to reach Europe during the early
1330s, travelling slowly along the overland trade routes. As no one
knew that the disease itself was also travelling slowly along the
same trade routes, there seems to have been no thought initially
that this catastrophe might also affect European countries. It was
only when the disease appeared in the Near East, and reports of
high death rates continued to reach European centers, that some
unease was felt. This caused a reassessment of these events as
likely indicators of impending calamity in Europe. The deadly disease was no longer something being visited solely upon "others,"
upon the "infidels." It was also striking down the "true believers"—
European Christians who traded in the Near East. It was in this
context that Villani began to record events which heralded the
arrival in Europe of this major outbreak of epidemic disease.

Villani took seriously the reports of terrifying events in far-off
lands. He recorded other accounts of the epidemic in the East that
also had a touch of the fantastic about them. In writing some of
these, he sometimes allowed his doubts as to their plausibility to
creep into his chronicle. Overall, however, he accepted that some
mysterious and deadly disease was raging in the East. He went
even further, asserting that the enormous death toll which arose
from the epidemic had been predicted by "the masters of astrology."
They had foretold that a great disaster would occur because of the
particular conjunction of the planets in that year.

Villani, however, did not see the movements of the stars and
the planets as the primary cause of disasters. Since he held completely orthodox medieval Christian views, he hastened to point out
that the primary cause of all calamities such as epidemics, floods,
and famines was to be found in human sinfulness. In the ultimate,
it was God who decided if such sins should be punished, and what
form the punishment should take. Astral signs, and other strange

occurrences were simply warnings of God's displeasure. If people took note of these warnings, and turned away from their sinful ways, they might avoid the full impact of God's wrath. Even as Villani was writing his chronicle, however, those portents of future disaster were being replaced by stark evidence of the arrival of the disease at the seaports of Italy early in 1348.[2]

The Black Death

The period 1348–1351 saw bubonic plague devastate the countries of Europe. The areas most severely affected were those which lay on important trade routes between Europe and the East, and from these to other trading centers in Europe. Nevertheless, many other areas, both urban and rural, also suffered greatly and the overall mortality rate was very high. By any standards it would be hard to escape the conclusion that this outbreak of epidemic disease, later to become known as the Black Death,[3] constituted a natural disaster of a magnitude never before encountered, and without parallel even to the present day.[4] At the end of 1351, as the first wave of the epidemic subsided, Pope Clement VI called for an assessment to be made of the number of deaths which had resulted from the plague in Christian Europe. The conclusion reached was that a total of 23,840,000 perished, some thirty-one percent of the pre-plague population of the area.[5] Even though medieval chroniclers in general are not noted for great precision in matters relating to statistics, there is now a considerable body of evidence, gathered from many different areas in Europe, which tends to support the estimates produced for Pope Clement.

Florence was one of the cities of Europe that was severely affected by the plague epidemic. The disease raged in the city and the surrounding countryside of Tuscany for some five months, from March to August of 1348. Estimates of the death toll in the city alone range from forty-five percent to seventy-five percent of the pre-plague population. Current research tends to accept a figure toward the upper rather than the lower levels of this range.[6]

Many of the inhabitants of Tuscany must have fallen easily before this new type of epidemic since severe famine conditions during the previous year had lowered their resistance to any disease. The famine followed in the wake of a serious crop failure, and people were so desperate for food that, according to one chronicler, ". . . there was no grass left on the ground that people did not eat."[7]

When the plague struck, people were stunned by the apparently inevitable death which its victims faced, and the horrible nature of the disease itself. One contemporary, Agnolo di Tura del Grasso, felt unable to describe the full horror of the situation: ". . . there is no human language which can describe such a horrible thing."[8] Predictably, terror reigned in every city struck by the epidemic, and everyone feared for personal and collective survival: ". . . everyone believed that it was the end of the world, and that neither medicine nor any other form of defence was of any use."[9] Petrarch wrote in anguish that "everywhere we see sorrow, on all sides we see terror . . . would that I had never been born or had died earlier!"[10] Nor are these reactions surprising given the way in which Petrarch described the plague's effects:

> In what chronicles did anyone read that dwellings were emptied, cities abandoned, countrysides filthy, fields laden with bodies, and a dreadful and vast solitude covered the earth? . . . we ourselves . . . can scarcely believe them [these things] and would consider them dreams except that we perceive them awake and with our own eyes and that after viewing a city full of funerals we return to our homes only to find them empty of our loved ones.[11]

With such a horrendous death toll, and the lacerating grief and hardship which this inflicted upon almost all families, everyone sought to understand what had caused this disaster.

Making Sense of Catastrophe

An immense strain was placed on the social fabric of the Florentine community by the impact of the Black Death. Death struck, apparently indiscriminately, across boundaries of age, sex, and social status. In a great many cases, the family unit, the central core of Florentine society, was torn asunder. Graphic accounts of the way in which the plague impacted on the community and on families can be found in many contemporary records. Boccaccio is one of the writers who spoke of the way in which the overwhelming fear of contracting the plague caused a breakdown in normal social relationships:

> It was not only that one citizen shunned another, and that almost nobody gave aid to their neighbours, or that people

rarely or never visited their relatives, keeping contact only from afar; but the great terror which this scourge struck in the hearts of men and women caused brothers to abandon brothers, uncles their nephews, sisters their brothers, and in many instances wives deserted their husbands. But an even more appalling, almost incredible thing was that fathers and mothers repudiated their own children, and refused to stay with them or care for them in any way.[12]

Boccaccio's account of the plague epidemic in Florence in 1348 is the most widely known and cited, mainly because it has been available in English translation for some centuries. Many later writers have seized upon his accounts of the abandonment of family members, often to the exclusion of other parts of Boccaccio's description of the plague in Florence. Because of this, desertion of relatives and friends, and headlong flight from plague areas to avoid infection tend to be the responses most widely identified with the Black Death. This simply ignores other contemporary evidence which shows clearly that these responses were far from universal, even if frequent.

Matteo Villani, who took over writing the *Chronicles* when his brother Giovanni died of plague in 1348, also referred to this "cruel inhumanity" in which family members deserted each other through fear of also becoming victims of the plague.[13] He also pointed out, however, that "many others who were ready to attend to their sick relatives and friends, escaped becoming ill." According to Matteo Villani, when others saw that it was not inevitable that one caught the plague from its victims, they turned to the stricken and offered help. As a result, many who otherwise would have died recovered from the infection. Petrarch also gave two instances in which relatives and friends stayed to tend victims of the plague. In one of these, he described how his brother Gherardo, a Carthusian monk, was the only survivor, apart from a dog, in a monastic community overwhelmed by the plague. His brother tended his fellow monks as, one after the other, they were taken ill. As they succumbed to the disease, it fell to Gherardo to carry out the burials for each one of them.[14]

Petrarch also wrote of the rapid demise of a friend who appears to have contracted the septicaemic form of the disease:[15]

> . . . this man, I say, having been suddenly seized by the illness of the plague which is devastating the world, spent the

evening with his friends and what remained of his ebbing life conversing with me and recalling our past friendship and relationship. He spent the night calmly amidst his excruciating pains, and was overtaken by sudden death that morning. And in keeping with the fatal times, before three days were over, his children and all his family followed him.[16]

This extract also illustrates the way in which whole families were sometimes eliminated by the disease. There is another contemporary account that underscores the lacerating grief and suffering, which accompanied the appearance of plague in a family.[17] Agnolo di Tura del Grasso poignantly described how he personally cared for his own children as they were dying from the plague. And when the end came, he found that there was no one who would undertake the burial. As a result, he recorded, "I buried my five children with my own hands."[18] To compound his feelings of anguish, he had to bury them, as many others were forced to do, where it was impossible to properly cover them with earth. As a result of this difficulty in burying bodies adequately, "throughout the city the dogs dragged forth and ate many of the bodies."

Surrounded by such scenes of death and misery, everyone sought explanations. Most contemporary writers commented on this speculation within the community, and the range of discourses on causation which emerged. In his prologue to the *Decameron*, Boccaccio provided the most extensive account of the Black Death in Florence which is available.[19] Within this chronicle of events, he set down the two views on the origins of the calamity that were most commonly espoused within the community. The "deadly pestilence," he declared, without expressing a definite opinion of his own, had fallen on the city either through the "the influence of the stars, or the righteous anger of God at our iniquitous way of life."[20] Almost universally, contemporary writers reflected the conviction which lay at the core of the dominant religious discourse that there was a direct causal link between human sin and divine punishment. Within this context, all illness and disease could be equated to some form of retribution for human transgressions. Petrarch believed that events showed that God's mercy had finally become exhausted by human faults, but he was perplexed as to the apparent severity of the punishment: ". . . we suffer punishment not only for our sins but for those of our fathers. I do not know whether we are worse than they, but we are certainly more wretched."[21] For

Giovanni Villani there was absolutely no doubt that God had visited the pestilence upon the people of the city and the surrounding countryside "as punishment for sins."[22]

Since the catastrophe was seen as a punishment for sinful behavior, individuals and community groups agonized over the ways in which they had offended, and sought to appease God's anger in the ways which their religious beliefs and traditions had provided for them. Even news that the plague had broken out in a neighboring city was sufficient to galvanize a community into ritual expressions of individual and collective repentance. When the plague appeared in Genoa, the Florentine authorities called for the whole community to display contrition and pious devotion in such a way that God could be persuaded to end the plague, and to protect the city and its surrounding countryside.[23] According to Villani, this appeal for intervention on behalf of Florence took the form of solemn processions throughout the city which lasted for three days. Despite these collective appeals for mercy, the progress of the plague was not impeded, and when it struck the city of Florence, Giovanni Villani himself became one of its victims. Nevertheless, the citizens of Florence did not see this lack of success as suggesting that appeals of this sort were ineffectual. It was taken to mean that the sins of the city and its inhabitants were so reprehensible that the sinners could not expect to escape their just punishment. Boccaccio also noted that there was frequent recourse to religious rituals seeking relief from the plague while the epidemic was raging in Florence. However, he noted that none of these efforts was effective in limiting the devastating effects of the epidemic. According to his account of the events, "countless appeals directed to God by devout persons, processions of intercession ordered by the city, and other kinds of petitions seeking relief were of no avail."[24]

Horror without End

The pandemic of 1348, the Black Death, engendered great fear in the minds of all in Florence. It was a completely unknown disease, its effects were swift and horrible, there seemed to be little anyone could do to avoid its depradations, and it was responsible for the deaths of a major proportion of the population. Unfortunately, the plague did not just disappear when the Black Death seemed to recede after some six months. It reappeared at all too frequent intervals, with Florence experiencing a further thirty-two epidemics of plague in the two centuries after the Black Death.[25] Generally, however, these later outbreaks were less severe than that of 1348. After this long period of threat from plague, there were only two further outbreaks, in 1631 and 1632, before the plague finally disappeared from Florence.[26] Much of the same situation existed throughout Europe where the plague remained endemic for an even longer period.

The frequent reappearance of the plague, with its inevitable patterns of illness and death on a mass scale, ensured that communities such as Florence remained apprehensive and fearful of the consequences for individuals, their families, and for the future of the whole city. Each outbreak of the plague tended to reinforce and extend ideas inherent in perceptions and practices established by earlier epidemics. In this way, perceptions of the body, particularly the "disordered" body, shifted progressively, with something akin to those we associate with the "modern body" emerging toward the end of the plague period.

Contemporary records over the whole period show that responses by individuals replicated or accentuated the responses evidenced during the period of the Black Death. Fleeing from the danger remained a primary response for many people. In the outbreak of 1527, for example, so many had fled from Florence that one writer likened it to "a city taken forcibly by infidels, and then abandoned."[27] The main difference which can be identified over the period of plague epidemics is that, while flight from the disease remained a primary response for many people, it was common later for families to flee together if they were so able.[28] No accounts of later plague epidemics refer to abandonment of relatives. Flight alone, however, provided no certainty that people could avoid the disease. Chronicles show that some families were forced to move a number of times in an effort to avoid "dangerous" locations, and even then some still became victims of the disease.[29]

Flight, of course, was only available to those who had the financial resources to make this possible. As a result, it was among the indigent, and those who could not leave Florence because of other responsibilities, that the death toll was the highest. This was how Boccaccio reported on the uneven incidence of death during the Black Death period in Florence:

> As for the common folk, and the greater part of the middle class, they were in a much worse situation, since the majority of them were obliged to stay in their houses either from

poverty or from the hope of survival. By remaining in their own sections of the city, thousands of them became ill each day, and being without anyone to assist them or to supply their needs, almost without exception they died.[30]

There is no reason to doubt this account of the impact of the plague on the poorer classes, during the period of the Black Death. All evidence points to a disproportionate death toll among the poor, a tendency which became even more pronounced during later epidemics. The fact that the death toll was slightly more evenly spread over the community during the Black Death arose largely because the plague struck so swiftly that many became victims before there was any opportunity to flee from the city. Later, with greater knowledge of the risks involved, those who could afford to leave the city often departed at the first rumor of a return of the disease. Flight from danger of any kind is a fundamentally human response. There were, however, other responses which were unique to the threats posed by plague epidemics. Many of these are central to the development of our argument.

A Community in Crisis

Because the Black Death impacted so widely on all levels of society, there was a greater upheaval in the social and political structure of Florence at that time than was evident in later epidemics. Given this pattern of stress placed on the institutions such as the church and the medical profession, it could be expected that the political power structure of the Commune would also be threatened. Yet, despite a significant number of deaths among members of the ruling classes, and within the ranks of elected officials, the government of Florence did not cease to function at any stage during the period of the Black Death. Formal meetings of the governing councils of elected representatives were suspended for the period during which the epidemic raged, due to the somewhat chaotic conditions prevailing in the city. However, a small group of officials was appointed to conduct the affairs of the city, and this ensured continuity of government throughout the six months of the Black Death.

As soon as the plague appeared in the city, the city authorities enacted measures which they believed would be useful in the control of the disease. Boccaccio recorded that "large quantities of garbage were removed from the city by officials appointed for this purpose, anyone who was ill was denied entry to the city, and a good deal of advice was given on ways to preserve good health."[31] Despite the tremendous upheaval that occurred throughout the community in this period, the administrative functions of the city were maintained, and many regulations aimed at controlling the spread of the epidemic were promulgated. In later epidemics, the government of the city remained even more fully under control. This pattern of governmental resilience was not unique to Florence but was also in evidence in other cities of northern Italy during the Black Death and later outbreaks.[32]

Despite the ability of some sections of the community to withstand the disruptive influence of the plague epidemics, many institutions in Florence underwent change in response to these powerful events. One such institution was the family unit.[33] While there was little fundamental change in the intrinsic values of this social group, two aspects showed marked shifts from previously well established patterns. These related to the ages at first marriage, often close to forty years for men and twenty-five years for women; and the birthrate. The size of family in Florence in the early-fourteenth century generally consisted of some four to six children.

After the Black Death, the number of marriages increased sharply as the citizens of Florence tried to re-establish a sense of community within traditional patterns. Matteo Villani observed this response, and explained it in terms of the sense of impending doom which prevailed, saying "filled with fear they married."[34] This urge to marry could be accepted just as easily as a way of satisfying the important need to maintain the continuity of the lineage within the Florentine family. In a general community sense, great value was attached to the important social and political connections which this provided. In addition, it was essential for the financial stability and continuity of a family business enterprise.

The relatively stable nature of the family unit over the plague period meant that it remained, essentially, a patriarchal and patrilineal institution in which male children were valued more highly than females. However, the scale of the losses within families and the trauma this caused brought two significant changes over the period of the plague epidemics. The first of these produced an appreciable lowering of the age at which the first marriage took place for both men and women, reduced to twenty-four years for men and sixteen years for women.[35] This process was somewhat reversed during the extended period of the epidemics, and later marriage once more became the norm. The second change lay in a sharply increased birthrate immediately following each epidemic in contrast to the great drop in the number of births during the progress of an epidemic.[36] Not only was the birthrate higher in the wake of each outbreak but the overall size of family increased markedly in some sections of the community. It was not unusual to find families of eighteen to twenty children among the more affluent levels of Florentine society. At other levels of society, however, the birthrate remained modest.[37]

There was yet another change in the social patterns of the family that arose directly from the problems created by the plague. During each epidemic, there was a substantial interruption to trade and manufacturing activities in Florence. With no work and no income, many members of the underclass became destitute, and unable to feed their families despite the distribution of grain and bread by the city authorities. This desperate situation caused many parents to abandon their children, and in line with the values prevailing at the time, more girls than boys were abandoned.[38] These unfortunate children often joined the roving bands of children orphaned by the plague, and existed on charity, or by begging.[39]

Bodies, Bodies, Bodies!

Contemporary documents on plague experiences provide a great deal of evidence as to the effects of the epidemics, and the responses of individuals and institutions to those experiences. What is universally described, however, and usually in graphic detail, was the community's encounter with death and disease on a scale unknown within human memory. And, of course, the long succession of plague epidemics to which Florence was subjected could not but focus attention on the fragility of human life, and the disintegration of the body when assailed by such a disease.

The shock and dismay felt within the community during the Black Death is captured in Petrarch's bewildered exclamation: ". . . how fragile is our body. . . ."[40] Contemporary accounts of the plague leave no doubt that the body became increasingly a focus of attention in a way not previously apparent. Chronicles and family memoirs of this period frequently contained comments on the body and its susceptibility to corruption, and, often included reference to current recommendations on how to withstand the inroads of disease. Even the early rumors that the plague epidemic was gradually moving closer to Europe were couched in terms which accented the corporeal impact of the outbreak. One chronicler claimed that: "India was depopulated, Tartary, Mesopotamia, Syria, Armenia were covered with dead bodies; the Kurds fled in vain to the mountains. In Caramania and Caesarea none were left alive. . . ."[41] According to another writer, the plague left 85,000 dead in the Crimea alone.[42] It was from this region, littered with dead bodies, that a bizarre incident provided the final link in the transfer of the disease from Asia to Europe in 1347.[43]

As the death toll soared, the Tartars in the Crimea region responded in a way common to most communities. They blamed the strangers in their midst for spreading the disease. In this instance, the dangerous Others were the Genoese who had established trading posts throughout the area for trade with the East. The Tartars attacked the Genoese and forced them to flee to their fortified trading post at Caffa (now Feodosiya), a port on the Black Sea. There the Tartar forces laid siege to the town, but found themselves seriously disadvantaged by an epidemic outbreak of plague which had finally reached that region.[44] Before withdrawing from the city, however, they appear to have decided that their opponents should suffer the same fate. In an action which seems to have been a precursor of biological warfare, they loaded the bodies of plague victims on to catapults and hurled them over the fortified walls. As a result, diseased and rotting bodies soon littered the streets of this small enclosed town. Very soon the plague broke out among the defenders and a great many died. The human body had become a weapon of destruction. The survivors decided to withdraw, and fled in their galleys from the Black Sea to the Mediterranean, unwittingly taking the plague with them.

After leaving a trail of disaster in the various ports at which they called along the Mediterranean, some of the galleys arrived in Sicily, others went on to Genoa, and some ended their journey at Marseilles. Giovanni Villani gave a graphic account of the fate of the crew of the eight galleys which set out from Caffa for Genoa. During the journey, according to Villani:

> . . . the majority of them [the crews] died, with only four [of the galleys] returning full of ailing men who were dying all the time. Of those who arrived at Genoa, all died, so corrupting the airs of the place where they had arrived. Whoever encountered them at close quarters died.[45]

While this account is generally in accord with other contemporary records of the arrival of the galleys, stressing the high death toll and the "corruption" caused by the corpses, one important aspect is missing. It is clear from other accounts that not all sailors died on arrival at Genoa. When the Genoese realized that the galleys had brought disaster, those that were still manned "were driven from Genoa, and after those cursed galleys had departed, they arrived at Pisa. . . ."[46] Once the plague had reached Genoa and Pisa, it spread rapidly throughout the peninsular, reinforcing the conventional wisdom that disease was always introduced into a community from elsewhere. It is not surprising then that communities such as Florence banned the entry to their cities of anyone who had been in Pisa, or other centers where the plague had been reported.[47] Little has changed. The dangerous Other is still the prime suspect when blame is apportioned for the transmission of disease.

As the plague epidemic moved from Pisa toward Florence and the neighboring cities of the north, each community in which it appeared was overwhelmed by the magnitude of the disaster. One of the most immediate problems was the large number of bodies of victims that had to be interred. As a result, the usual burial grounds soon became full and large ditches had to be dug to accommodate the corpses. There was little or no ceremony at such mass burials. The bodies were simply dumped into the pits, often without any religious rites. So apparently insensitive was the handling of the bodies, that one commentator asserted that "no more respect was shown to those who died than would be shown nowadays to goats."[48] In recording events in Pisa and Siena, Agnolo di Tura noted that for many of the victims there was no one but relatives to carry out the actual burial.[49] For others again there were no surviving relatives or friends, and many bodies lay about the streets in full view of the public, awaiting collection by those appointed by the city to remove such bodies. Ultimately, they were simply tossed into the nearest available ditch, and often poorly covered with soil so that sometimes "the wolves and wild animals ate the poorly buried bodies."[50]

The situation in Florence was similar, but even more daunting, because of the greater size of the city, and the very high proportion of the population that died of the plague. Boccaccio wrote of the "great multitude of bodies" which had to be buried, a number which he asserted were being added to "each day and almost every hour."[51] We have two accounts of the difficulties which arose from this enormous death toll in Florence.[52] As in Pisa and Siena, the conventional places for burials, the churchyards, were quickly filled and enormous pits had to be dug. Into these, according to Boccaccio, bodies were stacked in their hundreds, tier upon tier just as one placed "a ship's cargo," with a thin covering of soil placed between each layer of bodies until the pit was filled. Marchionne's description was even more bizarre. He likened the layering of bodies with a little soil to the process by which "one sprinkled layers of cheese when making lasagne."

The scene within the city itself was one which even more directly focused attention on the fragility of the human body and on attitudes toward death. Those who had no one to assist them, in particular the poorer classes of the city, lay about in large numbers wherever they had finally succumbed to the plague. Boccaccio described it thus:

> And many of them fell dead in the public streets, by day and night, with many others dying in their own homes. With regard to the latter, it was generally only the stench of their rotting bodies which signalled to neighbours that they had died. With these, and with all the others who were dying throughout the city, bodies were everywhere.[53]

Further, he asserted, "the whole atmosphere seemed to be filled and polluted by the stench of dead bodies, of sickness and of medicines."[54] And since the smell of rotting bodies fitted with the prevailing concept that corruption of the atmosphere could cause disease, most people were greatly afraid of even being near such corpses.[55] This fear persisted for a long time as accounts of later plague epidemics reveal. One incident in 1497 and another in 1527, refer to men who had died in the streets in the center of Florence being sidestepped, and left for many hours through the fear which plague engendered.[56] These accounts refer to individual victims of plague being shunned. There is little evidence that large numbers of bodies were left unattended in the streets during later appearances of the plague. However, many plague sufferers were still refused aid, due to the fear of the disease being passed on, during later outbreaks.[57]

Although the death toll was much lower in epidemics after the Black Death, the citizens of Florence were unable to free themselves from the sense of horror they felt at the manner of dying that was associated with bubonic plague. Apart from the revulsion felt at the bodily dissolution that had never been encountered on such

a scale before, there were other matters related to traditional rituals connected with death which troubled many of them. According
to Giulia Calvi, death from plague was perceived as fundamentally
disgraceful, because of the recourse to mass interments during epidemics.[58] This applied particularly to the middle and upper classes
since it meant that they lost identity, and had no tomb which could
be honored by their families. Further, since plague had progressively become associated with the poor in every way, dying from
plague, for members of these classes, was to die "like the poor and
the dishonored."

The most arresting feature of contemporary accounts of the
plague epidemics, especially that of the Black Death, is the constant reference to the great proliferation of bodies. Traditionally,
death had been a relatively private affair and the bodies of the
departed treated with respect and buried with dignity. Plague shat-
tered this pattern. Many died on the streets and their corpses lay
there rotting. Even for those who died at home, the disposal of their
remains became a public affair. Boccaccio claimed that when many
people died in their homes, neighbors, fearful of the decaying
corpse, hastened to place the bodies in the open streets "where, particularly in the mornings, anyone could see countless numbers of
them."[59] The enormous death toll meant that bodies were exposed
to the public gaze as never before. Furthermore, the inevitable processes of decay and dissolution of the body after death became all
too visible.

The Transformed Body

The fear that people felt at being close to a plague victim
turned to abject terror when the visible signs of the disease
appeared on their own bodies, or on those of members of their own
households. Although plague had been unknown to Europeans for
centuries, the disease spread so rapidly that everyone soon became
aware of the telltale indications of its presence on the surface of the
body. The plague was thus seen "as the visible externalized horror
of this transformed body."[60]

Several chroniclers gave precise details of the "signs" that
accompanied plague infection.[61] All of them referred to the primary
indicators, the well-known appearance of swellings or buboes under
the armpits and in the groin, that is, in the lymph glands. Some of
them added other details of the way in which the disease could be

identified. Boccaccio noted that the buboes could vary in size from that of an egg to that of an apple or even larger. He, along with Matteo Villani and Benedetto Varchi, also observed that after a few days small blisters could appear on other parts of the body. Sometimes these became reddish or black from bleeding under the skin. Marchionne and Boccaccio were the only chroniclers to refer specifically to the fever which usually accompanied this most common of the plague variants, bubonic plague. From experience people learned that with these "signs" upon the body a person may recover if they could survive the four days to a week cycle of the disease. The same experience taught them that some other "signs" exhibited by the body spelled certain death. Marchionne asserted that when some of them spat: "they spat blood mixed with saliva, and none of those who spat blood survived."[62] This description is now easily recognizable as the pneumonic form of the plague which could lead to death within a day or so. No chronicler recognized the septicaemic form of plague which could run its fatal course within hours. This is not surprising since there was no time for buboes or any other indicator to appear. However, the speed with which a person could die during an epidemic was well known. It is central to Boccaccio's lament that so many people seemingly in perfect health "took breakfast with their relatives, friends and companions in the morning, and then dined with their ancestors in the other world that evening."[63]

Death—The Body in Decay

Such direct encounters with death on a large scale helped reshape community concepts of mortality. From considering themselves mortal as human beings, individuals were forced to accept the reality of their own death, and the need to be well prepared against its unpredictability in time, manner, and place.[64] Even before the arrival of the plague, there had been changes in the perception of death, and it came to be represented, in the fourteenth century, as a construct. It was around 1340 that the first visual depiction of the concept of death occurred.[65] Death was frequently shown as a grotesque female figure featuring bat's wings and clawed fingers and toes. At the Monumental Cemetery in Pisa, Death is portrayed "flying over a group of corpses she has strewn along her path with her scythe."[66] A fresco, executed by Bartolo di Fredi in 1368, continues the thematic association between Woman, Sin, and Death. This fresco, entitled Inferno, is described thus:

The landscape of hell is bleak, rocky and thorny. A single sinner, seductively naked, her hands tied behind her back, wanders toward the black mouth of the cave from which a terrifying winged figure has just emerged. The female figure's elongated body is sketetal, her face diabolical; her hands hold a chain that once must have reached the sinner's hands. Her flaccid, wrinkled breasts and long white hair with bald patches underscore her repugnant femininity, further stressed by the gloss: '. . . I am the mortal enemy of all that is good / servant of the devil / woman of hell / mother of eternal pain'. Corporeal death, spiritual death, evil, and the devil combined to generate this monster that could be defined as the eternity of the torments of Hell.[67]

Visual representations of plague experiences affirmed the fragility of life in that period, and drew attention to the futility of human intervention to defer death. An Italian codice of the latter half of the fourteenth century developed this theme, employing three panels to depict the demise of a plague victim.[68] In the first, Death appears in the guise of an angel with a scythe in hand, hovering above a mass of corpses. The second panel shows a sick man sitting on a bed, drinking some medical potion. The final panel shows a coffin with funeral attendants, clearly inferring that the medicine had been useless. Within the whole community, attention became focused on the imminence of death, the unpredictability of its timing, and the need to make spiritual preparations for this eventuality.

Perceptions of death now embraced the idea of a life cut short. And the unavoidable spectacle of dead and decaying bodies lying about the city ensured that, after the Black Death, there was a new focus on the dissolution of the body after death. Instead of the traditional Christian concentration on the passage of the soul to heavenly peace, many now dwelt on the horrors of physical decay. The daily encounters with bodies transformed by disease, and bodies in various stages of decay and dissolution, ensured that the inseparability of body and soul, a central tenet of medieval religious dogma, became less dominant in discourses of the body.

The prevalence of macabre themes within the community can be deduced from their frequent appearance in the literature, and the art of the period. Although elements of the macabre can already be found in late-thirteenth century religious art, Italian artists employed this motif frequently after the Black Death.[69] One example of this usage, found in a number of places in Italy, offers three images of the body in progressive stages of disintegration.[70] In the first panel, the corpse is displayed with its limbs already bloated from the internal gases generated after death; the second panel shows another stage of decomposition with a view of worm-infested entrails. Finally, the third panel demonstrates the ultimate end of all human physical existence, a skeleton from which all flesh has vanished. Similar iconographic representations of death as cruel and repulsive were used north of the Alps. The figure of Death was usually shown partly as a skeleton, partly mummified. In most cases the abdomen was open, displaying the worms at work in the final stages of bodily disintegration. Death as physical decay also provided the theme for the poem 'La Danse Macrabré. In this widely circulated work, the only consolation that was offered was that this was the inevitable end for everyone, from princes to paupers.[71]

The Body Beautiful or the Body Vile?

This intense preoccupation with the body and its propensity to corruption by disease, and the horror of physical decay after death, persisted in community perceptions, in literature and in art into the fifteenth century. Progressively, however, further changes to images of the body emerged. These were due to a number of factors emanating from disparate sources. First, one could argue that a desire to suppress the horrors of the plague epidemics inspired a retreat from the images of diseased and corrupt bodies which had dominated that period. Second, the philosophy of the Renaissance humanists was taking hold in Florence. This involved, amongst many other things, a rediscovery of Graeco-Roman aesthetics in literature and in art. As a result, greater attention was given to the classical Greek appreciation of the human body. Their honoring of the body expressed a sense of human wholeness, which accorded with humanist ideals. The classical Greeks demonstrated pride in the body and saw it as something to be admired and kept in perfect physical condition. Such attitudes were clearly opposed to the medieval ascetic stance of rejection of the body, but in the second half of the fifteenth century, Florentine humanists sought to reconcile the differences. They were greatly assisted in this task by a change in religious iconography that had emerged in the middle of the thirteenth century. This modification arose from a decision by the church hierarchy that the frescoes, which depicted the cycle of human life in cathedrals and churches, should not end with the Apocalypse but with a portrayal of the Last Judgement.[72] To be consistent with the then prevailing doctrine of the resurrection of both the spirit and the flesh on Judgement Day, those who emerged from the tomb had to be portrayed with naked, perfectly formed bodies.

By a combination of all these factors during the fifteenth century, the image of the human body once more became a mirror of divine perfection, the instrument through which the soul carries out its functions while on earth. Such a perception of the body reflected neo-platonic ideas on the nexus between inner and outer beauty. In Castiglione's *The Book of the Courtier,* Pietro Bembo is quoted as saying:

> . . . beauty is a sacred thing, . . . I say that beauty springs from God and is like a circle, the centre of which is goodness . . . only rarely does an evil soul dwell in a beautiful body, and so outward beauty is a sign of inner goodness. . . . Therefore, for the most part the ugly are also evil, and the beautiful good.[73]

Nevertheless, in the discussion which followed these statements, it was conceded that despite the innate beauty of goodness, exceptions existed. There are, it was said, "beautiful women who are unchaste" and "handsome men can also become wicked." The clearest evidence that this change in the perception of the body as good had finally occurred is seen in the emergence of the Renaissance nude by the second half of the fifteenth century. The naked figure, long an object of shame and humiliation, could once more appear in triumph as an example of the perfection of God's handiwork.

Despite these shifts in perception, the more ascetically inclined within the clergy retained much of their earlier aversion to the physical nature of the body. And consistent with that stance, they remained convinced that there was a nexus between sin, particularly sins of the body, and the incidence of disease. These two divergent discourses on the body co-existed in Florence, and elsewhere, for a long time, creating a degree of ambivalence in many minds. Michelangelo, for example, was renowned in his own time as the leading exponent of the perfect nude body, the hallmark of late Renaissance art.[74] Nevertheless, in his poetry, he could still express a disdain for the body which was consistent with the then religious discourse on the body. In 1554, he wrote an epitaph in verse for the young son of a friend:

> The flesh turns to clay and here remain my bones,
> Stripped of my beautiful eyes and my cheerful face,
> . . .
>
> In what a prison lives the soul down here![75]

The views of Leonardo da Vinci were more extreme, and focused on his perception of the grotesque nature of human sexuality. In notes inscribed on one of his anatomical plates he declared that:

> The sexual act and the members employed therein are so repulsive, that if it were not for the beauty of the faces and the adornments of the actors and the pent-up impulse, nature would lose the human species.[76]

Although both perceptions of the body co-existed during the fifteenth and sixteenth centuries, it was the dominant religious discourse of the church which continued to inform the majority of individual and institutional responses to the plague and to shape community perceptions of the human body. And, in this context, Jacques Le Goff declared that, "Horror of the body was most acute in regard to the sexual functions . . . [and] the height of abomination, the worst of the body and of sexuality was the female body."[77] The depth of commitment to this concept becomes abundantly clear as we continue our review of the impact of the recurring plague epidemics on Florence.

CHAPTER 5

Castigating the Flesh

For I know that nothing good dwells in me, that is, my flesh. . . . I see in my members another Law at war with the Law of my mind. . . . Wretched man that I am! Who will deliver me from this body of death?

—Romans 7:18, 23–4.

The [female] sex poisoned our first ancestor, who was also husband and father [to the first woman]; it strangled John the Baptist and delivered brave Samson to his death. In a manner of speaking it also killed our Savior; for had [woman's] sin not required it, Our Savior would not have had to die. Woe unto this sex, which knows nothing of awe, goodness or friendship, and which is more to be feared when loved than when hated!

—Geoffroy of Vendôme[1]

The miserable flesh is put under the ground to be a meal for stinking worms. . . . But how contemptible is [a man] while he is alive? The Scriptures say that he is more loathsome than slime, [and] even worse, he is a sack of dung and foulness.

—Jacopo Passavanti[2]

Throughout the Christian West, there was an unquestioning acceptance of the view that plague epidemics were a manifestation of divine punishment. They were seen as a form of retribution for the sins of the community, or at least, for the transgressions of some members of the community. This perception grew in the wake of the Black Death and succeeding epidemics, and "sins of the flesh," particularly those of a sexual nature, were viewed as the transgressions most likely to provoke divine wrath and cause the plague to be visited upon the whole community. This propensity to focus on human sexuality, and the high price to be paid for indulging the body, arose from an extended period of theological debate, and from the fear engendered in every community which experienced the depradations of the plague. In this chapter we examine major shifts in religious discourse on the body during the Middle Ages, and their influence on community responses to the Black Death, and the subsequent outbreaks of plague, in western Europe.

The Church, Gender, and the Body

To the church, Woman was, by definition, inferior in all ways to Man. God had so ordained it. Woman was to be the helpmate of Man, but in the eyes of medieval theologians, this promise had not been fulfilled. Ever since the Fall, women had caused men trouble and grief. Women constituted an ever-present threat to the spiritual and physical well-being of men. Theologians such as Thomas Aquinas drew upon the pronouncements of Aristotle to support their conviction that women were inherently inferior mentally and physically, and that sexual relations were harmful to both the body and the soul. Giles of Rome, an influential theologian of the early fourteenth century, espoused the same views. He judged women to be so poorly endowed with reason that they surrendered to their passions more easily than did men.[3] He was convinced that women lacked depth and were naturally drawn to artifice and the superficiality of appearances, both of which were, of course, dangerous to men.

Denunciations of the human body, and the debilitating effects of sexual relations with women, were ever-present elements of clerical thought in the late medieval period. These attitudes emerged from the theological debates of that period which were notable for their intense preoccupation with the sexualized body. In general, it was the celibate clergy of the monastic orders who felt compelled to define the roles of men and women, and to classify which bodily activities were deemed morally acceptable and which were deviant and hence sinful. Furthermore, they sought to impose controls on the body, particularly the female body.

Most of the men who claimed authority to speak on these issues shrank from any direct contact with women, and their fear and loathing at the very thought of such "contamination" is patently obvious in their pronouncements. Enjoined to remain celibate, they "knew nothing about women, or, rather, about Woman, other than what they imagined. They represented her as a distant, strange, and frightening figure of profoundly contradictory nature."[4] Inevitably, their knowledge and understanding of women was extremely limited and frequently very distorted. Nevertheless, it was the "clerical gaze" which defined "woman" and the "body" for all western European communities. And for most of the Middle Ages, there was little in the way of challenge to these images since the clergy, or at least the better educated levels of the clergy, had a virtual monopoly on the written word. By and large, they also controlled the most common means of transmitting information and opinions—the pulpit. As a consequence, the distorted views of women held by the clergy received wide circulation and carried the imprimatur of the church.

To avoid the spiritual and physical dangers attributed to sexual activities, the lay world was offered perpetual chastity as an ideal way of life. Men, however, were informed that they could triumph over their sexuality, and could be seen as unblemished again "when virtue is won, evil defeated or restitution made."[5] On the other hand, women's lives could only be complete "when death assured perpetual virginity." In this context even marriage was presented as a second-best solution to the demands of human sexuality. Some clerics, however, offered women another possible pathway to salvation, one which allowed them to indulge their perceived weakness in sexual matters. To achieve this end, a woman should accept that it was her primary role in life to bear children, and in the words of one Dominican, "generate children continually until her death."[6] Nevertheless, while childbearing was lauded as a duty, the concepts of virginity or of great sexual restraint were elevated to new heights as a result of late medieval theological debate.

Religious discourse was also a powerful determinant of practices relating to the public display of the female body. Adorning the body with sumptuous clothing, jewelry and makeup was regarded as the antithesis of the Christian doctrine of bodily denial. This demanded a detachment from the corporeality of the body and a concentration on the inner aspects of spiritual life. Nevertheless, adhering to such dictates was recognized as difficult in daily life. Accordingly, clerics enjoined women living in the general community to practice restraint and decorum in their dress and presentation. Women were advised that their bodies were not for their own pleasure but to be held in sacred trust for their husbands and families. In essence, the body of a woman should be preserved and presented in such a way as to reflect her husband's station in life, and his status in the community:

> Just as a nun detached herself from her body to commit it to monastic seclusion and discipline, so a laywoman, though she dressed and made up with care, was no longer mistress of her own body. Her body belonged to the family, for whom it was displayed as a status symbol, and above all to her husband, for whom it had to remain inviolate, attractive and healthy.[7]

Women were also enjoined by church leaders to restrain their gestures and behavior in public places, lest they make an excessive display of the body. Norms of behavior, derived from the monastic tradition, were applied to women. Females of all ages were expected to exercise corporeal discipline by avoiding lively or animated actions or gestures. Modesty was highlighted as the hallmark of appropriate female demeanor.[8] These prescriptions directed against women led ultimately to an alienation from the body for all groups of women in society.

Voices of Dissent in the Middle Ages

The church had always given a place to women who were perceived as having the gift of prophecy. They were accorded much freedom to speak out provided there was no hint of dissent in their pronouncements. Women, however, had never been allowed to interpret doctrine or assume a didactic role. Nevertheless, by the late Middle Ages, many women, including nuns, mystics, and the Beguines (who were a lay "order" of women), began to voice their views.[9] The church was initially perplexed by the Beguines, but this turned to hostility as it became evident that they were commenting on matters regarded as the preserve of the clergy. Finally, the General Council of Vienne in 1312 decided that they were "afflicted by a kind of madness" in discussing matters of faith and sacraments, and decreed that they were to be "permanently forbidden and excluded altogether from the Church of God."[10] This response to the threat to established order from women's voices was typical of the way in which the church had imposed discipline since the Gregorian reforms of the seventh century.

After instituting controls on monks and the secular male clergy, the church increasingly turned its attention to imposing controls on women late in the Middle Ages. Jacques Dalarun concluded that a contradictory pattern evolved.[11] Certain women such as Bridget of Sweden and Catherine of Siena were given much freedom to express themselves on religious matters. Others such as the Beguines and mystics were viewed with grave suspicion. And while men outside the church enjoyed some freedom in expressing their religious convictions, provided they conformed to the orthodox, women's voices were perceived as a threat. Support for this perception was found in Paul's declaration in I Timothy, 2:12: "But I suffer not a woman to teach, nor to usurp authority over the man, but to be in silence." Dalarun considered that this hostility toward the voices of women led to the persecution of witches. We would argue that the levels of anxiety within the church about female sexuality, and the perceived need to regulate and control women's bodies and behavior, were also significant factors contributing to the persecution of women labelled as witches.[12] This resonates with the views expressed by Bryan Turner that "religion provided that regime by which the individual body and the body politic are controlled and ordered."[13]

The increasingly prescriptive nature of the way in which religious discourse sought to control bodies, particularly female bodies, engendered feelings of dissent within the lay community. In part, this reflected the persistence within most communities, particularly within the underclasses, of beliefs associated with pre-Christian religions honoring a female diety. Typically, these focused on those elements of human life that shared a relationship with the earth—cycles of fertility, life, and death. In this context, there was no justification for despising or denying the human body, and certainly not the reproductive capacity of the female. The role of women, and the importance of the reproductive processes, were, in fact, endorsed by these essentially agrarian religious beliefs. These were the views which underpinned the role of the "wise women" in the community. It was to these women that the underclass turned for midwifery services and advice on contraception and abortion.[14] They also served as community healers dispensing traditional herbal remedies.

While there are no direct accounts of the history of these old religious beliefs and practices, the frequency with which they are mentioned in the penitentials and in records of Church Councils makes it clear that they retained great popular appeal. For many within the community, these old beliefs were compatible with Christian doctrine since both had recourse to the supernatural to explain many earthly events. And both called upon some form of divinity for relief from suffering.[15] To the church, their continued persistence represented a challenge to its authority. It also viewed any adherents to the old religions as deviants and heretics. The church itself, however, faced mounting criticism for the gap which existed between the message it delivered and the practices of the hierarchy and the clergy.

There was ample evidence that many clerics were not conforming to the moral code which lay people were being directed to follow. It was openly acknowledged that deviant behavior in sexual and other matters was all too frequent within the hierarchy and among monks and priests. In some instances, it was the popes themselves who behaved in scandalous fashion. In the early eleventh century, Benedict IX was banished by the Romans for his licentious behavior.[16] Nevertheless, there were other popes who conducted vigorous campaigns against moral turpitude and vehemently denounced the sexualized body. Innocent III, whose pontificate from 1198 to 1216 is seen as the culminating point of temporal and spiritual supremacy for the papacy, declared that sexual intercourse was always accompanied by "the stench of the flesh."[17] Despite the many denunciations from the pulpit of sexual activities, the steady growth in the population of Europe up till the time of the Black Death, indicates that the lay population rejected the calls for abstinence or restraint, choosing instead to risk possible retribution for their sexual indulgence.

But there were other factors that stimulated dissent within the general population. One of these was the widely-held perception that the hierarchy of the church was remote from the experiences of daily life in most communities, and cared little for the laity. This is not surprising as bishops, archbishops, and cardinals were usually appointed from the families of the rich and powerful and lived in a state of great luxury. Further, for a long time, the church had been torn asunder, and its authority weakened by schisms within the Curia. This had resulted in the election of popes and anti-popes, often acting concurrently.[18] It was a combination of these two factors, the behavior of some of the clergy, and the uncertainties within the church, which disturbed many in the community. And it was this situation that fostered dissent and gave space for the development of conflicting discourses on religious issues. One outcome was the emergence of a distinctly anti-clerical attitude within the laity, a sentiment which did not undermine their fundamental religious convictions, or their faith in the church as an institution. The depth of the underlying religiosity of the general population is clearly shown by the fact that some two million pilgrims visited Rome during the Holy Year proclaimed by Boniface VIII in 1300.[19] Despite this fundamental goodwill toward the church, dissatisfaction with the inconsistencies between church pronouncements and clerical practice increased, and led to moves for reform of the church. Inevitably, these moves became associated with the general civic unrest which was a feature of the late medieval period.

Millennial Dreams

Many people experienced grinding poverty and hardship during much of the Middle Ages, living in a state perhaps more properly described as "destitution."[20] They endured oppression by feudal landlords, famines and epidemic diseases, wars and natural disasters. And despite the rhetoric, it seemed to many that the church was indifferent to their plight, that poverty still carried the "stain of sin."[21] Although this may not have been a completely fair assessment, it represented the perception of a significant proportion of the economically disadvantaged levels of European communities. Revolts against economic conditions arose with marked frequency during the twelfth to fourteenth centuries. Protests against their lot also took the form of popular religious demonstrations based on the chiliastic belief that at some point in time Christ would return to the world to right all wrongs, to punish the oppressors, and to ease the pain of sufferers.

The only hope that the majority of these people had was their belief that at some time the old world order, with all its inequities, would be overthrown and the oppressed would be able to live in peace and plenty. For this reason, prophecies which raised hopes that the promised millennium was close at hand were welcomed and frequently caused spontaneous outbursts of religious fervor, particularly among the poorer classes.[22] Most of these prophecies were linked to the appearance of unusual events which were widely accepted as apocalyptic signs—an eclipse, a flood, an earthquake, or an outbreak of epidemic disease. Any preacher who could claim prophetic abilities, and declare that the promised millennium was close at hand, was given a respectful hearing.

Nevertheless, it was not to the parish priest that large numbers of people turned for comfort and guidance. They flocked to hear the words of the many itinerant preachers who travelled from city to city in the late Middle Ages.[23] These preachers, frequently religious hermits with tenuous or no links with the church, were the most prominent purveyors of apocalyptic prophesies which fired the imaginations of urban communities. They operated outside the organized church, at times drawing the hostility of the hierarchy. However, it was only in rare instances that their messages suggested anything contrary to fundamental Christian doctrine. They did, however, frequently criticize the life-styles of the clergy as an affront to God. In the main, they concentrated on exhorting their listeners to avoid the perils of sinful behavior, and to seek timely expiation of sins before the end of the world arrived. It was their commitment to promoting a return to basic Christian moral values, and the implied promise in their message of better things to come, that commanded the allegiance of large numbers of people. Overall, the message of the roving preachers was not dissimilar to that of the mendicant friars, but they also tapped the feelings of dissent which many felt toward the practices within the organized church. Preaching in large open spaces within the cities, or in the countryside, they inspired a high level of popular religious fervor. They also created an atmosphere in which all manner of persons became readily disposed to participate in mass public rituals of repentance.

Rituals of Flagellation

During the thirteenth century, a new element entered into these collective penitential exercises inspired by roving preachers. Initially, it even attracted individual members of the church hierarchy and clergy. In 1261, a hermit in Perugia organized the first European procession of flagellants, bands of men who sought to purge their sins through scourging their bodies with spiked whips.[24] The call for public demonstrations of repentance in this manner was heeded by a great many people, indicating their belief that denial or torture of the body, or imitating the sufferings of Christ, provided a path to salvation. The Franciscan friar Salimbene gave an eye-witness account of these early events, describing the response to the hermit's call: ". . . all men, both small and great, noble and common, went in procession, naked, whipping themselves through the cities, led by the bishops and men in religious

Orders. . . . And so many went to confess their sins that the priests scarcely had time to eat."[25] A more detailed description of the method of self-flagellation shows the extent to which these men were prepared to inflict injuries upon their naked torsos in a quest for spiritual salvation:

> The men beat themselves rhythmically with leather scourges armed with iron spikes, singing hymns meanwhile in celebration of Christ's Passion and the glories of the Virgin. . . . At certain passages—three times in each hymn—all would fall down 'as though struck by lightning' and lie with outstretched arms, sobbing and praying. . . . After a while the men stood up, lifted their arms towards heaven and sang; then they recommenced their flagellation. . . . Each day two complete flagellations were performed in public; and each night a third was performed in the privacy of the bedroom. The flagellants did their work with such thoroughness that often the spikes of the scourge stuck in the flesh and had to be wrenched out. Their blood spurted on to the walls and their bodies turned to masses of blue flesh.[26]

It is difficult to comprehend the intensity of religious fervor that lay behind this wholesale attack on the body. Nor is it easy to understand the feats of endurance involved in continuing this self-castigation through an extended period of 33½ days, a period chosen to represent the number of years during which Christ is traditionally thought to have lived on earth.[27]

There were two factors that provoked this initial display of public and collective expiation of sins through bodily violence. First, the flagellants believed that they were acting on behalf of the community, and through their actions could gain divine intervention to relieve the suffering caused by the recent succession of severe famines, wars, and outbreaks of epidemic disease.[28] Second, it was a collective response to the apocalyptic prophesy of the Calabrian monk, Joachim of Fiore, who warned that the start of the millennium was then close at hand. Because of this, many felt the need to purge their sins and show the religious devotion and the solidarity of the group as a matter of urgency. After a period of intense involvement in these collective penitential rituals, the flagellant movement in Italy withered. However, the practice spread widely throughout Europe where the same rituals, with minor local variations, were employed.

When later the Black Death arrived in Italy, its first appearance in western Europe, it was widely regarded as another apocalyptic sign. To most communities, the very scale of the disaster showed that the end of the world had arrived. Consequently, the flagellant movement re-emerged with a heightened sense of religious zeal engendered by the horrors of the plague epidemic. So great was the fear of the disease that flagellant groups would form and practice their propitiatory rituals at the first indications that the epidemic might be approaching. Once again the flagellant movement spread rapidly from Italy to the rest of western Europe.

The second flagellant movement lasted from early in 1348 until about the end of 1349. During 1349, church and state authorities became alarmed at the threat to their power and influence which many of the flagellant groups seemed to pose. By contrast with the earlier demonstrations when the clergy, particularly in Italy, played some part in the proceedings, the flagellants of 1348 were led by laymen. The new flagellant groups expressed a great deal of criticism about the practices of the clergy and the hierarchy, and to some extent the authority of the church. Not surprisingly, the church began to see heresy in their activities. Secular authorities also were suspicious of their intentions, since traditionally all governments have been wary of any large assemblies of citizens, and especially when they voiced anti-establishment views. In this instance, church and state co-operated to ban public processions of flagellants. Furthermore, in October 1349, the Pope issued a Bull against the flagellant groups, and the secular authorities joined enthusiastically in their suppression. Apart from a few minor groups which survived in smaller areas, most penitents abandoned the flagellant movement and vanished into the communities from which they had come.

Some aspects of the flagellant movement bear closer study. Leaving aside the techniques of flagellation, which we have already discussed, other elements of their ritual procedures offer revealing glimpses of the constructions placed on the body by the dominant religious discourse of the mid-fourteenth century.[29] In addition, they indicate, through their prohibitions, the moral judgements which were applied to differentiate between the "ordered" male body and the "disordered" female body. Each flagellant was required to be clothed in a white robe with a red cross on front and back, and to wear a hood similarly marked. The uniform provided a means of confirming the solidarity of the group, and identified each flagellant as a member of a privileged group. The color of the uniform signified the desire of the group for spiritual and physical purity. The flagellant group adopted a range of measures involving bodily and social deprivation. During the whole period of the ritual self-abasement, the flagellant was not permitted to bathe, shave, or change his clothes. A participant was required to fast for most of the time, was not to sleep in a soft bed, and was not to speak to another flagellant unless so authorized by the lay Master of the group. And above all else, penitents were forbidden to have any dealings with women. This was to ensure that the flagellants could present themselves before God as pure in body and mind, uncontaminated by the "disordered" female body. They were to avoid any sexual contact with their wives, and they were not to be served food by a woman in any house where they were lodged. If a flagellant spoke even a single word to a woman, he had to undergo a ritual beating by the Master who then enjoined him to avoid the same sin again. And as unequivocal evidence of the prevailing perception that the female body was evil and a source of pollution, the whole flagellation ritual was deemed invalid, and had to be re-commenced, if a woman intruded while the assembled penitents were performing their self-scourging.

Channelling Subversive Voices

The medieval church had two ways of dealing with subversive voices—extermination and incorporation. Groups or individuals defined as deviant were pursued, persecuted, and executed. With the aid of the Inquisition, and the secular authorities, the church had no difficulty obtaining guilty verdicts, and removing or dispersing those dissenters who posed a threat to its authority. A prime example of the zealous pursuit of those perceived to be challenging the church is found in those accused of practicing witchcraft. In addition to being branded heretics, these women stood accused of sexual malpractices—procuring abortions, imparting contraceptive knowledge and depriving some men of their sexual powers. They were subjected to torture and execution on the flimsiest of evidence.[30] The Flagellants were among other groups whose challenge to the authority of the church incurred the wrath of that powerful institution. Many others in the later Middle Ages, a period of rising religious dissent, developed counter religious discourses which struck at some of the central elements of church dogma. There were, however, other groups whose dissent was of a less confronting nature, whose views represented a differing discourse without any challenge to the fundamental doctrines of the church. The less contentious of these groups were neutralized by being absorbed into the structure of the church. The Mendicant Orders provide an example of this incorporation of a group with a dissenting discourse. They sought a return to the ethics of poverty and universal brotherhood as practiced by the early Christians. It was beyond question that these were moral values established by the Gospels of the New Testament, but by the late Middle Ages there was clear evidence that the life-style of members of the hierarchy, and that of many of the clergy, fell far short of the standards set by the church as an institution. In these circumstances, it would have been difficult for the views of the mendicants to have been declared heretical, especially as there was never any challenge to matters of doctrine or to papal authority. Accordingly, they were brought into the formal structure of the church and given the tasks of eradicating heresy, and of preaching the gospel to the general population.

During the twelfth and thirteenth century, the mendicant friars themselves became involved in channelling other potentially subversive voices into activities of benefit to the church and the community. The possibility of revolt was founded in a wave of dissent apparent throughout Europe. It arose from a deep sense of religiosity within most communities facing many crises, and from a sense of dissatisfaction that the laity was totally excluded from participating directly in religious observances. For the most part, these moves did not represent challenges to the institution of the church or to orthodox doctrine. The advent of the mendicants, with their doctrine of simple Christianity, gave support and encouragement to groups of laymen to form brotherhoods devoted to religious rituals in which the secular clergy played little or no part. These associations were the confraternities common to most countries of western Europe in the late Middle Ages, and generally falling into categories defined by their specific objectives. One group concentrated on rituals which honored, and sought the protection of the Virgin Mary, the Queen of Heaven. Members of a second group of confraternities devoted their ceremonial activities to rituals of self-flagellation, although not with the violent public displays which we have described above. A third group focused on charitable works including care of the sick and dying, burying the dead, comforting prisoners condemned to die, and aiding the needy. We will confine our attention to the way in which Florentine confraternities of the *laudesi*, those who honored Mary; and the *flagellanti* or *disci-*

plinati, those who practiced self-scourging, responded to the epidemics of bubonic plague.

The *laudesi* gained their identification from the fact that their principal rituals involved singing hymns of praise to the Madonna, their patron saint. In essence they were upholders of the Marian cult which sought to glorify the pure body of Mary, the emblematic virginal condition which guaranteed a path to salvation. By paying homage, they anticipated that they could call upon the Virgin to intercede on their behalf, and be relieved of divine punishment which they otherwise deserved for their sinful behavior. On the other hand, the *flagellanti* focused on rituals to cleanse the impure human body by self-castigation, and return it to a state of purity. And it is clear from contemporary documents, that the sins which troubled the *flagellanti* most were the carnal sins. One fifteenth century Florentine of the ruling classes described his guilt and his self-scourging in graphic detail: "In my heart I repent that I am so filled with carnal sin. But with a scourge I lash my flanks again and again, whence, pouring forth, blood collects about me as I kneel upon the ground, and mixes with my copious tears."[31] The rituals of the *flagellanti* were conducted within their own meeting places, the only "public" nature of the exercise being that it was performed in the presence of all members gathered together. Nevertheless, there was a great degree of anonymity as the ritual was performed with all lights extinguished and the participants hooded and dressed in long gowns, open at the back.[32] After the self-scourging, the wounds were washed, and the participants retired to sleep overnight before emerging as "purified" bodies.

Ritual Responses to the Black Death

The sense of horror engendered by the plague epidemics focused attention on religious rituals which might deflect or minimize its impact on communities and individuals. Collective responses were deemed important for both purposes. Accordingly, there was an upsurge in membership of groups that pursued collective penitential exercises, and recourse to penitential processions involving the whole community.

Private Rituals of Repentance

From their beginnings in the twelfth century, growth of the confraternities in Florence was fairly slow, there being only twenty at the end of the thirteenth century. Their growth during the next two centuries was, however, remarkable, reaching a total of more than 100 by the end of the fifteenth century.[33] This is even more remarkable when we consider that due to deaths from plague in that period, the population had fallen from about 100,000 to some 37,000 to 40,000.[34] There can be little doubt that the ever-present fear of imminent death caused by the plague epidemics would have provided a great incentive to participate in penitential rituals which sought relief from what was perceived as divine punishment. There were also other benefits of membership which became more important in time of plague.[35] A sense of social cohesion could be restored, a member could rely on his brothers to aid him if he became a plague victim, to bury him if he succumbed, and to offer prayers for his soul thereafter. However, despite the fact that these benefits were available in every confraternity, it was the *flagellanti* group which showed the greatest growth in numbers, far outstripping other groups of confraternities in Florence by the end of the fifteenth century. This pattern supports a conclusion that the Black Death and the epidemics of the fifteenth century caused greater emphasis to be placed on the flawed nature of the human body and the need to punish it to deflect divine wrath and punishment. This conclusion is also supported by the fact that most orations and exhortations delivered at meetings of confraternities in the fifteenth century focused on two concepts. First, the corporeality of the body was treated as being responsible for sin, and second, flagellation was the most frequently mentioned penitential practice in these addresses.[36] Among the speakers who addressed confraternity gatherings, one declared that the remedy for the evils of the body was "to castigate, beat, and with whips and fasts to torment the body." A second speaker enjoined his listeners to "forget . . . your depraved, dissolute desires and vices and [with] whip ready, kneel." Yet another demanded similar action: "With the scourge in hand, remedy the injuries of your pus-filled body." These were not the words of clerics or of mendicant friars. They were from orations delivered by laymen who were well regarded humanist scholars of the early Renaissance period.[37] For this reason, they represented the prevailing perceptions of the "learned" and middle classes in Florence that the body was inherently vile and prone to sensual aberrations which undermined the quest for spirituality. And to remedy the position, they held that it was necessary to curb and chasten the body by penitential self-mortification of the flesh.

Public Rituals of Repentance

While the confraternities conducted rituals in private for their individual and collective purgation, and for deliverance from the evils of the plague and other menacing events, they also assisted in public rituals which aimed to demonstrate that the whole community wished to repent of their sins. This type of event was mentioned in the previous chapter in referring to the decision of the communal authorities of Florence to call for a penitential procession when plague first threatened the city. Such rituals were a regular feature of communal life in that period, being organized whenever a crisis affected or threatened the city. And since the aim of a penitential procession was to appease God, it was deemed necessary for the whole social body to be mobilized to demonstrate unity of purpose and total commitment to the undertaking. For this reason, the processions had to include all religious dignitaries and members of the religious institutions of the city—prelates, the secular clergy, the regular clergy, the mendicant orders, and men of the lay confraternities. Nuns took no direct part; their role was to pray. After the religious community representatives came the office bearers and the governing councils of the city, then all other men, and at the end of the assembly, the women. It was not until near the end of the fifteenth century that children played any role in penitential processions.

Calls for penitential processions originated generally from the communal authorities but occasionally from church leaders in the city. However, civic authorities rarely acted completely on their own initiative when threats to the community were perceived as stemming from divine wrath. Instead, they sought advice on the matter from religious persons, sometimes from the traditional clergy, but more frequently from holy men and women considered as seers. Their recommendations followed a fairly standard formula—demonstrate the pious devotion and repentance of the whole community with solemn processions, prayers, and orations, and ensure that all participate in the rituals. Once the form of the occasion had been decided, the arrangements were left in the hands of the clergy who determined the details of time, place and duration, and the type of clothing to be worn.[38] However, it is not the events themselves but the social constructions which lay behind them which are of particular interest to us.

While everyone was required to participate to show community solidarity, the sexes were rigidly separated, as indeed they were in churches also. This was designed to avoid any perception of laxness in sexual matters that would offend God and undermine efforts to appease Him.[39] The disruptive influence of the "impure" female body was clearly a matter for great concern. But the "pure" body and its inherent power was treated with great reverence. There is ample evidence of this attitude in the planning of processions. When seeking advice on the conduct of public rituals of repentance, the commune frequently turned to "virginal" women, nuns, and the occasional visionary laywoman. The latter, according to established precedent, was usually a widow of unchallengeable character, "with a reputation as a good woman who has always behaved perfectly, a virgin in body and mind, as her confessor testified."[40]

Theological debate around the concept of a "pure" and sacred body in opposition to the "impure" body commenced from the moment when "the Word was made flesh" (John 1:14). According to the doctrine of the Incarnation, it was then that Christ became a fusion of "perfect God and perfect Man," free from any stain of sin by the manner of His birth. The purity of His body and soul was confirmed by the doctrine of the Immaculate Conception which asserts that the Virgin Mary also came into this world with a pure body free from the stain of original sin.[41] For these reasons, the bodies of both Christ and Mary were perceived as most sacred, and venerated above all other symbols of corporeality. Mary was worshipped for her virginal state, and because, as the mother of God, she was the most powerful Saint in Heaven to whom prayers for intercession could be addressed. But in the ultimate, the pleas for relief were directed to God in the image of Christ. And it was the body of Christ that conveyed the most powerful images of the sacredness of the body, and was central to the Eucharistic rituals of the medieval church. For the people of that period, the celebration of the mass involved a supernatural transformation—the bread actually became the body of Christ, and those who partook of the bread participated in an act which Bynum described as "symbolic cannibalism."[42] Through this process, the "impure" body could absorb and be nourished spiritually by the "pure" and sacred body of Christ.[43]

These were the most widely accepted perceptions of the body of Christ in the late Middle Ages. There were, however, more complex constructs favored by some medieval theologians and mystics. In these, and despite the general association of maleness with Christ, His body was perceived as having a close affinity with female flesh since he had no human father and his body came solely from Mary.[44] Caroline Bynum concluded that this association of woman with the body of Christ was given additional emphasis by some mystics: "Indeed, they went so far as to treat Christ's flesh as female, at least in certain of its salvific functions, especially its bleeding and nurturing." These perceptions of an association with the female flesh also found their way into the iconography of religious art from the thirteenth to the sixteenth centuries, and into some medieval devotional texts. But, in the main, it was the mystics, male and female, not the general populace, who saw Christ's body as a female personification.[45] Overall, according to Bynum, "medieval people of both sexes could see the holy manifest in the same flesh which had lured humans into lust and greed during their lives and, after death, putrefied in the grave."

But incontrovertible evidence of belief in the power of the sacred, "pure" body is manifest in the central role accorded to images of the Virgin Mary, and to the sacred relics of holy figures by the Florentines in times of crisis. It was then that a collective sense of impending doom moved the whole community to look to their moral transgressions, to purge themselves of lust and other sins, and to seek divine help in their hour of need. Invariably, it was to the images and relics which possessed the powers of intercession granted to sacred and "pure" bodies that they turned. And while there were many images of Mary in the various churches and monasteries of Florence, there was one in particular which was credited with having the greatest influence with God. In times of severe crisis such as the plague epidemics, the greatly revered image of the Virgin held at a small church in the village of Impruneta, just outside Florence, was brought into the city to join the penitential processions.[46] Such was the faith in the powers of intercession of the Madonna of Impruneta that one historian, Varchi, claimed that her intervention had gained respite from the plague for Florence on at least two occasions.[47]

The sacred relics carried in the procession served the same purpose as the image of the Madonna. They also provided a bridge between earthbound human life and the supernatural, the only agency to which humans could turn for support or relief. The most highly prized relics were fragments of bones from the bodies of saints or other holy persons, which were believed to still retain the power of a sacred, purified body.[48] Appeals to these relics were based on the belief that relics represented the saints themselves, "living already with God in the incorrupt and glorified bodies mere mortals would attain only at the end of time."[49] So great was the demand for these symbols of the sacred body, that bodies of the early saints and martyrs were exhumed, broken into pieces and distributed about Europe. Every church, every monastery, every monarch or noble-man, and, later, every civic commune of the Middle Ages had relics, and competed for those relics which had established reputations for successful intervention with God. Even the power of the Pope, according to one writer, owed much to the fact that he was the cus-todian of the body of St. Peter.[50] The Florentine processions of ritual repentance drew upon these powers of the sacred body to intercede on behalf of the citizens to lift the burden of plague.

Changes in public rituals of penitence developed during the long succession of epidemics. Late in the fourteenth century, there was another outpouring of popular religious fervor in Europe when bands of white-robed penitents, known as the *Bianchi,* moved from town to town inspiring the local population to join their rituals. When some of these bands reached Florence, again facing a renewed outbreak of plague, they attracted many supporters. One contemporary chronicler attributed the events to the fact that "God is angered by the whole human race," and because neither "the civic leaders nor prelates nor the learned" had responded and cor-rected the sins of the world, God had called upon the "mass of ordi-nary people" to lead the way.[51] The same account reveals that the sexuality of the body was still seen as a barrier to moral purity. According to this record of the events, there was a strict require-ment that all men who participated must remain chaste through-out the period of the pilgrimage.

On arrival in Florence, the numbers of the *Bianchi* were aug-mented when the city authorities invited all girls and boys, as well as men and women, to join the *Bianchi* processions.[52] As a result, crowds of some forty thousand people joined the processions which paraded about the city daily for several days. The inclusion of chil-dren in penitential processions was unusual at that stage. Later, however, the composition of these processions changed significantly as a result of experiences during plague epidemics. The stimulus to change arose from the high loss of life among the children of Flo-rentine families and an enhanced perception of the worth of chil-dren which followed.[53] One outcome from this re-evaluation was the formation of lay religious confraternities for young boys, under the patronage of the older groups. Progressively, the boys' fraternities became an important element of the ritual processions of the city. They appeared only twice during late fourteenth century proces-sions but were regular participants by the middle of the fifteenth century.[54] When the boys took part in the processions, dressed all in white, they presented an image of asexual innocence. They portrayed an image of bodily purity indicative of a moral purity fitting them to be the new "saviors" of the community. By including the boys, the community hoped to convince God, through the contrasting images of the asexual young and penitent adults, that there was a collective recognition of the perils of the body.

Responses of the Clergy

The first response of the clergy was to reaffirm that the plague which was devastating the city was a punishment from God for the wickedness of the citizens. Florentines needed little reminding of this nexus, so firmly was it embodied in community discourse. However, when ordinary citizens observed that the mortality rate was just as high among the clergy and the members of the hierarchy, as among themselves, they were bound to entertain some doubts. The evidence forced them to ask themselves who were the real sinners who had so offended God that he had inflicted such a dreadful punishment upon the whole city. In this way, the plague began to pose problems for an institution which claimed complete supremacy in interpreting God's will and in determining matters of doctrine. Furthermore, the very severity of the continuing epidemics tended to challenge both the credibility and the authority of the clergy.

This was further challenged by the actions of some members of the clergy. One of the most serious questions faced by the clergy during the plague epidemics was their responsibility to their congregations. Arguments for and against flight from the plague continued to the end of the plague period.[55] Some were convinced that there was no neglect of priestly duties in flight from danger, and they fled. This group included priests, friars, monks, and prelates. Nor were popes averse to flight from the plague, as many references to the removal of the papal court confirm.[56] On the other hand, many others stayed to minister to their flocks as best they could. However, the whole problem was exacerbated by the high death toll among the clergy, with many citizens being denied spiritual support and the rites traditionally associated with priestly duties.

Some of the clergy displayed another disturbing characteristic—avarice. Many sought to profit from the disorder created by the plague, and although there were other professionals in Florence who showed the same greed, such behavior was rightly considered improper for priests and friars. Contemporary documents show

some of these people demanded an "exorbitant price" for performing their normal duties.[57] It was also asserted that they pressed
their services on the wealthier families: "Priests and friars used to
go to the rich in great numbers, and were paid so great a price [for
their services] that they all grew wealthy."

The great number of priests and friars who died from plague
meant that many churches and monasteries were left with few if
any to carry on the usual activities. Efforts to obtain replacements
attracted relatively few new novices, and often these were very
young and unexperienced, and of low educational standards. In
addition, many of them lacked a vocation, and a commitment to a
life of chastity. Even among the older clergy there were many
instances of sexual and other bodily indulgences that did not match
the rhetoric of the church on sins of the body. The sin of lust had
long been attributed to some of the clergy, but in this period it
became so entrenched in community perceptions that it found a
credible place in literature.[58] It is unlikely that the figure of the
cunning and licentious priest or friar could have become so prominent in Boccaccio's stories, or in Machievelli's play *La Mandragola*
unless this reflected community perceptions of the actual situation.[59] None of this helped to restore the reputation of the clergy
which had declined markedly as a result of some clerical responses
during the plague epidemics. It only reinforced the undercurrent of
anti-clerical feeling which had existed in Italy for a long time.[60]
Some appreciation of this feeling can be gained from the following
comment on priests by Buonaccorso Pitti, in the late fourteenth
century: ". . . the priests . . . were an unscrupulous lot at the time—
not indeed that I ever met an honest one either before or since!"[61]

The discreditable, or worse, responses to the plague shown by
many within the hierarchy and the clergy accelerated pressure for
reform of the church. Concessions then made were too little and too
late. As a result, the pent-up demands for change soon culminated
in the upheaval of the Reformation and the Counter Reformation.
Thereafter, the church ceased to be the spiritual centre of Chris-
tendom, and its status as a temporal power in Europe was greatly
diminished.

Regulating the Sexualized Body

With attention so heavily focused on the body and its fragility
as a result of the plague, it was inevitable that the nexus between

sin and disease, and sin and the body would be reinforced. Prominent preachers, particularly friars of the mendicant orders, became more strident in their denunciations of sexual behavior that they deemed to be deviant, and which in their opinions contributed to the incidence of plague. Some saw such behavior as not simply a contributing factor but a direct cause of the disaster. Among these, the two most prominent were Bernardino of Siena, who preached in Florence and Siena in the first quarter of the fifteenth century, and Girolamo Savonarola, a charismatic figure belonging to the end of that century. Both exerted great influence on their congregations and on the lawmakers of their times. Bernardino of Siena was always outspoken on issues concerned with human sexuality and sought to regulate almost any type of conduct within this area. In 1425 he delivered a number of sermons which touched on activities which he considered sexually deviant. In two of them he devoted the whole of the address to homosexuality. In the first of these he asserted, without qualification, that "God sends pestilences for sodomy."[62] And, in his opinion the city of Florence well deserved this punishment. So infamous for this vice was the whole of Tuscany, he declared, that anyone from the area was prohibited, by statute, from being employed as a teacher in Genoa.

In the second of these sermons he repeated his claim that God punished sodomy by causing a corruption of the airs which in turn led to outbreaks of plague.[63] He called on all fathers and mothers to observe "that it is a matter of great astonishment that at a very young age they [boys] are already contaminated by sodomy!" According to Bernardino, they were so young that "they haven't dried their eyes and yet they are contaminated and sodomites!" And as he continued to attribute to sodomites every vice in society, he blamed them for wars, and tempests in addition to the plague. His remedy, apart from inflicting harsh punishments on offenders, lay in parents ensuring that they discouraged anything which might lead their sons into such a vice. He gave an example of this in the abbreviated tights and doublets which some boys wore, "displaying too much flesh for sodomites [to see]."[64] He warned that tailors who made such clothing, those who wore it, and the mothers and fathers of the boys, would be held to have committed a mortal sin.

While Bernardino had a great deal to say about sodomites, he was just as direct and outspoken about heterosexual activities within the community. He accused wives and husbands of conniving to prevent birth, either by contraception or by procuring abortions.[65] On one occasion he declared that those who adopted such

practices were no different to sodomites since their actions also contributed equally to the shrinkage of populations throughout the
world.[66] And in terms of the religious discourse of the period which
labelled anal intercourse between men and women as "sodomy," he
castigated men who had intercourse with their wives in ways which
were "against nature and against the proper mode of matrimony."[67]
But, it would seem, Bernardino considered that most sexual intercourse was shameful, and that women and their lustful natures
had to bear much of the responsibility for the effects which sexual
indulgence had on men:

> Why do you believe that one is more ashamed of an act of
> lust than of any other sin though a great sin it may be?
> Because the intellect becomes bestial, because reason
> becomes clouded, and we are ashamed to have our reason
> overwhelmed by the flesh. . . . Many [men] have become
> foolish and forgetful through their wives, that is through
> lust.[68]

Bernardino frequently chastised women for their vanity, their use
of make-up, for tinting their hair, and their extravagance in dress.
Such women, he declared, acted like prostitutes not like good wives,
and undermined the resolve of men to lead chaste lives. And, as an
alternative, he extolled the superior virtues of virginity.[69]
Bernardino's remedy for the problems caused by the "vice of lasciviousness" was to encourage a denial of the body, to constrain its
passion by fasting, sober living, ensuring that wine was well-
diluted with water before drinking, and by "castigating the body
with hard work."[70] These prescriptions were consistent with practices associated with renunciation of the body originally devised to
reduce temptation for those leading a monastic life.[71] Bryan Turner,
in discussing the traditions of fasting within this context, concluded
that dietary practices "provided one of the principal means for the
control of the inner body, releasing the spirit from the cloying presence of the flesh."[72] By the late Middle Ages, however, practices
originally meant to save monastics and ascetics from temptation
were being proposed for the whole community as penitential practices.

Girolamo Savonarola, the other major preacher of the fifteenth century, was Prior of the Dominican Church of San Marco in
Florence from 1491 until his death in 1498. During this period the
city again experienced a succession of plague epidemics and, as a

consequence, a significant death toll.[73] Fear drove many people from the city on some of these occasions. Savonarola, like many of his predeccesors, saw the origins of the plague in divine punishment for the sins of the city, and for him, these were principally bodily sins. In one sermon he asserted that the problem was not confined to Florence as "one can see the whole of Italy corrupted by lust and sodomy."[74] For this reason, he declared, it was necessary to suppress "the desires of the flesh" if the city was to be freed from a pestilence such as had been described in the Bible. And for Savonarola these considerations drove him to institute a morals campaign to cleanse the city of its sins of lust and sodomy. For quite a long period he was able to exert a strong reforming influence on a community ready to accept the blame for the outbreaks of plague. Again like many of his fellow clerics, Savonarola made denial of the body an essential element of his prescription for Florentines. He asserted that paying too much attention to the body entangled one in the "temptations of the devil," and that living a sensual life, as did young men and boys, led to bodily and mental weakness.[75] In his precepts for living a good life, he declared that men must turn from the pleasures of the flesh and "live chastely, fleeing from women and other provocations to lust." These statements simply repeated the stereotypical view that the female body incited the male to indulge in practices which were dangerous and debilitating. The same view is implicit in his direction to men to avoid such places as dances and taverns, since these places were frequently gathering places for prostitutes. It appears that he believed that anywhere women were present represented a hazard which could put body and soul at risk. In effect, Savonarola revealed in these comments his abhorrence of any kind of sensory pleasure for the body. His sermons, and his efforts to constrain any behavior which contained elements of gratification, are a testament to the strength of his convictions on the matter.

Florence, Savonarola claimed, was full of lechery, the women and young men were totally lascivious, female servants were prone to immoral behavior and should be kept at home for as long as possible, and prostitutes should not be allowed to walk the streets.[76] He insisted that women and girls should be constrained in their contact with males and in public appearances. Women were enjoined to converse with men as little as possible, contenting themselves with prayers, and attending to the affairs of the house. And to underscore the polluting nature of sexual contact with women, Savonarola directed that to cleanse their souls from every stain of sin arising from the body or other vices, men "must stay separated from the act of matrimony for several days" before they went to communion. Apparently, even the sexual functions of the male body posed problems for Savonarola as he insisted that a man must abstain from taking communion if he had experienced "nocturnal pollution which comes in dreams."[77]

Forthright preachers such as Bernardino of Siena, Savonarola, and others of their kind, had always been able to influence community attitudes and, in particular, those of the lawmakers of the city. And since the community continued to accept that civil law should be in accord with divine edict, definitions of deviant behavior emanating from religious figures were frequently translated into statutes enforceable by officers of the state. Savonarola, accepted as the spiritual leader of Florence for several years, was able to take this process a little further. Based on his belief that the older members of the community were beyond easy redemption, he established bands of young boys with the same image of asexual purity and innocence as those of the earlier boys' confraternities.[78] They ranged in age from six or seven years to seventeen or eighteen years and paraded in white in processions composed of some 5,000 boys. Apart from their ceremonial activities, however, Savonarola encouraged the boys to directly eradicate sin in the city. This they did with great energy, reproving women in the streets for wearing unsuitable clothing or ornaments, and chastising gamblers. A diarist of the period described their actions thus:

> The boys were encouraged by the *Frate* [Savonarola] to take away baskets of *berlingozzi* [Lenten cakes], and the gambling-tables, and many vain things used by women, so that no sooner did the gamblers hear that the boys of the *Frate* were coming than they fled, nor was there a single woman who dared go out not modestly dressed. . . . The said boys went about everywhere, along the walls of the city and to the taverns, etc., wherever they saw gatherings of people; this they did in each quarter [of the city], and if anyone had rebelled against them, he would have been in danger of his life, whoever he was.[79]

Two years later the boys were bold enough to gather a "pile of vain things, nude statues and playing boards, heretical books, . . . mirrors and many other vain things, of great value," and burn them on a bonfire in the main city square, an early example of the "bonfire of the vanities."[80] It is not surprising that such violent and repressive actions against anything resembling sensory pleasure produced a reaction within the community. After several years the civic authorities of Florence and the Pope also turned against him and accused him of heretical preaching. Savonarola's seven years of spiritual and political power and influence ended on the scaffold and the stake.

Defending the Male Body

The Black Death created a crisis around the body. It heightened anxieties about the uses of the body, the public presentation of the body, and the co-mingling of bodies. These concerns extended far beyond the social practices developed to manage the succession of plague epidemics. Responses to the crisis led to the development of mechanisms which intensified and entrenched masculine control of Florentine society, and reaffirmed male supremacy in the use of and access to public space. As we have seen above, most responses to the plague had their origins in perceptions generated by religious discourse. However, their implementation was channelled through the male power structure of the church and the state.

The techniques of protection which emerged were explicitly directed at *defending* male bodies from polluting bodies—female bodies and plague-ridden bodies—physical entities which were conceptually linked through religious discourse. The female "disordered" body, however, was viewed as polluting on two counts. In a conflation of moral and physical dangers, it was perceived as posing a constant threat to men's spiritual health, and also acting as a potential conduit for the transmission of plague. Consequently, the male body, under siege, was placed at the center of religious and secular rituals aimed at warding off the contaminating influence of sexuality and disease. Men flailed their bodies in rituals of purification, and bands of boys roamed the streets policing the presentation of women's bodies in public space. Women's bodies, perceived as sexually threatening, were segregated within or excluded from public events in which men participated.

Within this same period, blighted as it was by the crises of plague epidemics, there were the stirrings of a struggle by women to be seen and heard. Women had been enshrouded in silence until the end of the thirteenth century, but after that their voices began to emerge in religious and secular arenas. There were a few prominent secular women of letters, for example, Vittoria Colonna, Isabella d'Este, Elisabetta Gonzaga, and Christine de Pizan.[81] Pizan, who was born in Italy but spent most of her life in France, was one of the pre-eminent literary figures of her time. While she was a prolific writer, one of her most notable works was *Le Livre de la Cité des Dames* [The Book of the City of Ladies].[82] In this polemical work, Pizan challenged the normative discourses about women contained in sermons, poetry and pedagogical treatises. She assumed responsibility for the defense of the "fragile sex," and wrote of a utopian city governed only by women. Not only did Pizan demonstrate that women could acquire and apply knowledge, but she asserted that women had, in fact, invented various forms of learning.

Most women who spoke out in this period were from the world of religion. These included nuns, female mystics such as Saint Catherine of Genoa, the Beguines, and tertiaries such as Saint Catherine of Siena.[83] Catherine of Siena achieved considerable prominence as an intensely devout prophetic mystic who was an ardent advocate of bodily renunciation. This included a conviction that illness and disease were conditions to be endured for spiritual enrichment. To Catherine, "the offer of a cure was a temptation."[84] After her death at an early age, she was accorded the honor of the triple halo and crown.[85] Contrary to Paulian injunctions against women speaking on religious matters or issues, Catherine of Siena was also a "preacher."[86]

Despite these exceptions, there was a concerted campaign to keep women silent. Régnier-Bohler provides us with a rationale for this drive to suppress the threat posed by women's voices:

> The fear of female language was linked to the fear of female flesh and desire. . . . Woman was sinful before the fact because she usurped language from man and with it invaded public and domestic space. She was dangerous too because of her charismatic and prophetic powers of speech, which reflected, from the thirteenth century on, female claims to a new relation with the sacred.[87]

The strenuous efforts of men to eliminate and contain the threat to their power posed by women resulted in an increased masculinization of Florentine society.[88] In the process, women generally lost ground despite the apparent prominence of the few. Misogynist views of women and their place in life became more entrenched.

Boccaccio, known generally for his apparent indulgence toward women's sexuality in the *Decameron,* later displayed a complete reversal of attitude when he asserted that: "The female is an imperfect animal, driven by a thousand passions, unpleasant and abominable to recall, let alone to ponder upon them. . . ."[89] Almost two hundred years later, Matteo Palmieri, a well-known Florentine historian, saw women's role as being a producer of male heirs:

> The principal use that is expected of a woman is [to produce] sons, and to continue families. The wife is like the fertile soil which, after receiving the seed, nourishes it and produces from it abundant and good fruit.[90]

These expressions of contemporary viewpoints can only confirm that women became even more disadvantaged during the period of the plague epidemics

Joan Kelly-Gadol, in her seminal work on women in the Middle Ages and the Renaissance, asserted that they had generally lost status and power, and had become less "visible."[91] Ian Maclean, in his *Renaissance Notion of Women,* drew the same conclusion.[92] In a more recent paper, David Herlihy argued that the only area in which women had gained greater recognition was as charismatic figures.[93] Silvana Vecchio concluded that there was only one new development which improved the perceptions of women—"the discovery that women had souls."[94]

Regulating the Bodies of Citizens

We prosecute Nicolosa, daughter of Niccolò Soderini, of the parish of S. Frediano, aged ten years. Nicolosa was discovered wearing a dress made of two pieces of silk, with tassels and bound with various pieces of black leather, in violation of the communal statutes. [She confessed through her procurator and paid a fine of 14 lire.][1]

. . . It has come to the attention of the above mentioned judge and his court . . . that this Salvazza, wife of Seze . . . has publicly committed adultery with several persons and has sold her body for money. . . . With respect to all these charges, the judge intends to discover the truth; and if she is found guilty of walking without gloves and bells on her head or with high-heeled slippers, to punish her according to the communal statutes; . . .[2]

[The commune] shut down the taverns, truly horrible places, where many evils and disorders of the city are born; put in place special strict regulations concerning the vain display and trinkets of women, . . . and especially the mode of dress of public women [prostitutes]; renewed the penalties for the sin of sodomy; prohibited anyone from disputing the Faith; ordered suitable punishment for blasphemers; [and] broke up all forbidden games; . . .[3]

The escalating fear of women's sexuality, so evident in strident denunciations from the pulpit, was equally manifest in the deliberations of the civic leaders of Florence. However, their concerns were motivated as much by the perceived challenge by women to male power and supremacy, as they were by moral issues. During the plague period, these issues had a major influence on the enactment of increasingly restrictive legislative measures directed against women. Two of the extracts cited above attest to this outcome—a child of ten years fined for wearing clothing deemed immodest, and a woman charged with acting as a common prostitute without wearing the required distinguishing clothes. The third extract lists a wide range of prohibitions and restrictions instituted during an outbreak of plague in 1527. Some of these were directed at women, but others targeted a wider section of the community. It is clear, however, that most of the activities subjected to restrictions involved some form of bodily indulgence, or sensory pleasure. Hence, embodying these restrictions in civic law represented a secularization of older moral laws promoting denial of the body, a constant in the teachings of the church.[4] And while ostensibly enacted for the whole community, there is little doubt that much of this legislation was aimed primarily at disadvantaged and marginalized groups within the community. It is this growing involvement in the control of the bodies of citizens, and the intrusion into the intimate affairs of individuals by the State, which we examine in this chapter.

The Commune

It was only during the eleventh and twelfth centuries, as imperial power declined, that the communes, or city-states, of northern Italy began to emerge. As a result, local landholders took over the administrative control of their cities from the bishops and others who had acted for the Empire.[5] Gradually, the emerging merchant class demanded a voice in government, adding their calls to those of the banking and professional groups. By the first half of the fourteenth century, the government of the commune had assumed a form which remained relatively unchanged well into the plague period. Nevertheless, there was much vying for position amongst those eligible for election to office, and many shifts of power within the various arms of government.

The general council of the commune was comprised of elected representatives from the various guilds, the major guilds having a greater influence than the lesser guilds. Much of the day-to-day administration of the commune rested with a form of executive committee, membership of which rotated frequently. As we noted earlier, the system, while republican, did not correspond to our concepts of a democracy. Power was always held by a relatively restricted number of groups which resisted the addition of representatives from other sectors.

Beyond this ruling elite, there was a very large section of the population which had little or no influence. It was only the sheer size of this underclass, and the threat that they could pose to civic stability, which gained them a modicum of consideration from the elected representatives. They were not permitted to organise into groups even for social or religious purposes, and they had no voice in government. It is not surprising that the poor were the perceived locus of incipient revolt, seething with bitterness against authority.[6] At the best of times, many in this group lived in poverty. Assessments of the numbers who lived under these conditions in the fifteenth century are startling. It has been estimated that some 16 percent of the population lived at the poverty level, and a further 30 percent barely subsisted.[7] On this basis almost half of the inhabitants of Florence lived precariously even at normal times. And their difficulties were compounded by the fact that many had to borrow to cover the costs of household goods and tools of trade, and so remained trapped in debt.

The underclass of Florence was described by the ruling elite as the *popolo minuto*, the "little people." This somewhat perjorative term covered four groups of people, classified by their type of employment. First, the cloth workers of the important textile industries; then artisans, apprentices, and semi-skilled tradesmen; and a third group, those who performed menial tasks as servants, grooms, and peddlers. At the bottom of the social scale were vagrants, beggars, prostitutes and their pimps, and criminals (professional and amateur) "who inhabited the shadowy precincts of Florence's underworld."[8] Whilst it is frequently assumed that women of the period were restricted to household duties and childbearing, this is not entirely correct. In fact, the Florentine economy relied very much on the work of women both inside and outside the home, an issue that conventional records tend to obscure on the assumption that most work was men's work.[9] There were many women who worked at least part time in the textile industries, in craft enterprises, and as small scale traders.[10] Naturally, none of these women had any representation, or exercised any influence, in the communal government.

With the advent of the plague, the commune had to deal with death and illness on a scale never before encountered, and the major disruption to community life that followed. Not the least of the problems was that posed by the desperate plight faced by the underclass. According to a contemporary account: "No trades were operating in Florence: all workshops were locked, all taverns were closed, only the churches and the apothecaries were open."[11] There was no work for many months, and a grave shortage of foodstuffs. Where food was available, prices soared.[12] For the ruling elite, this carried implications of grave unrest, and threats to their power and authority.

The Commune in Disarray

Even before the plague arrived in Florence, communal authorities decided to act. They feared that the devastation being experienced in Pisa and Genoa could quickly spread to their city. In an effort to avoid such an eventually, they turned to measures which had been invoked at any sign of a crisis in the past—public displays of repentance to placate God.[13] Despite these pleas for protection, the plague epidemic continued to spread and soon reached Florence. Faced with widespread sickness and a rapidly escalating death toll, civic leaders made strenuous efforts to control the spread of the disease.[14] Boccaccio's brief but clear account of the sanitary measures adopted by the authorities was referred to in an earlier chapter.[15]

In addition, travellers from areas where plague had been reported were denied entry to the city. And, as was customary in times of crisis, prostitutes and homosexuals, whose activities were perceived as an affront to God, were banned from the city. Many of these measures had already been in existence and were simply reintroduced, or enforced more rigorously. They were, however, only the initial responses of officials somewhat overcome by the magnitude of the emerging disaster, and endeavouring to maintain some semblance of stable government.[16]

However, it became extremely difficult to conduct the administrative functions of the city in a normal manner. Death took some members of the ruling councils, others became sick, and some fled the city. Archival records show that there were no formal meetings of the elected representatives of Florence from March to August 1348.[17] There is also evidence that there were no formal meetings of the Priors, those who cared for the day-to-day administration of the city, over the same period. The implementation of plague control measures was delegated to a special commission of eight citizens.

Contemporary accounts give a general indication of the way in which the normal functions of government were disrupted during the various plague epidemics. It is only in Boccaccio's account of the 1348 epidemic, however, that there is any detailed account of the way in which administrative functions were dislocated:

> Amidst so much affliction and misery, respect for the laws of God and man had almost vanished. Those who had the responsibility for administering the laws were either dead or sick, and had so few assistants that they were unable to fulfil their duties. As a result, everyone could behave as they pleased.[18]

No other chroniclers commented in any detail on this aspect of civic life in Florence during the Black Death. Hence, the extent of this apparent paralysis of public services has to be determined by recourse to other records. From the same records, we can establish, at least in broad terms, how the government of the city re-established order, and the legislative responses developed to limit the spread of the epidemic.

There was one exception to the suspension of the activities of the councils of the commune. This took place on July 17–18, 1348, solely to delegate all administrative powers of the commune to meetings of the Priors and the *Gonfalonieri* (the "Standard Bearers" representing the sixteen districts of Florence). This group was given the task of governing the city until August 30, when the next elections were due to take place.[19] There appears to have been a delay in that process due to the continuing presence of the plague. In the event, this *balia* (special magistracy) to which power had been delegated acted on their own initiative and introduced changes which had considerable political significance for the electoral system. As a result, the predominance of the middle ranking and minor guilds, which had existed from the second half of 1343 until the end of the Black Death period, was eliminated. In effect, the old ruling elite seized the opportunity created by the plague, and profoundly altered the political and administrative balance in Florence.[20] This had a considerable influence on the shape of later plague legislation which increasingly reflected the values and interests of the elite in Florentine society.

The group to whom powers had been delegated called a special meeting in August, 1348, adding sixty-nine citizens to their own number (the Priors, the sixteen *Gonfalonieri* ["Standard Bearers"], and the twelve *Buonuomini* ["Twelve Good Men"]). The enlarged meeting, which contained a majority of representatives from the major guilds, introduced new Provisions to reduce the number of guild representatives to be elected to the governing councils. The representation was lowered from twenty-one to fourteen, with the reductions being to the detriment of the lesser guilds. At the same time, representation of the lesser guilds amongst the nominated office bearers of the city was reduced, and they were excluded totally from the office of *Gonfaloniere di Giustizia* ("Standard Bearer of Justice"). The reductions were claimed to be necessary because the membership of these guilds had dropped markedly as a result of the plague. The argument seems a little specious given that a contemporary account of the difficulty in drawing sufficient names for office does not appear to differentiate between the various guilds:[21]

> When the Priors opened the bags and selected the marbles, they found many people had died. For the office of Standard Bearer of Justice, all who were selected had died.[22]

Overall, the plague provided the rationale and the opportunity for the major guilds to manipulate the electoral system, and to gain a predominant place for their interests in the policy decisions of the government.[23] This transfer of power lasted until 1378, when the wool workers of the city, the *Ciompi*, rebelled against working conditions and gained a more favourable representation for the lower ranks of society.[24] Even then, a government run predominantly by the lesser guild groups lasted only four years. The conservative ruling group then quickly and decisively re-established its position of power in the increasingly class conscious society characteristic of Florence at the end of the fourteenth century. This power shift, which followed directly in the wake of the plague, introduced a class bias into the control regulations.

Power, Poverty and Social Unrest

The advent of the plague magnified the potential for civil disorder in Florence, with considerable worker unrest in the period following the Black Death.[25] Threats of violence and disorder were present in varying degrees throughout the whole period of the plague epidemics, but were countered by a range of measures to constrain dissidents. A propensity for violence and disorder was not new, having been a notable feature of the cities of Tuscany in the century which preceded the arrival of the Black Death.[26] Reasons for this tendency to civil disorder have been suggested by many writers. An Italian writer of the sixteenth century, Giovanni Botero, believed that the social structure of Florentine society, and of other cities in the region, fostered this discontent.[27] According to Botero, this recourse to violence and civil disorder was most evident amongst two groups—the wealthy because of their arrogance and drive for power; and amongst the poor because of the desperate straits in which they lived. It was clear that the poor had nothing to lose and perhaps much to gain by armed revolt. By contrast, the middle classes had a real stake in maintaining a peaceful society because violence threatened their livelihood, and their more limited capital resources were at great risk in times of civil disorder. Although Florence in the early fourteenth century had a sizeable middle class, it was not able to provide an effective stabilizing influence to counter threats to the community posed by other groups, particularly the large body of poor people.

The plight of these people became even more desperate during each outbreak of plague. From the Black Death onwards all workshops were closed during plague epidemics and the working classes were without any income with which to support their families. Whilst some survived on charity, others turned to unlawful activities to support their families. This tendency to lawlessness, which had been noted by Boccaccio in 1348, was apparently still evident when plague reappeared in the 1520s.[28] In reporting on the reappearance of the disease in 1527, Lorenzo Strozzi noted that there was an accompanying increase in the incidence of crime in the absence of the keepers of the law.

Although the majority of the underclass suffered more severely during plague epidemics than at other times, there were some who benefited from the outbreaks. Much wealth was derived from the inordinate fees charged by some medical practitioners, priests and friars, apothecaries and food vendors. There was another group of people, who undertook menial tasks such as the digging of graves and the handling and burying of diseased bodies, who benefited from the plague. These people, the *becchini* who, according to Boccaccio, were drawn from the dregs of society, saw the frequent reappearance of the disease as an opportunity for financial gain from direct charges for their services, and from the illegal sale of the belongings of the dead. To mark their pleasure at the return of the plague in May 1527, they roamed through the streets crying "welcome to the plague, welcome to the plague" in a cruel parody of the traditional greeting for the return of spring— "welcome to May."[29]

This formed part of a response pattern which saw a Carnival-like inversion of the normative social order, through a temporary dependence on the "unrespectable poor."[30] Other evidence of this reversal of the social order showed the poor acquiring the abandoned belongings of the dead, dressing in their finery, and indulging a newfound taste for delicate foods.[31] Contemporary documents also show that servants and farm workers were reluctant to perform their usual tasks, and then only if paid considerably higher wages. Alarmed at these challenges to the social order and to the power structure of Florentine society, the state enacted laws to limit pay rises, and to reinforce the dress codes which helped to define social class boundaries.[32] Efforts by the state to limit the gains of the underclass were not very successful, but the partial inversion of the social order was of a relatively short duration. After that, a sense of powerlessness and deprivation once more became the norm for a significant proportion of the Florentine population.

Although the combination of unemployment, hunger, inflated food prices, and the great loss of life during plague epidemics could only raise the potential for social unrest and disorder, violent responses to authority were not common, and major riots were few. There is no evidence that women took part in any uprising.[33] Incidents such as those which involved officers of the Inquisition being stoned by the public, and the rescue of a thief about to be hanged, were rare.[34] Threats of violent disorder, however, lay just beneath the surface, and any gathering was likely to alarm authorities. Nevertheless, the only serious revolt of the working classes was the *Ciompi* rebellion of 1378. After a brief taste of power in communal office they were displaced by the traditional ruling groups which never again lost their grip on power. Following the *Ciompi* revolt and during all crises caused by plague, the state was ever watchful for signs of conspiracy which might lead to a challenge to its authority. For this reason, any place where groups of people gathered together, even for social occasions, fell under suspicion. The parish church was one of the places where the general populace congregated during the Middle Ages, but it became less popular for this purpose during the fourteenth century. One of the reasons for this trend was the loss of credibility suffered by the clergy after the Black Death. People chose to gather at other sites, such as places of work and at taverns.[35] By late that century, the tavern had become the place where "the laboring classes could forge their own plebeian culture."[36] It is not surprising then that taverns were closed by the state whenever a crisis, such as an outbreak of plague, occurred.

The poor posed a threat to the state and to civil order in two ways. First there was the threat arising from individual actions of a males within this class—those who engaged in criminal activities such as property offenses and violent behavior. Second, groups of poor males were viewed as menacing because of their potential for collective action, particularly of a political nature. And even though uprisings were few, the implied challenge to power from assemblies of disaffected poor was ever present in the deliberations of the councils of the State.

It is also true that men from the wealthier levels of the community could threaten instability through political conspiracies. Members of various influential families were constantly vying for positions of power in communal government. Times of plague created conditions conducive to the launching of coups as the government was preoccupied with the effects of the epidemic. An example of this was the conspiracy fomented in Bologna in 1400. Many citizens of Florence had fled there to avoid the plague, and a group of political exiles seized the opportunity to plan an attempt to overthrow the government. The plot was revealed, however, and many plotters paid with their heads, others were banished, and some fined. In response to this attempt, the city government increased its guards and appointed a special officer with responsibility to supervise the defence of the city against insurrection.[37]

Disciplining the Dissident Body

A fundamental transformation in the Florentine system of surveillance and control developed from late in the fourteenth century.[38] These changes emerged from the experiences of the Black Death, and particularly the threats to stability which arose from the *Ciompi* revolt of 1378. Progressively over approximately the next two centuries the apparatus of state control—surveillance, investigation, and punishment—became more complex and reached further into the community. New tribunals were established and given wide-ranging powers to investigate and punish. It was through these agencies that the state was able to control challenges to its power.

During most plague epidemics famine conditions also developed.[39] Not only was there a scarcity of food but, through lack of work, the poor could not afford to buy even the staples such as bread or grain. Under these conditions, the simmering discontent within the underclass surfaced in public protests. But even when the poor were gathered in protest only, the physical presence of so many bodies in one place at the same time alarmed city authorities, who imposed harsh crowd control measures on the inhabitants.[40] The response to the threat of disorder, real or perceived, by the city administration was twofold. It made use of both an incentive to conform, and a deterrent against riotous behavior. The first of these responses by the city was reflected in the distribution of grain, flour, or bread to the hungry poor during plague epidemics.[41]

The second response of the state was more repressive. Many members of the governing councils urged the adoption of harsh penalties as deterrents to any form of uprising by the starving poor. Precedents for such action were not lacking. Punishment under the law frequently resulted in disproportionate penalties being imposed on poor offenders because of their inability to pay the fine which the conviction usually incurred. In such cases, physical restraint or inflicting physical injury, even mutilation, upon the bodies of the poor was deemed appropriate. The judges did not disguise their reasons for handing down such disproportionate penalties. In sentencing a man for assault in 1382, a judge ordered that the man's left hand be amputated because it appeared that he was too poor to pay the fine that would have been applied in other circumstances.[42] In another case, eighteen men convicted of conspiracy to rescue a condemned thief were banished from Florence, instead of being fined, "because they were poor people."[43]

A similar attitude applied to deterrents and punishments during times of plague epidemic. Archival material on Council debates in 1417, confirms the degree of apprehension felt in government circles regarding the management of the poor, especially in the face of the crisis of plague epidemics:

> Antonio Alessandri said that on account of the plague which was imminent, it is necessary to provide for the preservation of our regime, keeping in mind the measures which were taken at similar times in the past. First, we should acknowledge our obligation to God, taking into account the poverty of many [citizens], that is, by distribut-

ing alms to the needy and indigent persons, appointing [for this task] men who are devoted to God and who lead good lives, and not those who are active in the affairs of state. But since not all are quiet, and in order to instill fear into some, foot soldiers should be hired who are neither citizens nor residents of the contado, and who will serve the needs of the Commune and not those of private [citizens]. . . .

Buonaccorso di Neri Pitti said that the poor should be assisted so they can feed themselves. Those of our indigent citizens who are capable of doing evil should be hired [as soldiers] and sent to those places where troops are stationed, and their salaries should be increased.[44]

Not all dissidents or potential troublemakers, even in periods of plague, came from the ranks of the underprivileged. The *Signoria* considered any organized group as potentially dissident. Despite their importance in crisis processions, even lay religious confraternities were disbanded on orders from the state on many occasions. The principal reason for such was the suspicion that they provided fertile grounds for fostering anti-government conspiracies. After the fears of uprisings noted above during the 1417 plague, and renewed outbreaks of the epidemic in neighboring Tuscan cities in the following year, it is not surprising that the state moved to eliminate any perceived potential for disorder. In 1419, an order for the dissolution of all types of confraternity gave as the reason that "the Lord priors . . . [desired] . . . to remove all suspicion from the minds of the authorities. . . ."[45] The decree, however, did allow the formation, with the consent of the Priors, of new confraternities whose members were to be "prohibited from . . . interfering by word or deed in matters pertaining to the Commune of Florence, to the Merchants' Court, to any guild . . . or to the administration of them."

Despite the misery which had to be endured by the *populo minuto*, it was kept in check by the actions of the government during all plague epidemics. The state learned to combine charitable relief with a show of force on such occasions, but it recognized the dangers inherent in an excessive display of repressive power. Nevertheless, the repeated recourse to armed surveillance gradually broke down the inherent dislike of Florentines for officials with broad police powers and accustomed them to an increase in the level of state intervention in their lives.[46] The officers charged with responsibility to contain plague exercised considerable authority in enforcing the regulations. They were able to impose penalties ranging from fines to whipping and imprisonment, even banishment, for noncompliance. The frequency with which these controls were imposed, and the diligence with which they were enforced helped further to condition citizens to a new regime of surveillance.

Disciplining the Female Body

Whilst the poor became one of the principal targets of the new systems of surveillance and constraint, another disadvantaged group, women, fell increasingly under the gaze of the law makers. These regulations directed at women were frequently based on a perceived need to curb their sexual behavior for the good of the male-dominated community. Such restraints applied to women generally, and not solely to those practicing prostitution. All women were seen as "wayward in body and restless in spirit," and needing to be in someone's custody, ideally the custody of a male.[47]

For this reason, unattached women were viewed with great suspicion. In Florence, the age gap between men and women at marriage ensured that many women would become widows at an early age. The result was that by the age of 50, one half of the women in that city had been widowed.[48] Many lived with married sons and helped with the management of the household, but others lived alone. If young women posed a threat to men and society, old women, particularly those living outside male custody, were seen as highly dangerous to the whole community.

A separate discourse emerged on the perils associated with old women. It drew on Aristotelian and Galenic views that postmenopausal women were extremely dangerous because various excess humours were no longer cleared through menstruation but passed to the outside of the body through the eyes.[49] This provided the basis for the assertion, referred to in an earlier chapter, of Albertus Magnus, that old women could poison infants by staring at them in their cradles. He also claimed that poor old women were even worse because their diet was based on coarse, hard to digest food, which made them more poisonous, not to themselves, but to those they gazed upon. It is not difficult to see the origins of the "old hag" as a witch, versed in all the black arts, in these beliefs.[50] These notions fuelled the witch hunts, and the demands for placing restraints on women's bodies generally.

Not only were women subject to regulation of their own bodies, but they were blamed for sexual behavior in which the male was a willing participant, if not the initiator. Samuel Cohn described an incident in which a servant girl in Florence was charged with attempting to poison the wife of her patron so that she could live with him to "satisfy her immoderate sexual appetites."[51] Only the servant girl was punished, being publicly whipped through the streets to the place of execution where her nose was cut off before she was burned at the stake. This incident highlights the way in which severe punishment was inflicted upon women's bodies for perceived sexual transgression. In this case, the level of punishment equated that of more serious crimes in which men were the offenders.

Apart from the extreme physical punishment which could be meted out to women, they were subjected to other techniques of constraint and confinement. Pressure from the church and a male-dominated society removed them from the public sphere and confined them to the custody of husbands, fathers, or other male relatives, within the private space of the home. Young women, and frequently girls, could be placed under "protective" custody through consigning them to a convent, or sending them to be servants with wealthy families. The convent, which required a lesser dowry than was necessary to attract a suitable husband, was the destination for many younger daughters of families with limited means. Girls from the underclass with no dowry were more likely to be sent into service where their wages might augment the incomes of their families.

During the sixteenth century, a new phenomenon emerged, institutions which provided "assistance," correction and supervision of women.[52] They included institutions for reformed prostitutes, and refuges for the *malmartitate*, those whose marriages were particularly difficult. In each of these cases, a women could be admitted of her own accord, or be consigned there by a husband, another relative, or the state. These institutions placed particular groups of women under constraint and surveillance, but the techniques of discipline which they employed were applied to women generally in Florence. Whilst at some levels of society the constraints were less onerous, the methods of regulation and surveillance reduced all women's participation in public life, and confined them increasingly to the demands of procreation.

The Diseased Body: Exclusion and Inclusion

Whilst we can identify the broad range of controls introduced in Florence to limit the spread of plague in 1348, detailed accounts of theses measures do not appear to have survived. However, records for the same period from Pistoia, a hillside town under the influence of Florence, still exist and are more explicit. It is likely that they reflect the types of regulation which were also in force in Florence. They include all the features we have identified in broad terms—prohibitions on the use or sale of clothing and other belongings of a plague victim, bans on travellers from places where the plague was present, and the reenforcement of traditional sanitary regulations.[53] In addition, however, they specifically prohibited the transport of dead bodies to the city for burial, and required that the bodies of those who had died within the city be enclosed in wooden coffins so that the *fetor* (stench) of the decaying bodies could not escape. To further reduce the risk of contamination from the diseased corpse, the city statutes required that it be buried, enclosed as specified, at a depth of at least two and one-half arms lengths. Obviously, as the death toll mounted it became impossible to adhere to these requirements in the disposal of bodies. Nevertheless, the regulations as framed were clearly based on the fear that the diseased bodies of plague victims could contaminate the surrounding air, and so spread disease by the "miasmas" which were central to Galenic theories of disease transmission.

Despite this evidence of state legislative responses to the plague of 1348, the appointment of officers to enforce the health regulations was regarded as an emergency measure only.[54] As each epidemic appeared, authorities renewed, and gradually amplified the range of control measures at the disposal of their enforcement officers. Each time the plague struck the city, an *ad hoc* group was appointed for the duration of the crisis to implement the measures to limit the impact of the disease.

In creating temporary magistracies only to fight plague, Florence acted in the same way as other cities in northern Italy during the fourteenth and fifteenth centuries. Even in 1448, after a further sixteen epidemic outbreaks of plague had been experienced in Florence, and in response to yet another plague epidemic, it is clear that no permanent organization existed to deal with disease control. In that year, the responsibility for containing the plague: "to preserve health, keep off the plague and avoid an epidemic," was given to an existing magistracy, the *Otto di Custodia* (the

"Eight for Security"). The authority of the "Eight" to act on plague matters was to be exercised for three months only, and was to be in addition to their already important duties as a major law enforcement agency. This magistracy had been created in 1378 after the collapse of the *Ciompi* revolt, and was essentially a bureau of political police with very wide powers of enforcement.[55] On behalf of the commune, the "Eight" were authorized to arrest, investigate, impose fines, and, as they often did, to inflict capital punishment.[56]

There is a clear inference in the appointment of this group that the state recognized the need for strong action to enforce health regulations. In effect, by adding plague control to the responsibilities of the "Eight," the state caused a convergence of the penal and public health systems. As a consequence, plague officials were equipped with an extensive inventory of ways with which to discipline the diseased body. It was also during the 1448 epidemic that the *Signoria* first mentioned the term "contagion" as a means of spreading the disease, although most earlier state health regulations relating to the epidemic implied that the plague could be transferred by bodily contact with, or close proximity to a diseased body. State control measures introduced subsequently clearly reflected the final adoption of this concept.[57] This differed from the medical discourse on disease causation, a contrast we will review in the following chapter.

It was only in 1527, during the plague epidemic which lasted from 1522 to 1528, that the need for a permanent commission for plague control was recognized in Florence.[58] A magistracy of five officials "who could in no way refuse, or proffer excuses, or claim any privileges whatsoever in order to excuse themselves from such office," was created.[59] Details of the wide-ranging measures which they introduced are to be found in the accounts of the plague written by Benedetto Varchi.[60] He recorded the many regulations which had been introduced at that time. These were to be enforced by "health officers" (*gli uffiziali di sanità*) who were given the same authority as "the magistracy of the Eight" (*i signori otto di guardia e balia*). As we have already noted above, the magistracy of the "Eight" carried the authority in the Florentine community for much of the law enforcement. The many penalties which they could impose were also granted by the commune to the newly appointed health officers. Once again penal provisions could be applied to the disciplining of the diseased body, this time however, through the actions of a permanent health board. This great responsibility placed upon the health officers was to be performed without salary, solely "for the love of God" (*per l'amore di Dio*). The measures adopted by this group, which Varchi noted were more often called "the Plague Officers" (*gli ufficiali del morbo*), represented a consolidation of all previous control measures, and became the pattern for the future.[61]

Confining the Diseased Body

The primary control measure involved confinement.[62] Varchi explained that plague had appeared first in a poor district because a "common man" (*plebeo uomo*) had just returned from Rome where an epidemic was raging. As soon as the disease was discovered, the district was "closed and barricaded" (*chiusa e sbarrata*), to prevent anyone entering or leaving the area. Clearly, the "impure" bodies of the poor were to be segregated from the "pure" bodies of the rest of the community. To ensure that no one had any excuse to leave their detention zone, the Commune provided food daily for those so confined. In this outbreak, which commenced in 1522, the disease was not contained as the authorities had hoped, and plague rapidly spread to the wealthier districts due, according to Varchi, to the "wilful disobedience of the regulations" (*malvagità*) by one of those infected.[63] As the plague spread, a system of classification as to the bodily condition of the citizens was introduced to enable surveillance mechanisms to be enforced. Two categories requiring surveillance were defined: those already with the disease, "those declared as infected" (*i quali si nominavano infetti*), and those who had conversed with or had other direct contact with an infected person, "and those were called suspects" (*e quelli si chiamavano sospetti*).[64] Those classed as "suspects" were still permitted to move about their quarter of the city, but, generally, they were restricted in their movements in other parts of the city. Furthermore, they had to carry a distinguishing sign at all times, namely, to wear across the shoulders a white handkerchief, towel, or band. The houses in which they lived, and those where plague had been experienced also had to be clearly identified. For these houses, the sign that plague had been or was present was a white ribbon tied to the bell at the front entrance.[65] The intentions of these requirements were clear—for effective surveillance and control, the "infected" and the "suspected" bodies needed to be made visible.

As the hospitals for plague victims became full during the prolonged epidemic of the 1520s, the Plague Officers ordered construction of huts along the outside of the city walls, some 600 of them, to accommodate additional plague sufferers. This also proved insufficient, and temporary hospitals were created in some churches and convents outside the city. In addition, the "suspects" were given accommodation in another group of church and convent buildings. It appears, however, that some of this group, particularly those from the more privileged classes, were not obliged to remain in these areas. Nevertheless, they remained under surveillance since they bore the sign of their classification as "suspects."[66] Evidence suggests that controls aimed at identification of plague victims or those suspected of having been in contact with plague infection, were more rigorously applied to the lower classes in Florence. Some medical practitioners assisted in this process of discrimination since they were reluctant to report instances of plague when their patients came from the more powerful and privileged levels of Florentine society.

A pattern of control measures gradually evolved during the succession of plague epidemics which were experienced in Florence over a period of approximately two centuries. Coupled with the regular use of armed force to inspire conformity, they represented a code of practice which had achieved the status of a norm for community control. One method of control, that of identification, followed plague victims to the grave. Whilst Florence had maintained a register of deaths since 1385, it was little more than a record of burials performed by communal gravediggers in the earlier periods during which the records were kept.[67] However, in response to the long sequence of plague epidemics in the fourteenth and early fifteenth centuries, the Florentine authorities introduced new regulations for recording deaths in 1424.[68] These required that all plague deaths, and those suspected of being caused by plague, be reported to the Health Officers. It was believed that this information would help to identify the areas where plague was active, and allow the city authorities to take action to limit the spread of the disease. Certificates as to plague as the cause of death were required from medical practitioners after they had examined the bodies of the deceased.

By the middle of the fifteenth century, this practice fostered an enthusiasm for more statistics, and most large cities of northern Italy had extended the requirements for reporting, and identifying the cause of all deaths in the community.[69] It is apparent that the period from the fourteenth to the sixteenth centuries saw a consolidation of plague controls which functioned also as social control mechanisms. The evidence of their application to processes of identification, classification, segregation, and confinement, offers support for Foucault's general hypothesis as to the origins of the control mechanisms of the modern carceral state.[70] However, our research indicates that these processes were already in place well before the late seventeenth century outbreak of plague which Foucault used as the basis for his thesis.[71] There is also another difference between the two systems of control being compared. The measures used in the fifteenth and sixteenth centuries in northern Italy stemmed from religious and moral considerations, significant elements of which still underpin twentieth century social and legal systems for the regulation of the body. Without denying the underlying conclusions drawn by Foucault, we suggest that his theories of body control discount such factors, and appeared to flow from later Cartesian concepts of the body as a mechanism which can be disciplined to improve its efficiency within society.[72]

Targeting the Poor

Whilst the measures which we have just discussed were meant to apply to the whole community, it is clear from the application of the controls that many of them were directed principally at specific groups within the community. Comments of contemporary writers highlight the entrenched views of the ruling elite that controls should be directed primarily at the indigent classes. As a result, the poor were seen as the main agents by which the plague was spread, and control measures increasingly focused on methods of confining their bodies in places as far removed as possible from others in the community. Ludovico Muratori wrote at length on methods which should be employed for the control of plague. He was convinced that the most efficacious method lay in:

> putting into quarantine all the low class people of the city, because experience too often shows that it is by these people, not by the nobility or the more wealthy, that the disease is easily disseminated and introduced into the homes of the more prudent citizens. That means, those who wish to leave the city may do so when ordered to leave within so many days, [then] the poor and the lower class people must be locked in their houses[and remain there] under pain of death, . . .[73]

The class bias of this statement is patently obvious. It is the bodies of the poor which pose the main threat of disease transmission. It is the bodies of the poor that must be subjected to confinement. It is this stigmatized group which is threatened with legally sanctioned punishment for any infractions of the confinement edict. And this punishment is, in fact, extreme—death.

The stigmatization of the poor by the wealthier classes owed much to their perceived Otherness. However, relegating them to the margins of society was also tacitly accepted by the ambivalent attitude of the church toward the poor and the afflicted. Despite the rhetoric of the Christian ethos, religious discourse held that the condition of the poor was so ordained by God. And, as to acts of charity, their important function was to enhance the spiritual standing of the donor.[74] In the words of a Dominican friar: "See, therefore, how necessary are the poor and afflicted! . . . If there were no poor, no one would be able to give alms, or show compassion or the virtue of pity."[75] But, as we have already seen, the influence of the church extended to all areas of community life, not just to shaping perceptions of the poor. It determined all moral boundaries and hence it defined concepts of deviance. Its edicts were frequently translated into civil law. Hence, any societal group which differed significantly in perceptions and practices from those endorsed by the church or the ruling elite was likely to be stigmatized as deviant and to be the victims of measures to control or restrict their activities. Carmichael has drawn particular attention to the poor in Florence as such a group specifically targeted by plague controls which became, effectively, social controls.[76] However, other groups were also stigmatized in this way and became the target of special control measures, as we will see below.

Two factors contributed to the gradual consolidation of the view that the plague was essentially a disease of the poor, a group representing close to half the population of the city.[77] In the first instance, there was the perception of "otherness" which prevailed in the minds of the wealthier toward the impoverished. The latter endured a more precarious life style, had inferior housing, and because of this, lived in more squalid conditions generally. As we have seen from the attitude of Muratori, their bodies were seen as corrupt and capable of contaminating others. Further evidence of the perception by the elite that the poor were vectors of the disease can be seen in other contemporary comments. In his *Ricordi*, records of his family and events of his time, Giovanni di Pagolo Morelli described the way in which the 1348 plague spread. He had no hesitation in locating its origins amongst the lower classes who were, in his opinion, responsible also for spreading the disease to the rest of the community. According to Morelli, it was only by mid-July, some five months after the outbreak commenced, that it spread "to the respectable people and those who lived orderly lives"[78] During a later epidemic, Alessandra Strozzi, a member of a prominent Florentine family, noted that the plague had appeared again, but only amongst the "manual laboring classes."[79] In the following year, she again revealed the perception of her class that a connection existed between the plague and the poor. She noted that in that year the epidemic "does not affect the better class of people."[80] Varchi's description of the plague epidemics from 1522 to 1527, already referred to above, clearly states that the outbreak had been caused by a *plebeo uomo* ("common man"), who had just returned from Rome where there had been an outbreak of plague.

The second factor which led to the perception of plague being a disease of the poor was the evidence that the death toll was highest amongst the poor during an epidemic. Boccaccio recorded this fact in relation to the 1348 epidemic, and perceptively identified the primary reason for the disproportionate number of deaths amongst the poor and the majority of the middle classes as an inability to flee due to their financial constraints.[81] All contemporary accounts of the succeeding plagues give clear evidence that the wealthier classes fled with their families as soon as an epidemic threatened.[82] Not only did the poor have to remain in the midst of each plague epidemic, but when confined in crowded and, arguably, insanitary temporary hospitals, they would have been very susceptible to any other disease in the vicinity. Add to these disadvantages the inadequate diet on which the poor had to exist at the best of times, and near starvation during periods of plague, and it was inevitable that the poor would have succumbed in very large numbers during an epidemic.

During the fifteenth century, the commune explored the possibilities for establishing separate hospitals for plague victims. Initially, this was proposed as a work of charity which would be pleasing to God, and so save the city from further pestilential diseases.[83] However, it is likely that the traditional isolation of lepers in leprosaria would have lent support to separating plague victims from other ill people. In practice, segregation was already being practiced in existing hospitals by mid-fifteenth century, those with plague being separated from other patients . By the end of the century, however, and after the experience of several outbreaks of plague, the first separate plague hospital, the *spedale del morbo*, was established.[84]

Since the poor predominated amongst those stricken by the plague, the plague hospitals became, in the main, establishments in which the bodies of the poor were confined and regulated. In addition, the plague officers exercised their most diligent surveillance upon the bodies of the poor because of their perceived threat to the rest of the community. This construction of the bodies of the poor as the principal vectors of disease, and as a public health threat, led to some very harsh treatment being meted out by the Plague Officers. Arguably, the starkest expression of this focus on the disadvantaged as both the main plague victims and a threat to the community, is reflected in an incident during the 1498 epidemic. Luca Landucci, a Florentine apothecary whose diary recorded the event, was greatly troubled by what he saw as "a brutal thing and a harsh remedy," noting that ". . . the Plague Officers went through the hospitals evicting the poor, and wherever they found them throughout the city they drove them all from Florence. . . ."[85] To complete this exercise in persecution of the poor who were suffering from the plague, the Plague Officers set up a system of ropes and pulleys outside the Armourers' Guild to torture any of those that they had expelled should they try to return to the city.

Outsiders as Dangerous Others

We have already noted that regulations were introduced at the first appearance of the plague in 1348 to prevent travellers from entering Florence if they had been in areas affected by plague. This practice was maintained throughout subsequent plague epidemics, and those who wished to enter the city had to obtain an entry permit. Authorization was required not only for travellers, but also for traders who wished to bring their goods into the city. With the latter, it was recognized that it was not only the bodies of travellers which might be vectors of the disease, but cloth and foodstuffs were also believed capable of transmitting plague. Penalties for those who disobeyed these plague control regulations were similar through Tuscany. In neighbouring Siena, for example, anyone who entered the city, even from its own surrounding areas if plague was reported, was liable to a fine and ten lashes of the whip for each and every time he or she entered the city.[86] It was also common practice in most Tuscan cities to limit itinerant traders to an overnight stay only, even when an entry permit had been granted. In practice, however, the system which regulated entry to a city was not applied consistently. Foreign dignitaries, ambassadors, and their entourages were allowed unimpeded access to and from Florence, even if they had come from plague affected areas.[87]

Florentine regulations on entry to the city increasingly defined certain categories which were to be excluded under the plague control regulations. Typical of these were the instructions given to exercise control over "the quantity of ruffians who arrived at the city gates on the roads from Pisa."[88] Even more specifically, those appointed to the commission to implement plague control measures in 1494 were required to keep out "rogues, swindlers, the poor, beggars, and particularly foreigners."[89] There is an unmistakable note of class bias in this stigmatized group since all of these people fell within the most disadvantaged groups in society. It is also to be seen in the discriminatory way in which the entry controls were implemented. In practice, the rules were often ignored where they might limit entry of persons of power and influence, but of lesser rank than the foreign dignitaries mentioned above.

The list of those prohibited entry did, however, include another category—foreigners—to whom particular attention was to be paid. There was no qualification in this listing as to whether or not the traveller had come from a plague stricken area. Some cities made a distinction between foreigners coming from a plague area and those coming from an area unaffected by the disease. Siena imposed a penalty of a fine and ten lashes of the whip for any foreigner who could not prove that he or she had come from an area free from plague.[90] It was also an offense for an Sienese citizen to harbor anyone who had come from an area where plague was present. Again, the perceptions of "otherness," which still colors many views in our own times, placed foreigners generally in a suspect group. The influential merchant Datini revealed a similar fear of foreigners as vectors of disease when he warned his wife that they should not obtain any slaves from Roumania.[91] The same perception of foreigners as the "dangerous others," as the bodies which harbored disease, underpinned the travel control regulations of other cities in northern Italy in times of plague. Both Perugia and Venice linked the coming of the plague to immigrants from Albania and Slavic regions, and either banned their entry to the city, or expelled such people already resident.[92]

Managing Polluted Bodies

It was in the fourteenth century that there was a significant growth in the state regulation of sexual behavior. Until that time, ecclesiastical courts had exercised almost total authority over cases involving sexual deviance. During the plague epidemics, many towns and cities adopted new statutes restricting sexual behavior. In keeping with the dominant discourses about women's voracious sexual appetites, women were presumed to require greater regulation than men. This discourse persisted despite the fact that men were more likely to be prosecuted for sexual offenses.

Legal and community concern about sexual behavior focused on matters such as the incidence of male homosexuality and the social function performed by female prostitution.[93] Prostitution was not illegal in Florence, nor was street soliciting prohibited provided the prostitute wore the required identification—gloves, hat with bells, and high-heeled slippers.[94] Generally, prostitution was seen as a necessary evil, sinful but for the good of the community in reducing rape and discouraging homosexuality. In accepting this viewpoint, one shared by many other European communities, the Florentine government was undoubtedly influenced by the declarations of Thomas Aquinas on the subject. He compared prostitution to the sewer in a palace. According to Aquinas, if the sewer did not function, the palace would be filled with pollution. Similarly, if prostitution were eliminated, the world would be filled with "sodomy" and other crimes.[95]

In 1403, the government of Florence decided to extend its control over the activities of prostitutes by appointing a group called the *Ufficiali dell'Onestà* (Officers for Decency) to supervise the activities of prostitutes, and establish a public brothel in the city with prostitutes recruited from outside Florentine territory.[96] One of the stated aims of this move was to reduce the levels of homosexual activity, perceived as prevalent within the community. There were two reasons for this decision, both influenced by the effects of the long succession of plague epidemics. Prominent preachers had long asserted that the bodily activities of both prostitutes and sodomites were sinful and grossly offensive to God, and brought punishment upon the whole community. As a result, the general perception within the community was that prostitutes and sodomites had, by their offensive practices, contributed to the outbreaks of plague which had been experienced in Florence since 1348. It was for this reason that there was an almost ritual banishment of these groups whenever plague appeared in the area.

The second factor that contributed to the efforts to divert young men from the practices of sodomy toward heterosexual relationships was the great concern felt for the low level of population replacement after massive plague losses. Despite the patterns of new marriages and the sharp increase in birthrate after each epidemic of plague to which we have referred in an earlier chapter, the population base of Florence had been drastically reduced by plague deaths. While the government of the city sought to re-establish the community by attracting migrants from other areas, it believed that an increase in population by reproduction was preferable. It feared the loss of power and prestige that Florence would suffer if the population of the city could not be rebuilt quickly. To remedy the position, the young men of Florence had to be encouraged to see procreative sexual relations with women as desirable and sodomy as reprehensible.

The *Signoria* decided to establish two more public brothels in 1415.[97] According to the decree that authorized this action, the brothels were to be located in places within the city where they gave no offense to neighbors, and prostitutes were to remain within the new establishments where "the exercise of such scandalous activity can be best concealed, for the honor of the city. . . ." Those who practiced prostitution without wearing the required garb, and those who lived off the profits of prostitution by renting out premises to be used by prostitutes were prosecuted. Employing the double standard traditionally associated with morality, the state saw the use of female bodies for private gain as illegal, but acceptable if directed toward an aim which it saw as of benefit to the community. The government of Florence still banished prostitutes from the city during periods of crisis, such as when plague struck, in the fifteenth and sixteenth centuries. In common with many other northern Italian cities, it also imposed stricter controls on movements of these women from the latter part of the fifteenth century.[98]

Although there was still no perception that there was a causal link between sexual intercourse and plague transmission, authorities generally became aware that the living conditions of the marginalized groups of society might well encourage the spread of plague. As an example of this trend, Venetian authorities denounced prostitutes as a health risk to the whole community in 1486, on the basis that they lived in unclean places and that they did not discriminate between healthy and infected customers.[99] Once again we encounter the state defining an "inner" and an "outer" group within society. The "diseased" body as a threat to the "healthy" body, is now accompanied by the dichotomy of the "unclean" body and the "clean" body. By 1490, prostitutes in Venice were not allowed to ply their trade when plague threatened but were rounded up and lodged in a Rialto warehouse. Those who refused to move, or resisted in any way, were punished with incarceration, fines, and public whippings. Florence adopted similar methods to restrict the movements and activities of prostitutes in 1504.[100] The same fears were expressed that the "unclean" bodies of prostitutes might transmit plague.[101]

There is no reasonable evidence to suggest that the establishment of public brothels did anything to alter the extent of homosexual activity in Florence. Contemporary writers and prominent preachers continued to claim that while the practice had been well known in Florence for a long time, it had reached alarming proportions among the young men of the city by the fourteenth and fifteenth centuries.[102] We have already seen some examples of the way in which the Franciscan preacher Bernardino of Siena constantly railed against sins of the flesh, hurling blunt and unambiguously worded accusations at his listeners, male and female. He preached many times on the evils of sodomy which, he asserted, was prevalent in all of Tuscany, and claimed that this practice was responsible for the plague epidemics which continued to strike fear into the minds of all Florentines. Since these sermons were delivered in 1425, more than twenty years after the introduction of public brothels in Florence, it is obvious that Bernardino did not believe that the aims of the state to reduce homosexual practices had been successful. Antoninus, Archbishop of Florence from 1446 to 1459, also denounced "sodomitic practices," although his definition of "sodomy" covered all non-procreative sex.[103] Even later, as we have already seen, the Dominican friar Girolamo Savonarola constantly railed against the prevalence of homosexuality in Florence. This persistent denunciation of the practice by such prominent preachers, who warned of the dangers it posed for the city, put considerable pressure on the authorities to take strong action against "sodomites."

At this time, it is difficult to ascertain whether male homosexuality was more prevalent in Florence than in other European cities of the period. There is plenty of evidence that other cities of Europe were also accused of being centers of sodomy.[104] And, until recently, historians have been unable to agree on the actual extent of male homosexuality in Florence.[105] These debates have now been overtaken by the work of Michael Rocke, who argues convincingly, from archival material, that homosexuality was prevalent among the youth of Florence in the early Modern period.[106] It is not surprising then that contemporary perceptions among Florentines, constantly beset by plagues and other crises, was that sodomy was a major problem which had to be tackled by legislative measures to protect the city from divine punishment. There was also another factor which pressured authorities to act. Sodomy posed a direct challenge to the patriarchal and patrilineal traditions of Florentine society by threatening the institutions of marriage and the family which underpinned the whole power structure of the state. This combination of moral pressure, and a desire to maintain the political *status quo*, produced an increase in state efforts to regulate the bodily activities of sodomites.[107]

Male homosexuality had been illegal in Florence for a long period, denounced by many but often treated with some tolerance by authorities. As crises such as the plague epidemics arose, old sanctions against the practice were reintroduced, or new statutes promulgated. New regulations were introduced, for example, in 1415, 1418, 1432, 1494, 1527, and 1542. At various times over the period we are reviewing, penalties included in these regulations for sodomites ranged from fines to whipping, sometimes castration, and ultimately to hanging or burning.[108] Despite the severity of the penalties contained in the statutes, evidence shows that authorities maintained an ambivalent approach to efforts to eradicate sodomy.[109] In some areas at least, officers of the state had no compunction about using homosexuals to assist in the task of surveillance of the population. In Siena, homosexuals were encouraged to act as spies, reporting any infringements of the law, or rumors of discontent or treachery. As a reward, they received a quarter of any subsequent fines imposed.[110] Further reflecting the ambivalent position of the authorities toward offenders, penalties actually applied were usually lighter than the code might permit. In addition, when new statutes were being introduced, penalties were actually lowered on many occasions.

The most significant move against sodomy in the fifteenth century, however, was the creation of new magistracy, the *Ufficiali di Notte* (Officers of the Night). This was established in 1432 with the sole task of prosecuting the crime of sodomy.[111] Finally, it was disbanded after some seventy years due to strong opinion that its activities were drawing too much attention to the problem, and adversely affecting the reputation of Florence. While the magistracy existed, the Officers of the Night conducted a great number of investigations into accusations of sodomy. However, as charges could be lodged anonymously, doubts must be held as to the validity of some of the accusations. Furthermore, as we have seen earlier, accusations of sodomy routinely accompanied charges of heresy, and were also often levelled at political enemies. Taking these factors, and the incomplete nature of the records of trials and convictions into account, there is no firm basis for assessing the effectiveness of the magistracy.

Florentine authorities viewed homosexuality as a threat to society on the grounds of sexual immorality. Prostitution was viewed in a similar light, but less subject to penal sanctions. However, both prostitutes and sodomites had been subject to some form of regulation since the early part of the fourteenth century. Somewhat curiously, the legislation under which their activities were controlled formed part of the traditional sanitary legislation. This did not infer, in any way, that there was any obvious connection, at that time, between sexual activity and disease transmission. Rather, the city statutes actually included morals controls in the guise of sanitary regulations, based solely on the perception that the activities of prostitutes and sodomites were sinful and would attract God's wrath. For that reason, control of their sexualized bodies was considered to be necessary for the well-being of the whole community. The same general sanitary legislation under which prostitutes and sodomites were controlled also included regulations which aimed to restrict other types of behavior seen as morally deviant. These required strict separation of men's and women's days at the public baths. The statutes declared that strict separation was necessary "to reduce sin and vice resulting from clandestine mixture of the sexes."[112]

There is a strong suggestion of gender bias in the legislation which sought to regulate public bathing, and in those statutes which aimed to control prostitutes and homosexuals. The origins of this bias are to be found in the complexities of the Judeo-Christian view of women. Within that tradition, they have been variously worshipped, coveted, feared, and hated. The elements that caused the fear and hatred lay in the perception that it was solely the seductive nature and insatiable desires of women which led men into sexual passion and to their downfall.[113] Prostitutes, then, could be seen as the extreme manifestation of all female characteristics, desirable but dangerous. Homosexuals, on the other hand, were consistently seen as some aberration of the female sex, another inferior group. In one of his sermons, San Bernardino attributed to homosexuals the stereotypical female characteristics of being "prone to jealousy and envy . . . [and] to all forms of gossip and tale-bearing."[114] In similar fashion, Marsilio Ficino, the Florentine humanist, warned that men must guard against appearing *muliebris* (womanish).[115] Confirmation of this community percep-tion of homosexuals as aberrant females can be found in the terms applied to the "passive" partner in homosexual activities in cases before the Officers of the Night in Florence. They were referred to as if they were females, or with perjorative feminine labels such as *cagna*, *bardassa*, and *puttana* (bitch, harlot, and whore).[116] On the contrary, the masculinity of the "active" or dominant partner was never called into question. He had not broken the traditional taboo on a male adopting a "female" or "receiving" role.

In any periods of crisis, and certainly when plague threat-ened, existing sanitary or other regulations for the control of the sexualized bodies of homosexuals and prostitutes were more rigor-ously enforced. Often, as we have already seen, both homosexuals and prostitutes (but not their clients) were expelled from the city.[117] By excluding the contaminating influence of these "deviant" groups from the enclosed space of the city, the morally conforming mem-bers of the community might be spared from the plague. Prostitutes and homosexuals were joined with the poor, and foreigners as "dan-gerous others," who became the collective targets of blame for the whole community.[118] It was only the prostitutes and homosexuals who were seen as morally deviant. In one sense, however, Florence was more liberal in its stigmatization of "dangerous others" during periods of plague. There is little evidence in that community of the persecution of groups such as the Jews and lepers, who were blamed for the spread of bubonic plague in many other parts of Europe.[119]

Regulating the Decorated Body

While clothing and jewellery designated the social status of the wearer, it was a woman's appearance that attracted the great-est attention during the plague epidemics. Dress was an indicator of social position, and was an important device for manifesting and claiming social privilege. Moreover, the association between the decorative and ephemeral nature of clothing and the corruptible and finite character of female flesh intensified the vehement opposition to the apparent decadence of female finery. Bernardino of Siena frequently railed against women's vanity. In one sermon he declared:

> The vanity of women is the destruction of a city, because of the cost of such merchandise as velvets and other cloths, bonnets, pearls, silver and other adornments. You know that what I say is true. . . . The extravagant dowries that must be given are the undoing of those who provide them . . . and if a women does not have a suitable dowry, a man looking for a wife will not take her. And therefore [men] give themselves to the vice of sodomy, turning in one way or another to every vice that there is.[120]

Driven by Bernardino's denunciations and their own convictions, the members of the Florentine communal government formulated new sumptuary regulations again in 1433. The officials charged with the responsibility for enforcing this legislation were known as "the officials to restrain female ornaments and dress." While these controls had their origins in trade and economic considerations (the preservation of the local textile industry and the reduction in imports of expensive fabrics), the new regulations embraced the abhorrence of female sexuality so evident in Bernardino's condemnations. The sumptuary controls were rationalized in the following way:

> [The lords Prior recognize the need] to restrain the barbarous and irrepressible bestiality of women, who, not considering the fragility of their nature, but rather with that reprobate and diabolical nature, they force their men, with their honeyed poison, to submit to them. . . . But women were created to replenish this free city, and to live chastely in matrimony, and not to spend gold and silver on clothing and jewelry . . . and in order that the city be reformed with good customs, and so that the bestial audacity of these women be restrained, [the regulations are approved].[121]

These controls were so strict that they tended to lessen the social distinctions between women expressed through dress and appearance. Class differences, encoded within the visual presentation of the body, were rendered irrelevant in the drive to homogenize the appearance of all women. This according to Diane Hughes, reflected a "progressive sexualisation and demonisation of women's fashion."[122] While women's responses to these imposed controls ranged from defiance to acceptance, it is clear that women suffered the formal loss of a principal social signifier.

Hughes concluded that, in enacting sumptuary legislation, the leaders of the Florentine community were drawing attention to the "carnal sexuality which costume flaunted rather than covered."[123] It was evidence, according to Hughes, of the perception that there was a socially dangerous sexuality associated with "flesh, decomposition, and women." Given the examples we have cited, it seems obvious that many of the control measures introduced by the state in response to plague epidemics carried a strong gender bias, one which reinforced the stereotypical misogynist views which existed in the community—woman as temptress and betrayer, the downfall of man. They also confirmed the significance to the ruling elite of limiting any expression of bodily desires, public or private, and of controlling the public presentation of the body.

Of Pure and Impure Bodies

Plague epidemics provided the basis for many other types of interventions by the state. While some of the statutes were introduced directly by the *Signoria*, much of the intervention in community activities was effected through the Plague Officers whose authority and prestige increased steadily as the range of control measures expanded.[124] To limit the entry of plague infection, they created road blocks on important inter-city links, and, despite strong protests from merchants, prohibited the passage of much commercial traffic. By the late fifteenth century, they also curtailed assemblies of all kinds to limit the spread of infection. The regulations that prohibited many public gatherings were based on the prevailing public health discourse in Florence. This discourse perceived bodily contact with a plague sufferer, or even conversing with such a person at close range, as a means of disease transmission. Direct handling of clothing or other possessions belonging to anyone who had died of plague carried the same threat, so resale of such items by grave diggers was prohibited. As we have already noted, the implication contained in public health discourse that disease was transmitted by bodily contact was at variance with the prevailing medical discourse. The latter remained linked, at that stage, to "miasma" theories of transmission. We will address this issue in more detail in the next chapter.

Many in the community, particularly church authorities, were opposed to this intervention by the state since it often resulted in suspension by the Plague Officers of traditional festivals and other kinds of religious gatherings. Such actions also challenged the traditional crisis processions held during periods of plague. On some occasions, the *Signoria* overruled such prohibitions, but in general, the decisions of the Plague Officers prevailed despite hostility in important and powerful levels of society.[125] There were also occasions when the *Signoria* itself acted directly to prohibit demonstrations, ostensibly to limit the spread of plague, but really to limit opportunities for provoking unrest among the people.[126] According to Landucci, the *Signoria* used this ploy in 1497 with the aim of preventing the Dominican friar Savonarola from preaching.[127] By this time, Savonarola was seen as a threat to the stability of government, not the saviour of the community which had been his earlier image. On this occasion the *Signoria* prohibited all sermons in the churches of Florence for the period during which the Priors were in office. They went further and caused all the seats to be removed from Santa Maria del Fiore, the large cathedral of Florence, again claiming that it was a precaution against the spread of plague. That this was a specious argument is highlighted by the fact that such action, by itself, would not have eliminated the contaminating influence of a large assembly of bodies. The political motivation of the decree is further revealed by the fact that there were no reports of the plague in the vicinity at that time.

All evidence points to a conclusion that the plague epidemics provided scope for the state to develop and refine new techniques for the regulation of the diseased or "disordered" body. It defined categories of "pure" and "impure" bodies to which it allocated clearly defined positions within the spatial configurations of the community. The city walls marked the limits of mobility of those classed as "outsiders," although discrimination along class lines further refined the degrees of movement permitted. High ranking outsiders such as ambassadors and wealthy and powerful foreigners were allowed unimpeded access to the enclosed space of the city, despite the fact that some of these people had come from plague-affected areas. Clearly, the bodies of the wealthy and privileged were not seen to be inherently contaminating. On the other hand, the itinerant poor, roving beggars, and all others classed as "foreigners" were denied entry at the gates of the city by armed guards.

These actions were based on the conviction, heightened during the plague periods, that the bodies of the poor and non-privileged "outsiders" represented a serious threat of contamination to the "pure" bodies within the Florentine community. After all, "only a thin line separated the wanderer who carried the plague stupidly and irresponsibly but without malevolence from the evil outsider who might well be the agent of a foreign power, sent to spread the disease by poisons and noxious substances."[128]

For those who usually lived within the enclosed space of the city, two modes of body control were employed by the state in response to the plague—confinement and banishment. Diseased bodies, or those suspected of being contaminated by plague, were confined within their homes, within barricaded and guarded districts, or in hospitals. On some occasions destitute plague sufferers were expelled from the city, but it was the sexualized bodies of prostitutes and male homosexuals which were regularly banished from the enclosed space of the city by state decree. Within both religious and civic discourses, any form of non-procreative sexual activity was sinful and likely to attract God's wrath. The bodily activities of prostitutes and homosexuals, however, were considered to be particularly offensive to God. Many were convinced that their behavior had brought divine punishment in the form of plague epidemics in earlier times, and would do so again unless they were publicly repudiated by the Florentines. As a consequence, both religious and civic discourses dictated that the bodies of prostitutes and homosexuals be excluded from the community to prevent plague corrupting the entire social body.

Overall, the succession of plague epidemics provided the opportunity for the state to significantly and permanently extend its field of influence in community and church affairs.[129] State controls increased considerably in the areas of health, community social activities, and in medicine. In the process, "disordered" bodies subject to state control came to include diseased bodies, the bodies of the poor, and those of any travellers from outside. Sexualized bodies were also perceived as being "disordered," women's bodies in general, but especially those of prostitutes, and those perceived as being aberrant forms of females—homosexuals. The corollary to this, and one of the most enduring outcomes of the plague period, was the creation by the state of a much-enlarged bureaucracy to administer the new control measures. This flowed inevitably from the conviction, implicit in the Florentine political system, that community problems of all kinds could be resolved by government intervention.[130] According to one writer, 1348 was the year that "marked a historical moment at which governmental regulation was initiated on a large scale."[131] The following chapter will explore in greater detail the involvement of the state in the development of the medical profession, and in the expansion and regulation of health services in the community.

The Diseased Body Confronts Medicine

This kind of [poisonous] vapour is formed in the air, in time of plague epidemics, by the malign influence of the stars, particularly Mars and Saturn. . . .

—Marsilio Ficino[1]

Nowhere in the world do medical practitioners have an answer or a real cure for this pestilential disease, not by means of natural philosophy, or the physical sciences, or through knowledge of astrology.

—Matteo Villani[2]

[To avoid getting the plague during an epidemic] Those that are well must drink two fingers of their own urine each morning at dawn . . . and each evening, before the meal, eat some rue with a mouthful of bread dipped in vinegar. Continue while the risk [of plague] persists, and refrain from sexual intercourse. . . . Women who are still well, should do this also. If they are menstruating, they should take some of this [menstrual blood] from a healthy woman. Children, who cannot take the urine should be given a little rue each morning and evening.

—Consiglio dei Dieci[3]

The arrival of the Black Death created problems for medical practitioners that they had never before had to face.[4] It challenged all current theories of disease causation, and it threw into question the professional competence of medical practitioners and the effi-

cacy of remedies which were traditionally prescribed. It also undermined the privileged status claimed by these practitioners in the
control of the disordered body. As a result, many people turned to
methods of treatment and prophylactic measures offered by people
who were not recognized by the medical guilds. And on this score
there was no shortage of advice available from community healers,
and a coterie of *arrivistes* who offered all manner of pills, potions,
and charms to ward off the plague. The end result of these various
challenges to medical theory and practice was a complete restructuring of the Florentine medical profession and fundamental
changes in the diagnostic and treatment methods employed by
these practitioners. In the process, the body in general, and the disordered body in particular, were viewed within an entirely new conceptual framework. These innovations, which are easily recognized
as precursors of modern-day practice, were not unique to Florence.
They emerged at much the same time, and also largely, although
not solely, in response to the plague in other centers of northern
Italy, and were then adopted in other European centers. This followed a precedent first established during the late Middle Ages
when students from all over Europe came to Italy to study
medicine. At that time, there was a revival of interest in early medical theory and practice which later became critical to the establishment of new regimes for the treatment of the diseased body in
western Europe. This ostensibly *new* knowledge was in fact drawn
from three areas of medical practice—Greek, Roman, and Arabian—and was modified by cultural and social imperatives over
many centuries.

In this chapter we identify major changes in medical theory
and practice that stemmed directly from plague experiences. We
argue that these included the medicalization and institutionalization of the body, and the medicalization of bodily disorders. These
changes marked a significant shift in treatment regimes for the
body. They also signalled a major turning point in the history of the
body—dealing with the body as an object in medical practice.

Medicine and Medieval Concepts of the Body

The dominant discourse which shaped medical theory and
practice during most of the Middle Ages was that developed within
the church. This religious discourse defined the human body as an
integral part of a mighty universe which functioned entirely in

accordance with a divine plan. Consequently, the human body must inevitably be attuned to the rhythms of the universe and must be affected by any disturbances to the natural harmony of the cosmos. In this context, the body represented a microcosm within the macrocosm of the universe. And since the whole of the universe was God's handiwork, the way in which the human body functioned was accepted as being beyond comprehension. (As we have observed earlier, a corollary to this thesis envisaged both the universe and the body as completely enclosed systems, sealed by the Creator at the dawn of time.) Accordingly, it was deemed inadvisable, even sacrilegious, to seek to explain or delve into the secrets of the body. Such attempts, it was believed, might well be construed as a challenge to God's authority and attract divine punishment.

These concepts ensured that for most of the Middle Ages, hypotheses concerning the internal organs of the body and their functions owed more to teleological definitions than to any real knowledge of internal anatomy. This situation did not change to any degree until the latter centuries of the Middle Ages. As a consequence, for most of the medieval period, medical management of the disordered body had to rely on "reading" the external signs on the body's surface. Medical practitioners believed such signs indicated and guided in the diagnosis of particular internal disorders. In part, this practice rested on a tradition of long standing which held that the external appearance of a person was a reflection of his or her inner condition—moral and physical. Applied to medical practice, this meant that for the medical practitioner of the Middle Ages the body represented an envelope "filled with some invisible and mysterious matter in which all kinds of ills develop . . . finally emerging in the form of spots, buboes, and ulcers but also as liquids. . . ."[5]

These emanations and eruptions from the disordered body were somewhat problematic for medieval medicine, strongly influenced as it was by the teachings of the church. The uncertainties created stemmed from the contradictions inherent in different strands of Christian religious discourse. At one end of the spectrum, there was the evidence of biblical authorities who exalted in the sacred nature of the human body.[6] To them, it was an example of God's work; it was the precious vessel which enclosed the human soul during its earthly existence. The opposing view represented the body as vile, as polluting to those who handled it.[7] As a result, medieval medical treatises on the management of the disordered body reflected fears of contamination, and the moral loadings which were implied by Christian doctrine. Even toward the end of the Middle Ages, treatises such as that of the noted French surgeon Mondeville revealed a "scarcely disguised moral approach to illness."[8] By way of an example of this stance, Mondeville referred to the bodies of the sick as "impure," and expressed the view that leprosy was not only a "vile disease" but it was also to be considered "shameful."

In broad terms, these were the fundamental concepts that informed medical theory and practice through to the late Middle Ages. Bodily disorders were simply viewed as manifestations of divine retribution for sinful behavior. As such they were attributed to supernatural rather than natural causes, and treatment regimes were shaped accordingly. Overall, there is little evidence that mainstream medical practice during the Middle Ages gave any serious attention to alternative theories of disease causation such as we discussed in chapter 2. All of this changed, however, when the West rediscovered long-forgotten concepts of medical theory and practice, late in the Middle Ages.

A Challenge to Monastic Medicine

After several centuries during which the church dominated medicine in western Europe, the opportunity for a revival of secular medicine emerged in the ninth century. A group of physicians, a *"civitas Hippocratica,"* settled at Salerno, near Naples, and established the first European school of medicine since the days of the Empire.[9] Its location close to Greek speaking communities living in Sicily and southern Italy ensured that it could draw on the knowledge of Greek medicine which remained. In addition, it drew upon sources of Hebrew and Arabic medicine, the latter proving to be critical to the international reputation which the School of Salerno acquired. It was through this channel that western Europe again encountered Greek medicine, in particular the interpretations of Galen, with further additions and commentaries from Arabic sources. At this juncture, Western medicine was introduced to the discourse on causation which attributed disease to unfavorable conjunctions of the stars and planets. The use of minerals and precious stones for medicinal purposes was also revived, so advancing the development of alchemy.

Students came to Salerno from around Europe to absorb the new knowledge. The graduates, who included laymen and women as well as clerical medical practitioners, then returned home to apply the new practices. It should be stressed at this point that lay practitioners of the late Middle Ages still held firmly to the church position that bodily disorders were a punishment for sin. The revival of true secular medicine was yet to come. The great age of Salerno lay in the eleventh and twelfth centuries during which it not only trained many practitioners, but, through its teachers, produced over 100 medical treatises which aided even wider dissemination of Salernitan knowledge. This was important for the development of medical practice since only a minority of practitioners completed their training in this way, even after the founding of the new universities of Europe, first at Bologna, then Montpellier, Padua and Paris.[10] The new ideas were spread throughout the continent, reviving an interest in medical practice outside the monastery.[11] There is evidence, in fact, that there was a great proliferation of healers of all kinds, both lay and clerical, from the early twelfth century.

The medical philosophy that was reintroduced into Europe from about the ninth century was essentially secular in character. It explained the diseased body in terms of internal imbalances of the four bodily humours—blood, phlegm, yellow bile, and black bile—representing the four basic properties of hot, cold, moist, and dry. Galen saw any imbalance as due to adverse external influences, generally identified as "miasmas."[12] He recognized that not everyone succumbed to these adverse conditions, even during epidemics, and explained this by individual predisposition arising from "non-natural" conditions—essentially conduct factors over which each person had control. Cures, then, relied on eliminating the external source of trouble and following a regime that would restore the humoural balances within the patient. The first involved removing "pestilential atmospheres" such as those that arise from dead bodies, stagnant water, and emanations from swamps. The personal factors were to be corrected by diets, exercise, blood letting, purging, and vomiting, together with moderation in drinking and sexual activities.

Nowhere in Galenic precepts or practice was there any reference to divine causation or the need to placate angered deities. Consequently, there was considerable room for conflict between such divergent medical discourses as that based on the dogma of the church and that following Galenic principles.[13] Nevertheless, a fusion of ideas was possible using as a basis those concepts which appeared to be shared by both areas. The church, for example, had a long tradition associated with the disciplining of the body. But it was also possible to find common ground on this issue within the empiricist Hippocratic tradition. They held that it was "not only sick people, those who had already allowed their bodily passions and appetites to go untamed, but also those who seem healthy," who were in need of discipline.[14] For this reason, it was considered that dietary control not only aided bodily health but could be used as a means of improving the "moral tone" of all human life.

Accordingly, Galenic admonitions to be temperate in eating and drinking, and to exercise restraint in sexual relations, were close enough to advice offered by the church. Further, diet restrictions, purging, induced vomiting, and blood letting could be envisaged as practices consonant with the renunciation of the flesh advocated by many Christian theologians. The essential difference lay in the recognition or otherwise of divine intervention in human affairs. In this case, a reconciliation was achieved by continuing to recognize the omnipotence of God and His role as First Cause in earthly events, and by retaining a strong and prescriptive moral code as an element of medical practice and patient care. In addition, the integration of Galenic medical theories and practice into religious discourse on human disabilities required that pain and suffering be recognized as examples of God's instruments of warning and instruction for sinners.[15]

Another element of Greek and Arabic medicine challenged Christian attitudes toward body fluids and discharges. While the dominant religious discourse of western Europe displayed an abhorrence of blood, the *Greek Herbal* supported the medicinal value of blood, both animal and human. There was, however, some ambivalence as to this usage. Some claimed that while menstrual blood applied externally relieved certain complaints, it could also render infertile those who touched it.[16] Despite this potential threat, and religious protestations about pollution associated with handling blood, medieval medical practitioners accepted its value in treatment regimes. According to Pouchelle, "the most reputable medical men also used blood as a medicine. Animal blood, but also human blood, and even the much-feared menstrual blood."[17] Blood was also used as preventative medicine, as we have seen at the beginning of this chapter, with the recommendation to drink menstrual blood as a plague precaution. Further, the most frequent medical procedure of the Middle Ages involving blood was undoubtedly blood letting, one of the techniques used to restore the perceived humoural imbalance of the patient.

Medieval medical practice also made extensive use of other body fluids and discharges for diagnosis and treatment regimes, hence challenging the perception of the church that they were polluting agents. Medical practitioners cautiously examined body secretions and excretions for their color, consistency, cloudiness, odor, and sometimes taste as a means of identifying the ailment and determining the appropriate treatment. And apart from the widespread practice of viewing the condition of a urine sample, drinking urine was believed to have a proven therapeutic value.[18]

Christian discourse held that tending the sick was an act of charity and, in general, monastic medicine had been founded on this principle. However, many secular medical practitioners saw medical practice in the same way as Pliny the Elder, that is, "lucrative beyond all the rest."[19] Those, no doubt, would have agreed with the choice made by the well-known Greek physician, Asclepiades, who had turned to medicine because he could not earn enough as a rhetorician. In the end, the difficulty posed by seeking payment for medical services was resolved by the church gradually withdrawing from this area of medicine.

Shifting the Focus of Medicine in the late Middle Ages

Throughout the twelfth and thirteenth centuries there was a marked increase in the number of persons practicing medicine. These included both clerical and lay practitioners, some trained at the new university medical schools, but the majority having acquired their skills through a form of apprenticeship to a more experienced practitioner. Beyond these, there were many others of more limited training who practiced forms of community medicine at the local level, serving those who could not afford to pay for treatment. Many monks with medical skills became increasingly involved in medical practice outside the monastery, and despite the church views on Christian charity, received payment for what was essentially secular medicine. This attracted criticism from church authorities, not for the medical services that they rendered, but because it distracted them from their true religious calling and led them into the sin of avarice. As a consequence, edicts emanating from a series of church councils forbade monks and priests from practicing medicine "for temporal gain."[20]

The church also became concerned at the involvement of clerics in medical procedures that appeared to be in conflict with concepts of the body in religious discourse. Procedures that were seen as particularly problematic included the letting of blood to correct bodily humoural imbalance, and the spilling of blood during surgical interventions. This disquiet culminated in limitations being placed on the activities of clerics. The Council of Trent in 1163, and the Lateran Council of 1215, banned all clerics from offering any treatment which involved the shedding of blood.[21] This meant that all forms of surgery—including dentistry, all blood letting, and cauterisation of wounds—had to be left to lay medical practitioners. In regard to dealing with the whole body, the position of the church was somewhat contradictory. It appeared to be quite acceptable for the church to call for the torture, the dismemberment, and the burning of the bodies of heretics, criminals, and those who resisted papal authority in secular matters. In fact, many of these procedures were carried out by arms of the church such as the Inquisition. However, in general, the church saved itself from being guilty of spilling blood and taking life by the expedient of turning its victims over to the state for execution.

The re-emergence of lay medical practice in the city-states of northern Italy led to a statutory requirement that those who wished to practice medicine, in cities such as Florence, had to belong to one of the professional or trade guilds of the city. There were no options, and the city authorities dictated which guild medical practitioners should join. In Florence, the relevant guild was comprised of three main divisions—medical practitioners, apothecaries, and a disparate group of small merchants.[22] Our interest is in the subgroup covering medical practitioners which we will refer to as the "medical guild." Even in the area of lay medical practice, however, the church continued to exert a strong influence through the thirteenth and fourteenth centuries by virtue of its involvement in the admission of applicants to the medical guild. For example, in 1314 the guild statutes required that candidates for membership be examined by a panel consisting of the six consuls of the medical guild and four friars. It was only in 1349, after the Black Death, that ecclesiastical representatives were eliminated from this examining body.

Despite the revival of lay medicine, religious discourse continued to shape medical perceptions of the human body and of sickness. Insisting on a recognition of the relationship between sin and sickness, the Fourth Lateran Council of 1215 decreed that lay medical practitioners called to a seriously ill patient must refrain from giving any treatment until the patient confessed and sought forgiveness for his or her sins.[23] This meant that both in principle and in practice, the priest, as doctor of the soul, must take precedence over the secular medical practitioner. This Lateran decree was also incorporated into the statutes of the City of Florence in the mid-fourteenth century, at the height of the Black Death, and later that century it became one of the requirements of the medical guild statutes. While there is some evidence that this was applied with less enthusiasm in later periods, regard for church dictates on sinful behavior ensured that the requirement to limit treatment until a patient had confessed remained on the statutes until the late sixteenth century.[24]

The "Sealed" Body

One of the fundamental tenets of the Christian faith that continued to inform medical theory and practice in the West was the concept that the body was an enclosed system, sealed by the Creator. On this premise, it was axiomatic that there should be no intrusion into the body envelope by human agencies. This conclusion was largely in accord with Arabian commentaries which discouraged contact by hand with the human body, believing such an action to be both unholy and unclean.[25] The sealed body image, with its oppositions between the inside and the outside of the body, was important in both medical and religious discourses on the body. Both converged in the conviction that it was necessary to preserve the closure, or at least to ensure the integrity of the inner parts of the body by regulating entry or exit through the various body openings. Medical theory advanced two fundamental reasons for monitoring the functions of the real and metaphorical body openings. First, it was necessary to control that which may be voided from the body, since both undue retention of bodily excesses, and excessive evacuations were perceived as dangerous to health. According to then current beliefs, the former could lead to leprosy, the second to death if the vital life force, blood, were to escape.[26] The second reason for exercising control of body openings was to prevent the invasion of the body by agencies which could create internal disorders.

Religious discourse, on the other hand, saw body openings, real or metaphorical, as entry points for sin. The five senses of the body were believed to represent potential entry points, and of course, genital and anal orifices were those which provided the greatest threat. However, in their efforts to restrict the entry of any stimulus to sinful behavior through body openings, theologians directed their most intensive drive for control at women's bodies. To clerics at least, the female anatomy was comprised of an excess of openings and, as a consequence, the female body was a greater source of threat than that of the male. Further, for many within the church, the body of a woman was a repository of pollution, and would be less of a threat to men if it remained permanently sealed, that is, in a state of virginity. It followed, then, that the metaphor of the female body as a "sealed vessel" was consistent with the general community perception that the body of the female represented both pleasure and peril, and needed to be controlled. This perception was reinforced by the frequent use in contemporary literature of metaphors of woman's "sealed body," likening it to a walled castle, or a fortress, to which a man laid 'siege'. In this they followed the erotic style of Solomon, in the *Song of Songs* (4:12) : "A garden inclosed is my sister, my spouse; a spring shut up, a fountain sealed." While clerics generally wished the "fortress" to withstand attack, most lay writers hinted at the pleasures of breaching the defenses, using such unambiguous metaphors as "opening" and the "hole in the door" as they described the pursuit of women. All of this underlines the preoccupation with sexuality, in particular that of women, which was a feature of late medieval theology, medical inquiry, and the general community.

Although there was a continuing debate about human anatomy, it was largely a sterile repetition of concepts and opinions from the distant past. Human anatomy for most medical practitioners was that which Galen had described. They believed that he had already established all there was to know about the interior of the body. Clearly, this left much to be desired since Galen had only dissected pigs and apes. Nevertheless, in general, physicians believed that everything they needed to know to diagnose an ailment, and to prescribe remedies, could be gained from observing the external surface of the body and examining its discharges. They had only to "read" the body. They had no need to probe what lay inside the envelope of the body. Hence, in the late Middle Ages, examining the pulse, a urine sample, perhaps other bodily discharges, and a general observation of the patient, were the main diagnostic tools applied to the disordered body. From these indications the physician decided which of the bodily humours was out of balance, and which restorative medication or dietary regime should be used. All other procedures that required manipulating the patient's body were left to the surgeon.

It was the image of the body as an enclosed system that

allowed for a distinction to be drawn between the two areas of medical practice—that of the physician and that of the surgeon. The surface of the body was visible, and could be "read" for indications of disorder. Naturally, disorders that originated within the body envelope could not be directly identified and physicians had to rely on secondary evidence inscribed on the surface of the body, that is, on the externalization of the internal disorder of the body. Leprosy and plague were, of course, examples of disorders that could be readily identified by the disfigurement of the outside of the body. For many other diseases, medical practitioners had to rely on their training and experience to identify which external indications gave evidence of inner disorders. Because of the specialized knowledge this implied, the physician was considered to be a member of a learned, theoretically oriented group, while the surgeon was seen as belonging within the ranks of the skilled and practical artisan.[27] The surgeon was limited to intervention at the site of a problem where physical injuries such as cuts, fractures, or skin eruptions were obvious. Although this broadly defined the division of late medieval medical practice, and the way in which treatment of the diseased body was conducted, it does not tell the whole story. Some practitioners offered themselves as both physicians and surgeons, although this does not appear to have been common.

As a general rule, most practitioners adopted a very conservative approach to medical practice, limiting themselves to those areas in which they had developed skills. The majority showed little curiosity about what lay within the envelope of the body. By the late Middle Ages, however, there was a marked resurgence of interest in learning across many disciplines, a development usually referred to as the Twelfth Century Renaissance.[28] Nevertheless, this interest was evident only in limited areas in the field of human anatomy since there were strong traditional church and secular objections to any interference with the human body. It was widely held that the body was not only a microcosm within the pattern of the universe, but it also paralleled the functioning of human society. Hence, any interference with the body was not only a threat to the human concerned but posed a symbolic danger to the natural order, and to the stability of society at large.

Gazing into the Body—First Steps

As early as 1209, there are records indicating that autopsies were being officially conducted in Italy to provide evidence for papal verdicts as to the cause of death.[29] These are the first known recorded instances of public dissections since the Alexandrian period, and clearly, they were for forensic purposes rather than to advance knowledge of human anatomy. It was in 1286, at Cremona, that we have the first recorded instance of an autopsy for medical, as opposed to forensic, purposes. In this instance, the autopsy was conducted to investigate deaths caused by an outbreak of epidemic disease. The account of this investigation is contained, almost as an aside, in the chronicle of Salimbene, a Franciscan friar.[30] Salimbene noted that there had been a great outbreak of disease in the Cremona area, and many men and chickens had died as a result of this epidemic. According to the friar, one physician felt impelled to investigate and find the cause of these deaths. To this end, he had some dead chickens "opened up" and found a "cancerous growth" on each heart. He pursued his investigation by having a man who had died from the same disease "opened up" and found that there was a similar growth on the man's heart. While this appears to have been a first tentative step toward pathologico-anatomical investigations of epidemic disease, Salimbene was not very interested in the medical implications of the case. His main concern seemed to lie in the likely shortage of chickens for the pot that would follow the epidemic outbreak.

There is evidence that at least two further autopsies were carried out for forensic purposes at Bologna toward the end of the thirteenth century. On these occasions the procedure was employed to assist in proceedings in the civil jurisdiction of the city. However, there is no evidence to suggest that the practice was anything but unusual. The general conservatism among lay and ecclesiastical authorities dampened any enthusiasm to open up human cadavers and gaze inside at the contents of the body. For that moment, medical practitioners had to be content with the "sealed body" instead of the "revealed body." One of the issues that made dismemberment of bodies so problematic was the concern as to what would happen at Judgement Day when body and soul were to be reunited. Nevertheless, northern Italy continued to be the area in which interest in the body and its innermost secrets gradually overcame conservative practice. As early as the thirteenth century, Guglielmo Saliceti (better known as William of Saliceto) reintroduced the use of the knife in surgery at Bologna, displacing the reliance of Arab practitioners on cautery only.[31] And it was while Mondino de' Luzzi was lecturing at the University of Bologna, that he published his *Anatomia* in 1316. This was a treatise to accompany practical exercises in dissection.[32] Although it was based closely on Galenic concepts of anatomy, it remained one of the most important texts used for teaching anatomy until the end of the sixteenth century, appearing in more than forty editions. There is evidence, also in Bologna, that the growing curiosity as to what lay within the body envelope led to some unofficial probing. It was here, in 1319, that several people were charged with the crime of "body-snatching."[33]

Although these activities imply that considerable gains were being made in knowledge of the human body, that is not a totally correct assumption. Attempts to penetrate below the surface of the body were still viewed with suspicion as they were seen as an unwarranted intrusion into the mysteries of God. And many were content to accept Galen's descriptions of the body and its functions as the only information required for the practice of medicine. By and large, his explanations and recommendations still guided medieval medical theory and practice, and dissections of the late Middle Ages tended to "find" within the body that which Galen had declared to be so.[34] Even in the face of new evidence to the contrary, many physicians were reluctant to accept that Galen's descriptions of human anatomy could be incorrect. So blind were many to practical experience that one medical lecturer even maintained that the human body must have changed since the first century A.D.[35]

While dissection had never been formally prohibited by the church, there were many implied barriers to the process of gazing inside the body. Nevertheless, once these perceived moral barriers had been breached, simultaneously with the actual "breaching" of the body envelope, the tide could only flow one way. All that was then required for dissection to become an essential part of the study of anatomy was a recognition that more information on the body and its functions had become critically important. Such a situation emerged unexpectedly in the mid-fourteenth century and changed the form and practice of Western medicine.

The Plague Body Confronts Medical Practitioners

Before the advent of the Black Death, the citizens of Florence appear to have had complete faith in the competence of the medical practitioners who served that community. And, in turn, those practitioners were completely confident of their ability to treat the range of bodily disorders which they encountered. Apart from leprosy, with which medical practitioners had little involvement until it was disappearing from western Europe, there are no records of major epidemics after the sixth century. Nevertheless, there seems little doubt that other diseases such as typhus, smallpox and dysentery were encountered during the Middle Ages, but nothing to really challenge the efficacy of medieval medicine.[36] This situation changed dramatically and swiftly in 1348 with the arrival of the Black Death. Plague was, without doubt, a disease which was beyond the experience and comprehension of practitioners whose approach to medicine was circumscribed by the principles and practices laid down by Galen.

For physicians of the mid-fourteenth century, plague was particularly perplexing since it appeared in three distinct forms. The most common manifestation was in the bubonic form where large and painful swellings, sometimes the size of "a common apple," became evident in the areas of the lymph glands.[37] Those who contracted this form of the plague were likely to be severely ill for some four or five days before either succumbing to the disease or recovering from it. Less fortunate were those who became victims of the pneumonic form of the plague, a variant which was spread readily through droplets from coughing or sneezing. For these people, death was inevitable, and not long in coming. The most virulent form of the plague was the septicaemic variation, which usually proved fatal within twenty-four hours of the onset of the disease, and before buboes had time to form.[38]

Given its reliance on a medical discourse based largely on divine causation, and the limited range of diagnostic and treatment techniques available, it is not surprising that medieval medicine had no counter for bubonic plague, a disease for which the causative organism, and means of transmission were not fully identified until the late nineteenth century.[39] In the event, medical practitioners simply continued to apply the traditional methods of diagnosis and treatment which they had employed for any other illness when plague struck Europe. This was equally true whether they were among the minority who had studied medicine at a university or were among the majority of practitioners who filled the ranks of the empirics.

Models of Disease Causation in 1348

By the beginning of the fourteenth century, members of the medical guilds of Florence and other European centers had, in the main, adopted a common theory of disease causation. This incorporated the essential elements of three of the discourses on causation discussed in chapter 2. The First Cause, beyond any dispute, was God. Illness and disease could only strike if it were His will. This epitomized the Christian view that bodily disorder represented divine punishment for the sinful behavior of the afflicted. At a secondary level, the appearance of disease was attributed to adverse stellar conjunctions corrupting the air which humans breathed. This aspect of fourteenth century discourse on causation encapsulated two distinct conceptual approaches—Galenic theories of humoural imbalance, and the "miasmic" transmission of disease through the creation of "pestilential atmospheres"; and the concepts of astrological influence introduced with Arabian medicine.[40] As we noted earlier, these disparate views had been accommodated by accepting that the Christian God reigned supreme in all matters concerning the universe.[41] Finally, it was believed that an individual could increase his or her propensity to illness or disease by adopting an intemperate life-style. Overall, the dominant model on disease causation in the mid-fourteenth century recognized four contributory factors: divine punishment; heavenly bodies; corrupt air; and a harmful mode of life. This discourse provided the sole basis for the diagnostic and therapeutic regimes of guild medical practitioners as they attempted to combat the plague epidemics.

Perspectives on Healing

The accepted approach to treating a bodily disorder in the late Middle Ages was to identify the ailment by "reading" the signs on the outside of the body, and examining excretions, particularly the urine of a patient. Effectively, the "medical gaze" was still confined to viewing of the outer surface of the body envelope. From such evidence, medical practitioners deduced which of the humours was out of balance and sought to rectify the imbalance through the use of dietary practices, blood letting, and drug therapies whose antecedents reached back to the *Greek Herbals*.[42] An alternative to this regime was employed when the imbalance was considered to be due to the effects of a "poison." In such a case, the "poison" was countered with a "contrary," another poison. Muratori referred to this procedure when he noted that on the recommendation of the most distinguished physicians, Pope Adrian VI carried a disc of arsenic close to his heart to ward off the plague.[43]

To ensure that any remedial treatment was effective, patients were also advised to conduct themselves in such a way as to maintain good health in times of plague. Such advice included injunctions to be moderate with the intake of food and drink, and in taking exercise and bathing. Almost invariably this advice was supplemented with dire warnings which reflected the age-old fear men have had about women—the debilitating effects of sexual relations. We see a clear example of this perceived threat in a document compiled by the College of Physicians of Paris in 1348. This canvassed the causes of plague, its treatment and precautionary measures to be adopted.[44] This information enjoyed wide circulation in Europe. The advice given on precautions to be taken concluded thus:

> To have relations with females is the worst, and is deadly: and not only through having carnal relation with them; but even to have them in bed with you prevents you from protecting yourself [from the plague], . . .

Similar advice was still being given in the fifteenth century. The blunt advice of the noted Florentine philosopher, Marsilio Ficino, also educated in medicine, was to "abstain from coitus" to reduce the risk of plague.[45]

A further aid to the treatment of the disordered body in the early fourteenth century relied on the use of astrological predictions and almanacs, which had been introduced through the incorporation of Arabian medicine into Western practice. Physicians used this information in prognosis, and to determine the most propitious times for administering medication. Similarly, surgeons frequently consulted astrologers to ascertain the most advantageous times and conditions before undertaking surgical procedures.[46]

Caring for the Plague Body

There was widespread disillusionment and condemnation of medical practitioners for their apparent inability to apply the knowledge and power they claimed to have to treat the diseased body. Until the arrival of the Black Death, medical practitioners had been credited with being privy to the "secrets" of medicine and with being the only members of the community capable of "reading" the body to determine the cause of serious disorders. For minor ailments, the general community did not need to rely on members of the medical guild for the diagnosis and treatment. By longstanding tradition, most people could do that for themselves, or at least, need go no further than consult the local community healers or "wise

women" skilled in domestic cures for common complaints. Plague
changed this situation completely. Now anyone could read the signs
on the body which were the basis for a diagnosis of bubonic plague.
When swellings appeared in the groin or the armpit, and the
patient had a high fever, there was no need to consult a physician.
The victim, or his or her relatives or friends, could recognize the
signs for themselves. And, as for treatments prescribed by medical
practitioners, these had been shown to be of little use. As the chronicler Marchionne declared: "neither physician nor medicine was of
any use; either the illness was still unknown or the physicians had
never studied it; there seemed to be no remedy for it."[47]

As a result of their difficulties in combatting the epidemic, the
reputation and community standing of medical practitioners suffered a marked decline, even though some of them tried hard to
ease the suffering of their patients. Those who attracted the
strongest criticism were the physicians who had claimed that their
university training gave them an elite status even within the medical guild. Criticism came from many levels of the community. Matteo Villani declared that their claims to learning in the field of
medicine were a "sham," and Petrarch heaped scorn on their inadequate medical knowledge, and their claims to be considered among
the intellectuals of the community.[48] Among Florentine chroniclers,
only Giovanni Morelli seems to have recommended adopting the
counsel of "worthy physicians," but even in this instance the advice
related more to establishing a healthy life-style as a preventative
measure rather than to measures for treatment of the plague.[49]

For many people, their disillusionment with the abilities of
medical practitioners was compounded by a sense of betrayal when
many practitioners refused to attend to the sick, or provided only
perfunctory services for exorbitant fees.[50] Further, many medical
practitioners fled from plague areas, not only during the period of
the Black Death, but whenever there was a further outbreak of
plague. Even during the last of the Florentine epidemics in the
early sixteenth century, according to the historian Varchi, medical
practitioners were among the first to depart.[51] Accordingly, they
remained for a long period, the targets of critical comment as to
their competence and professional conduct. Evidence that this attitude was prevalent in many communities can be found in contemporary literature such as, for example, in the satirical writing of
Pietro Aretino in the 1530s.[52]

The perceived incompetence of medical practitioners to deal
with the plague led many people to turn to unorthodox methods of

treatment. Since no one understood the nature of the disease, nor the vectors of transmission, it is possible that people may have gained as much benefit from such treatments as from advice given by a member of the medical guild. This recourse to alternatives to conventional medicine was evident well after the passing of the Black Death. A letter written by a Florentine notary in 1400 bears this out.[53] He claimed that his local bishop sought advice from a "poor person" when he gained no relief from the medication prescribed by his medical practitioner. The unorthodox advice he was given suggested that he mix a well-cooked onion with some butter and apply this to the buboes. The outcome, according to the notary's letter, was that the bishop was cured immediately.

Another example of the widespread lack of faith in conventional medicine can be found in an account left by Enea Silvio Piccolomini (later Pope Pius II) of his own experiences as a plague victim almost fifty years later.[54] Piccolomini, accepting that there was no real cure for the plague, elected to be treated by "an unlettered German" who was known to be "more fortunate" in his treatment of patients instead of "a learned, but ill-fated" Parisian medical practitioner. Piccolomini also recorded a popular belief in the community that some herbs were more useful than conventional medical treatment for the plague.[55] Clearly, this reflected the persistence of an underlying belief in popular medicine and miraculous cures that came to the surface again under the crisis conditions of the plague epidemic. The same conditions provided an opportunity for many who had never practiced medicine before to offer amulets, charms, incantations and herbal preparations which were claimed to ward off or cure plague.[56]

To compound the crisis of confidence which medical practitioners faced, they also became peripheral to the state management of the plague crises. In some measure, this arose from a divergence between medical discourse and public health discourse on the transmission of disease during an epidemic in the community. There was, however, no significant difference between the two groups on the theory of causation. As we have already noted in the previous chapter, state regulations to contain the spread of the epidemic followed the basic ideas of pre-existing health and sanitation measures. These stemmed from an intuitive concept of "contagion," although that term was not used formally until the fifteenth century. Medical discourse, as opposed to public health discourse, favoured Galenic concepts of humoural imbalance and "miasmas," as a theory of disease causation, and discounted theories which assumed "contagion" as a vector of disease transmission. This position was maintained until long after public health discourse adopted the "contagion" definition formally. Accordingly, medical practitioners played no part in determining state policy on disease control, and were never appointed to the health boards created to implement government measures.

The government of Florence did, however, see a role for medical practitioners that could not be filled by others. Not only was there a need to have them take responsibility for the formal diagnosis of plague, and to issue death certificates as to the cause of death, but the provision of palliative care was also seen as a medical practitioner's role. However, the ranks of the medical profession were greatly reduced by the plague, and among surviving practitioners there were many who were loath to visit and treat plague victims. To remedy this situation, the state adopted two measures which had a significant impact on the practice of medicine in Florence. First, it simply ordered certain practitioners to attend to plague sufferers, and insisted that they remain in quarantine with the victims while the epidemic persisted.[57] Given the ease with which the disease was transmitted, this was often a sentence of death for any practitioner given this onerous task. Second, the state sponsored an influx of practitioners from outside Florence, and overrode the statutes of the medical guild to ensure that those who wished to practice medicine in Florence could do so with no other requirement than the payment of a fee. Neither action was popular with Florentine medical practitioners, but the second of these incursions into the affairs of the medical guild was viewed with alarm by its members. In the judgment of guild members the outcome was that "many idiots, totally ignorant of the art of medicine who used to work as blacksmiths, and at other mechanical occupations" were permitted to practice.[58] The physicians with university training were particularly incensed, since this action only added to the then prevailing opinion that medical practitioners did not know how to care for the diseased body. It inspired them to fight vigorously to regain the privileged position they once held in Florentine society.

Reclaiming the Diseased Body

From early in the fourteenth century, the medical guild of Florence had all the hallmarks of a professional organisation. The guild had the sole power to issue or withhold licenses to practice, that is, it claimed for its members the exclusive rights to treat the diseased body. It justified this monopoly in the field of medicine by virtue of its claimed specialized knowledge and technical competence. To maintain exclusivity, members had to undertake not to divulge privileged medical information to anyone outside the guild, and to provide mutual assistance and support to fellow members in professional and personal matters—requirements characteristic of similar professional organizations in more recent times. The reputation and power which membership of the guild delivered, at least to its more prominent members, ensured that medicine, particularly the role of the physician, was considered to be an appropriate and desirable career for members of the socially elite families of Florence.[59] In addition, members of the guild were eligible for election to various councils and positions of authority in the government of the city-state of Florence.

While some members might well have gained this access to political power through their family status, most members of the guild did not have these connections. The basis for their power and influence, both in the field of medicine and in politics, lay in the perception that medical practitioners possessed privileged knowledge and expertise. It is not difficult to recognize in this connection between knowledge and power in Florentine society a manifestation of the interrelationship between these factors, which Foucault identified as a fundamental element of power structures in society.[60] But in this particular instance, the community realized that, despite their protestations, medical practitioners did not have the necessary knowledge with which to combat bubonic plague. As a result, the basis for the power and status of medical practitioners was undermined, and the actual power that they exercised over the diseased body was diluted. In addition, their general status in the community and their access to political power suffered a marked decline that lasted for some two centuries.

The medical guild addressed the problem of the reduced status of practitioners and the loss of community confidence in several ways. It sought to raise professional competence and to improve the ethics and conduct of its members. The main drive for restoration of the status and reputation of medical practitioners came from the university-trained physicians within the guild. However, the real aim of their endeavors was to distinguish themselves from all others who offered medical attention. They wished to be recognized as an elite group within the guild, holding prime responsibility and authority with regard to treatment of the diseased body. Not only did they try to marginalize the empirics (those qualified by experience only) who were members of the guild but they also sought to separate themselves from university-trained surgeons.[61] They drew support for their views on the latter from Galen's statement that surgery was "only a means of treatment," an implication that surgeons were simply artisans and inferior to the intellectually-oriented physicians.[62] Support for their drive for recognition as an elite group came from two perhaps unexpected sources: the state and the church. The most significant impetus came from a decision of the state. This resulted in profound and permanent changes in the way the human body was viewed and treated.

New Knowledge—New Power

In June 1348, at the height of the epidemic in Florence, the city authorities recognized that physicians were not able to deal adequately with the outbreak of plague because they had insufficient knowledge of the disease. Accordingly, the *Signoria* authorized and paid for autopsies to be performed on several victims of plague, "to be able to understand more clearly the diseases [affecting] the bodies."[63] This is the first recorded instance of an officially sanctioned dissection in Florence. It was not for forensic purposes as had been the main reason in the past, but to gain a better understanding of the disease which appeared to be destroying the city. And it seems that this was not an isolated attempt to advance knowledge of the disease. Later that month there is an entry in a list of public expenditures "for giving more corpses to physicians who requested them," for autopsies on plague victims.[64] This major break with traditional attitudes to the body, and uncertainty about church reactions, must have given the members of the *Signoria* some concern as to their decision. At the same time as authorizing the dissections, they sought and paid for papal letters of indulgence to absolve those who conducted autopsies for pathological investigations during the Black Death.[65]

Florence was not alone in overcoming the traditional reluctance to explore the inner secrets of the human body. Other northern Italian cities such Perugia, Venice, Padua, and Bologna also authorized autopsies for the same purpose and at about the same time. All evidence leads to a conclusion that the Black Death had caused this break with the traditional view of the body as sacrosanct and not to be violated. Finally, the "sealed body" had become the "revealed body," open to the medical gaze. And once the barriers that impeded gazing into the body were overcome, the study of anatomy became an essential element of medical education. In this area, the Florentine experience was typical of similar developments in medical education in other cities of northern Italy even though the timetable of events varied slightly. In 1349, the commune required that all medical practitioners, not just students, should attend regular public lectures and discussions at the University of Florence.[66] By 1372, the guild itself adopted statutes that called for discussions to be held twice a month, and to include topics of interest to young practitioners.[67] It also required that dissections be held twice a year so that knowledge of anatomy could be improved. These requirements were supplemented by statutes of the University of Florence which, in 1388, stipulated that two dissections be held each year for the benefit of senior students of medicine. These procedures were to be performed upon one male and one female body. (The corpses, those of foreign criminals executed in Florence, were supplied by the commune).

This evidence from contemporary sources invites alternative conclusions or interpretations to those drawn by several current theorists. Many such writers appear to overlook, or be unaware of, the emergence of new and fundamentally different perceptions of the body in northern Italy in response to the epidemics of bubonic plague. Indeed, they locate their arguments on these issues in a much later period. Herzlich and Pierret, for example, claimed that even "at the beginning of the seventeenth century, dissections were rare and difficult to carry out."[68] Michel Foucault implied much the same in *The Birth of the Clinic*.[69] While he acknowledged the innovative work done by Giovanni Morgagni in pathological anatomy, this took place at Padua in the middle of the eighteenth century. Most of Foucault's other references to pioneering work focus on French anatomists. There is no acknowledgment of the early work in this field triggered by the plague epidemics, nor of the way in which this was applied in hospital practice in the fourteenth and fifteenth centuries. These, we would argue, represented some of the most significant paradigm shifts in the history of perceptions of the body.[70]

We suggest also that there are other misconceptions to be found in the literature on the sociology of the body. In *Regulating Bodies: Essays in Medical Sociology,* Bryan Turner offered a persuasive argument that the practice of dissection should be viewed as an extension of the punishment regime since it was usually performed upon the bodies of executed criminals.[71] While it is true that many of the corpses supplied for dissection were those of criminals, we see this only as a function of their availability. From the evidence discussed above there is no doubt that the dissections were authorized to gain information, not to inflict symbolic punishment. The sole purpose of these autopsies was to find out more about plague, its causes and effects, for pathologico-anatomical purposes.

Medicalizing the Body

Although the study of the human body and its internal structure for medical purposes was accelerated by the acceptance of the practice of dissection, it was some time before the Galenic inheritance was fully challenged, and direct observation of the body was accepted as the basis for a knowledge of anatomy. In some measure this was accelerated by the pursuit of new knowledge across other disciplines such as art, literature, science, and in exploration of New World, at the same time as the boundaries of medical science were being expanded. This thirst for knowledge, which characterized the underlying thrust of the Renaissance, was evident first in Italy before it spread to the rest of Europe. While our immediate focus in this chapter has been on perceptions of the body in the field of medicine, we should not overlook the contribution made to the study of anatomy by artists of the Renaissance. Both Michelangelo and Leonardo da Vinci conducted dissections to learn of skeletal and muscular structure, although they had no great interest in the way in which the body functioned. Leonardo, however, adopted an approach which represented a new, objective and scientific approach to the human body.[72] He was uninfluenced by the ideas of Galen or late medieval anatomists, and recorded in many detailed anatomical drawings precisely that which he saw during the more than thirty dissections he performed himself. There is little doubt that such an approach would have assisted medical theorists to observe for themselves instead of accepting without question inherited concepts of human anatomy.

While general community attitudes to the body were gradually being modified by these developments, our main concern at this point is with the outcomes for medical theory and practice. In the field of anatomy, the use of dissection in medical education proceeded apace, first in Italy, then in France and other European centers, and challenges to Galenic pronouncements on human anatomy became more frequent. This reached its full flowering in the work of Vesalius, completed when he was a lecturer at the University of Padua in the mid-sixteenth century. His treatise, *De Humanis Corporis Fabrica,* published in 1543, marked a major break with ancient anatomy. It was the first large-scale, original survey of human anatomy and physiology since Galen. Accordingly, Vesalius is credited with being the founder of the modern science of anatomy, and an early and important proponent of medical science based on direct observation rather than inherited concepts.[73]

As a consequence of these developments, medical practitioners could once more claim to be the custodians of esoteric knowledge about the human body that the general public could not share. But it was the physicians who finally established themselves as the main beneficiaries of this outcome. As early as 1392, they formed a separate College of Physicians within the guild of Florence for those holding a university degree. And by the end of the sixteenth century, it was no longer possible to be a member of this College unless one had the necessary financial backing to study at a recognized university, and to acquire the library of books and the equipment deemed necessary for a physician. In effect, they had established their supremacy over all other practitioners, an outcome mirrored in the medical professions of most northern Italian cities. As a consequence, they claimed the sole right to deal with the diseased body. However, their claims to exclusivity did not rest solely on their possession of specialized knowledge. They were aided considerably by two other developments which also emerged during the period of the plague epidemics.

Marginalizing Women in Medical Practice

Women had long been among those who provided medical attention, most acquiring their skills by practical experience and through the handing down of traditional knowledge. Others gained more formal medical training in the same manner as did men. For example, women were among those who studied medicine at the medical school of Salerno. Women who acted as general practitioners were also to be found on the registers of the Florentine medical guild. Of the latter, most were daughters or widows of medical practitioners who had given them their practical training. However, by the end of the Middle Ages, men began to create obstacles to the participation of women in medicine. As the new university medical schools emerged women were not permitted to enroll. University trained physicians made strong efforts to marginalize all women who offered treatment for the sick, and to limit the fields in which they could practice medicine. And even in the traditional area of midwifery, their competence was challenged, and men gained the right to check on the work of midwives and ultimately to largely displace them.[74]

Some of the most virulent attacks were directed at the "wise women" of the community who offered a wide range of treatments for simple ailments, attendance at childbirth, and advice on contraception and abortion. Physicians were assisted greatly in these attacks by the antagonism shown toward these women by the church, and the denunciations of midwives as witches in the *Malleus Malleficarum*. As we have noted earlier, this was a period in which figures in authority fostered the view that older women, particularly those outside the control of a male, were very dangerous. For this reason, it was relatively easy for male medical practitioners to undermine women, usually of mature age, who practiced community medicine, as well as those who were members of the guild.[75] As a result of this pressure, women became marginal in professional medical practice and only continued their work in community medicine because of their ready availability and their low cost to those of the poorer classes.

Institutionalizing the Body

The status of the physician, and the power which he could exercise over the diseased body, were also enhanced by virtue of the major changes which occurred in the hospital system during the period of plague epidemics. Florence, like its neighboring cities, had a system of small charitable hospitals in operation before the arrival of the Black Death. These establishments were hospices rather than hospitals since they provided care and shelter, instead of treatment, for a wide range of people, including travellers in need of accommodation.

The Black Death, and the succession of epidemics of plague which followed, accentuated the need to treat the sick, and hospitals gradually changed the basis on which they operated. More hospitals were established and finally, at the end of the fifteenth century, one solely for plague victims was opened in Florence. With the expansion of the hospital system, and the greater focus on curative rather than palliative care, new opportunities for physicians and surgeons were created. By the early sixteenth century, physicians had become central to the functioning of hospitals, and as such were able to exercise a great deal of control over the bodies of those confined within these institutions.[76] Senior physicians visited the hospitals daily to examine patients and to discuss their progress and treatment with resident staff. The latter, consisting of junior physicians and nursing staff, administered the medication and other treatment regimes prescribed by the visiting physicians. Surgeons also visited daily to attend to skin disorders, wounds, or other matters deemed to be within their province.

The important role in hospitals played by physicians can be well demonstrated by one example. At Santa Maria Nuova, a Florentine hospital with 230 beds, the staff of physicians numbered nine, of which three were junior residents under the supervision of the six salaried physicians who visited daily.[77] This system has a marked resemblance to that which has operated in hospitals in this century. And in the regulation of the diseased bodies of the patients, there are further parallels. Hospitals employed the same system of identification, classification, and of course, confinement which had been developed by the state to control the spread of plague. The bodies of the sick were confined in an institution and placed under the control of a medical bureaucracy, which included medical practitioners and administrative staff.

Bryan Turner concluded that the modern hospital system operates according to Foucault's concept of panopticism, and that it is "symbolic of the social power of the medical profession, representing the institutionalization of specialized medical knowledge."[78] While agreeing with this conclusion, the evidence which we have advanced extends this interpretation—that this was the period in which the body itself became de-personalized and institutionalized through the hospital system. Further, we suggest that the basic form and nature of the modern hospital system had already emerged in the latter part of the plague period, rather than in the seventeenth or eighteenth centuries as Turner implied.[79]

The Body Becomes an Object

Although the restructuring of the medical profession was an important outcome of plague experiences, equally significant were the changes which occurred in the perceptions of the body and of disease. Before the Black Death, and for some time after that, the human body was seen as an integral part of the divine plan for the universe, as an element of human existence inextricably linked to the soul. The catastrophic nature of the Black Death focused attention on the fragility of the body when faced with an outbreak of epidemic disease. It also challenged and found wanting all existing discourses on causation and treatment. From the efforts to find causes through dissection, new views of the body began to emerge. The image of the body as a microcosm attuned to the universe in accordance with a divine plan gave way to an image of the body as an object which could be manipulated, adjusted, and repaired at the hands of the medical expert with privileged knowledge of the body's secrets. This perception anticipated and paved the way for the seventeenth century exposition of the Cartesian view of the human body.

These changes also ushered in the era in which the medical model of bodily disorders would take precedence over all others. In the first instance, this represented the final move in the secularization of medicine when the priest was replaced by the physician. It allowed scope for new discourses on causation, and the re-definition of bodily disorders as sickness rather than as punishment for sins. And with the medicalization of the body, physicians could persuade patients to reconfigure their illness experiences in terms of medical theories on bodily disorders which the practitioner had been trained to accept. Just as Galen's ideas of anatomy had given way to the results of objective investigation, medical discourse gradually accepted the concept of contagion as a means of disease transmission. This concept was an important change of direction for medical science, and played a vital part in understanding the next outbreak of epidemic disease—syphilis.

PART III

Fin-de-siècle Forebodings

Our Apocalypse is not real it is *virtual*. Neither does it belong to the future, its incident is *in the here and now*.
. . .

Now that the aristocratic illusion of origin and the democratic illusion of the end increasingly drift apart—we no longer have the choice to advance, 'to abide in our present destruction, nor to withdraw, only a last ditch effort to confront this radical illusion.

—Jean Baudrillard[1]

CHAPTER 8

The Danger of Touch:
The Body and Social Distance

May 14, 1496.The plague has returned in many places in
Florence.

May 28, 1496.A certain ailment has appeared here, one
called "French blisters." They are like a severe form of
variola, and seem to have no cure. They are continuing to
spread.

July 8, 1496.And now that complaint called "French blisters" is starting to increase even more, so that the city is
full of it, with almost all who have the complaint being
grown men and women.

December 5, 1496. Another house with plague has been
discovered after we have had some months free of it. At
the same time, the "French blisters" have spread
throughout Florence and the surrounding countryside. It
is also in every city in Italy, and this affliction lasts a long
time. Those who try to cure themselves have to endure
much pain in all their joints, only to find that the problem
returns. Few people have died from this complaint, but
they have had to suffer great pain and torment.[1]

Toward the end of the fifteenth century many areas of western
Europe were still coping with recurring outbreaks of plague. But to
the dismay of many, it was during this period that a new scourge
appeared. First called the "French blisters," but soon known by a
variety of names, this scourge was the disease we identify today as
syphilis. Like the plague before it, this apparently new disease
appeared first in Italy. From this point, its progress across Europe—

indeed across the whole of the known world—was disturbingly swift.

In this chapter, we review the way in which this new epidemic finally consolidated the discursive and procedural shifts set in place by the earlier major epidemics. Beyond this, we argue that syphilis, through its own particular characteristics, was responsible for significant shifts in perceptions of the body, of disease, and for fundamental changes in medical theory and practice. Further, we contend that syphilis produced profound and lasting effects on attitudes toward sexuality and gender relations.

These new outcomes were due, in part, to the fact that syphilis displayed features markedly different from leprosy and plague. The first of these was its persistence. Unlike the earlier scourges, syphilis did not gradually disappear after wreaking great havoc upon afflicted communities.[2] Over time, it entrenched itself permanently in almost every community in the known world, becoming the first of the "social diseases" of modern times to appear. The second characteristic that made it different was its propensity to develop mutant strains. From early in the sixteenth century, observers commented on this ability to mutate. Both of these characteristics are still evident today.[3]

New or Old?

The diary of Luca Landucci, cited above, described how this disease spread rapidly throughout Italy. As a keen observer, Landucci was able to identify the main characteristics of this outbreak. It bore a resemblance to smallpox, already well known to European communities, but it was more painful, and seemed to have no cure. It appeared to be confined to adult men and women, a factor which soon led to the conclusion that "it is never or only with great difficulty that one can be infected other than through coitus."[4] However, the new disease proved to be more lethal than Landucci predicted. Later evidence showed that there was a significant death toll during its first few years in Europe when the disease was at its most virulent.

Members of the general community had no doubt that they were witnessing the arrival of an entirely new bodily disorder. Syphilis presented indications not previously seen, or even referred to, in popular discourse. The signs were inscribed on the outer surface of the body, appearing initially on or about the genitals, and later spreading to other parts of the body. At that stage, pustules appeared on the normally visible parts of the body—the face, hands, and legs—signalling the presence of the disease to even the most casual observer. But it was from the first indications—the lesions in the genital region—that the general population sensed that the disease was not only novel, but that it must be linked in some way to sexual activities.

Within the medical profession there was considerable debate as to whether the disease was, in fact, novel, or whether it had been known in earlier periods. At the outset, many medical practitioners were loath to accept that the disease may be new since they retained a residual faith in the authority of Galen. They believed that Galen and his contemporaries had already catalogued any ailment that could possibly be encountered. Accordingly, they thought that they had only to search the old texts more diligently to be able to find a solution to the current dilemma. This attitude lingered, despite the fact that plague experiences had already shaken the absolute reliance previously placed in Galenic theories.

Debate about the novelty or otherwise of syphilis continued within medical circles. It was spurred, at least in part, by the new spirit of inquiry which was evident in Italy during the Renaissance.[5] In particular, it drew upon an increasing recognition of the need for "objective" and "analytical" examination of all available evidence, an approach which lay at the core of the new "scientific" ethos of the age. Under the influence of such an approach, and in the absence of any unambiguous evidence to the contrary, a consensus emerged that syphilis was "either completely new or unknown until this age in our hemisphere."[6]

It was not until some thirty years after the first outbreak that a connection was drawn between the expeditions of Columbus to the New World and the introduction to Europe of the new disease. Indeed, the discovery of the Americas provided a convenient explanation for the origins of syphilis. It drew an association between a new disease and a new part of the world, an area inhabited by "a race with black faces and black hair," many of whom had "hideous bodies scaly with scabs, [and] flowing with pus."[7] And the skin color of the "American Indians"—reported as "black"—was reaffirmed as a signifier of cultural and moral inferiority.[8] Comments such as those by Amerigo Vespucci bear this out:[9]

> They have as many wives as they desire; they live in promiscuity without regard to blood relations; mothers lie with sons, brothers with sisters; they satisfy their desires . . . as beasts do.[10]

Attributing the source of the infection to the immorality of non-Christian races provided an explanation which proved quite satisfactory to European communities, since it freed them from association with the origins of such a loathsome disease. To them, it was clearly a new disease. It had originated in a faroff land where the intemperate sexual behavior of a non-Christian race had spawned this vile disorder of the body.

Since then the Columbian connection has remained the most popular theory on the origin of syphilis, although argument has continued to the present time. A strong counter-argument has been raised for its existence in Europe before the fifteenth century, despite the fact that there are no known, unequivocal accounts of such a disease having been observed.[11] Recent recourse to osteo-archeological examination of skeletal remains for syphilitic lesions has also proved somewhat inconclusive. For this reason, suggested evidence of lesions in European skeletons of pre-1500 origin is doubtful, while skeletal remains from South America show definite evidence of exposure to syphilis.[12]

However, there is yet another theory. This posits that syphilis could have existed in different forms before the fifteenth century in Europe, America, Africa, and Asia.[13] According to this theory, the disease had gone unnoticed within a range of skin complaints. It is further suggested in this so-called Unitarian theory that the American mutant was a more virulent strain than any that had existed in Europe before and that it was spread rapidly through communities with no previously acquired immunity by the troop movements of the late fifteenth century.[14] The much earlier spread of leprosy is believed to have occurred in a somewhat similar manner, having been introduced into western Europe by the returning Crusaders. However, we make no deductions on the origins of syphilis. Our interest focuses on the way in which communities and the institutions of power responded to contemporary constructions of the disease.

The "French Disease"

The Florentine historian Guicciardini included an entire, if rather brief, chapter in his *History of Italy* describing the arrival of the new disease and the way in which it had "spread throughout the whole of Italy."[15] According to Guicciardini's account, responsibility lay with the army of the French King Charles VIII who led an invasion into Italy in 1495.[16] He described how, after reaching and occupying Naples for a short period, the French army was forced to withdraw. Then as the army travelled northward, the troops spread syphilis wherever they went. No one has ever seriously disputed this account, although just how the troops became infected in the first place was a matter of considerable debate. And since the path of the disease mirrored that of the retreating French forces, the disease became known in Italy as the "French blisters," or more popularly, the *mal francese,* the "French disease." Understandably, the French were disinclined to accept responsibility for the spread of syphilis, claiming that the army which had invaded Italy had acquired the malady in Naples. Accordingly, they called it the "Neapolitan disease."[17]

The new disease acquired many different names as it was spread across Europe by mercenaries of the French army returning to their home countries. As a result, by 1496–7 syphilis had been introduced into France, Spain, Germany, England, and Scotland as well as throughout Italy.[18] And most other countries of western Europe reported outbreaks of the disease by 1502. Each community in which the disease appeared blamed some other country for the outbreak. Apart from it being called the French disease by the Italians, and the Neapolitan disease by the French, the Germans called it the French sickness or disease, the Poles described it as the German sickness, and the Russians knew it as the Polish sickness. Across the channel, the English labelled it the French sickness, or more commonly the French pox, and later just the great pox. The Flemish and Dutch, and the inhabitants of Northwest Africa referred to the disease as the Spanish sickness, and the Turks saw it as the Christian disease.[19]

One element is common to this variety of names—the new disease was always perceived as an evil introduced from outside the community, from a neighboring country, or even more menacingly, from an enemy country.[20] Syphilis, it seems, confirmed all pre-existing perceptions of the threats posed by the dangerous Other who came from outside the community group.

The Libertine as Other

It was not only the "stranger," the person who came from another area, or from religious groups such as Muslims and Jews, who was consistently targeted as the dangerous Other. There were

also groups within the community who were perceived as a threat
to the rest of the population. We have already seen how homosexuals, prostitutes, and indeed the poor, were repeatedly marginalized
and more closely regulated during periods of plague. Syphilis introduced another category of dangerous Other—the male whose reck-
less pursuit of sexual relations outside the bounds of marriage
exposed him to the new disease.

During the first few years of the epidemic, when syphilis was
viewed as a just punishment for unbridled sexual indulgence, men
could expect little sympathy if they contracted the disease. Even
among medical practitioners there were some who were reluctant
to offer treatment since they questioned whether one should "work
against the will of God, who had punished them by the very means
in which they had sinned."[21] In such an atmosphere, men who
placed themselves at risk of becoming infected were considered not
only sexually irresponsible but also deviant. After such men could
no longer hide the fact that they had contracted the disease, they
were frequently shunned by their erstwhile companions.

This is exactly what happened to Joseph Grunpeck, a young
cleric from Augsburg, who visited Rome in 1498. After attending a
banquet at which, he noted with some irony, Venus as well as Bacchus and Ceres were also present, he became infected with
syphilis.[22] After some lapse of time, he became so pale and languid
that he was forced to confess his predicament to his friends. Following this revelation, he noted bitterly, "my dear friends turned
their backs on me as if some pursuing enemy had his sword at their
throats, without giving a single thought to the obligations of fel-
lowship and friendship."[23] It is arguable that Grunpeck was a foolish young man rather than a libertine, but his experiences demonstrate how, in the early years of the epidemic, a man who became
infected with syphilis could be excluded from the social body.

The general perception that men who avidly pursued sexual
pleasures were worthy of condemnation, and were, in fact, culpa-
ble, is shown clearly in the early iconography of syphilis. The first
known example of the visual representation of syphilis was an
illustration by Albrecht Dürer. This was published in 1496 in a
pamphlet on syphilis written by Theodorius Ulsensius.[24] In this
illustration, Dürer offers a caricature of the syphilitic as a *boule-
vardier* whose face and neck, hands and legs are covered with the
pustular signs of the disease, and not the image of a solid, God-fearing burgher who conforms to societal norms. The figure is a French
gallant, dressed extravagantly in a large plumed hat, voluminous

cloak, elegant shoes, and with long flowing hair. The symbolism is clear. It is the womanizing libertine, in this instance identified as a stereotypical Frenchman, already associated in German popular discourse with sexual excess and deviance, who is the target of condemnation.

A similar inference can be drawn from one of Leonardo da Vinci's anatomical sketches on human sexuality.[25] In this work which is undated, but belongs to the period in which syphilis first appeared, Leonardo showed a sectionalized view of a male figure engaged in sexual activity. Around the sketch there are many annotations in the artist's handwriting, and among these is one that states: "By means of these figures, the causes of many [health] perils, sores, and diseases can be shown."[26] Given the period in which the sketch was executed, and the obvious association with the sexual act, Leonardo's comments seem to affirm the ethos of the age. By electing to depict the male with an atypically long flowing hair style, Leonardo appears to be defining the self-indulgent male as a culprit rather than a victim.

The Male as Victim

Syphilis appeared at all levels of society, infecting princes, prelates, and paupers, but its incidence was particularly notable among the ranks of the more influential male members of the community. Within these influential circles, there was an attempt to minimize the social stigma attached to becoming infected. Hence, an account was constructed that explained male infection as stemming solely from contact with women. By such means, blame and responsibility were diverted from men, and men were able to depict themselves as victims rather than as transgressors. This fantastic invention completely discounted the fact that women also contracted the disease.

This promotion of masculine vulnerability was reflected in a reworking of the visual images of the disease. The iconography of syphilis progressively focused more attention on the suffering male. Men were represented as martyrs rather than satyrs, as the primary victims of the disease rather than its disseminators. Women, on the other hand, were increasingly portrayed as being responsible for this insidious invasion of men's bodies.

The element of moral condemnation in community discourse remained, but over time, was directed more stridently at women and their "rampant sexuality." This permitted men to indulge their sexual appetites without attracting opprobrium, and to think of themselves as "unfortunate" if they became infected with syphilis. Shifting the blame from the male to the female gave men the freedom to speak openly of their sexual adventures and to treat syphilis as simply another hazard to be faced in their intimate dealings with women. Some revealed all in their autobiographies. The Florentine sculptor Benvenuto Cellini, for instance, described in great detail his encounter with syphilis and the misery he suffered during more than fifty days of treatment, when he wrote of his life in the sixteenth century.[27]

In the succeeding centuries, European literature made considerable use of the *motif* of the libidinous male who became infected with syphilis from a diseased female.[28] Admittedly, some of these works allowed for a token acknowledgment of the moral implications. However, redefining men as the victims paved the way for women to be held primarily responsible for the spread of sexually transmitted diseases.

Woman as Other

The transfer of culpability from men to women drew extensively on the prevailing social construct of Woman that had been inherited from the Middle Ages. A succession of pronouncements and interpretations by theologians, and other male figures of authority, fuelled men's ignorance and fears of women, and reinforced long-held beliefs as to the dangers women's bodies posed for men. For example, Marbode of Rennes declared that:

> Woman . . . was a temptress, a sorceress, a serpent, a plague, a vermin, a rash, a poison, a searing flame, an intoxicating spirit . . .[29]

While this pronouncement represents an extreme point of view, it is well within the spectrum of traditional perceptions that defined Woman as the source of all evil and corruption.

Several of these perceptions of Woman intersected and reinforced each other in the late fifteenth century. The most general of these was the portrayal of Eve as the archetypal Woman—devious, seductive, and responsible for all the trials and tribulations of the world. This, of course, was central to Christian theology, and had been instrumental in shaping community discourse on women in general. During the latter part of the Middle Ages this image was strongly reinforced by a revival of interest in the Greek Creation myth. In this myth, Pandora, the first woman, was characterized as being "as foolish, mischievous, and idle as she was beautiful—the first of a long line of such women."[30] Like Eve who succumbed to the blandishments of the serpent and partook of the forbidden fruit, Pandora was headstrong and disobedient. She had been entrusted with a precious jar whose contents were to remain untouched; but was unable to contain her curiosity. Despite the admonitions, she recklessly opened the jar and so released upon the world all the ills to which humanity has since been prone. This parallels the account in Christian tradition of trouble and misery introduced into the world by Eve. Indeed, like Eve, Pandora was seen to be the archetypal representation of the sexuality of women, the essentially flawed attraction that undermined men's resolve and exposed them to spiritual and physical peril.

This construction of Woman was given added emphasis by an interweaving of fable and medical theory on the physiology of women. During the latter part of the Middle Ages, a cultural theme from a distant past emerged as a popular literary *topos*. This was the tale of the Poison-Damsel, or the Venomous Virgin, discussed earlier in chapter 2. The story proved to be extremely popular and was translated into every language in the West. It had an enormous influence on European literature with the myth of the Poison-Damsel being adopted, and also adapted by many writers.[31] In the thirteenth century, the Florentine Brunetto Latini, one of Dante's mentors, included a modified version of the myth in his collection of stories, "The Treasures of Brunetto Latini."[32] And during the thirteenth and fourteenth centuries, the myth of the Poison-Damsel was included in the *Gesta Romanorum* (The Deeds of the Romans).[33] These myths and tales, purporting to relate to the past glories of Rome, were compiled by monks for their own pleasure, and, more pertinently, for use in discourses from the pulpit. It is likely that it was through this usage that the Poison-Damsel *topos* was indelibly imprinted upon the minds of late medieval communities. The story served to remind men of the ever-present dangers they faced in their encounters with women. The Poison-Damsel represented this danger in a very specific way. She was always described as beautiful and alluring, drawing men irresistibly to her kisses, caresses, and sexual embrace. The myth created an image of instant sexual death for the incautious male.

Death by intercourse was but a variation of the Poison-Damsel theme. A notable example of its use is found in Machiavelli's comedy, *La Mandragola,* published in 1518, in the midst of the syphilis epidemic.[34] In this work, we encounter the stereotypes of Renaissance comedy—the old man with a young and beautiful wife whose sexual favors are being sought by a handsome fellow of her own age. The elderly husband believes that the wife must be barren since there are no children from the marriage. A conspiracy centered around the eager young suitor persuades the old husband that there is a potion available which will cure the condition although there is a serious problem—the first man to have intercourse with the wife after she has taken the draught will die. The solution proposed, and finally accepted by all parties, is that a substitute man must be found, someone plucked from the street to face this certain death by intercourse. In the manner of all comedies, the "stranger" is of course the ardent young man appropriately disguised, and the couple arrive at a happy compromise. The relationship posited between sexual intercourse and the resulting death of the male participant was a potent theme in the early sixteenth century. Moreover, it was completely in harmony with community (and religious) discourse on women. We will explore this in more depth later.

Venomous Venus

Fabulous accounts, such as those of the Poison-Damsel, which suggested that women could acquire an immunity to poison, were paralleled in late medieval medico-theological discourse on women's physiological processes.[35] Medical theorists, and theologians who appear to have been greatly concerned with women's reproductive cycles, declared that menstrual blood contained some kind of poison. In effect, they defined Woman as "a 'machine' capable of producing a certain dose of poison every month."[36] However, women were said to be able to develop an immunity to this poison, and it was only others who were at risk in contact with them.

This belief found its strongest expression in community discourse as well as in medical and theological circles, in an abhorrence of sexual intimacy during menstruation. For some, the outcome of such a union would be a monstrous birth, a sure sign of divine displeasure, and a portent of disaster. Others postulated that intercourse at such a time would produce leprous children.[37]

Men's fears of women's bodies could only be heightened by the threats apparently posed by menstrual blood. They saw themselves at risk while women remained unaffected due to their natural immunity to the poison in such blood. This was a protective mechanism that men could never hope to enjoy. Hence, it established an uncrossable frontier between the sexes. It also convinced men that they were always at peril in their sexual encounters with women.

All of these themes intersected in discourses on the transmission of syphilis which began to emerge in the late fifteenth century. The generally held view of medical authorities was that a "poison" was involved, that "it [syphilis] involved the introduction of a poison into the body."[38] And given the link between the disease and the sexual act, this was not an unlikely association to be perceived by medical men steeped in the classical foundations of humanist education. They would have been well aware that in Latin the words *venus* (representing sexual love), and *venenum* (originally a magical potion or love philtre, and later, a poison or venom) are linked etymologically. Most medical writers of the late fifteenth century speculated on this apparent connection as they pondered the nature of syphilis. They also theorized about the nature and origin of the "poison" that caused the condition which Leoniceno, the eminent Professor of Medicine at Ferrara called the "love disease."[39] And with perceptions grounded in the prevailing discourse on women's physiology, it is not surprising that it was frequently concluded that syphilis arose from contact with the menstrual flow. This concept is clear in the way in which one medical authority expressed his convictions. Writing in 1504, he proclaimed that "it [syphilis] is a morbid condition originating in a total infection of the substance of the blood, linked with a poison contained in the *menstrues*."[40]

The notion of an association between women, and a poison that caused syphilis, was soon reflected in community discourse on the new disease. It drew upon the causal relationship between the sexual act and syphilis, and reinforced long held beliefs about the dangers women's bodies posed for men. Nowhere is this clearer than in Fracastoro's counsel for those who wished to avoid becoming infected by syphilis: "Nevertheless, keep away from Venus, and above all things avoid the soft pleasures of love making—nothing is more harmful. . . ."[41] The "well of love" had become a "poisoned spring and a deadly trap."[42] It was but a small step for men to start directing the blame for transmission of syphilis toward women.

Such convictions not only shaped the social construction of syphilis in the early sixteenth century but defined patterns of gender relationships. They inspired changes in acceptable standards of behavior between the sexes and in the norms to be observed in the presentation of the body both in private and in public. These matters will be addressed in more detail later. For the moment, however, we turn to other important issues—the damage wrought upon the body by syphilis, and the changes in perception of the body which followed.

The "Serpentine Disease"

Syphilis has the distinction of being the first major disease from the pre-modern period to have been observed and documented from its initial appearance. Between 1497 and 1501, that is, at the very beginning of the epidemic, some dozen significant medical treatises appeared on the subject.[43] During the sixteenth century and beyond, many writers speculated on the origins of the new disease, and gave detailed accounts of its characteristics and treatment. This extensive documentation of the disease was due in no small measure to the fact that syphilis arrived in western Europe not long after the printed book had supplanted the manuscript, so allowing information and images to be recorded and circulated more readily.[44]

As might be expected, most of the writers were medical practitioners who described the progress of patients under their care. Among this group, however, there were some who were well qualified to speak from firsthand knowledge since they also had contracted the disease.[45] Beyond the clinical observations that they recorded, contemporary medical writers often provided insights into the social construction of this disease through the metaphors they employed in their writing. One of the frequently used metaphors characterized syphilis as the "serpentine disease." A renowned Spanish medical practitioner explained his use of the term as follows:

And as far as the name morbo serpentino (serpentine disease) is concerned, in point of hideousness there is no better object of comparison than the *serpent*. For just as the animal is hideous, fearsome and terrible, in like wise is the malady hideous, fearsome and terrible. It is a grave malady which ulcerates and corrupts the flesh, breaks and destroys the bones, and cuts and shrinks the tendons, and for all these reasons I give it this name.[46] [Our emphasis]

Fracastoro also used the serpent metaphor in his literary, but medically impeccable, account of the disease. This described the vectors of transmission, the progressive deterioration of the sufferer, and the various methods of treatment in use at that time. The "serpent disease syphilis," he declared, attacked the body through the actions of "the fine seeds of the invisible contagion, those whose habit is to snake inside the body in astonishing ways," and to treat it, one had to "burn out the nasty seed and slay the crawling serpent plague." Without such treatment, according to Fracastoro, the patient's condition would deteriorate because the disease would continue "quietly snaking through his guts bringing destruction."[47] Not only was the disease caused by a "poison" inherent in the menstrual flow, but its progress was likened to the insidious nature of the serpent. This construction challenged the concept of the "sealed body," the ideal body impervious to external influence. Now the body was vulnerable to this sinister condition, "snaking" into the body through orifices which both medicine and theology were anxious to guard, and then wreaking havoc within the body envelope.[48]

The Body under Attack

Plague and syphilis emphasized different aspects of the way disease affected the human body. Plague epidemics had focused attention on the fragility of life, on the unpredictability of both the time and the place of one's demise, and on the inevitable dissolution of the body after death. On the other hand, syphilis concentrated community attention on the way in which disease could disfigure and distort the body, and even destroy body tissues and bones, while a person continued to survive. In this sense, syphilis evoked memories of leprosy.[49] Fracastoro described the subsequent progress of the disease in graphic detail:

> slowly a caries, born amidst squalor in the body's shameful parts, became uncontrollable and began to eat the areas on either side and even the sexual organs. . . . Then as it spread it caused intolerable pain in the joints . . . unsightly sores broke out over all the body and made the face horrifyingly ugly. . . . Moreover the disease gnawed deep and burrowed into the inmost parts, feeding on the victims' bodies with pitiable results: for on quite frequent occasions we

ourselves have seen limbs stripped of their flesh and the bones rough with scales and mouths eaten away yawn open in a hideous gape while the throat produced feeble sounds.[50]

The horrendous damage to the bone structure of the body, described by Fracastoro, left many sufferers permanently and terribly deformed. According to Guicciardini, these people were rendered "useless, and subject to almost perpetual torment."[51] But before it produced such crippling effects, syphilis rendered the body visually repugnant. The body was frequently afflicted with suppurating sores that created an unbearable stench. As a consequence, many feared to come close to a syphilitic, believing that they may become contaminated either by the "corrupted airs" surrounding the sufferer or from direct contact with the patient's body. It is hardly surprising, then, that Benedetto, a Venetian medical practitioner, was led to exclaim that "the entire body is so repulsive to look at and the suffering so great, especially at night, that this sickness is even more horrifying than incurable leprosy or elephantiasis. . . ."[52] Nor should it surprise that Erasmus should rank the "French [pox]" or "Spanish pox" as the worst disease known to the world because "this scourge brings in its train all the terrifying aspects of other illnesses: disfigurement, pain, infection, the risk of losing one's life, and a treatment that is both difficult and extremely unpleasant. . . ."[53]

Syphilis was at its most virulent, and more likely to prove fatal, during the first five to seven years following its arrival in Europe. From early in the sixteenth century the severity of the epidemic was somewhat diminished, and by mid-century syphilis had settled into the all-pervasive and insidious pattern that is closer to the characteristics with which we are more familiar today.[54] Those who chronicled the progress of the disease through the first half of the sixteenth century voiced the general conclusion, now shared by modern writers, that the disease had been transmuted into a less severe and less contagious form of syphilis.[55]

Nevertheless, the horrors associated with the "serpentine disease" became deeply imprinted in community consciousness everywhere. Like leprosy which had preceded it, syphilis became a dreaded and reviled disease. These two scourges became, according to Susan Sontag, "the first illnesses to be consistently described as repulsive."[56] But because syphilis was more widespread within any community than leprosy had ever been, community responses to the new epidemic were more acute. The overwhelming response of universal revulsion stemmed from the fact that syphilis transformed the body into something shameful and revolting, into something quite alienating. This community reaction led to a resurgence of the perception that the human body was vile and disgusting, a thing to be denied and hidden. It also fuelled the climate of moral repression that became a notable feature of the sixteenth century. And in the field of medicine, investigations into syphilis accelerated advances in medical theory and practice that had begun tentatively as a result of plague experiences.

From Sin to Social Scourge

Although the practice of medicine had embraced significant shifts in both theory and practice by the end of the fifteenth century, elements of earlier concepts co-existed with the new ideas. In addition, some old ideas were revived in the early stages of the syphilis epidemic. One of these was a renewed emphasis on a causal link between sin and bodily disorder. To some degree, this countered theories of disease causation that had begun to attribute bodily disorder to earthly rather than divine influences. It brought to light a parallel between leprosy and the new disease. Both were disfiguring diseases perceived to be associated with sexual activity. Syphilis, like leprosy, was perceived as God's punishment for unbridled sexual indulgence. This conviction persisted in some medical circles well into the sixteenth century. As late as 1575, the noted French surgeon Amboise Paré declared that it was "God's wrath, which allowed this malady to descend upon the human race, in order to curb its lasciviousness and inordinate concupiscence."[57]

Although medical practitioners looked increasingly to factors other than divine punishment to explain the emergence and spread of syphilis, moral condemnation continued to underpin medical attitudes toward the disease. In fact, a moral loading was evident in many of their deliberations on bodily disorders in general. This is consistent with the cultural ambience of the period, and the role which the medical profession, particularly physicians, played in society. By the beginning of the sixteenth century, medical practitioners had largely regained the status that they had lost during the plague epidemics. Once more they were able to join the other main institutions of power—the church and the state—as the arbiters of community standards. The medical profession was also able to assist in implementing measures that repressed or curtailed any expressions of sexuality that were deemed a threat to social order.[58] Syphilis was understood to be such a threat, and as the nexus between sin and syphilis disappeared, medical practitioners were able to re-define the disease as a "social scourge," a menace which had to be controlled by medicine and the state.[59] As a result of such moves, the medical profession emerged as one of the major instruments of social control.[60] As a consequence, whatever measures the medical profession saw fit to adopt, or whatever new developments in medical science were applied, the effects were felt across the whole community.

The Fine Seeds of the Invisible Contagion

Syphilis arrived in Europe at the start of a period marked by innovative thinking, and the application of newfound "scientific" knowledge on anatomy and physiology to the treatment of the disordered body.[61] This spirit of inquiry was evident in many parts of Europe, but particularly in Italy, France, Germany, and Switzerland. Considerable effort was directed to investigating the "causes" of syphilis and speculating on its methods of transmission. This culminated in the publication, by Fracastoro in 1546, of new theories on disease causation and transmission.[62] According to Fracastoro's argument, all diseases were caused by "invisible seeds" that could be spread in various ways—by direct contact between bodies; by contact with materials contaminated by, and carrying the "seeds" of a disease; or from a distance (for example, becoming airborne).[63] The notion of disease being caused by "seeds" was not entirely novel, having enjoyed some currency before Fracastoro propounded his ideas.[64] However, it had never been developed into a coherent and consistent hypothesis, and it had never displaced the "miasmic" theories of disease causation.

Fracastoro's outstanding contribution to medical theory was his ability to analyze the available evidence and to produce from that a theoretical position that can be described as a "germ theory." The emergence of this theory, embodying a logical exposition of three classes of contagion, ultimately led to the demise of Galenic "miasmic" theories of disease transmission. Fracastoro also applied his hypothesis to a detailed review of all the known major diseases. This led him to posit a theory as to the way in which each of these diseases could be transmitted, and then to propose appropriate treatment regimes for each disease. His treatise is notable for its clarity of expression and his "scientific" approach, which were unusual for his time. Because of this, he has been called the father of modern pathology, and his work described as showing "a perception . . . of the meaning of the experimental method many years before the treatises of Francis Bacon and René Descartes."[65]

While some conservative elements of the medical profession clung to old concepts, the theories of Fracastoro were accepted and elaborated upon by many of his contemporaries. It was a watershed in medicine, one which finally disentangled medicine from its earlier teleological associations. And with this final step in the secularization of medicine, the focus of attention shifted from primary causes to the study of methods of transmission, and the ways the spread of disease could be limited. When this was applied to syphilis, the responses of the medical profession and the community at large were shaped by Fracastoro's "germ theory" and his contention that contagion was of critical importance in the transmission of the "seeds" of disease. It became imperative that direct bodily contact with an infected person should be avoided to prevent transmission of the infection. However, it was not always possible to determine who may have been infected with syphilis. For this reason, the maintenance of a safe distance from any potentially contaminating source became an important factor in the daily life of the community.

Understandably, attention focused initially on that most intimate of bodily contacts—sexual intercourse. Men had repeatedly been advised by medical practitioners to refrain from, or at least exercise great restraint, in sexual relations during times of epidemics, or periods of illness. This recommendation had reflected the idea that intercourse had a debilitating effect, and that men could make themselves more vulnerable to disease if they were sexually imprudent. With the arrival of syphilis, sexual intercourse was not only considered inadvisable, it came to be seen as positively dangerous. Consequently, medical advice was now couched in stronger terms: "I recommend once more that you should avoid any form of intimate contact with women who are infected with this dangerous malady. . . ."[66] In effect, this recommendation warned against sexual relations with all women because it was difficult to determine who was infected in the early stages of the disease. Medical practitioners frequently made this point, referring to the way in which signs of the disease could be less visible in women than in men.[67] This dilemma is illustrated in the following comments:

> There persists, within the private parts of women, lesions
> which remain remarkably virulent for a long time; they are
> particularly dangerous because they are less evident to the
> eye of the man who wishes to cohabit with women in com-
> plete safety.[68]

It is clear that the principal concern expressed in this passage
related to the men. They were presented not as sexual predators, but
as unwitting and unfortunate victims. And, by inference, the blame
in such situations was directed at the women involved. Even in Fracastoro's fairly objective account of syphilis, during his exposition of
the mechanisms of contagion, the focus is on the outcome for men.
Referring to the fact that coitus was the principal method by which
syphilis was transmitted, Fracastoro declared that "through such
means, the majority of men were infected."[69] Evidence also suggests
that this bias led many medical practitioners to concentrate more
attention on males than on female patients infected with syphilis.[70]

Fracastoro's work on disease transmission recognized that,
apart from direct contact between bodies, it was possible to become
infected by indirect means, that is, by touching articles such as bed-
ding, clothing, or wood already carrying the "seeds" of the disease.[71]
State health officials had subscribed to these possibilities during
the plague, but it was only in the sixteenth century that medicine
came to accept the concept of indirect contagion. Apart from recognizing the relevance of Fracastoro's theories on indirect means of
disease transfer, medical practitioners were persuaded that indirect contagion must be possible because there were cases of
syphilis, such as those occurring in infants, which could not be
explained in terms of sexual activity. Such infections, it was concluded, arose from ingesting breast milk from the mother or from a
wet-nurse already infected. With older children there was yet
another possibility—that the infection had been acquired through
the sharing of eating or drinking utensils. Shared bathing facilities
also became suspect, particularly public baths, since these were frequently meeting places for prostitutes, and water was seen as a
means of spreading the infection. Such attitudes were not confined
to community responses. They also entered into medical discourse
on syphilis. As a consequence, medical practitioners warned of the
dangers involved in touching the belongings of infected persons,
and in bathing the body in any way which shared facilities with
others. It was only much later that bathing regained medical support, and then it was for therapeutic purposes.

Medicine and the Vulnerable Body

Until the late fifteenth century, the action of touching a body could be interpreted on two levels—as a sensual and erotic act, or as an act of healing. The first reading links touch with an earthly or "bestial" kind of love which, according to the Florentine, medically trained philosopher Marsilio Ficino, was a disorder akin to madness.[72] Indeed, for Ficino, sensual love was the "most serious disease of all" when compared with "leprosy, pneumonia, consumption, . . . and plague."[73] The second reading of touch encompasses the biblical laying on of hands—credited with miraculous cures—and the careful ministrations of those tending the sick.

The advent of syphilis prompted a major shift in the understanding of touch. The sexualized touch became a dangerous and polluting agent, perhaps even the touch of death; and the application of "healing hands" fell into disuse.[74] Nevertheless, the practice of medicine still required some degree of direct contact with the body, and new protocols and methods had to be devised to deal with a potentially dangerous situation.

Physical examination of the disordered body had been a regular component of medical practice from ancient times, although the early procedures bore little relationship to the present day submission of the patient's body to the hands of the medical practitioner.[75] Galen's examination of the disordered body, and his use of touch, were fairly limited—feeling the pulse, taking the temperature, and palpating the body, in particular the abdomen.[76] The pulse was taken with the finger, the temperature with the palm of a hand, and palpating the body usually involved the use of both hands. Little changed in this procedure, until the Renaissance period. Other physical aspects of the examination process were also rather limited—visual inspection of the eyes, the tongue, the complexion, and the taking of samples of bodily excretions. This marked the limits of the physician's direct involvement with a disordered body.[77] Touch played a very small part in the procedures. On the other hand, surgeons had always dealt more directly with the disordered body. Touch and manipulation were essential aspects of their remedial work—resetting broken bones, dressing wounds and skin eruptions, and some of the early surgical interventions.

With the arrival of syphilis, physicians also were obliged to perform more detailed examinations of the body, and the mechanism of touch became hazardous for both surgeons and physicians despite the use of spatulas and the like to limit direct contact with a syphilitic body. Practitioners and patients found that it was now necessary to examine and touch areas of the body not normally exposed to view. This ran counter to the growing general cultural trend, and the growing reticence about sexual matters which developed in the sixteenth century.[78] The medical gaze now extended to the most intimate parts of the body, so making the patient even more vulnerable and subordinated to the power of the medical practitioner. A new patient/practitioner relationship had to be defined to cover this situation. It conferred on the practitioner the privileged right to ask intimate questions, and to examine and manipulate the body in ways which in other circumstances might constitute offensive and even sexually provocative behavior.[79]

The powerful position of the practitioner in this new relationship with the patient was further enhanced by an innovation in medical education in the sixteenth century. It was during this period that medical students began to receive clinical training within hospitals for the first time in modern Europe. This program was initiated by Giovanni da Monte, professor at the University of Padua from 1540 to 1551.[80] Da Monte taught clinical method to medical students during visits to hospitals. Patients, mainly from the lower socioeconomic levels of the community, were physically examined in public before an audience of students—touching the body to check the pulse, the temperature, and for palpation. These clinical procedures also required that the patient be interrogated to elicit information "about his customs and habits, what trade he exercises, whether he has anything specific in his nature, such as avoiding cheese or wine, etc."[81] Da Monte then proceeded to interpret his findings in front of the students.

During the physical examination, the interrogation and the subsequent discussion on his or her condition, the patient was a passive participant (apart from the need to provide answers). His or her body was subjected to public examination in a way that could only reinforce the power disparity between patient and practitioner. The patient had to surrender his or her body and, in the process, experience their bodies as devalued and vulnerable. In addition, the probing for intimate details created a new level of medical surveillance. This involved an intrusion into the intimate affairs of the patient remarkably similar to that implicit in the relationship between a priest and a parishioner.[82] In effect, the new practice— intimate probing by the practitioner and pressure on the patient to reveal all—paralleled the rituals of confession, and many of the elements of control and discipline that were associated with the role of the priest. Inevitably, these new measures further consolidated the medical practitioners' position of sovereignty with regard to the patient's disordered body.

Epidemics have always created conditions conducive to the enhancement of medical authority. The new clinical procedures discussed above represent but one example of the way in which medical power was reinforced by the syphilis epidemic. Since the disease did not disappear, but remained endemic in most communities, it became the focal point for much medical debate, and experimentation on the bodies of patients. This outcome, according to one writer, was that "never before has a disease threatening the human race produced such a degree of theoretical elaboration."[83] On another level, syphilis provided the rationale for medical surveillance and intervention on a long-term basis. This need arose, in part, from the high number of cases involved, and the propensity of syphilis to reappear in those who believed that they had been cured. It was further exacerbated by the significant numbers of people who had been so disabled by syphilis that they required considerable ongoing medical attention for the rest of their lives. Some of this latter group could never hope to be restored to health as they had suffered such impairment as loss of "the lips, the nose, eyes and the external genitals."[84] As well, many suffered such damage to the skeletal structure that they became totally crippled.[85]

To care for those severely affected by syphilis, special institutions were established, first in Italy, and then in other parts of Europe.[86] In Italy these establishments were known as hospitals for the *incurabili* (incurables), a name which reflected the prolonged period during which syphilis affected many of its victims.[87] In most instances, these hospitals were sponsored by religious charitable organizations, and had the primary objective of serving the poorer classes of the community.[88] Fear of contamination provided a strong motivation for the establishment of special hospitals for syphilitics. By isolating them from other patients, cross-infection by direct bodily contact could be minimized. Further, the revolting stench of syphilitics was perceived as a potential vector of disease transmission, not only facilitating the spread of syphilis, but perhaps causing an outbreak of plague. It was this fear that caused the authorities in Venice, in 1522, to order the compulsory confinement in hospital of all syphilitics found begging in the town.[89] Civic authorities throughout Europe soon found the hospitals for the "incurables" useful for the enforced segregation of the more marginalized in society. Simply to become infected was enough for vagrants and beggars to be segregated from mainstream society.[90] It was not necessary to have a chronic condition, the original basis for admission to hospitals for the incurables.

The responsibility for the surveillance and management of the inmates of these hospitals was entirely in the hands of medical practitioners. Not only did this reinforce medical sovereignty over the disordered bodies of patients, but it transferred to these practitioners a large measure of responsibility for social control measures instituted by civic authorities. It positioned medical practitioners even more strongly within the ranks of those who exercised power within the community.

As far as treatment regimes were concerned, the medical profession had to deal only with the physical manifestations of syphilis in the first stages of the epidemic. However, there is evidence that, as the sixteenth century progressed, many patients who were thought to have been cured, showed symptoms of the tertiary stage of the disease.[91] Typically, such patients exhibited signs of mental as well as physical deterioration.[92] Some writers of the period hinted at a connection between syphilis and the condition of "madness" which began to attract greater attention as the century progressed.[93] However, the possibility of such a link was generally discounted within the medical community.[94] It was not until the nineteenth century that the connection was finally posited and accepted.[95]

In the event, "madness" presented the medical profession with a new type of disorder which could be brought under its management. The physical and emotional manifestations of this disorder were so diverse that it lent itself to a claim by the medical profession that its diagnosis should be left to the privileged professionals. With the medical profession already well positioned by the sixteenth century to claim this prerogative, the diagnosis of "madness" became, and has since remained largely within, the province of the medical practitioner. This outcome underscored the powerful position that physicians had been able to attain. It reinforced the conclusion that their privileged position delivered to them a degree of social power that derived as much from their control over the definition of illness, as from their control of treatment regimes for the disordered body.[96]

Dangerous Bodies

The sixteenth century saw increasing concern over prostitution in the major centers of Europe.[97] This concern revolved around two main issues—an apparent marked increase in the number of women engaged in prostitution, and the arrival of syphilis.

The historical record suggests that the prevalence of prostitutes was most evident in those cities, associated with international commerce, which had a large floating population. Other cities, like Rome, attracted a large number of women who took up prostitution (or worked as high-class courtesans) because of the preponderance of males in a city frequented by so many nominally celibate members of the clergy.[98] Indeed, the scale of prostitution in Rome in the sixteenth century was such that the Pope had to rescind an order banishing prostitutes from the city because of popular revolt, and because of the damage this would do to the city's finances.[99]

Statistics on the scale of prostitution are, of course, most unreliable. First, many operated outside the law and frequently changed their names to avoid detection. Because of this they could not be accounted for accurately in any census figures. Second, the number of prostitutes plying their trade could easily be exaggerated by arbitrarily attributing this occupation to women who, ostensibly, engaged in other pursuits. According to Partner, some writers classed as prostitutes any woman not otherwise given an occupation in a census. Further, other researchers frequently labelled as prostitutes all washerwomen and women listed in a census by forename and place of origin only. In such cases there was no direct evidence that they operated as prostitutes.[100] Nevertheless, there was a general consensus among contemporary writers that prostitutes were operating in greater numbers at the end of the fifteenth and into the sixteenth centuries, and the legislative responses of authorities lend support to this conclusion. To those who made and enforced the laws, prostitutes represented the worst features of uncontrolled female sexuality which had to be brought under control for the good of the state.

The issue that caused most disquiet among civic authorities was the changing profile of the prostitution trade, long tolerated as a "necessary evil," and even legally sanctioned in many of Europe's main cities.[101] This position continued as long as authorities believed that they could maintain adequate control over the activities of prostitutes—by strict supervision, and sometimes, as in Florence for example, through direct ownership of public brothels. However, as women entered prostitution in greater numbers, they tended to operate outside the officially condoned limits, and thus attracted increasingly rigorous policing and prosecution.[102] Many young girls also turned to prostitution in a period when employ-

ment opportunities were few.[103] They operated outside the law, rely-
ing for protection on the services of an older woman, a "madam," or
female pimp—a new role in society.[104]

By the end of the fifteenth century, prostitutes were not only
seen as a challenge to the established social order, but began to be
directly linked to another threat to society. After the initial rapid
spread of syphilis, prostitutes became identified, and feared, as the
ultimate manifestation of the "Venomous Venus." They began to be
targeted as the principal means by which the disease was spread.
The part that men played in spreading syphilis through venal sex
was minimized, although some writers did address this issue. Erasmus touched on it in one of his *Colloquies*. In this homily, entitled
"The Young Man and the Harlot," Erasmus described how a young
man, a former client, persuaded his erstwhile paramour to abandon
her trade lest she become infected with syphilis:

> . . . and you make yourself a public sewer that every Tom,
> Dick and Harry—the dirty, the vile, the diseased—resorts
> to and empties his filth into! If you haven't yet caught the
> new contagion called the Spanish pox, you can't long escape
> it.[105]

This use of a "public sewer" image suggests a strong link with the
declaration of Thomas Aquinas that while prostitution was repugnant, it was like the sewers of a palace, necessary for the maintenance of normal life.[106] For Erasmus, however, this sexually intimate contact could no longer be viewed as socially tolerable. It was
now fraught with considerable danger since it promoted the transmission of the "new contagion"—syphilis. And, as he pointed out, a
man could infect a prostitute just as readily as one might contract
the disease from a woman during such a sexual encounter. Erasmus was one of few writers who openly warned that men's promiscuous behavior encouraged the spread of syphilis.

Proposals for dealing with prostitutes ranged from the punitive to the practical. That of Martin Luther was punitive in the
extreme: "If I were judge . . . I would have such venomous syphilitic
whores broken on the wheel and flayed because one cannot esti-
mate the harm such filthy whores do to young men."[107] There is no
hint of censure here for the young men who entered into such
liaisons, nor was condemnation of the male apparent in other proposals for limiting the spread of syphilis. Civic authorities initially
reacted as they had with the plague, banishing prostitutes from

cities on the basis of moral and public health considerations. Later they adopted more practical measures such as the closure of publicly-owned brothels, taverns and public bathhouses. The latter two venues fell under this edict since they were considered to be meeting places for clients and prostitutes who operated outside the law. Prostitutes were also required to undergo health checks. An example of this requirement was that proposed in 1500 by the physician Gaspare Torella for the city of Rome. He submitted to Pope Alexander VI that regular examinations of prostitutes be instituted and that those found infected should be taken to hospitals for treatment.[108] Among many other cities to adopt health checks for prostitutes, Faenza adopted the following statute in 1507:

> women desiring to devote themselves to prostitution should present themselves at the office of the Guard so that it may be known if they come from a suspect locality and if they have a healthy body; and no one of them should be permitted to serve who had the French disease.[109]

The same intensified surveillance of prostitutes is revealed in the 1552 Venetian edict which required those who were "ulcerated and afflicted with the French disease should go for treatment to the places designated for them."[110] All European authorities followed this pattern of directing prostitutes to hospitals for syphilitics for examination and treatment. They joined other marginalized groups in being subjected to compulsory segregation while under treatment.

Overall, regulatory measures were directed more at prostitutes than at other groups. Throughout Europe governments moved to stamp out prostitution. By the middle of the sixteenth century, many countries had made prostitution, and activities associated with it, a criminal offense.[111] Limiting the spread of syphilis may have provided the initial impetus, but the atmosphere of rigid morality that gathered strength during the first half of the sixteenth century provided further motivation for the elimination of prostitution. Behind these factors lay the fear that prostitutes represented the ultimate threat posed by women—they flaunted their sexuality and ignored the behavioral norms set by men in authority. Uncondoned sexuality, that is, any sexual activity outside the bounds of matrimony, was considered dangerous. It challenged and upset established order and had to be brought under control.[112] In the ultimate, prostitutes represented for men all the dangers inherent in the figure of the Poison-Damsel—seduction and gratification concealing danger, the erotic touch combined with the kiss of death.

Whereas syphilis in the hands of the medical profession had been translated from a sin to a "social scourge," prostitution became a "social problem" demanding the attention of both state and church authorities. "Penitent prostitutes" and other women and girls believed to be at peril of becoming prostitutes, were admitted or committed to institutions established for this sole purpose.[113] These institutions—sometimes labelled convents, sometimes refuges or hospitals, appeared first in Italy during the sixteenth century, and then spread to other Catholic countries of Europe. Ostensibly to aid "fallen women," they also provided a solution for the state, and for some families, to bring other women under control. Those who were deemed to be sexually deviant, and others who were simply defying male authority, could be placed under surveillance and corrective control in these refuges. Such institutions became the prototype for the various asylums and refuges that were later used to control refractory women. They also predated the establishment of those institutions that underpin Foucault's theories of panopticism in the carceral society.[114]

Toward the Modern Body

The danger of touch, already recognized to some degree from experiences with leprosy and plague, was given greater emphasis as a result of the syphilis epidemic. It was underscored by the concepts propounded by Fracastoro in his new theories of contagion. This fear of bodily contact prompted a significant reappraisal of many attitudes to the body and its functions in the late fifteenth and sixteenth centuries. As a consequence of this reappraisal, there was a resurgence of the medieval mistrust of the body, its appetites, and its weaknesses in resisting temptations. This fostered a new era of censorious morality and prudery which became most evident during the sixteenth century. Not all of this could be attributed only to responses to the syphilis epidemic. Discourses on the body had already undergone many changes as a result of experiences during the plague epidemics. In the main, these changes were confirmed and consolidated during the syphilis epidemic. However, the new disease also prompted additional changes that stemmed solely from its particular and unique characteristics.

Other circumstances were also at work in reshaping community perceptions of the body and bodily practices. Notable among these was one particular community response to events during the plague periods. It was plainly evident that there was a wide discrepancy between the standards of morality required by the church and those adopted by many of the clergy.[115] Sexual indulgence among those enjoined to be celibate, at all levels of the church, was one of the issues which drew serious criticism. Dissatisfaction with this situation, both within the church and in the community at large, intensified earlier tentative moves for reform of the church. Ultimately, pressure for strict observance of the essentials of Christian morality within the church culminated in the schismatic events of the sixteenth century. The early decades of that century witnessed the dramatic events set in train by the Catholic Reform movement and the Protestant Reformation. Then, by mid-sixteenth century, European communities felt the full force of the Counter-Reformation, a vigorous, even draconian, campaign to re-establish Papal authority over the remaining part of the church congregation. One of the most notable aspects of the Counter-Reformation was its strict and intransigent stance on moral issues. This was particularly evident in its censorious and repressive attitude toward the body and anything even suggestive of sexuality. And as the Protestant Reformation promoted similar views on such matters, communities throughout Europe entered upon an era characterized by constraint and prohibition with regard to the body and bodily practices.

The coincidence of these two factors—community responses to syphilis and the prescriptive moral ambience of the sixteenth century—reshaped all discourses on the body. One of the most enduring outcomes of this process was that the perceived association between sexuality and disease became firmly entrenched in discourses which informed both medicine and the community generally. In a wider sense, this reshaping of discourses on the body produced a range of body images that influenced the everyday lives of the whole community.

The Repudiated Body

The main physical manifestations of syphilis were so loathsome and repulsive that the image of the "vile body" was revived. Once again the body and its functions were viewed as abhorrent and offensive. In particular, the parts of the body between the waist and the knees were perceived as shameful and a source of embarrassment. This attitude is patently clear in Fracastoro's poem on syphilis when he declared that the disease was born in the "shameful parts" of the body (*enata pudentis*).[116] He continued to express this viewpoint in his later work on contagion. In this he noted that one of the names given to the new disease was *pudendagra* because it originated in those parts of the body that caused shame and embarrassment.[117] It is apparent from these observations that the sense of shame which had become associated with the disease, and with those who contracted it, had also been extended to the body's genitalia. Fracastoro's comments also indicate that this negative attitude toward the body's sexual functions had become well entrenched in medical as well as community discourse during the course of the sixteenth century.

This heightened sense of shame associated with the sexuality of the body found expression in many ways. In the main, it can be seen in measures designed to conceal those features of the body that gave evidence of its sexual nature. The church led the way on this matter, but its precepts rapidly entered into community discourse on the body and its presentation. Nudity became anathema to the church. And in the community at large it soon became viewed as something vulgar, sometimes even attracting harsh punishment.[118] The pronouncements of the Council of Trent, which formed the framework for the Counter-Reformation, required, among many other things, that all traces of sexuality and sensuality be removed from works of art. As a consequence, the image of the "body beautiful" which had been retrieved from Greek antiquity by the Renaissance no longer conformed to the new prescriptive norms. Contemporary artists, and those of the past, were criticized for depicting the human body naked instead of decently clothed.[119] Drapery, or appropriately placed foliage, was painted on the art works of the past, and statutes of naked male figures suffered amputations to destroy shameful portrayals of the body's sexuality.

Sexual identity was furthered disguised by changes to the definitions of what constituted seemly attire and decorous behavior. Erasmus, in a work published in 1530, and ostensibly addressed to young boys, revealed the extent of the prevailing preoccupation with rendering the body asexual:

> Transparent clothing has always been strongly disapproved of both for men and women, since the second function of clothing is to cover what gives offence to men's sight.

It was once held to be somewhat effeminate not to wear a belt, but nowadays nobody is at fault for this, because with the invention of underwear, shirts, and hose, the *private parts* are concealed even if the tunic fly open. Furthermore, clothing too short to conceal, when one is bending over, those parts that modesty requires to be hidden, is distasteful in every society.[120] [Our emphasis]

It would be misleading to conclude that because Erasmus prepared his guide to good manners for boys, the rules did not have wider applications. They represented normative standards to be applied throughout any civilized community, even though, in a practical sense, they could hardly be adopted by the less affluent in society. Nevertheless, they underpinned the progressive privatization of the body that commenced in the sixteenth century. With this came new standards for modesty—we would argue, prudery—which even extended to the confines of the bedroom: "Whether undressing or rising remember to be modest and see that you do not reveal yourself to another's sight what custom and nature require to be covered."[121]

The denial of the body, in the name of modesty, was to be taken even further, according to Erasmus:

To expose, save for natural reasons, the parts of the body which nature has invested with modesty ought to be far removed from the conduct of a gentleman. I will go further: when necessity compels such action, it should none the less be done with decency and modesty *even if there is no observer present.*[122] [Our emphasis]

This is a clear example of the way in which people came to view bodily functions as coarse and unbecoming rather than as instinctive and natural. They dissociated themselves from the body itself, its natural functions and, in particular, from its sexuality. Shirts, underwear, and nightgowns allowed a discreet veil to be drawn over that which was now considered to be vulgar. And sexual matters, once more burdened with a sense of guilt and shame, entered into a forbidden zone from which they have never fully re-emerged. As one writer has aptly described the denial of the body which emerged in the sixteenth century: ". . . a 'conspiracy of silence' begins to descend on sexual matters, and what might be called a 'conspiracy of invisibility' descends upon the 'private' parts of the body."[123]

The Gendered Body

Women became early targets of the new morality and the atmosphere of prudery that swept through Europe during the sixteenth century. It was a process that unfolded in parallel with the increasing tendency to lay the blame for the spread of syphilis at the feet of women. It also drew on a cluster of stereotypical images of women, long fostered by misogynist theologians and medical theorists. These images portrayed the female as an insidious temptress, bent on seducing the unsuspecting male. She was the daughter of Eve, the Poison-Damsel, the one who used her body to weaken or destroy that of the male. These perceptions were also reinforced by iconographic representations of women as inherently erotic figures. For instance, Hans Baldung, a German artist of the sixteenth century conceptualized the Fall, not as an act of disobedience, but as an erotic act. By depicting Eve as a lascivious nude figure, he represented the Fall as caused by her sexuality, reversing the traditional view that the descent into sexuality followed the Fall.[124] Such a portrayal in the sixteenth century also suggested a conflation of two critical themes—Woman as the cause of the doom of the human race, and the then current perception that women's bodies carried the threat of syphilis.

The myth of women's rampant and insatiable sexuality was supported by medical theory, which held that their inherently sexual nature demanded erotic fulfilment as a biological necessity.[125] Such exercises in self-delusion enabled men to reinforce their notions of self-esteem and self-importance by casting off their sense of weakness and projecting it on to women.[126] In this way, they constructed images of masculinity and femininity that maintained the male as the dominant force in sixteenth-century society. Men validated this position by recourse to religious discourse that defined the characteristics of strength and weakness, and stability and instability. Christian doctrines portrayed women as inherently weak, unreliable and unstable, unable to control the passions to which their bodies were subject. Men, on the other hand, were viewed as inherently capable, strong and stable, able to exercise rational control over their bodies and affairs generally. It was the corrupting influence of women's bodies, according to religious discourse, that threatened to disrupt an orderly existence. The syphilis epidemic only exacerbated men's fears. A new dimension to the threat posed by women's bodies, and the temptations they offered, had appeared.

Renewed efforts were made to counter what was perceived as the pernicious influence of women. A process of redefining or restating the bounds of socially appropriate gender roles within the community was instituted. And while it was women's sexuality that provided the initial catalyst, it was the broader implications of the relationship between gender and power that fuelled the main drive to redefine femininity.[127] The persons who felt particularly threatened by women were those who also shaped societal behavioral norms; that is, men in positions of authority—men who dominated the civic power structure, men of the medical profession, and men who claimed to speak on behalf of the church. There was also another group of men—the artists—who exercised considerable influence on public perceptions of women. During the sixteenth century, they increasingly portrayed the female body as "quintessentially grotesque," and when they sought to show the male body as grotesque, "they did so by giving it female characteristics."[128] From a perspective of self-interest, all acted to maintain the long association of masculinity with power by supporting measures that limited feminine intrusion into the male domain of authority. In addition, socially acceptable ideals of femininity were reshaped to confirm the perception that women were fragile, lacking in intellectual ability, and only interested in trivial matters.

Sixteenth century women were enjoined to act in a "feminine" way and not to mimic the ways of men. Just what this entailed became clear from Baldesar Castiglione's *Il cortegiano* (The Book of the Courtier), published in 1528.[129] In this work, which achieved wide circulation and acceptance in Europe, Castiglione declared:

> . . . above all, I hold that a woman should in no way resemble a man as regards her ways, manners, words, gestures and bearing . . . so it is well for a woman to have a certain soft and delicate tenderness, with an air of feminine sweetness in her every movement, which, in her going and staying and whatever she does, always makes her appear a woman, without any resemblance to a man.[130]

Continuing his discussion on desirable feminine attributes, Castiglione called for a woman to be thoroughly domesticated, able to take good care "of her husband's belongings and house and children," and display "the virtues belonging to a good mother."[131] Further, she should aim to be decorative "since women are permitted to pay more attention to beauty than men . . . keeping herself all the while dainty and pretty."[132] Nevertheless, a woman should not appear to be immodest or to be flaunting her femininity, particularly in dress and ornamentation, lest these actions inflame the passions of an unsuspecting man. The sumptuary laws provide ample evidence of the limits men placed on displays of femininity—women should be feminine but not provocative.[133]

As Castiglione's work became so popular throughout Europe, we can assume that it functioned as a reliable guide to contemporary perceptions of the ideal feminine qualities which men sought in women. Although the book was based on court life in northern Italy, it became a guide for people at all but the poorest levels of society. The image of the ideal woman that emerges from this contemporary commentary on social standards is that of a woman destined to be confined to the private space of the home and excluded from the public space. This latter was to remain the domain of the male in society. Although there were some notable exceptions, it is hard to conceive of many women having any life other than as a submissive, useful and ornamental adjunct to her husband.[134]

Other forces at work in society tended to reinforce this relegation to the private domestic sphere, already becoming evident toward the end of the plague period.[135] Both the Protestant Reformation and the Catholic Counter-Reformation movements accented the sanctity of marriage, and elevated the virtues of motherhood to new heights. This was emphasized even further by a mid-sixteenth century edict of the Council of Trent that all marriages were to be solemnized in a church.[136] Before that time, wedding ceremonies, if they were held at all, were frequently only civil affairs. From the sixteenth century, matrimony became the only situation in which religious authorities of any persuasion could countenance sexual relations, and then only for the purposes of procreation.

So, along with societal pressure to conceal and repudiate the body's sexuality, chastity and sexual restraint became an imperative for women, and, arguably, but a desirable objective for men. And increasingly, moral arbiters imposed on women the task of imparting to their progeny, particularly their daughters, the virtues of chastity, sobriety, and the paramount importance of feminine values.[137] This resulted in a major reshaping of social relationships between the sexes, and a concurrent redefinition of the ideals of femininity. On this point, we argue that the social construction of gendered bodies that emerged during the sixteenth century produced images of masculinity and femininity, which still inform both institutions and social practices during the twentieth century. We also see these outcomes as providing the grounds for that long-enduring image of femininity—the rather weak and ineffectual "little woman" who was beholden to, and dependent on, a masterful and wise husband.

The Civilized Body

Many of the responses to the threat of syphilis laid the foundations for major changes in patterns of social behavior that appeared during the sixteenth century. Clearly, they were not the only influences at work for change. However, many of them so changed societal attitudes to the management of the body that they became codified within the canons of socially acceptable behavior. In essence, many measures taken to protect the body from infection were translated into maxims for the presentation of the body in a seemly and decorous manner. And these guidelines not only became *de rigueur* for civilized behavior in public, but were also considered appropriate for personal conduct within the private sphere.

The danger of touch in the age of syphilis impelled people to avoid direct contact with others. This sense of fear even extended to being in close proximity to other people in confined spaces, or within crowds in a public area. Two examples of this type of response may suffice to illustrate the point. In 1529, Cardinal Wolsey was arraigned before the English Parliament to answer the charge that "knowing himself to have the foul and contagious disease of the great pox . . . [he] came daily to your grace [Henry VIII], rowing in your ear, and blowing upon your most noble grace with his perilous and infectious breath, to the marvellous danger of your highness."[138] The second example is taken from a dialogue in one of the *Colloquies* of Erasmus, and highlights contemporary perceptions of the perils of staying in a crowded inn:

But nothing seems to me more dangerous than for so many persons to breathe the same warm air, especially when their bodies are relaxed and they've eaten together and stayed in the same place a good many hours. Quite apart from the belching of garlic, the breaking of wind, the stinking breaths, many persons suffer from hidden diseases, and every disease is contagious. Undoubtedly many have the Spanish or, as some call it, French pox, though it's common in all countries.[139]

It is obvious from these passages that the dangers associated with being in close contact with other persons had become indelibly imprinted upon the community consciousness. As a consequence, the recognition that syphilis, and other diseases, could be spread by contagion prompted a demand for the preservation of personal space. These factors also led to the introduction of notions of appropriate social distance, concepts relatively unknown in the crowded confines of medieval and early Renaissance cities. These innovations formed part of the sixteenth century trend toward "privatizing" the body.

Preservation of an adequate social distance in interpersonal relationships was but one of the ways to reduce the risk of infection. Fracastoro's theories of contagion had persuaded people to accept that syphilis could be acquired in a variety of ways. As we have already seen, sexual intercourse was accepted as the main method of transmission. It caused many people to enter matrimony with some trepidation.[140] However, there was widespread recognition that other direct, and indirect, means of transmission also called for people to be vigilant in their behavior. As a result, other avoidance measures which were adopted also led to marked changes in bodily practices and social behavior. In due course, these were accepted as guidelines for the socially acceptable presentation and management of the body. Mouth to mouth contact was recognized as one of the means of transmitting syphilis, so kissing on the mouth, a gesture of affection between friends as well as lovers, declined in popularity.[141] And for the same reason, the sharing of drinking cups and eating utensils became unacceptable.[142]

Public bathhouses, as we have already noted, were closed for fear of syphilis being transmitted through contact with water already contaminated by others. Similar establishments, such as those providing steam baths, were shunned by the public if they had not been officially closed.[143] The community at large developed a growing distrust of water as a potential threat to the maintenance of good health. As a result, the use of water for bathing the body was virtually abandoned during the sixteenth century.[144] Powders and perfumes gradually took the place of water in cleansing the body, at least in the circles that could afford such preparations. In a related development, clean linen became an acceptable substitute for a clean body. These two changes in cultural practices created an even sharper division between social classes during the sixteenth century. Those who could afford clean linen, perfumes, and powder could disguise their body grime and odor, and give every outward appearance of respectability. For the remainder, their unwashed and malodorous bodies, and their filthy clothing, gave proof of their inferior status in the community. It is arguable, however, whether, when bathing was abandoned, the perfumed body was any more hygienic than that which simply went unwashed.

Other outcomes of syphilis also contributed to changes that can be seen as part of the process of "civilizing" the body. One of the readily visible effects of syphilis, one which wounded vanity rather than anything else, was a loss of hair, perceived as an important indicator of masculinity. Commenting on this outcome, Fracastoro noted that ". . . the loss of hair on the head and other places makes men ridiculous, some without beards, others without eyebrows, while others again become completely bald-headed."[145] Such an obvious indicator of a syphilitic condition was clearly a source of considerable embarrassment, and men and women took to wearing wigs to hide the effects of their ailment. Some have attributed the emergence of the widespread custom of wearing wigs, even over a full head of hair, to the problems caused by *alopecia syphilitica*.[146] Conversely, if a lack of hair marked those who suffered from syphilis, the ability to display a good growth of hair should prove that one was wholesome, as well as unambiguously masculine. Many men started to grow beards for this purpose.[147] It seems evident that the disgrace and humiliation which became associated with syphilis provided a powerful stimulus to changing many social practices, and some of the ways in which the body was presented.

These developments clearly originated in community responses to the syphilis epidemic. However, they intersected with attitudinal changes that reflected the new morally repressive perceptions of the body, and the reshaping of gender relationships. Together they produced new images of the body, and a code of behavior for its presentation, which can properly be classed as expressions of a "civilizing" process. Erasmus addressed these issues in his treatise "On Good Manners for Boys."[148] But where Castiglione's book, *Il cortegiano,* provided a guide to courtly behavior, Erasmus' work became accepted as a guide for those of the new middle classes who wished to adopt socially acceptable standards of deportment.[149] These books belonged to a new genre of manuals of deportment and good manners which emerged in the sixteenth century. Both were translated into many languages, and received with great acclaim in western Europe.[150]

Erasmus dealt with many issues—how to carry the head, control of facial expressions, how to wear the hair, the need to wash the hands after going to the toilet, and the way to clean the teeth. He discussed, with a frankness rarely encountered, the natural functions of the body. Urinating, breaking wind, and purging the bowels, he declared, should be performed in private, with decency and modesty, even if there were no observer present. Much of what Erasmus sought to impart arose from his conviction that "it is seemly for the whole man to be well ordered in mind, body, gesture, and clothing."[151] Everything he recommended was aimed at presenting the body, in appearance and deportment, as reflections of the inner quality that comes from a well-ordered mind. He insisted, however, that all of this should be accomplished with restraint and due modesty, an echo of Castiglione's call for *disinvoltura*.[152]

The history of manners is a subject that has been explored and charted in *The Civilizing Process,* the magisterial work of Norbert Elias.[153] To substantiate his conclusions, Elias drew on many contemporary accounts of social behavior commencing with the social patterns of the early Middle Ages. When he came to discuss the significant changes that occurred in the sixteenth century, he frequently cited the views expressed by Erasmus . Elias considered that the treatise of Erasmus accurately reflected the changing expectations people of the time had of each other in their interpersonal relationships. He also concluded that it was in that particular period that the thresholds of shame and embarrassment were markedly raised.[154] For Elias, these were the signs of a society in transition, of a period in which "coarse" and "vulgar" behavior were being redefined, when instinctive and natural behavior came to be judged as indelicate and unseemly. They were signs of a "civilizing" process.

Elias set out to identify the process by which by Western society became "civilized." He traced the various shifting patterns of personal conduct that were translated into normative standards for socially appropriate behavior. One of the most important factors, he suggested, was "the decisive role played in the civilizing process by a very specific change in the feelings of shame and delicacy."[155] We suggest that this was one of the elements present in community responses to syphilis. It arose from the nature of the disease, and its effects on the body. Syphilis also changed many bodily practices, involved in the presentation and management of the body. In addition, it reshaped the way in which people related to each other. All of this leads us to the conclusion that community responses to syphilis played a pivotal role in the evolution of the "civilized body" during the sixteenth century.

The Subordinated Body

By the sixteenth century, two apparently contradictory images of the body co-existed. The foundations for both of these can be linked, in the main, to responses to the major epidemics which we have investigated. First, we have the image that emerged from the Renaissance period—the body as secular and private.[156] It owed much to the gradual shift during the plague period from the perception that the body was an instrument of God to the view that the body was responsive to influences other than divine intervention. The "private" nature of the body became more evident during the epidemic of syphilis when the new notions of "civilized" behavior were also being formulated.

Overlaid on this image was that of the "subordinated body," the body constrained by limitations imposed upon it by those exercising power in the community. Our review has shown that illness experiences during each epidemic provided many opportunities for this type of intervention. In the event, they also proved to be powerful influences in the reshaping and transforming of social patterns of domination and subordination. State responses to the plague elevated intervention in the lives of citizens to a markedly increased level. It is clear also that many of the measures aimed at controlling the spread of plague soon became instruments of social control, directed particularly at the marginalized sections of society. Further, regulations introduced as temporary measures were progressively transformed into permanent legislation. State authorities rarely surrender regulatory powers over the citizenry once these are on the statute books.

A similar pattern emerged during the syphilis epidemic. In that period, however, authorities focused much of their attention on the sexuality of the body. Obviously, there were genuine health risks that demanded some regulatory controls, but one of the overriding considerations appears to have been the perception that unrestrained sexuality posed a threat to society. In particular, it was women's sexuality that was seen as the most threatening since it challenged and undermined the male-dominated power structure of the community. Women's fertility also attracted the attention of those in authority—the state, the church, and the medical profession. And although both the state and the medical profession had, in the main, unshackled themselves from the limitations of religious dogma, they made common cause with the church on issues of morality. They were convinced that women's sexuality needed to be controlled, and their fertility channelled into procreation within matrimony. All other expressions of sexuality were to be denied. The state and the medical profession have continued to act as a powerful duopoly in the community since the sixteenth century. They have claimed the right to intervene in the life of citizens in all matters pertaining to sexuality. And following the precedent set during the syphilis epidemic, this intervention has been particularly evident in areas that have been labelled "social diseases."

The image of the "subordinated body" was further reinforced by the sovereignty over the disordered body that the medical profession had secured by the sixteenth century. By that time, medical practitioners had gained an almost exclusive license to examine and treat the human body. In the process, patients had conceded to medical practitioners unfettered access to the most intimate parts of their bodies, and the right to probe deeply into their personal habits and their innermost thoughts. To further emphasize the way in which the body had become a "subordinated body" in the area of medicine, we have only to consider that the power of practitioners stemmed from the almost exclusive right they had gained to differentiate between a healthy and a disordered body. It was the medical practitioner, then as now, who affixed the labels "healthy" or "ill." It was he who determined whether or not a patient's body should be subject to his manipulation or treatment.

The Body Redefined

From the tenth to the sixteenth centuries, western Europe witnessed three major epidemics. Each left its own particular mark on the popular consciousness. Each initiated significant changes in discourses on the body, on disease and its causation, and on bodily practices. Each contributed to progressive changes to images of the body as community perceptions were modified by experiences of death and disease. We suggest that the image of the body that emerged from the sixteenth century, reflecting the various discourses current in the community, was itself multifaceted. It represented the point of intersection of the variety of images that we have just identified—the repudiated body, the gendered body, the civilized body, and the subordinated body. This composite image of the body mirrored the perceptions of a society in transition from the Middle Ages to the early Modern period. According to Elias, when people of the twentieth century look back to the way the body was portrayed and presented in the sixteenth century, they would see some aspects as being "utterly medieval," but accept others as being indicative of "exactly the way we feel today."[157] We agree—the era of the modern body had commenced.

Corporeal Catastrophe:
Bodies "Crash" and Disappear

In the countdown to a millennium, a rise in apocalyptic thinking may be inevitable.

—Susan Sontag[1]

Who says the human presence on this earth was ever sustainable? Why do we continue to believe so strongly in our competency to manage the risks we compound daily?

—Andrew McMurry[2]

The transition from one century into another often generates anxiety about the future, instigating speculation about the trajectory of social and technological "progress" and calling forth either utopian or dystopian visions. This has been evident throughout modern history.[3] In many ways, the prevailing mood at the close of the twentieth century is bleak. The coming turn-of-the-millennium is surrounded by signs and portents of disaster. Economic, social, and ecological problems have accumulated to the point where the commercial practices of the West are almost unsustainable, and the daily lives of many are blighted by crime, violence, and disease. The institutions of government, church, and medicine are no longer seen as benign, and the promise of science and medical knowledge to provide a superior standard of living, and a cure for many diseases, has not been upheld. Further, the discourse of optimism has been replaced by a trend toward cynicism and disengagement. Consequently, many dominant social institutions are no longer viewed as authoritative, relevant, and useful. Instead, the individual is in

233

retreat, in fear of contact with others and overwhelmed by a sense of dread about what the future may hold. Isolation—psychic and social quarantine—now seems for many the best strategy for survival.

In this chapter, we consider the ways in which contemporary images of the "disordered body" reflect the western cultural traditions that emerged in response to the three major epidemics we have investigated in earlier chapters. The influence of the apocalyptic tradition, and its reinterpretation in the postmodern era, are reviewed against the global problems associated with old and new diseases in the "age of the epidemic." We also examine the ways in which the traditional concepts of "contagion" have been reconfigured to form part of the postmodern lexicon, now encompassing not only "disordered bodies," but all manner of social problems, that is, disorders of the "body social." We argue that constructs of Otherness follow a similar pattern of redefinition, now extending beyond categories of human "difference" to embrace biomedical constructs of viruses as "foreign," as "intruders" into the biological self. We further argue that postmodern constructs of the "disordered" or diseased body, and bodily practices that stem from these constructs, are the outcome of the atmosphere of uncertainty and disengagement which characterizes the end of the twentieth century. They also reflect a tension between a hedonistic focus on the human body as "project," and the deconstruction of the corporeal implicit in our engagement with the cyber age.

Our Imminent Doom

Traditional understandings of apocalypse conceptualize this as a religious event of great moment: a cleaving of good and evil, and true and false. Apocalyptic events supposedly result in the expulsion of the evil and the false, and their obliteration in a "second death" (Book of Revelations).[4] As McMurry observes, these conventional interpretations have drawn upon "millennial expectations, notions of inexorable decline, the implicit moral bankruptcy of humankind since Adam and Eve, or linear or cyclical visions of history."[5] As we have already seen in earlier chapters, soothsayers of doom are not just a twentieth-century phenomenon. Indeed, the production of doom-laden prophecies increases at the ends of centuries, and of millennia.

The Center for Millennial Studies divides the reactions to the millennium into two types: those which predict momentous change (described as Roosters); and those which predict minimal change (known as Owls).[6] Not surprisingly, there are many more Roosters than Owls.[7] Roosters include religious groups which claim that a cataclysm is upon us, and environmental groups which predict natural disasters as a result of human intervention into complex ecosystems. Of course, Roosters also include philosophers and scientists who evince ideas of significant change. The philosopher, John Leslie, recently published a book entitled *The End of the World*, in which he argues that the probability of human extinction is relatively high.[8] Leslie builds on the Doomsday Argument first put forward by the mathematician, Brandon Carter, and elaborated upon by the astrophysicist, J. Richard Gott. Leslie points out that 99.9 percent of all of the species that have ever lived are now extinct—suggesting that *species* can be regarded as mortal. Leslie asks: why should humans be any different?

However, the traditional apocalyptic script, based on biblical exegesis, has been rewritten in modern times. While the Four Horsemen of the Apocalypse—War, Famine, Pestilence and Death—are still with us, we can detect shifts away from the prior conceptions of cataclysm. For some, the apocalypse of the mass-mediated postmodern age is now mere simulation. They suggest that the real and the simulated have fused, that the hyperreal has been born, and that the apocalyptic hermeneutic itself has vanished.[9] Sontag notes:

> Apocalypse is now a long-running serial. . . . Apocalypse has become an event that is happening and not happening . . .

> Reality has bifurcated, into the real thing and an alternative version of it, twice over. There is the event and its image. And there is the event and its projection.[10]

There is also the secularization of apocalypse: the calculus of disaster applied to lived experience. There is a desire, acknowledged in film and other entertainment media, to contemplate the end of the world. Catastrophe, in this context, is viewed as an exciting, and perhaps compelling, prospect leading to the destruction of matter and the production of meaning. Apocalypse, says Joe Sartelle can be "exhilarating as well as dreadful."[11] Further, Sartelle asks: "What does it say about the United States as a national culture that we have come to take such pleasure in imaging our own annihilation, over and over in such varied and compelling forms?" There is, for example, a subcultural movement that embraces all that is rejected or repressed—in short, all that is abject. While it is marginal, this movement taps the nerve of a wider cultural sensibility in contemporary America. This alternative subculture has been labeled "apocalyptic" because it is fascinated by all the signs of societal collapse—the excessive, the deviant, and the bizarre. One book that captures the flavor and feel of this movement is Adam Parfrey's *Apocalypse Culture*.[12]

The last fifty years of the twentieth century have been witness to the threat, and subsequent avoidance, of nuclear apocalypse. Now, humanity seems to be defeated not by its own weapons but by the failure of its institutions and the degradation of the social and natural environment. And catastrophe still remains a seductive possibility.

Sexual Apocalypse

The anxieties and fears about millennial change, or the movement from one century into another, may be condensed into specific bodily conditions. The physical aberrations implied in disease may symbolize the dystopian mood pervading society at this time. Just such a social upheaval characterized the end of the fifteenth and the beginning of the sixteenth centuries. As we noted in the previous chapter, the arrival in western Europe of the syphilis epidemic created widespread concern and anxiety at every level of society. And much later, at another turn-of-the century, syphilis again became a significant social issue.

Elaine Showalter argues that the closing decades of the nineteenth century were typified by syphilis—a disease perceived as a masculine affliction, a vulgar and hideous condition that exposed the male body to ridicule and revulsion.[13] The prostitute was construed as the main danger to the physical integrity of the male body. Her "putrid" body was viewed as a vector of contagion and an agent of corruption. The prostitute's body, as a foul and polluted vessel, threatened the survival of individual men.[14] This discourse of pollution was also applied to other women, rendering relations between the sexes tense and sometimes hostile.

At the close of the twentieth century, it is HIV/AIDS, among other viral conditions, that characterizes the prevailing mood. HIV/AIDS has delivered us again into an era of "venereal peril."[15]

Yet, unlike syphilis, it is a public issue politicized by those affected by it. HIV/AIDS has engendered a culture of activism, of resistance to medical stereotyping and political neglect. Also, the representation of HIV/AIDS in the media and in medical discourse has been the site of prolonged and bitter struggle.

HIV/AIDS also differs from syphilis in other important ways. Arguably, HIV/AIDS has introduced a new quality into twentieth-century thought—a "viral consciousness." Viruses are now characterized as "a menace in waiting, as mutable, as furtive, as biologically innovative."[16] HIV/AIDS is governed by twin metaphors: the idea of the virus *invading* the individual body; and the idea of the virus *polluting* the body of another as it is transmitted. The body's functions are subverted by the unwanted intrusion of the virus, yet the "viral enemy" is forever within, irrespective of whether or not the individual displays the signs of invasion. HIV/AIDS connotes disgust because it is perceived, like leprosy and syphilis, as an *organic* disease, implying mutation, decomposition, and decay. This threat to identity and to sexual difference may move beyond the individual body and may engulf society, undermining the social and economic order.

Showalter notes that both syphilis and HIV/AIDS are "symbolic sexual diseases that have taken on apocalyptic dimensions and have been interpreted as signalling the end of the world."[17] Both illnesses have occupied similar ideological niches at the ends of the nineteenth and twentieth centuries.

The Age of the Epidemic

The panic inspired by the apocalyptic threat of HIV/AIDS has, according to Linda Singer, radically altered the social and political landscape.[18] We are now living in the "age of the epidemic." Central to this ethos is the "logic of contagion." Contagion now shapes and guides social relationships: "communication has become communicability: access is now figured as an occasion for transmission and contagion."[19] In addition, the "logic of contagion," and its associated anxiety and dread, set the scene for the extended reach of the regulatory apparatus in society—that exercised by the state, and that appropriated to itself by the medical profession.

In the "age of the epidemic," there is a continual stimulation of anxious affect, sparking a "crisis of contagion" that radiates across many arenas of social life, justifying and necessitating a regulatory response to these new "contagious" social problems.[20] These problems are invariably the kind of intractable social difficulties that cause offense to the economic or political elites. The attribution of the term "epidemic" to the problem legitimizes the introduction of more intrusive and more punitive measures. Consequently, we have "epidemics" of drug abuse and youth violence. In fact, we can find examples of the literalization of the terms "epidemic" and "contagion" in the literature on social problems, implying that the problematic individuals are in some way "diseased." One example of the metaphoric use of the term "contagious" is the following :

> Violence is contagious. . . . It is clustered in space; it esca-
> lates over time; it spreads from one person to another. The
> evidence for this is consistent, persuasive, and vast.[21]

However, we can also see how the trope of contagion has been taken up elsewhere with great enthusiasm. Aaron Lynch has recently published a book entitled *Thought Contagion, How Belief Spreads Through Society*.[22] In this work, Lynch argues that the biological concept, "meme," can be applied to the explanation of the dissemination of particular patterns of belief throughout society. Taken from the work of the evolutionary biologist, Richard Dawkins, the concept "meme" is broadened to include social behavior. Lynch explores the idea of "thought contagion"; he says, "Like a software virus in a computer network or a physical virus in a city, thought contagions proliferate by effectively 'programming' for their own retransmission."[23] Lynch enumerates the mechanisms for this "retransmission"; each of these involves a "carrier" or host who serves to increase the size of the population "infected" with the belief in question.

In this instance, we have an illustration of the ascendancy of contagion—of the use of this concept as a theoretical explanation for social phenomena. However, when the epithet "epidemic" is applied to an issue or problem, a different dynamic is at work. Firstly, it opens up the possibilities for intervention. For example, there has been an intensification of surveillance and regulation within sites linked to erotic or social danger since the advent of HIV/AIDS.[24] We have witnessed the strengthening of legal controls over sex work, gay activity, and intravenous drug use. The bodies of these individuals have become "fetishized as vials of contagion and death."[25] These new forms of power redefine the nature and uses of pleasure, and produce and limit a variety of deviant behaviors. Further, bodies in general are now inserted within this proliferative "logic of contagion," and cultural knowledge about corporeality responds to this new epistemic frame by extending the "logic of contagion" throughout the social field. As Singer notes: "At this juncture, the boundaries of bodies have become liminally engaged by the culture of simulations, the terrains of representations and images, disciplines and practices, gestures, ideologies and institutions."[26]

Women's bodies, in particular, have been reinscribed with a new catalogue of dangers, and have been subjected to a novel array of regulatory prescriptions and practices. We can note that pregnancy, as a reproductive spectacle, has attracted significant attention in recent years.[27] The hegemony of the "logic of contagion" has multiplied and skewed the meanings attached to pregnancy. There has been an increased emphasis placed on a monogamous, heterosexual, and domesticated sexuality. Yet, at the same time, the introduction of innovative reproductive technologies has destablized the dominant constructions of parenthood and kinship. Pregnancy is now firmly located within the "cultural narratives of surveillance," and both law and social practice look over women's shoulders.[28] Women's bodies are fragmented into specific parts and functions, each one requiring vigilant monitoring. This naturalizes the interventions that are defined as vital in the "age of the epidemic."

"Hystories": Epidemics of Hysteria
in *Fin de Siècle* Culture

Elaine Showalter, the literary critic and historian of medicine, has developed a bold thesis in her recent controversial book, *Hystories*.[29] Showalter suggests that western society is afflicted by a wide range of hysterical syndromes that are circulating in a climate of millennial angst.[30] Showalter claims that mass hysteria is now evident in western cultures. This takes the form of syndromes, or mini-epidemics, such as chronic fatigue syndrome, Gulf War syndrome, multiple personality disorder, recovered memories syndrome, alien abductions, and ritual abuse syndrome. These conditions, according to Showalter, are the analogue of the hysterical conditions reported last century.

Showalter believes hysteria eventuates "when someone expresses stress, powerlessness, and unhappiness through physical or sensory symptoms which have no clinical explanation."[31] She concedes that those who suffer from the conditions listed above do experience psychological pain or discomfort. However, she asserts that the causes of such conditions are largely cultural:

> Nothing could be a better breeding ground for hysteria than the interaction between 1990s millennial panic, new psychotherapies, religious fundamentalism, and American political paranoia. And with our mass media, telecommunications, and e-mail, we've never had a better means of spreading hysteria to epidemic proportions.[32]

Showalter asserts that, in order for a hysterical epidemic to emerge, the following must be in place: a medical practitioner or other authorized knower, who defines, names, and publicizes a disorder; a vulnerable individual reporting vague symptoms, who learns of the disorder and begins to believe she is suffering from it; and a cultural environment, complete with self-help books, confessional television shows, and the Internet, to spread information about the new disorder and that feed the cycle of its growth.

Speaking of the 'X-Filing' of western culture at the close of the century and the millennium, Showalter says:

> Alien abduction myths are hysteria exaggerated to the highest level. While most Americans find it silly, there are Harvard professors and best-selling writers who are dedicating their lives to convincing people that alien abduction is real. People who claim to be abductees suffer from genuine conflicts that need to be treated seriously and psychologically. Perhaps women are seeking external explanations for their own sexual dreams, unconscious fantasies, and sensations, in a culture that still makes it difficult for women to accept their sexuality. Or maybe we're witnessing the birth of a folk religion, with aliens functioning much like the angels who have sprouted all over the country as the millennium approaches. We have to look not to invisible alien invaders but inside our own psyche to face the hidden anxieties and myths.[33]

Elaine Showalter argues that hysteria, in its multiple contemporary cultural manifestations, is highly 'contagious'. Yet, hysteria, according to Showalter, is primarily a response to the conundrums of subjectivity, gender, and social communication that confront us at the end of the twentieth century.

Medusa's Revenge

Everybody knows that pestilences have a way of recurring in the world.

—Albert Camus[34]

London: A public health expert warned yesterday that the human race was vulnerable to the emergence of a catastrophic new plague that could kill millions world wide.

—*The Weekend Australian*[35]

Two books, published in 1994, stirred both controversy and fear in the United States and beyond. Richard Preston's *The Hot Zone* was a bio-thriller which told the story of the entry, into the U.S. in 1989, of the virulent and dangerous Ebola virus.[36] The virus had been carried in the bodies of monkeys imported from the Philippines; the primates were housed in a facility located near a densely populated area of Washington D.C. The book recounts, in the vivid prose typical of popular crime fiction, the frantic struggle of scientists and military personnel associated with the Centers for Disease Control (CDC) and the United States Army Medical Research Institute of Infectious Diseases (USAMRID) to detect, control, and eradicate the source of the infection.

The book begins with a quotation from the Book of Revelation (Apocalypse): "And the second angel poured his vial upon the sea, and it became as the blood of a dead man." The book describes, in horrific detail, the destruction of the human body by the Ebola virus. It tells how organs and tissue liquefy, and how the skin rips open and hemorrhagic blood pours out. It documents how the virus kills a massive amount of bodily tissue while the host is still alive. The effects of the virus transform "virtually every part of the body into a digested slime."[37] Further, every opening in the body bleeds, yet the blood does not clot even as it gushes out of the body. Not surprisingly, the victims of the Ebola virus are known as "bleeders."[38] The body becomes a "city under siege" before it finally "crashes and bleeds out." The Ebola virus is variously labelled by the author as "a monstrous life form" and as "the replicative Other."[39]

The *Hot Zone* is replete with colorful imagery. For example, a cluster of related viruses is coded female—the "three filovirus sisters" (Marburg, Ebola Zaire, and Ebola Sudan) are described as both " devastating and promiscuous."[40] Part of predatory Nature, these viruses are also characterized as sexually threatening. Marburg apparently possesses a "special affinity for the testicles and the eyes." Moreover, reminiscent of the science fiction film, *Alien*, a team of scientists comes upon the "red chamber of the *virus queen* at the end of the Earth."[41] [Our emphasis]

The language of metaphor further extends the relationship between viruses and femaleness: both Marburg and Ebola become snake-like before the eyes of the awed scientists.[42] Karl Johnson, the scientist who discovered the Ebola virus at the CDC, described the virus particle as a "waving confrontational cobra."[43] Preston pushes this observation further; he writes:

> He saw the virus particles shaped like snakes. . . . They were white cobras tangled among themselves, like the hair of Medusa. They were the face of Nature herself, the obscene goddess revealed naked.[44]

The effects of these viruses upon the body, documented so vividly in *The Hot Zone,* resonate with dominant cultural fears about the disappearance of difference, the collapse of the binary oppositions of gender. Arguably, the reduction of the body's interior into a visceral stew, encased in a porous membrane, and leaking vast quantities of blood and tissue, may provoke a fear of feminization. It may do violence to the culturally-sanctioned notion of the controlled and ordered male body, uncontaminated by feminine similarity or association.

It may also be associated with an apocalyptic vision of the future. In *The Hot Zone*, Richard Preston claims that, as a consequence of the environmental damage wrought by humans, "Earth is mounting an immune response against the human species. It is beginning to react to the human parasite, the flooding infection of people."[45]

This apocalyptic message is represented in many sites within popular culture. Mass-market entertainment echoes these ideas about vengeful Nature in films such as *Not of This Earth* (1995).[46] In this improbable drama, an alien (played by Michael York) has arrived on Earth to find a cure for the plague affecting the beings of his distant planet. The alien—who is impersonating a human being—asks a nurse in his employ:

> Auto-immune diseases: they are new to this world, yes? And they come at a time when billions of breeding humans

are despoiling this world of all other forms of life. So, is it possible, then, that this world sees human beings like you— and me—as a virus destroying its body so that it fights back with these new fatal diseases, its vaccine against the human virus.

The trope of the protective and benign Mother Earth has been displaced, to a large extent, by the concept of Earth (or Nature) as a dangerous, and perhaps frightening, entity. Laurie Garrett, the author of *The Coming Plague*, the second influential book published in 1994, argues that pathogenic microbes are emerging as a result of the destruction of natural ecosystems, the decline of species diversity on land and in the ocean, and the rise of megacities.[47] According to Garrett, global warming will continue to provide opportunities for greater infectivity by insect-borne diseases. The movement of viruses between species will also increase, and microbes will become more virulent if the host population is numerous and, hence, expendable. "The history of our time will be marked by recurrent eruptions of newly discovered diseases," says Garrett.[48]

Popular culture is brimming with representations of "the viral condition."[49] The film, *Outbreak* (1995), starring Dustin Hoffman and loosely based on Preston's *The Hot Zone*, showcased the heroic endeavors of scientists in the face of "the greatest medical crisis in history."[50] The press advertisement for the film invited the audience to "try to remain calm" while they contemplated the visage of a fanged primate who carries "a deadly virus." Poised to attack, the poisonous monkey conjures up fears of the alien, strange Other; it is menacing Nature incarnate. In this context, the masculine bravado displayed by the lead scientist in *Outbreak* is both understandable and commendable. An objective detachment from both behavior and process becomes a strategy not just of containment and control, but also of rationalization and denial. Without a hint of irony, Garrett refers to the real-life scientists who study epidemic disease as "infectious disease 'cowboys'."[51] It is as if these scientist-heroes are operating at the edges of a new frontier.

This masculinized struggle for survival against the malicious interventions of nature is also outlined in vivid detail in the sequel to *The Hot Zone—The Cobra Event*.[52] In this book, Richard Preston describes a secret, counter-terrorist operation involving a genetically-engineered and highly contagious virus released in New York by a disgruntled scientist. Significantly, Preston labels this the *cobra* virus: the deployment of bio-weapons is referred to as "black" biology.

Like Ebola and her sister viruses, cobra plunders the body of its host, causing massive bleeding, violent seizures, and bodily disintegration. The viral amplification process culminates in self-cannibalization. The horror of corporeal catastrophe fills the pages of the text as the scientists from the Centers for Disease Control try to identify and track the spread of the virus.

This representation of viral invasion and bodily collapse has its parallel in real-life events. The United States' Department of Defense is currently spending $US50 million to provide crisis training for police, fire, medical, and ambulance workers in the event of a chemical or biological weapons attack (a CBW event). Specific cities are preparing for the possibility of a nuclear, chemical, or biological weapons attack. New York City began this training in earnest in 1998. U.S. President, Bill Clinton, recently announced a comprehensive strategy to strengthen U.S. defenses against terrorist attacks during the twenty-first century—including attacks on infrastructure, computer networks, and through the use of biological weapons. With regard to the latter, Clinton announced that the entire armed services will be inoculated against anthrax, and that medicines and vaccines to fight biological attacks, will be stockpiled.

It is now widely accepted that a major bio-warfare terrorist attack cannot be prevented and that thorough preparation and training are our only defense. Jeffrey D. Simon notes: "By improving our readiness to respond to biological terrorism, many lives can be saved and terrorists denied their goal of creating panic and crisis throughout the country."[53] The U.S. President recently declared that it is necessary to "approach these twenty-first century threats with the same rigor and determination we applied to the toughest security challenges of this century."[54]

Out There: The Epidemic Threat

How accurate are the mass-market representations of disease and social upheaval? There is certainly a tendency in these cinematic or text-based bio-thrillers to focus on the most deadly and the most fearful epidemic threats. The swiftness with which these depicted viruses strike, and the fatal consequences of their presence, charges the narrative with a high level of suspense. The audience experiences the vicarious thrill of the imagined brush with bodily catastrophe while savoring the victory of escape or rescue from a painful demise. The emotional rollercoaster ride offered by these fictional or "true-life" representations both distorts and obscures the contemporary reality of disease morbidity and mortality. Yet, these representations capture the tangible mood of anxiety and concern evinced by many scientists and public health organizations.

We know, for example, that infectious disease is the leading cause of death worldwide.[55] Of the 52 million deaths recorded by the World Health Organization (WHO) in 1995, 17 million were reportedly caused by infectious diseases.[56] Further, the WHO estimates that up to half of the world's population is at risk of contracting, and perhaps dying from, endemic diseases. The infectious diseases that killed the most people in 1995 were: acute lower respiratory infections (4.4 million); diarrheal diseases (3.1 million); tuberculosis (3.1 million); malaria (2.1 million); Hepatitis B (1.1 million); and HIV/AIDS (approximately one million). Especially worrisome episodes in 1995 included epidemics of dengue fever (including dengue hemorrhagic fever), and epidemics of cholera, yellow fever, diptheria, and Ebola. The latter occurred in Zaire and killed about eighty percent of sufferers.[57]

Tuberculosis, once a disease almost under control, is now making a deadly return, particulary in so-called developed nations. Moreover, drug-resistant strains of tuberculosis, malaria, cholera, diarrhea, and pneumonia are appearing. Many of the previously powerful antibiotic agents are ineffective in the treatment of these new strains. Lack of restraint in the utilization of these drugs by medical and hospital staff has greatly increased bacterial resistance to antibiotics. The WHO has declared: "In the race for supremacy, microbes are sprinting ahead."[58]

It was Joshua Lederburg who remarked that viruses are our main competitor for supremacy on Earth.[59] There is a ring of truth to this: there have been many new viruses identified in the last twenty years.[60] In addition, we are now contending with "emerging" infectious diseases.[61] Many social, political, economic, and environmental factors are responsible for the appearance and dissemination of infectious diseases. These include: human demographics and human behavior; ecological intervention; technological change and development; reductions in the public health system and breakdowns in public health measures.[62] Population growth, rapid urbanization, overcrowded and unhygienic living conditions, war or civil conflict, mass movement of people, deforestation and reforestation, agricultural practices including the building of dams, globalization of the food industry, international air travel, and the contraction of funding for public health programs are all significant determinants of the emergence and spread of infectious diseases.

Morse maintains that "this relentless march of microbes" is accelerating because "the conditions of modern life ensure that the factors responsible for disease emergence are more prevalent than ever before."[63] Microbiologist Alison Jacobson sounds an even starker warning:

> Within the last decade there has been an ever increasing awareness of the Darwinian struggle with which the human species is engaged. Microbial and viral predators abound, in no less abundance than before, and still present a constant threat to individual survival as well as to the success of the population at large. . . . The last two years have been accented by several striking episodes of disease emergence, such as multi-drug resistant tuberculosis, acute coccal infections, the rodent-borne pneumonic hantavirus in the United States. . . . Against the newer threats is a perpetual backdrop of a multiplicity of infections, which cycle throughout their ecological niches and are encountering opportunities in our modern world to spread with a frightening vigour.[64]

The Director-General of the World Health Organization has simply said: "We are standing on the brink of a global crisis in infectious diseases."[65]

Differentia: Immunology and Alterity

> Closed off, guarded against infection, beware the surface; any exchange of fluid, that is, any disclosure of an open, leaking body, threatens.
>
> —Allison Fraiberg[66]

> Under the auspices of bio-power, biological knowledge increasingly presents itself as the ground of self-realisation and governance in relation to life in general.
>
> —Adrian Mackenzie[67]

Susan Sontag maintains that it is with the development of medical technologies, which revealed the disease-causing agents to the human eye, that we can begin to detect the appearance of the military metaphors of anatomy and treatment.[68] A new level of scrutiny was implied in the early accounts of cellular pathology, and an accompanying visualization of this biological derangement was made possible by the invention of the microscope. It is now commonplace to encounter conceptions of the functioning of the human body, and medical interventions, in terms of this militaristic imagery. The immunologist, John Dwyer, for example, provides the following popular account of the immune system in his book *The Body at War* [sic]:

> Let's imagine that we are examining a particular security system that has been designed for an ultra-important, indeed ultra-secret, industrial complex. . . .
>
> If an individual brought in for an identity check is recognised as an intruder, he is indeed in a lot of trouble . . .
>
> the Generals will have called in and despatched may highly trained soldiers that can recognise this particular type of intruder. . . .
>
> Execution, clean and simple, in a security station designed for the purpose is the ideal.[69]

In this imaginary account, the biological components of the human immune system are described as a "sophisticated, integrated army."[70] Of course, such descriptions simply expose to public view the structures of metaphoric thought which underlie much current biomedical discourse.

This discourse about anatomy and functioning, in which militaristic imagery dominates contemporary constructions, may serve as a consolatory device. The struggle between good and evil, and inside and outside, so clearly articulated in Dwyer's popular account, is also about the erection of boundaries between self and Other. We should note, then, that the immune system, in its quest to identify and expel or exterminate unwanted "intruders," is dedicated to recognizing the essential characteristics of the biological self. According to John Dwyer, the "biological miracle of immunity" is the development of "a way of knowing the differences between the millions of components that make up our own special body (self) and anything else (non-self)."[71] In most instances, these "non-self" phenomena are viewed as dangerous to "self"; they include "those viruses, fungi, bacteria and parasites that invade and will kill us if we do not kill them."[72]

Donna Haraway argues that this biomedical discourse, in which the immune system is understood to be an internal military machine, maps out the boundaries around self—associated with all that is *normal*—and Other—associated with all that is *pathological*.[73] However, this is not necessarily a simple or straightforward exercise. As Mackenzie states:

> The corporeal negotiations of material differences carried by the immune system intimately determine what is properly one's own body; they regulate a body open to and capable of responding to an indefinite variety of "others"—living, non-living, or on the borderline between the living and the dead (e.g. viruses) . . . [but] there is no single borderline between what is foreign and what is recognized as belonging, no simple dividing line between drug and toxin, nourishment and parasite.[74]

Yet, the aggressive defense of the organism's biological integrity persists: the central dilemma of modern immunological thinking focuses upon the discrimination between what is "self" and what is "foreign."[75] It also attends to the danger of the disintegration of these boundaries—the spectre of non-recognition or non-defeat, of mergence, looms large. Haraway refers to the "constant danger" posed to organisms that live in the exotic locations of "jungle" or "at the bottom of the sea" of "losing their individuality by fusion."[76] Of course, Haraway is correct in assuming that women, in this discursive environment, are also in danger of losing their individuality. Women possess an ambiguous status as individuated beings; this is especially pronounced during pregnancy. Women's bounded individuality is challenged by the presence of the developing fetus, and it is compromised at the point of birth.

This biomedical discourse of immunology is a catalyst to the reconfiguring of the body in the postmodern age. In contrast to the constructions of the body which held sway in the nineteenth century, we live today with a "postmodern immune-system mediated body," a body which is "a biotechnological communications system."[77] Bodies have become cyborgs or "cybernetic organisms" comprised of "hybrid techno-organic embodiment and textuality."[78] The cyborg is a blend of metaphor, machine, text, and body.

What does this imply for our understandings of disease? In this new perspective on corporeality, disease is viewed as a disturbance of communications, a breakdown in data recognition or data management resulting from the transgression of the boundaries of the biological self. Contrastively, in the imagined terrain of the healthy body, the essential characteristics of self are clearly and unequivocally marked off from non-self. At the molecular and cellular level, the biological self is viewed as singular, homogeneous, integrated. The healthy, biological self continues to replicate these characteristics. When microbial "enemies"—bacteria, fungi, parasites, and viruses—enter the sacrosanct space of the biological self, they introduce elements of disorder—heterogeneity, plurality, and variability. The failure of the warrior-like immune system to recognize the "intruders," or the inability of the system to "defeat" them, produces the state of chaotic communications which characterizes infectious disease.

The Body Disappears?

> The rhetoric of clean bodily fluids is really about the disappearance of the body into the detritus of *toxic bodies, fractal subjectivity, cultural dyslexia, and the pharmakon* as the terror of simulacra in the postmodern condition.
>
> —Arthur Kroker, Marilouise Kroker, David Cook[79]

Today, we are witness to the retreat of the flesh, and the continual replacement of *matter* by *machine*. We live in the age of the technologized body, in which the body is being redesigned by medicine to assume a greater range of machine-like qualities or functions, and in which machines themselves are coming to resemble the human body more closely. Bionic bodies, comprised of manufactured "spare parts," are now a reality; surgery conducted via a computerized screen is now firmly on the agenda. For example, it is widely predicted that surgery in which a medical practitioner manipulates instruments, controlled by a technological device and projected into a three-dimensional computer image, will shortly be available.

This blend of computer technology, fiber-optic communications and high-tech medical diagnostics heralds the arrival of the "digital surgeon." Such developments radically extend the authorized power of the medical profession, and enhance its capacity to shape contemporary perceptions of health, illness, and disease. This is manifest in a number of different sites. By extending the spatial and geographical reach of the surgeon, operations can be conducted on patients at a great distance. Biomedical data can be transmitted quickly and efficiently and, of course, surgeons can acquire new skills and techniques through virtual technologies.

The human body has already been digitized for medical practice. The Visible Human Project, funded by the National Library of Medicine in the U.S., was initiated in 1991. Its aim was to develop a digital database of the complete human male and female cadavers. The long-term goal of the Visible Human Project is "to produce a system of knowledge structures which will transparently link visual knowledge forms to symbolic knowledge formats."[80] Reminiscent of the earlier urge to peer inside the body through dissection, this project has utilized computer imaging technologies to produce highly detailed "digital portraits" of both a male and a female body. The male selected for digitization was a 39-year-old convicted felon, Joseph Paul Jernigan. Jernigan was executed in August 1993, by lethal injection.

The process of preparing Jernigan's body for digitization was detailed and exhaustive. First, the cadaver was sectioned into quarters, and then sliced into almost two thousand strips. The strips were photographed, scanned using X-ray Computer Tomography, and imaged using Magnetic Resonance imaging techniques. Once they were stored digitally, the images were stacked one on top of the other in layers. With the completion of the process, the highly visible "digital man" was born.

In November 1995, the digitized image of a female cadaver was made available. The woman chosen for this exercise was an anonymous patient who died at 59 years from a heart attack. Unlike the Visible Man who was visualized at resolutions of one millimeter in three dimensions, the Visible Woman was visualized at resolutions three times more detailed. The Visible Woman consists of over 5000 cross-sectioned digital images and full-body radiographic images. Needless to say, the real-life bodies of both the Visible Man and the Visible Woman were destroyed in this process of converting matter into digital data.

Commercial opportunities abound in the wake of the Visible Human Project. Products available include the Digital Humans CD-ROM from Multimedia Medical Systems, and the Dissectible Human CD-ROM and printed atlases from Engineering Animation Inc. and Mosby.[81] (U.S. National Library of Medicine, 1996). Multimedia Medical Systems (MMS) has dedicated a website to the Digital Humans CD-ROM. On the Digital Humans CD-ROM home-page, MMS vigorously promotes the virtues of their product in the language of opportunistic hard-sell:

> Do not attempt to adjust your monitor! . . .
>
> Using the enclosed 3D glasses, the anatomy can be exam-ined by interactively rotating parts of the body while the glasses bring the structures to life.[82]

Perhaps not surprisingly, there have been applications to develop entertainment media based on the Visible Human Project. One of these is a computer game modelled on the film *Fantastic Voyage* in which the participants can travel through the human body in a micro-spacecraft. On a more serious note, it is possible to download a computer program, called the Visible Human Explorer (VHE), which affords a cyber-tour of the digitized body. It is also possible for a computer user to create his or her own "visible man" or "visible woman" by employing the Visualization Toolkit devel-oped by the Duke University Medical Center.[83]

For the first time, it is now possible to electronically interact with a computerized representation of the human body. It is possi-ble to inspect, dissect, rotate, reassemble, or animate any part of the digitized bodies. Further, it is now possible to "see" the simu-lated structures of the human body in more detail than ever before. Manufacturers of "spare parts" now have an accurate model of human anatomy on which to base their designs. Medical students can now observe and dissect the body without exposing themselves to the nauseating presence of a cadaver. Medical researchers can investigate the traumatic impact of car crashes or can simulate dis-ease processes. And surgeons can explore new surgical techniques without risking the lives of patients. Here, the human body is devoid of its capacity to horrify, to pollute, or to contaminate. The digitized body does not spill blood or other bodily fluids; nor does it threaten the well-being of other bodies. Safely stored as digital data, this body is closed and clean—an ordered body presented in a predictable and controllable format.

These medical maneuvers have been accompanied by a compat-ible cultural trend: the dematerialization of aspects of human expe-rience and human interaction. The "electronic frontier," for example, is often conceptualized as a "body-free environment"—a "place of escape from the corporeal embodiment of gender and race."[84] Virtual reality provides a hyperreal environment in which consciousness is mapped onto a constructed self.[85] The text-based virtual environment of the MUD (or Multi User Dimension of Dungeon), for example, is an imagined community populated by constructed or invented characters.[86] In MUDs, gender is a malleable construct. McRae reports that in LambdaMOO, players can adopt the Spivak gender which allows players to subvert the restrictions of gendered normativity. In this environment, gender is self-selected. And bodies, transformed into patterns of information, become "flickering signifiers, characterized by their tendency toward unexpected metamorphoses, attenuations, and dispersions."[87] Yet sexualized violence is scripted into a proportion of the interactions that occur in MUDs.[88] And identity deception of all kinds is commonplace on the Internet, with cross-gender representation being the most frequent occurrence.[89]

Indeed, fantasies about a new relationship to embodiment are now woven throughout both popular and elite culture. The science fiction writer, Pat Cadigan, has written about a future world in which a male character abandons his body and escapes into the circuitry of the Internet. The character exists only as consciousness, separate from and independent of his body. The performance artist, Stelarc, repudiates corporeality, suggesting that the body is obsolete: "The body is neither a very efficient nor very durable structure. It malfunctions often and fatigues quickly; its performance is determined by its age. It is susceptible to disease."[90] Confronted by the obsolescence of the body, Stelarc recommends that it be redesigned. The body should be emptied out, hardened, and dehydrated: "the hollow body would be a better host for technological components." Stelarc envisions a future in which the body is wired directly into the Internet, and in which the consciousness "attached" to that body could be shared. Hence, the Net-connected body could be manipulated and controlled by another from a great distance: "a body that quivers and oscillates to the ebb and flow of Net activity. . . . A body whose proprioception responds not to its internal nervous system but to the external stimulation of globally connected computer networks." This is a vision not dissimilar to Deleuze and Guattari's concept of the Body-Without-Organs, the discursive space in which biology and social practices collide.[91]

Speaking of Stelarc's 1995 performance, entitled Fractal Flesh, Brian Massumi notes:

> In the cyborg fourth dimension, the serial probings, sensitizations, expressions, transductions, relays, and transmissions of

the body are coaxed into co-presence with each other. All of the operations are held in ready reserve, as randomly accessible openings. The body as RAO (random-access-openings) can connect in any number of ways to itself, its objects, and other bodies. It can open, split and reconnect at any point, inside or out. It is not longer an objective volume, but an extendability. Its dimensionality has increased beyond the three of spatial presence: from the three-dimensions of the voluminous, to the fourth dimension of the extensile. Except that this "fourth" dimension is actually fractal, between dimensions.[92]

Stelarc advocates a "post-evolutionary" and, indeed, posthuman future. He declares that: "The body must burst from its biological, cultural and planetary containment."[93] This future will embrace an increasingly technologized existence: the body will incorporate technology rather than wear it as external paraphenalia. Today, according to Stelarc, technology defines the limits of the human, establishing the centrality of the body/machine interface.

Why the production of fantasies of dematerialization, this "flight from the flesh"? Balsamo is undoubtedly correct when she points to the cultural precedents and accompaniments to these fantasies.[94] She acknowledges that we are surrounded by "a palpable fear of death and annihilation from uncontrollable and spectacular body threats: antibiotic resistant viruses, radon contamination, flesh-eating bacteria." The advent of the technologized body could be viewed as a strategy of denial: "the popularization of new body technologies disseminates new hopes and dreams of corporeal reconstruction of physical immortality, it also represses and obfuscates our awareness of new strains on and threats to the material body." After all, the technologized body is a world away from the open, porous and leaking female body, or the contaminated and dangerous diseased body. The technologized body is synonymous with order, control and cleanliness.

Of Unknown Places and Safe Spaces

The body is terra incognita. . . . Its curious matter is the unruly subject that our sovereign will can only pretend to govern. It is an anarchic substance that we all possess and are possessed by.

—Vicky Kirby[95]

It was Susan Bordo who suggested that the dominant intellectual culture of the seventeenth century was revolutionized by the experiences of war, famine, poverty, and plague.[96] She further suggested that the corporeal experiences of injury, deprivation, suffering, and death were associated with the crystallization of new beliefs and values concerning the natural world and, also, of course, femaleness. Bordo describes this process as the masculinization of knowledge: the "'re-birthing' and 're-imaging' of knowledge and the world as *masculine*."[97] Hence, Bordo argues that Cartesian rationalism was a defense against the anxiety of separation from the organic female universe of medieval cosmology. She also argues that the vigorous pursuit of scientific goals was a manifestation of the "flight from the feminine."

However, as we have shown in earlier chapters, there was a perceptible embrace of interiority, and its corollary of individuality, within the major cultural transformations which emerged during the fourteenth to the sixteenth centuries. And with the establishment of the social and psychic regime of the bounded self came the heightened suppression and marginalization of the body and its processes. In addition, the two-sex model, which gained acceptance during the Enlightenment, assisted further in the marking out of corporeal and social boundaries.

While we agree with Bordo's suggestion that such remarkable transformations in individual and collective experience occurred as a result of the overwhelmingly negative impact of bodily catastrophes of various kinds, we nominate epidemic disease as the most significant of this catalog of disasters. We argue that the bodily disorders associated with epidemic disease, and the social unrest which accompanied and followed these epidemics, were perhaps the greatest catalysts to the changing perceptions, constructions, and experiences of both the corporeal and the carnal. Further, we argue that the masculinization of the dominant intellectual culture had its origins not in the seventeenth century, but in the late fifteenth century. It is during this time that we can detect early but clear signs of the "flight from the feminine." The Cartesian revolution of the seventeenth century was, in our opinion, an extension and a deepening of this crisis around gender, knowledge and experience. We argue that the epistemic and ontological status of the gendered body was irrevocably affected by the major epidemics which swept through the West from the tenth century onward.

We also argue that we are witnessing a similar historical shift at the end of the twentieth century—an intensification of the "flight from the feminine" provoked by the reappearance of particular infectious diseases, the emergence of new virulent viruses, and the apparent failure of science and medicine to deal effectively with these events. There is now a pronounced and profound fear of feminization—of the loss of individuality, of the dissolution of bodily boundaries, and of gendered social divisions. There is a concurrent strengthening of the desire to engage with the body—to "build" it, to sculpt and reshape it through diet, exercise, or surgery—in short, to control the fleshy abundance of the body and to deny its "openness." There is a parallel desire to construct alternative realities, whether virtual, social, or imaginary, to afford an escape from the presentation of the "grotesque" body and its association with the "monstrous-feminine." This fear of touch, of bodily contact, and of proximity, translates into a desire for disembodied communication and a desire for the hardening or stripping out of the body. Moreover, at the very moment when the body is again under threat, and in crisis, we are surrounded by a rising tide of masculinist thought and a public assault on the political rights of women. We argue, finally, that this remasculinization of the social is not coincidental, but is associated with the shattering of illusions of mastery and control propagated by Cartesian science and, also, the spectre of corporeal extinction.

Notes

Part I. The Body: Constructs and Constraints

1. From the Last Conversation (Phaedro) of Socrates, in Plato, *The Last Days of Socrates*, trans. Hugh Tredennick (Harmondsworth: Penguin, 1982),135.

2. Jean-Paul Sartre, *Being and Nothingness*, trans. Hazel Barnes (New York: Washington Square Press, 1966), 428–60.

Chapter 1. Imaging the Body

1. Chris Shilling, *The Body and Social Theory* (London: Sage, 1993), 74.

2. Elizabeth Grosz, *Volatile Bodies* (Sydney: Allen and Unwin, 1994).

3. Rene Descartes, *Discourse on Method and The Meditations* (Harmondsworth: Penguin, 1982), 53.

4. Descartes, 65, 73.

5. See Sara Kay and Miri Rubin, eds., *Framing Medieval Bodies* (Manchester: Manchester University Press, 1994) for a collection of essays on various ways in which the medieval world perceived the body.

6. The influence that these events had on community perceptions of the body will be explored in detail in later chapters.

7. Descartes, 163.

8. For this purpose, a computer was featured on the magazine's cover for January 3, 1983.

9. Other potential threats to health have been documented in a World Health Organization report, *Climate Change and Human Health*, issued in

July 1996. Due to global warming the report estimates that there could be an extra 50 to 80 million cases of malaria each year; worsening air pollution causing a higher incidence of heart and respiratory diseases; and a higher incidence of asthma and hay fever due to higher airborne concentrations of pollen and spores. By 2050, it is estimated that several thousand more deaths a year from heat stress will occur in each of the world's major cities.

10. See, for example, Arthur W. Frank, *The Wounded Storyteller* (Chicago: Chicago University Press, 1995).

11. Bryan S. Turner, *The Body and Society* (Oxford: Blackwell, 1984); and Michel Feher, Ramona Naddaff, and Nadia Tazi, eds., *Fragments for A History of the Human Body*, 3 vols. (New York: Zone, 1989).

12. Bryan S. Turner, "Recent Developments in the Theory of the Body," in *The Body: Social Process and Cultural Theory*, eds. Mike Featherstone, Mike Hepworth and Bryan S. Turner (London: Sage, 1991), 1.

13. Turner, 4.

14. Turner, 11.

15. John O'Neill, *Five Bodies* (Ithaca: Cornell University Press, 1985), 12, 152.

16. The importance of this action for O'Neill lies in his conviction that: "society is never a disembodied spectacle, we engage in social interaction from the very start on the basis of sensory and aesthetic impressions." See O'Neill, p. 22.

17. Arthur W. Frank, "Bringing Bodies Back In: A Decade Review," *Theory, Culture and Society*, 7, no. 1 (1990) :131–62.

18. For one reading of the influence of feminism on perceptions of the body, see Moira Gatens, *Imaginary Bodies: Ethics, Power, and Corporeality* (London: Routledge, 1996).

19. Arthur W. Frank, "For a Sociology of the Body: An Analytical Review," in *The Body*, 39.

20. Frank, *The Body*, 39–40.

21. Writers who adopted the highly theoretical approach include Barthes, Lacan, Foucault, and Baudrillard. A work typical of the second approach is *Fragments for A History of the Human Body*, already cited in this chapter.

22. Val Plumwood, *Feminism and the Mastery of Nature* (London: Routledge, 1993), 42–43. Plumwood offers an extended list of contrasting pairs to support her argument.

23. Anthony Synnott, *The Body Social: Symbolism, Self and Society* (London: Routledge, 1993), 39.

24. Aristotle, *Economics*, cited in Synnott, 43.

25. Claude Thomasset, "The Nature of Woman," in *A History of Women in the West*, Vol. II, *Silences of the Middle Ages*, ed. Christiane Klapisch-Zuber (Cambridge, Mass.: Belknap Press of Harvard University Press, 1992), 43–44.

26. See Thomas Laqueur, *Making Sex* (Cambridge, Mass.: Harvard University Press, 1990), in particular chapter 2, for an extended discussion of this issue.

27. Cited in Thomasset, 46. Avicenna (980–1037) was an Arab philosopher and physician whose medical system was highly regarded in western Europe for a long period.

28. Laqueur, 35–43.

29. Laqueur, 62.

30. See Nancy Duncan, ed., *Body Space* (London: Routledge, 1996) for a collection of essays that investigate the contextualization of gender relations through spatial considerations.

31. Stephanie Garrett, *Gender* (London: Tavistock, 1987), 10.

32. Lois McNay, "The Foucauldian Body and the Exclusion of Experience," *Hypatia*, 6, no. 3 (1991): 135.

33. Cited in Synnott, 55–56.

34. See for example, Synnott, 38; and Garrett, 7–9.

35. Garrett, 7.

36. See Richard Ekins and David King, eds., *Blending Genders: Social Aspects of Cross-Dressing and Sex Changing* (London: Routledge, 1996).

37. Bryan Turner, "Recent Developments in the Theory of the Body," in *The Body*, 20. See also, for example, Vicki Kirby, "Corporeal Habits: Addressing Essentialism Differently," *Hypatia*, 6, no. 3 (1991): 4–23.

38. Shilling, 108.

39. Shilling, 104.

40. This is extensively covered in Norbert Elias, *The Civilizing Process*, trans., Edmund Jephcott (Oxford: Blackwell, 1994). Elias discusses another aspect of the learning process in "On Human Beings and their Emotions: a Process-Sociological Essay," in *The Body*, 103–25.

41. Shilling, 107.

42. William Simon, *Postmodern Sexualities* (London: Routledge, 1996).

43. See, for example, Bryan Turner, "Recent Developments in the Theory of the Body," in *The Body*, 1–35.

44. Bryan S. Turner, *The Body and Society* (London: Sage, 1984), 114.

45. Shilling, 76–78, 90.

46. Shilling, 77.

47. O'Neill, 137.

48. O'Neill, 138.

49. Elizabeth Grosz and Elspeth Probyn, eds., *Sexy Bodies: The Strange Carnalities of Feminism* (London: Routledge, 1996).

50. This is a topic extensively canvassed in Ivan Illich, *Medical Nemesis: The Expropriation of Health* (London: Calder and Boyars, 1975).

51. O'Neill, 120.

52. Michel Foucault, *Discipline and Punish: The Birth of the Prison* (Harmondsworth: Penguin, 1979), 224.

53. Martin Hewitt, "Bio-Politics and Social Policy: Foucault's Account of Welfare," in *The Body*, 228.

54. Bryan S. Turner, "Recent Developments," *The Body*, 23.

55. Roberta Park, cited in Shilling, 112.

56. Shilling, 112.

57. Bryan S. Turner, *Medical Power and Social Knowledge* (London: Sage, 1987), 80.

58. Turner, 89.

59. Turner, 102.

60. Turner, 109

61. Synnott, 231.

62. Foucault used this expression in his *Discipline and Punish*, 136.

63. Drew Leder, ed., *The Body in Medical Thought and Practice* (Dordecht: Kluwer Academic Publishers, 1992), 3.

64. Synnott, 28.

65. Bryan S.Turner, *Regulating Bodies: Essays in Medical Sociology* (London: Routledge, 1992), 32–33.

66. See Mike Featherstone, "The Body in Consumer Culture," in *The Body*, 182–87.

67. See, for example, K. R. Dutton, *The Perfectible Body* (London: Cassell, 1995).

68. Synnott, 29.

69. Leder, 23–27.

70. See, generally, Mary Douglas, *Purity and Danger: An Analysis of the Concepts of Pollution and Taboo* (London: Routledge and Kegan Paul, 1984). See also William Ian Miller, *The Anatomy of Disgust* (Cambridge, Mass.: Harvard University Press, 1997).

71. See Mikhail Bakhtin, *Rabelais and His World*, trans. Helene Iswolsky (Bloomington: Indiana University Press, 1984), for a development of the concepts of the "classical body" and the "grotesque body." See also Francis Barker, *The Tremulous Private Body: Essays on Subjection* (London: Methuen, 1984) for an analyisis of changing perceptions of the body in the seventeenth century based on a review of selected texts.

72. See, for example, John and Jean Comaroff, *Ethnography and the Historical Imagination* (Boulder: Westview Press, 1992), 73.

73. Comaroff, 74.

74. Mary Russo, "Female Grotesques: Carnival and Theory," in *Feminist Studies / Critical Studies*, ed. Teresa de Laurentis (Wisconsin: Indiana University Press, 1986), 217. See also Mary Russo, *The Female Grotesque: Risk, Excess and Modernity* (London: Routledge, 1995) for a broad overview of the concepts associated with the female "grotesque" body.

75. See Margaret Miles, *Carnal Knowing: Female Nakedness and Religious Meaning in the Christian West* (New York: Vintage Books, 1991), 152–55 for a discussion on the ramifications of viewing the female body as "grotesque."

76. Janet Wolff, *Feminine Sentences: Essays on Women and Culture* (Cambridge: Polity Press, 1990), 127–29.

77. Cited in Synnott, 56.

78. Wolff, 126–27.

79. Russo, 213.

80. Susan Bordo, "Eating Disorders: The Feminist Challenge to the Concept of Pathology," in *The Body in Medical Thought and Practice*, ed. Drew Leder, 198–201.

81. O'Neill, 142.

82. Cited in Dick Pels and Aya Crébas, "Carmen—Or the Invention of a New Feminine Myth," in *The Body*, 363.

83. Shilling, 1–4.

84. Community preoccupation with the skin as a factor in defining the individual is canvassed in Marc Lappe, *The Body's Edge: Our Cultural Obsession with Skin* (New York: Henry Holt and Company, 1996).

85. Shilling, 3.

86. Jean Baudrillard, *America*, trans. Chris Turner (London: Verso, 1988), 35.

87. Ibid.

88. See Deborah Lupton, *Food, the Body and the Self* (London: Sage, 1996) for a wide-ranging analysis of the relationship between food and embodiment in the late twentieth century.

89. Cited in Mike Featherstone, "The Body in Consumer Culture," in *The Body*, 177.

90. Michel Maffesoli, *The Time of the Tribes: The Decline of Individualism in Mass Society*, trans. Don Smith (London: Routledge, 1996).

91. Two recent works investigate why anorexia nervosa is primarily a "woman's illness," and why some women are so attracted to cosmetic surgery. See Kathy Davis, *Reshaping the Female Body* (London: Routledge, 1996); and Morag MacSween, *Anorexic Bodies* (London: Routledge, 1996).

92. Philip Mellor and Chris Shilling, *Re-forming the Body: Religion, Community and Modernity* (London, Sage, 1997).

93. Susan Bordo, *The Flight to Objectivity* (Albany: State University of New York Press, 1987), 5.

94. Bordo, 9, 101–105.

95. Bordo, 9.

96. Bordo, 110–11.

97. Ernest Gellner, *Reason and Culture: The Historic Role of Rationality and Rationalism* (Oxford: Blackwell, 1992), 74.

98. See Sheldon Watts, *Epidemics and History: Disease, Power and Imperialism* (New Haven: Yale University Press, 1998) for an epidemiological account of six major types of epidemics that have occurred from the fourteenth to the twentieth centuries.

99. All translations from Latin, Italian, and French, of primary or secondary source material cited throughout this work, are by James Hatty unless otherwise specifically acknowledged in the relevant notes.

100. The apocalyptic tradition is being reinterpreted for the postmodern world by contemporary writers. See, for example, Andrew McMurray, "The Slow Apocalypse: A Gradualistic Theory of the World's Demise," *Postmodern Culture*, 6, no. 3 (May 1996), published electronically by the Oxford University Press, and available at http://jefferson.village.virginia.edu/pmc/contents.all.html, INTERNET ; and James Berger, "Ends and Means: Theorizing the Apocalypse in the 1990s," PMC, 6, no. 3 (May 1996). Berger reviews three recent works on the Apocalypse: Lee Quimby, *Anti-Apocalypse: Exercises in Genealogical Criticism* (Minneapolis: University of Minnesota Press, 1994); Stephen D. Leary, *Arguing the Apocalypse: A Theory of Millennial Rhetoric* (New York: Oxford University Press, 1994); and Richard Dellamora, *Apocalyptic Overtures: Sexual Politics and the Sense of Ending* (New Brunswick: Rutgers University Press, 1994).

101. Linda Singer, *Erotic Welfare: Sexual Theory and Politics in the Age of the Epidemic*, eds. Judith Butler and Maureen MacGrogan (New York: Routledge, 1993), 118.

Chapter 2. Banishing "Unclean" Bodies

1. Cited in James A. Brundage, *Law, Sex, and Christian Society in Medieval Europe* (Chicago: Chicago University Press, 1987), 424.

2. We follow a convention that views the Middle Ages as the period from 300 A.D. to 1300 A.D. This places the start of the period at about the time of the Roman Emperor Constantine's adoption of Christianity as the state religion (324 A.D.) and his conversion to Christianity (327 A.D.). The year 1300 brings us to events which, for many, marked the start of the Italian Renaissance—the lives of the three great figures of early Italian literature, Dante (1265–1321), Petrarch (1304–74), and Boccaccio (1313–75). Some prefer to consider the Middle Ages as starting with Sack of Rome (410 A.D.) and extending into the fifteenth or sixteenth centuries. In our view this places undue emphasis on the later flowering of the Renaissance in France and England.

3. The one-sex model of human anatomy, and related issues, are discussed at length in Thomas Laqueur's work on *Making Sex: Body and Gender from the Greeks to Freud*, previously cited.

4. Laqueur, 26.

5. Quoted in Laqueur, 26.

6. Peter Brown, *The Body and Society: Men, Women and Sexual Renunciation in Early Christianity* (NewYork: Columbia University Press, 1988), 9–10.

7. Laqueur, 26.

8. Laqueur, 57–58.

9. Bryan Turner, "Theoretical Developments in the Sociology of the Body," *Australian Cultural History*, no. 13 (1994): 22.

10. The Latin expression is quoted by Eleanor Commo McLaughlin, "Equality of Souls: Inequality of Sexes: Woman in Medieval Theology," in *Religion and Sexism: Images of Woman in Jewish and Christian Traditions*, ed. Rosemary Radford Reuther (New York: Simon and Schuster, 1974), 263, n. 56.

11. Danielle Jacquart and Claude Thomasset, *Sexuality and Medicine in the Middle Ages*, trans. Matthew Adamson (Princeton: Princeton University Press, 1988), 14.

12. Jacquart and Thomasset, 14–15.

13. Claude Thomasset, "The Nature of Women," 54, also refers to the etymological association drawn between the Greek word *mene* (moon) and menstruation.

14. Jacquart and Thomasset, 14.

15. Nel Noddings, *Women and Evil* (Berkeley: University of California Press, 1989), 37. See also H. R. Hays, *The Dangerous Sex* (London: Methuen, 1966).

16. McLaughlin, 129–30.

17. Quoted in Brown, 441. This work provides an extensive review of the impact of Christianity on the way in which the body and its sexuality came to be viewed as abhorrent.

18. While Graeco-Roman secular medical practice declined markedly after the fall of the Roman Empire, the principles of human anatomy expounded by Galen were preserved in the writings of such people as Isidore of Seville (560–636).

19. Quoted in Brown, 19.

20. We review the impact of religious discourse on the lives of women, throughout the Middle Ages, in later chapters.

21. Rosemary Radford Reuther, "Misogynism and Virginal Feminism in The Fathers of the Church," in *Religion and Sexism: Images of Woman in the Jewish and Christian Traditions*, ed. Rosemary Radford Reuther (New York: Simon and Schuster, 1974), 156–57.

22. Quoted in Laqueur, 30.

23. Jacques Dalarun, "The Clerical Gaze," in *A History of Women in the West: Silences of the Middle Ages*, ed. Christiane Klapisch-Zuber (Baltimore: Belknap Press of Harvard University Press, 1992), 19–23.

24. Thomasset, 62.

25. It is of interest that the Greek word "herpes" has the same root as the Latin *serpens* (serpent), and is used to describe a skin infection often associated with the genital region.

26. Quoted by Bernard S. Prusak, "Woman: Seductive Siren or Source of Sin?," in *Religion and Sexism: Images of Woman in the Jewish and Christian Traditions*, ed. Rosemary Radford Reuther (New York: Simon and Schuster, 1974), 93.

27. An extensive review of the legend and its antecedents appears in N.M. Penzer, *Poison-Damsels* (London: C.J. Sawyer, 1952). There is also reference to many of the variations on the myth.

28. There is no evidence that the work is really that of Aristotle but he was such a revered figure in the late Middle Ages that anything that bore his name was treated as factual. The tale of the Poison-Damsel was included in this collection, representing something of a discourse on the value of moral restraint for a king.

29. Based generally on Penzer, 25.

30. While both Socrates and Archimedes appear as joint participants in most European versions of the story, biographical information shows that Socrates died in 399 B.C., before Archimedes was born (384 B.C.). However, the inclusion of the two figures from the Greek Classical period most revered by the medieval west, gave the story a stamp of authenticity.

31. Thomasset, 65.

32. Brown, 6.

33. John Chrysostom, *de virginitate* 14.1, cited in Brown, 6.

34. Brown, 6.

35. Charles-Edward Amory Winslow, *The Conquest of Epidemic Disease* (Madison, Wisconsin: University of Wisconsin Press, 1980), 9.

36. Winslow, 3, citing F.H. Garrison, *An Introduction to the History of Medicine*, 4th edn. (Philadelphia: Saunders, 1929).

37. Carlo Ginsburg, "Folklore, magia, religione," 30, records that in the more remote rural regions of Italy there is ample evidence of gestures, rites, and the use of conjuration to ward off evil, which are relics from an ancient folkloric religious past. Another example can be found in a work,

otherwise rather outdated in attitude, by Walter Starkie, *Raggle Taggle* (London: John Murray, 1949), 60. Starkie referred to the belief of nomadic Gypsy tribes in Hungary "that illness and pain is caused by malignant spirits that lie in wait for the unwary, and the duty of the shaman or wizard is to drive them away."

38. Ovid, in his *Metamorpheses*, recorded that Juno caused a pestilence to descend upon a community that had honored her rival. Homer's *Iliad* claimed that Apollo caused a deadly plague to strike a community that had been discourteous to his priest.

39. This nexus between sin and disease as a punishment can still be seen in the responses of fundamentalist Christians to the scourge of AIDS in the late twentieth century.

40. Winslow, 73, citing from Galen's commentaries on Hippocrates, which included his own interpretations and extensions of the original theory. Galen also described in great detail the steps Hippocrates took to eliminate the "miasmas" which he believed were responsible for the Plague of Athens (Winslow, 72).

41. Winslow, 40–51.

42. Eugenio Garin, *Lo zodiaco della vita* (Rome-Bari: Laterza, 1976), deals at length with the often heated debate that was a feature of the period between the fourteenth and the sixteenth centuries concerning the acceptance or rejection of the belief in astrological influences on human existence.

43. Howard Clark Kee, *Medicine, Miracle and Magic in New Testament Times* (New York: Cambridge University Press, 1986), 2–4.

44. A more detailed explanation of these divergent discourses is presented in Richard M. Zaner, "Parted Bodies, Departed Souls: The Body in Ancient Medicine and Anatomy," in *The Body in Medical Thought and Practice*, ed. Drew Leder (Dordecht: Klumer, 1992), 101–22.

45. Kee, 32–33; Nancy G. Siraisi, *Medieval and Early Renaissance Medicine* (Chicago: University of Chicago Press, 1990), 3; and Zaner, 105,114.

46. Kee, 41–42.

47. Siraisi, 4–6.

48. The once mighty and imposing city of Rome ceased to be the capital of the Empire in the late fourth century, and for extended periods, was not even the papal seat. The process of decline continued for centuries, and by the late Middle Ages, could be described as "only a large, medieval village, smelling of cows and hay. . . . One Spanish traveller remarked that outside one or two small populated quarters Rome was so empty of people

that 'there are parts within the walls which look like thick woods, and wild beasts, hares, foxes, [and] deer . . . breed in the caves'." See Peter Partner, *Renaissance Rome 1500–1559* (Berkeley: University of California Press, 1979), 4–5.

49. Augustine, Saint, *The City of God*, trans. G. Walsh, ed. V. J. Bourke (Garden City, NY: Doubleday-Image Books, 1958), Book XXII, Chapter 22, 521–22.

50. Gregory of Tours, *The History of the Franks*, trans. Lewis Thorpe (Harmondsworth: Penguin, 1982), IV.31, 227.

51. Gregory of Tours, V.6, 263–64.

52. Leprosy still represents something of a problem in some countries in the twentieth century. In India, where there are still a large number of leprosy cases, the disease is known as the "illness of untouchability." It also provides grounds for divorce, and sufferers may be barred from using public transport. It was only in 1996 that Japan closed its leper colony where victims had been kept in isolation from the rest of the population. In the U.S., where the incidence of leprosy has been slight and erratic since 1942, there are an estimated 4,000 cases. Most of these are from groups born in other parts of the world and now settled in the U.S.

53. The "serpent" metaphor, discussed earlier, appears again, albeit fleetingly, with the terms "leper" and "leprosy." Sufferers were observed to have scaly skin, areas of which were frequently shed in the manner of serpents. The names given to the sufferer, and to the disease, reflect this— being derived from the word *lepra*, meaning scaly. This, in turn, is related to *lepein*, "to peel." Some also gave credence to the belief that a poison was responsible for the disease. One of the remedies used for leprosy, prepared by boiling adders with leeks, suggests some support this notion. It implied adherence to the Greek medical tradition of treating a reputedly poisonous material with a "contrary."

54. Thomasset, 66.

55. Quoted in Thomasset, 66.

56. It was only in the late nineteenth century that the Norwegian physician and bacteriologist, Armauer Hansen, identified the bacillus responsible for leprosy. Since that discovery, the disease has frequently been referred to as Hansen's Disease.

57. Recent research leads to the view that the organism responsible for leprosy can be transmitted by mice, bed lice, and mosquitoes.

58. Frederick F. Cartwright, *A Social History of Medicine* (London: Longman, 1977), 14.

59. A more detailed account of the various types of leprosy, their physical indications, and the potential progress of the disease can be found in Saul Nathaniel Brody, *The Disease of the Soul: Leprosy in Medieval Literature* (Ithaca: Cornell University Press, 1974), 21–33.

60. Brody, 61.

61. Rules for conduct at the leprosarium at St. Albans, in England, quoted in Brody, 78.

62. There is an extended account of these matters and the position of the leper in society in Brody, Chapter II. See also Cartwright, 27–28.

63. The fourth Lateral Council of 1215 extended this process of indicating "Otherness" to Jews. They were required to wear a colored disk on their clothing, usually yellow, but sometimes red or green. See Carlo Ginsburg, *Ecstacies: Deciphering the Witches' Sabbath*, trans. Raymond Rosenthal, ed. Gregory Elliot (London: Hutchinson Radius, 1990), 38.

64. Mary Douglas, *Risk and Blame* (London: Routledge, 1992), 84.

65. Ginsburg, 33–39.

66. Ginsburg, 35.

67. Cartwright, 27, Brody, 69.

68. Ginsburg, 34.

69. Erving Goffman, *Stigma* (Englewood Cliffs, NJ; Prentice-Hall, 1965), 4.

70. Foucault, *Discipline and Punish*, chapter 3, "Panopticism."

71. The Fourth Horseman of the Apocalypse represented Pestilence—deadly epidemics such as plague. The other Horsemen represented War, Famine, and Death (as inevitable).

Part II. Apocalyptic Angst

1. Dante Alighieri, *La Divina Commedia*, ed. Natalino Sapegno, Vol. I, "Inferno" (Hell), Canto III, 1–3, 9, 10–11. Dante describes the entry into Hell, and the eternal punishment to be endured by unrepentant sinners after Judgement Day. [Our translation]

Chapter 3. Florence: A "City of the Wicked"

1. Augustine, Saint, *The City of God,* 2 vols., trans. John Healey, ed. R.V.G. Tasker (London: J.M. Dent, 1945), Vol. II, 26, 264.

2 Odo of Cluny, cited by Jacques Dalarun, "The Clerical Gaze," 20.

3. Bono Giamboni, *Il libro de' vizi e delle virtudi,* cited in Francesco De Sanctis, *Storia della letteratura italiana,* 2 vols., 7th edn. (Milan: Feltrinelli, 1978), Vol. I, 81–83.

4. For the purposes of this study, we have borne in mind that almost all surviving documents, whether official documents or personal chronicles, were compiled by men. Furthermore, these individuals came solely from the ranks of the educated and ruling classes of their communities. While there are some contemporary documents that reflect the attitudes of a few women, these also are weighted toward the opinions and practices of the socially elite of the community. The voices of the vast majority of the inhabitants in a city such as Florence are never heard, and alternative strategies have to be devised if the aim is to present a balanced view of the times. This is a problem being addressed by an increasing number of writers on social history. Some examples of works which have explored areas of unrecorded history are: Roy Porter, "The Patient's View: Doing History from Below," *Theory and Society,* no. 14 (1985):175–98; Joan W. Scott, "Gender: A Useful Category of Historical Analysis," *American Historical Review,* no. 91 (1986): 1053–75; Elisabeth Schüssler Fiorenza, *In Her Memory: A Feminist Theological Reconstruction of Christian Origins* (New York: Crossroad Publishing, 1989).

5. Giovanni Villani, *Cronaca,* 4 vols., ed. F.G. Dragomani (Frankfurt: Minerva, 1969).

6. Villani, VII, 36. Florence was not alone in believing itself to be the legitimate inheritor of the glories of the Roman Empire. Other cities, notably Venice, also claimed to being the logical successors to the grandeur which had been Rome. During the Middle Ages, the city of Rome had been reduced to little more than a village.

7. Villani, XI, 94.

8. Cited by J.K. Hyde, *Society and Politics in Medieval Italy* (London: Macmillan,1982), 157–58.

9. W. Southern, *Western Society and the Church in the Middle Ages* (Harmondsworth: Penguin, 1979), 46. The figure of 120,000 is supported by the research of D. Herlihy and C. Klapisch-Zuber, *Tuscans and Their Families* (New Haven, NY: Yale University Press, 1985), 176, 183 (Table 16). Other sources suggest estimates ranging from 90,000 to 100,000, the latter representing a modern consensus of opinion.

10. Hyde, 153.

11. Joseph L. Baird (trans. and ed.), *The Chronicles of Salimbene de Adam* (Binghamton, NY: Center for Medieval and Early Renaissance Studies, 1986), 212–13.

12. Lay religious confraternities, largely inspired and sponsored by the mendicant friars, will be discussed in more detail in later chapters. The work of the mendicant Orders of the Dominicans and the Franciscans is discussed below.

13. See Charles Homer, *The Renaissance of the Twelfth Century* (Cambridge, Mass.: Harvard University Press, 1982), 212–18, for an overview of the application of canon law in the late Middle Ages.

14. Vern L. Bullough, "Heresy, Witchcraft, and Sexuality," *Journal of Homosexuality* 1, no. 2 (1974): 185.

15. See Ann G. Carmichael, *Plague and the Poor in Renaissance Florence* (Cambridge: Cambridge University Press, 1986), 96–97 for a broad account of the types of sanitary regulations operating in Florence in the early fourteenth century.

16. By their nature, sermons could be expected to accent moral issues, but much of the literature was also essentially didactic in style. One way or another these exhortations to improve the moral tone of a city and so deflect divine retribution, reached all of the community. For the majority, the message came through sermons, and through the visual representations of the Christian doctrine in the frescoes that adorned the walls of churches. The written word was much less accessible, since it was still only to be found in manuscript form, some of it in the vernacular, but much still written in Latin. However, if we refer to some of the surviving sermons of the day, and to the works of both clerical and lay writers of the period, we can identify the factors which created considerable tension and a sense of foreboding on moral issues in cities such as Florence.

17. II John, 2, 15–16.

18. Cited by Natalino Sapegno in Dante Alighieri, *La Divina Commedia,* 3 vols., ed., Natalino Sapegno (Florence: La Nuova Italia, 1982), Vol. I, .8, n. 32.

19. Giordano da Rivalto-Moreni, *Prediche* (Florence: Pietro Gaetano Viviani, 1738), 6.

20. Giordano, 10.

21. Giordano, 14.

22. See for example, Matteo Griffoni [Mathhhaeus de Griffonibus], "Memoriale historicum de rebus Bononiensium," in *Rerum italicarum scriptores,* Vol. 18, Pt. 2, eds. L. Frati and A. Sorbelli (Città di Castello: Lapi, 1902). Other chroniclers will be cited on the matter in later chapters.

23. Michael J. Rocke, "Sodomites in Fifteenth Century Tuscany: The Views of Bernardino of Siena," *Journal of Homosexuality,* no. 15 (1988): 25, note 3; John Boswell, "Towards the Long View: Revolutions, Universals

and Sexual Categories," *Salamagundi,* nos. 58–59 (1982–83): 103, note 31; and Vern L. Bullough and James Brundage, eds. *Sexual Practices and the Medieval Church* (Buffalo, NY: Prometheus Books, 1982), 62–63; 66. Clearly, the wide definition covered a range of same-sex activities, including anal intercourse, male or female.

24. John Boswell, *Christianity, Social Tolerance, and Homosexuality* (Chicago: Chicago University Press, 1980), 293, 295.

25. Michael Goodich, "Sodomy in Medieval Secular Law," *Journal of Homosexuality,* 1, no. 3 (1976): 299–300.

26. The mendicant Orders of friars are discussed in more detail below. They relied for their sustenance on alms from the citizens of the cities in which they established their communities.

27. For other examples, see also II Peter 2:10; Gal. 5:16,17; Thes. 4:3–5; I Cor. 5:9; 6:13, 18.

28. Jacopone da Todi, in *Poesia italiana del Duecento,* ed. Pietro Cudini (Milan: Garzanti, 1978), 270.

29. Cassian's arguments for chastity and the struggle to achieve this, are discussed in detail in Michel Foucault, "The Battle for Chastity," in *Western Sexuality: Practice and Precept in Past and Present Times,* eds. Philippe Ariès and André Béjin, trans. Anthony Forster (Oxford: Basil Blackwood, 1985), 14–25.

30. Morton W. Bloomfield, *The Seven Deadly Sins* (Michigan: Michigan State University Press, 1967), 71.

31. Brundage, 422, footnote 26, cites a table from a survey of medieval religious tales which shows that sexually explicit themes were very popular.

32. Brundage, 152–53.

33. The general merging of the concepts of the Seven Cardinal Sins and the Seven Deadly Sins did not fully occur until the fifteenth and sixteenth centuries. See Bloomfield, 43–44, 157.

34. Dante Alighieri, *La Divina Commedia,* 3 vols., ed. Natalino Sapegno (Florence: La Nuova Italia, 1982). Dante, a contemporary of Giordano, was not solely a writer of great renown, but had close association with many activities within the Florentine community. He played a not insignificant role in civic affairs—in various minor offices, as an ambassador, and for a brief period in 1300, as one of the six Priors of Florence.

35. Domenico Cavalca, *Specchio de croce,* cited by Carlo Ginsburg, "Folklore, magia, religione," in *Storia d'Italia,* Vol. I (Turin: Einaudi, 1974), 621.

36. Steven Runciman, *Byzantine Style and Civilization* (Harmondsworth: Penguin, 1975), 33.

37. The Florentine diarist, Luca Landucci, reported that the Dominican friar Girolamo Savanarola regularly preached to gatherings of 14,000 to 15,000 during the late fifteenth century. See Luca Landucci, *Diario Fioremtino dal1450 al 1516 di Luca Landucci,* ed. I. del Badia (Florence: Studio Biblos, 1969), 63, 94.

38. See Southern, 272–99, for an account of the rise of the mendicant friars.

39. Baird, 217.

40. Vern L. Bullough, "The Sin against Nature and Homosexuality," in *Sexual Practices and the Medieval Church,* eds. Vern L. Bullough and James Brundage (Buffalo, NY: Prometheus Books, 1982), 55. See also Michael Goodich, "Sodomy in Ecclesiastical Law and Theory," *Journal of Homosexuality,* 1, no. 4 (1976): 427–34.

41. Brundage, 416–19. It should be noted that sexual offenses covered a wide range of behaviors involving both sexes, and many of these warranted only relatively minor punishments such as penance. The term should not be confused with its present day connotations.

42. Southern, 296–99.

43. Jean-Louis Flandrin, "Sex in Married Life in the early Middle Ages: The Church's Teaching and Behavioural Reality," in *Western Sexuality: Practice and Precept in Past and Present Times,* eds. Philippe Ariès and André Béjin, trans. Anthony Forster (Oxford: Basil Blackwood, 1985), 115. See also Jean-Louis Flandrin, *Sex in the Western World: The Development of Attitudes and Behaviour,* trans. Sue Collins (Chur, Switzerland: Harwood Academic, 1991), particularly chapters 6, 7, and 8.

44. Cited in Millard Meiss, *Painting in Florence and Siena after the Black Death* (Princeton, NJ: Princeton University Press, 1978), 26.

45. Baird, 156.

46. Dino Compagni, "La cronica di Dino Compagni," in *Classici italiani,* Series II, Vol.XXIX (Milan: Istituto editoriale italiana, 1913), 164.

47. Anonimo Fiorentino, "Cronica volgare di un Anonimo Fiorentino," in *Rerum italicarum scriptores,* ed. Ellina Bellondi (Città di Castello: Lapi, 1915), Vol. XXVII, pt.1, 52.

48. Villani, XI, 2, 209–17.

49. Villani, XII, 73, 84.

Chapter 4. Disordered Bodies in Abundance

1. Giovanni Villani, XII, 84.

2. In Florence at that time, a new year commenced on 25 March. Consequently, contemporary records refer to the arrival of the plague in 1347, since it appeared in the city at the beginning of March. We have used modern day conventions in referring to these events.

3. This well-known term for the plague outbreak of 1348–50 emerged well after the event. See Stephen D'Irsay, "Notes on the origin of the expression 'Atra Mors'," *Isis*, no. 8 (1926): 328–32.

4. An overview of the psychological impact of the plague upon the people of Florence is contained in James Hatty, "Coping with Disaster: Florence After the Black Death," in *Disasters: Image and Context*, ed. Peter Hinton (Sydney, NSW: Sydney Association for Studies in Society and Culture, 1992), 153–65. For a general account of the origins and spread of the plague epidemics, see Élisabeth Carpentier, "Autor de la peste noire: famines et épidémie dans l'histoire du XIVe siècle," *Annales E.S.C.*, no. 17 (1962): 1062–92.

5. R.S. Gottfried, *The Black Death—Natural and Human Disasters in Medieval Europe* (London: Robert Hale, 1983), 77. The epidemic of bubonic plague also devastated many areas of the Far East, the Near East, and northern Africa. There is no reasonable way of estimating the overall death toll in these areas. See Michael W. Dols, "The Comparative Communal Responses to the Black Death in Muslim and Christian Societies," *Viator*, no. 5 (1974): 269–87; and *The Black Death in the Middle East* (Princeton, NJ: Princeton University Press, 1977).

6. See F.W. Kent, "The Black Death of 1348 in Florence: A New Contemporary Account?" in *Renaissance Studies in Honor of Craig Hugh Smyth,* Vol. I (Florence: Giunti Barbèra, 1988), 123, and notes 31 and 32, for a brief survey of the variations in estimates of the population and the death toll. In neighboring Siena, the death toll, according to an anonymous chronicler, was three out of every four people in the city. See Anon. "Cronaca Senese," *Rerum italicarum scriptores,* Vol. XX, Pt. 6, eds. A Lisini and F. Iacometti (Bologna: Zanchelli, 1931), 148.

7. Agnolo di Tura del Grasso, "Cronaca Senese di Agnolo di Tura del Grasso," in *R.I.S.,* Vol. XV, Pt. 6, eds. A. Lisini and F. Iacometti (Bologna: Zanichelli, 1931), 552.

8. Agnolo di Tura, 555.

9. Ibid.

10. Francesco Petrarca, *Rerum familiarium libri I–VIII*, trans. Aldo S. Bernardo (Albany: State University of New York Press, 1975), 415.

11. Petrarca, 417. See also Francesco Petrarca, *Le senili,* trans. G. Fracasetti, ed. Guido Martelloti (Turin: Einaudi, 1976), 97, for other comments that the plague seemed to signal the end of the world.

12. Giovanni Boccaccio, *Decameron*, 2 vols., 3rd edn., ed. Mario Marti (Milan: Rizzoli, 1979), Vol. I, 13.

13. Matteo Villani, "Cronica di Matteo Villani," in *Chroniche di Giovanni, Matteo e Filippo Villani* (Trieste: Lloyd Austriaco, 1858), Vol. II, Book I, 2.

14. Petrarca, *Rerum familiarium libri IX–XVI,* trans. Aldo S. Bernardo (Baltimore: Johns Hopkins University Press, 1982), XVI, 2.

15. Plague appeared in three forms. The most common, the "bubonic" form, was recognizable from the buboes (large swellings) which appeared in the lymph glands. This form was not always fatal. Those who did not succumb suffered greatly for some five or six days before recovering gradually. A second form of plague was the "pneumonic" variation where the disease settled in the respiratory system. The third variation was the "septicaemic" type where the bacilli population grew rapidly in the whole bloodstream. The latter two forms always proved fatal, sometimes within a day of becoming ill. Further information on the variations of plague and their methods of transmission can be found in William McNeill, *Plagues and Peoples* (New York: Anchor/Doubleday, 1976), 123–25; 166–68.

16. Petrarca, VIII, 8.

17. Feelings of grief and pain at the loss of children within the family are recorded in several contemporary accounts. See, for example, Gregorio Dati, "Il libro segreto di Gregorio Dati," in *Scelta di curiosità letterarie dal secolo XIII al XIX,* Vol. XXII, Disp. CII (Bologna: Commissione per i testi di lingua, 1968), 40 and 95; and Giovanni di Pagallo Morelli, *Ricordi,* 2nd edn., ed. V. Branca (Florence: Le Monnier, 1969), 174 and 455–59. A more recent commentary on responses to the death of children at the start of the fifteenth century is contained in Alberto Tenenti, "Témoignages Toscans sur la mort des enfants autor de 1400," in *Annales de Démographie Historique* (Paris: Mouton, 1973), 133–34.

18. Agnolo di Tura del Grasso, 555.

19. Boccaccio, *Decameron*, already cited.

20. Boccaccio, Vol. I, 10.

21. Petrarca, 418.

22. Giovanni Villani, Book XII, 84.

23. Ibid.

24. Boccaccio, 10.

25. Jean-Noël Biraben, *Les hommes et la peste en France et dans le pays européens et méditerréens*, 2 vols. (Paris: Mouton, 1975–76), Vol. 1, 394–97.

26. Biraben, Vol. 1, 399–400.

27. Lorenzo Strozzi, "Descrizione della peste di Firenze dell'anno 1527" (previously attributed to Macchiavelli), in Niccolò Macchiavelli, *Opere di Niccolò Macchiavelli* (Italia [Firenze]: 1826), Vol.VII, 33.

28. Morelli, 168–72; and Landucci, 125–27.

29. Dati, 96–97; and Buonaccorso Pitti, "The Diary of Buonaccorso Pitti," in *Two Memoirs of Renaissance Florence,* trans. Julia Martines., ed. Gene Brucker (New York: Harper and Row, 1967), 22 and 87–88.

30. Boccaccio, 14–15.

31. Boccaccio, 10.

32. See studies on Orvieto and Siena contained in William Bowsky, ed. *The Black Death: A Turning Point in History?* (New York: Holt, Rinehart and Winston, 1971); Élisabeth Carpentier, "Orvieto: Institutional Stability and Moral Change," 108–13, and William M. Bowsky, "Siena: Stability and Dislocation," 114–21; and generally, William M. Bowsky, "The Impact of the Black Death upon Sienese Government and Society," *Speculum,* XXXIX, no. 1 (1964): 1–34.

33. Frances and Joseph Gies, *Marriage and the Family in the Middle Ages* (New York: Harper and Row, 1989), reviews many of the responses to and changes which resulted from the Black Death. See particularly chapters 11 and 14.

34. Matteo Villani, I, 4.

35. Herlihy and Klapisch-Zuber, 81; 86–88.

36. Herlihy and Klapisch-Zuber, 81–82; 232–46.

37. Herlihy and Klapisch-Zuber, 253–54.

38. For a general overview of the problem of abandoned children in Florence, see Richard E. Trexler, "The Foundlings of Florence, 1395–1455," *History of Childhood Quarterly,* I (1973): 259–84. The whole problem was exacerbated by the fact that periods of famine often followed epidemics of plague. See also for a general overview of the way in which abandoned or unwanted children were cared for by others, *in loco parentis.*

39. BenedettoVarchi, *Storia fiorentina,* 3 vols., ed. Lelio Arbib (Florence: Editrice del Nardi e del Varchi, 1828–41), 473–74.

40. Petrarca, VIII, 420.

41. J.F.C Hecker, *The Epidemics of the Middle Ages,* trans. B.G. Babington (London,1859), 21.

42. G. Vernadasky, *The Mongols and Russia* (Yale, 1959).

43. It is unlikley that this was the only point of transfer of the disease, but it is the one most documented and almost certainly the only way in which plague entered Europe through Italy.

44. Biraben, Vol. I, 53 provides a detailed account of the progress of the plague through the Far East, and of the events at Caffa. See also Philip Ziegler, *The Black Death* (London: Collins, 1972), 15–16, citing Haeser, *Archiv für die gesammte Medizin* (Jena), Vol. II, 48–49; and Gottfried, 36–37.

45. Giovanni Villani, XII, 84.

46. Agnolo di Tura, 552.

47. Agnolo di Tura, 553; Boccaccio, 10

48. Boccaccio, 15.

49. Agnolo di Tura, 553.

50. Agnolo di Tura, 555.

51. Boccaccio, 15.

52. Boccaccio, 15, and Marchionne di Coppo Stefani, "Cronaca fiorentina di Marchionne di Coppo Stefani," in *Rerum italicarum scriptores,* Vol. XXX, pt.1, ed. Niccolò Rodolico (Città di Castello: Lapi, 1903), 231.

53. Boccaccio, 15.

54. Boccaccio, 12.

55. The theories of disease causation expounded by Galen and by Avicenna dominated late medieval medical discourse. Both had claimed that "corruption of the air," which was one of the main causes of disease, often arose from decaying matter. Among the examples offered, they listed "corpses left unburied on the battlefield," and the rotting carcasses of animals. See, for example, Winslow, 71–74; and Anna Montgomery Campbell *The Black Death and Men of Learning* (New York: AMS Press, 1966), 44–52, particularly the footnotes to those pages.

56. The first man, sitting in the *Mercato Nuovo,* was recorded by Landucci, 158; the second, lying in the middle of a bridge, by Lorenzo Strozzi (previously attributed to Machiavelli), in Niccolò Machiavelli, *Opere di Niccolò Machiavelli* (Italia [Florence]: 1826), Vol.VII, 39.

57. Landucci, 28, recorded the plight of a boy suffering from plague who had been left in the street, and no one could be found to carry him to a hospital (1478).

58. Giulia Calvi, "The Florentine Plague of 1630–33: Social Behaviour and Symbolic Action," in *Maladie et Société (XIIe–XVIIe siècles),* eds. N. Bulst and R. Delort (Paris: Editions du CNRS, 1989), 333–34.

59. Boccaccio, 15.

60. Claudine Herzlich and Janine Pierret, *Illness and Self in Society,* trans. Elborg Forster (Baltimore: Johns Hopkins University Press, 1987), 73.

61. Giovanni Villani, XII, 84; Matteo Villani, I, 2; Marchionne, 230; Agnolo di Tura del Grasso, 555; Boccaccio, 10; and Varchi, Vol. I, 471.

62. Marchionne, 230.

63. Boccaccio, 16–17.

64. Philippe Ariès, *Western Attitudes to Death: From the Middle Ages to the Present,* trans. Patricia Ranum (Baltimore: Johns Hopkins University Press, 1985), 52. The whole work provides a useful overview of the changing nature of death in the West.

65. Chiara Frugoni, "The Imagined Woman," in *A History of Women in the West: Silences of the Middle Ages,* ed. Christiane Klapisch-Zuber (Cambridge, Mass.: Harvard University Press, 1992), 336–422.

66. Frugoni, 363.

67. Frugoni, 363–67.

68. Alberto Tenenti, *Il senso della morte e l'amore della vita nel Rinascimento* (Turin: Einaudi, 1989), 51.

69. While the macabre became an iconographic element of Italian art, it was not as frequently used as it was north of the Alps. A general review of the iconography of the plague is contained in John B. Friedman, "He hath a thousand slayn this pestilence: The Iconography of the Plague in the Late Middle Ages," in *Social Unrest in the Late Middle Ages,* ed. Francis Newman (Binghamton, NY: Center for Medieval and Early Renaissance Texts, 1986), 75–97.

70. Tenenti, 414.

71. The text of this poem, and illustrations to match each section, are included in Edward F. Chaney, ed. *La Danse Macabré des Charniers ds Saints Innocents à Paris* (Manchester: Manchester University Press, 1945).

72. Kenneth Clark, *The Nude: A Study in Ideal Art* (London: John Murray, 1956), 305.

73. Baldesar Castiglione, *The Book of the Courtier,* trans. George Bull (London: Penguin, 1976), 330–32.

74. See the work of his contemporary and friend, Giorgio Vasari, *The Lives of the Artists,* trans. George Bull (Harmondsworth: Penguin, 1988), 325–442.

75. Michelangelo Buonarrotti, *Rime* (Milan: Rizzoli, 1954), 61.

76. Cited in Sander L. Gilman, *Disease and Representation* (Ithaca: Cornell University Press, 1988), 62.

77. Jacques Le Goff, *The Medieval Imagination,* trans. Arthur Goldhammer (Chicago: Chicago University Press, 1988), 83.

Chapter 5. Castigating the Flesh

1. Cited by Dalarun in "The Clerical Gaze," 19.

2. Jacopo Passavanti, *Lo specchio della vera penitenza* (Milan: Silvestri, 1825), 252. The original of this work of the Florentine Dominican friar Passavanti, the *Trattato della penitenzia*, was written in Latin about the same time as Boccaccio's *Decameron*, that is, just after the Black Death.

3. Cited in John H. Mundy, *Europe in the High Middle Ages 1150/1309* (London: Longman, 1980), 221.

4. Dalarun, 16.

5. Caroline Walker Bynum, "The Female Body and Religious Practice in the Later Middle Ages," in *Fragments for a History of the Human Body,* 3 vols., eds. Michel Feher, et al., Part I, 175.

6. Silvana Vecchio, "The Good Wife," in *A History of Women in the West*, ed. Christiane Klapisch-Zuber, 121, citing Nicholas of Gorran (died 1295).

7. Carla Casagrande, "The Protected Woman," in *A History of Women in the West*, ed. Christiane Klapisch-Zuber, 94.

8. Women were also the recipients of much advice about the consumption of food and beverages. This advice became increasingly strict from the end of the fourteenth century. Proscripotions and prescriptions, once reserved for nuns and widows, were sometimes extended to married women. Restraint and denial signalled obedience to God's wishes and acceptance of the necessary virtue of sobriety. Of course, should a wife ignore this lofty advice, a husband was quite within his rights to dispense a dose of corporal punishment. See generally, Silvana Vecchio, "The Good Wife," 105–35.

9. Dalarun, 40–41.

10. Southern, 330.

11. Dalarun, 42.

12. From the fourteenth to the seventeenth centuries Europe was the setting for an unrelenting drive against those suspected of practicing witchcraft. The witchhunt caused the deaths of some 200,000 to 500,000 people, mostly women. For some contrasting interpretations of the witchcraft craze, see Nachman Ben-Yehuda, "The European Witch Craze of the 14th to 17th centuries: A Sociologist's Perspective," *American Journal of Sociology*, 86, no. 1 (1980): 1–31; Ginsburg, *Ecstacies;* Hugh Trevor-Roper, *The European Witch Craze of the Sixteenth and Seventeenth Centuries* (London: Penguin, 1978).

13. Bryan S. Turner, *Religion and Social Theory* (London: Heinemann Educational, 1983), 47.

14. Barbara Ehenreich and Deidre English, *Witches, Midwives, and Nurses: A History of Women Healers*, 2nd edn. (New York: Feminist Press, SUNY, 1973), 3, 13–14; Jacquart and Thomasset, 114–15.

15. Vestiges of pre-Christian religious beliefs and practices can still be found in the twentieth century, co-existing with orthodox Christian practices, in the more remote rural areas of Europe.

16. In the fifteenth century, the Borgia Pope Alexander VI surpassed all others in sexual indulgence. Having produced offspring from his mistress while still a Cardinal within the Curia, he added several more after becoming pope. Another occupant of the papal throne, Julius III, was so well known for his homosexuality that he was the subject of much public ridicule. Julius III was pope from 1550 to 1555. See Partner, 203.

17. Cited in Laqueur, *Making Sex*, 61.

18. This was further exacerbated by the Great Schism which lasted from 1378 to 1417, and the long period (over a century) during which the papacy was located at Avignon.

19. See R. Krautheimer, *Rome: Profile of a City 312–1308* (Princeton: Princeton University Press, 1980), 159.

20. Michel Mollat, *The Poor in the Middle Ages: An Essay in Social History,* trans. Arthur Goldhammer (New Haven: Yale University Press, 1986), 1.

21. Mollat, 74.

22. For further reading on this topic see, for example, Sylvia L. Thrupp, ed., *Millennial Dreams in Action* (The Hague: Mouton, 1962), 31–43; Robert E. Lerner, "Medieval Prophecy and Religious Dissent," *Past and Present,* no. 72 (1976): 3–4, and "The Black Death and Western Eschatological Mentali-

ties," in *The Black Death: The Impact of the Fourteenth-Century Plague,* ed. Daniel Williman (Binghamton, NY: Center for Medieval and Early Renaissance Studies, 1982), 77–105; Southern, 304–309.

23. See Southern, 273–77 for some examples of itinerant preachers.

24. Biraben, Vol. I, 67; Ronald E. Weissman, *Ritual Brotherhood in Renaissance Florence* (New York: Academic Press, 1982), 50; and Norman Cohn, *The Pursuit of the Millennium* (Fairlawn, NJ: Essential Books, 1957), 125.

25. Baird, 474.

26. Cohn, 132–33.

27. Biraben, Vol. I, 66; Cohn, 128.

28. Some writers have mistakenly identified outbreaks of plague as one of the causes of this event. See, for example, Cohn, 126; and, more recently, Synnott, 16. Bubonic plague did not reappear in Europe until 1348.

29. Conditions relating to the ritual are drawn, in the main, from Cohn, 131–32. Other references appear in Southern, 308; and Biraben, Vol. I, 66.

30. With papal approval, two Dominican friars produced a manual on the detection, prosecution, and punishment of women practicing witchcraft. Arguably, it is one of the most rabidly misogynist documents ever published. In the spirit of the times, however, it was widely read and endorsed. See H. Kramer and J. Sprenger, *The Malleus Maleficarum of Heirich Kramer and James Sprenger*, trans. Montague Summers (New York: Dover, 1971). The title of this work translates as "The Hammer of the Witches."

31. Antonio Lanza, ed. *Lirici Toscani del '400* (Rome: Bulzoni, 1973), 387.

32. Weissman, 95.

33. John Henderson, "Confraternities and the Church in late Medieval Florence," in *Voluntary Religion: Papers at the 1985 Summer Meeting and the 1986 Winter Meeting of the Ecclesiastical Society,* eds. W.J. Shiels and Diana Wood (Oxford: Ecclesiastical History Society and Basil Blackwell, 1986), 70.

34. John Henderson, "Penitence and the Laity," in *Christianity and the Renaissance,* eds. Timothy Verdon and John Henderson (Syracuse, NY: Syracuse University Press, 1990), 233.

35. The statutes of each confraternity clearly defined the responsibilities of members toward their fellow members in need, in ill health, at

their death, and for the souls of departed members. As one example, see Luciano Orioli, *Le confraternite medievali e il problema della povertà* (Rome: Edizioni di storia e letteratura, 1984), 26–28, for the statutes of the "Compagnia di Santa Maria Vergine e di San Zenobio di Firenze."

36. Ronald E. Weissman, "Sacred Eloquence: Humanist Preaching and Lay Piety in Renaissance Florence," in *Christianity and the Renaissance*, eds. Timothy Verdon and John Henderson (Syracuse, NY: Syracuse University Press, 1990), 250–71, particularly 258–62. The citations are drawn from this source.

37. Weissman stated that humanists frequently addressed confraternities on the matter of sin and purgation and identified those whose views he cited. He also concluded that the humanists who spoke in this way had reconciled Christian beliefs on sin and redemption with the Platonic concept of purgation and elevation to a higher spiritual plane.

38. Richard Trexler, *Public Life in Renaissance Florence* (New York: Academic Press, 1980), 358.

39. On several occasions women and children were also excluded from crisis situations because they were perceived as less intelligent and would detract from the seriousness of the situation. See, for example, Landucci, 92–94; and Varchi, XL, 67.

40. Trexler, *Public Life*, 349, citing contemporary assessments of the requirements for seers and prophets who might be consulted by the commune.

41. The doctrine of the Immaculate Conception was hotly disputed among theologians for many centuries, and although widely accepted in practice, it was not finally incorporated into formal church doctrine until the decree of Pius IX, in 1854.

42. Bynum, 164. See also Jennifer Ash, "The discursive construction of Christ's body in the late Middle Ages: resistance and autonomy" in *Feminine, Masculine and Representation*, eds. Terry Threadgold and Anne Cranny-Francis (Sydney: Allen and Unwin, 1990), 75–105.

43. Piero Camporesi, "The Consecrated Host: A Wondrous Excess," in *Fragments for a History of the Human Body*, eds. Michel Feher, et al., Part I, 227.

44. Bynum, 175–76.

45. Bynum, 176.

46. One example, among many contemporary references to this image being brought to Florence, is found in Anon., "Diario d'Anonimo Fiorentino," in *Documenti di storia italiana*, Vol. VI (Florence: Deputazione sugli studi di storia patria, 1876), 341.

47. Varchi, 469.

48. The power inherent in the bodies of saints and martyrs was a long established element of church dogma. For a detailed explanation of the origins of the Cult of the Saints, and appeals to God through saints as intermediaries, see Peter Brown, *The Cult of the Saints* (Chicago: Chicago University Press, 1981).

49. Bynum, 163.

50. Southern, 30.

51. Giovanni Sercambi, *Le croniche di Giovanni Sercambi,* ed. Salvatore Bongi (Lucca: Giusti, 1892), 291, 303; and 319–21. Extensive accounts of the *Bianchi* processions can be found in Sercambi, 291–371; Weissman, *Ritual Brotherhood,* 51–55; and Iris Origo, *The Merchant of Prato* (London: Cape, 1957), 316–26.

52. Anonimo Fiorentino, "Cronica volgare di Anonimo Fiorentino," 242.

53. The changing perceptions of childhood in this period have been the subject of research by many writers. See, for example, Philippe Ariès, *Centuries of Childhood,* ed. Robert Baldick (New York: Random House [Vintage], 1962); Jean-Noël Biraben, "La médicin et l'enfant au Moyen Age," in *Annales de Démographie Historique* (Paris: Mouton, 1973), 73–75; F. Bonney, "Jean Gerson: Un nouveau regard sur l'enfance," in *Annales de Démographie,* 137–42; and Christiane Klapish-Zuber, "Attitudes devant l'enfant," in *Annales de Démographie*, 63–67; and "L'enfance en Toscane début XVe siècle," 99–122.

54. Trexler, *Public Life,* 376.

55. Extracts from an exchange of letters between a cardinal and a bishop which cover the arguments raised for and against flight can be found in Dorothy M. Schullian, "A Manuscript of Dominici in the Army Medical Library," *Journal of the History of Medicine,* III, no. 3 (1948): 395–99.

56. There were many passing references to such flights. An instance of a direct reference appears in Matteo Palmieri, "Historia fiorentina," in *Rerum italicarum scriptores,* Vol. XXVI, Pt. 1 (Città di Castello: Lapi, 1906), 160.

57. Marchionne, 230–33.

58. Mundy, 310–12, records the longstanding belief that homosexuality was prevalent among monks in the Middle Ages.

59. Many of the stories in Boccaccio's *Decameron* focus on this issue, while Machiavelli's Frate Timoteo is a willing accomplice in persuading the

young wife of an old husband to be seduced by a youthful lover. See Nicolò Machiavelli, *La mandragola* (Turin: Einaudi, 1980), also available in various translations.

60. Denys Hay, *The Church in Italy in the Fifteenth Century* (Cambridge: Cambridge University Press, 1977), 65.

61. Gene Brucker, ed., Julia Martines, trans. "The Diary of Buonaccorso Pitti," in *Two Memoirs of Renaissance Florence* (New York: Harper and Row, 1967), 25.

62. Bernardino da Siena, *Le prediche volgari,* ed. Ciro Cannarozzi (Florence: Rinaldi, 1958), Vol. II, 98–112.

63. Bernardino, Vol. IV, 270–90.

64. Bernardino, Vol. V, 42–43.

65. Bernardino's intense preoccupation with controlling female sexuality, particularly women's reproductive capabilities, is evident in his rather personal crusade against witches in Italy. He regularly denounced their supposed involvement with abortions and contraception from the pulpit. He claimed that his sermons delivered in Rome had been instrumental in bringing about the conviction and burning at the stake of two women. See Ginsburg, *Ecstacies*, 297–98, and Iris Origo, *The World of San Bernardino* (New York: Harcourt, Brace and World, 1962), 172.

66. Bernardino, Vol. III, 271.

67. Bernardino, Vol. III, 126. Another preacher of the period Giovanni Dominici warned women against "unnatural positions" like "a beast or a mule"; see Herlihy and Klapisch-Zuber, 251.

68. Bernardino, Vol.V, 44.

69. Bernardino, Vol. II, 82–97; Vol. V, 199–235.

70. Bernardino, Vol. V, 48.

71. Bernardino, of course, was not alone in advocating renunciation of the body. Another exponent of this view, for example, was St. Catherine of Siena, noted for her own adherence to an extremely limited food intake. In her letters, she frequently enjoined others to follow her example. See Catherine of Siena, *The Letters of St. Catherine of Siena,* Vol. I, trans. Suzanne Noffke (Binghamton, NY: Center for Medieval and Early Renaissance Studies, 1988).

72. Turner, *Religion and Social Theory*, 118.

73. Luca Landucci, whose diary covers this period, made frequent reference to outbreaks of plague in the city, and the fear that this engendered. Landucci himself fled from the city with his family on a number of occasions.

74. Girolamo Savonarola, *Prediche sopra Giobbe,* ed. Roberto Ridolfi (Rome Belardetti, 1957), 442, 445.

75. Girolamo Savonarola, *Operette spirituali,* ed. Mario Ferrara (Rome: Belardetti, 1976), Vol. II, 151–53; and 192–93.

76. Girolamo Savonarola, *Prediche sopra Amos e Zaccaria,* ed. Paolo Ghiglieri (Rome: Belardetti, 1972), Vol. III, 121, 149, 233.

77. Savonarola, *Prediche sopra Amos e Zaccaria,* 162.

78. For an extended account of the activities of these groups see Richard C.Trexler, "Ritual in Florence: Adolescence and Salvation in the Renaissance," in *The Pursuit of Holiness in Late Medieval and Renaissance Religion* eds. C. Trinkaus and H. Oberman (Leiden: Brill, 1974), 200–64.

79. Landucci, 123–26.

80. Landucci, 163.

81. Vittoria Colonna, a poet, was a close friend of Michelangelo, and a member of a significant group seeking reform of the church. Isabella d'Este was recognized widely for her erudition, her patronage of the arts and literature, and her interests in statecraft. Elisabetta Gonzaga was noted for her cultural interests, and her ability to govern the city-state of Mantua, on behalf of her husband, during his many absences.

82. Christine de Pizan, *The Book of the City of Ladies,* trans. Earl Jeffrey Richards (London: Pan Books, 1983).

83. The religious convictions and support for renunciation of the body of Catherine of Genoa were recorded by friends and supporters. See Anna Antonopoulos, "Writing the Mystic Body: Sexuality and Textuality in the *écriture-fémine* of Saint Catherine of Genoa," *Hypatia,* 6, no. 3 (1991):185–205. Tertiaries were those who were committed to a life of religious observance, generally adhering to the rules of one of the monastic orders, but without taking the vows of any such order. Catherine of Siena, later canonized, was a tertiary of the Dominican Order.

84. Bynum, 167.

85. Frugoni, 418 and 533 (note 49).

86. Frugoni, 418.

87. Danielle Régnier-Bohler, "Literary and Mystical Voices," *A History of Women in the West,* ed. Christiane Klapisch-Zuber, 429.

88. See Lauro Martines, "A Way of Looking at Women in Renaissance Florence," *Journal of Medieval and Renaissance Studies,* no. 4 (1974):15–28. An even wider analysis of the forces at work in the community during this period can be found in Barbara Diefendorf, "Family Culture, Renaissance Culture," *Renaissance Quarterly,* no. 40 (1987):660–81.

89. Giovanni Boccaccio, "Il Corbaccio," in *Letteratura italiana: Storia e testi,* Vol. 9, ed. Pier Giorgio Ricci (Milan: Riccardo Ricciardi, n.d.), 496. This work was written in 1355.

90. Matteo Palmieri, *La vita civile,* ed. Gino Belloni (Florence: Sansoni, 1982), 156–57. This work was written 1464, but published posthumously in 1529.

91. Joan Kelly-Gadol, "Did Women have a Renaissance?," in *Becoming Visible: Women in European History,* eds. Renate Bridenthal and Claudia Koonz (Boston: Houghton-Mifflin, 1977), 139–64.

92. Ian Maclean, *The Renaissance Notion of Women* (Cambridge: Cambridge University Press, 1980).

93. David Herlihy, "Did Women have a Renaissance?: A Reconsideration," *Medievalia et Humanistica,* no. 13 (1985): 2–22.

94. Vecchio, 135. See also Eleanor Commo McLaughlin, "Equality of Souls, Inequality of Sexes: Women in Medieval Theology," in *Religion and Sexism, Images of Woman in the Jewish and Christian Traditions,* ed. Rosemary Radford Reuter (New York: Simon and Schuster, 1974), 213–65.

Chapter 6. Regulating the Bodies of Citizens

1. Record in Florentine archives of a prosecution under the Sumptuary Laws in 1378. Cited by Gene Brucker, ed. *The Society of Renaissance Florence* (New York: Harper and Row, 1971), 181.

2. Record in Florentine archives of the prosecution of a woman for acting as a public prostitute without wearing the required distinguishing clothing. Brucker, 192.

3. Morals controls introduced or reaffirmed during the plague period of 1527. See Varchi, Vol. I, 223–24.

4. Despite the difficulties in differentiating clearly between religious and secular responses, we have elected to review these responses in different chapters for specific reasons. First, there had already been some irreversible shifts of power from church to state before the advent of the Black Death. Second, we aim to evaluate evidence which suggests that plague responses accelerated this process, and, among other outcomes, they resulted in the incorporation into state regulations of the moral code of the church.

5. J. K. Hyde, *Society and Politics in Medieval Italy* (London: Macmillan, 1982), 48–60.

6. Samuel Kline Cohn, Jr., *The Laboring Classes in Renaissance Florence* (New York: Academic Press, 1980), 159; and Gene Brucker, "The Flo-

rentine Popolo Minuto and its Political Role," in *Violence and Disorder in Italian Cities 1200–1500*, ed. Lauro Martines (Berkeley: University of California, 1972), 175.

7. Marvin Becker, "Aspects of Lay Piety in Early Renaissance Florence," in *The Pursuit of Holiness in Late Medieval and Renaissance Religion,* eds. Charles Trinkaus and Heiko A. Oberman (Leiden: Brill, 1974), 189.

8. Brucker, "Popolo minuto," 157.

9. Martines, "A Way of Looking at Women in Renaissance Florence": 17.

10. Claudia Opitz, "Life in the Middle Ages," in *A History of Women in the West* ed. Christiane Klapisch-Zuber (Cambridge, Mass.: Belknap Press of Harvard University Press, 1992), 295–97; 300–301.

11. Marchionne, 232.

12. Marchionne, 230, 231.

13. See chapter 4, n. 23.

14. The day-to-day administrative control of the Commune was in the hands of the *Signoria*, a group of officers elected for this purpose, and holding office for a relatively short period only. The purpose of this limited duration of authority was to avoid powerful groups gaining control of the city. In practice, however, these office bearers were always drawn from a limited range of eligible persons within the ranks of the ruling elite.

15. See chapter 4, n. 31.

16. For general accounts of communal actions during the 1348 epidemic, see Aliberto B. Falsini, "Firenze dopo il 1348. Le conseguenze della peste nera," *Archivio storico italiano*, no. 129 (1971): 437–49; and Gene A. Brucker, "Florence and the Black Death," in *Boccaccio: Secoli di vita* (Ravenna: Longo, 1977), 21–30.

17. Guidobaldo Guidi, "I sistemi elettorali agli uffici della città-repubblica di Firenze nell prima metà del Trecento (1329–49)," *Archivio storico italiano*, no. 135 (1977): 414.

18. Boccaccio, *Decameron*, 12.

19. There is evidence of a similar suspension of meetings of the Councils and the administration of the state being left to a smaller group for some two months in 1498. See Rachel Erlanger, *The Unarmed Prophet: Savonarola in Florence* (New York: McGraw Hill, 1988), 203).

20. Guidi, 419; and Falsini, 475–77.

21. Names of citizens eligible for office were included in locked bags. In a form of lottery, marbles which identified these citizens were drawn from the various bags under public scrutiny.

22. Donato Velluti, *La cronica domestica di Messer Doanato Velluti*, eds. Isidoro del Lungo and Guglielmo Vopli (Florence: Sansoni, 1914), 199.

23. Guidi, 414–15, 422.

24. See Lauro Martines, *Power and Imagination: City-States in Renaissance Italy* (Harmondsworth: Penguin, 1983), Chap. IX, for an account of the transition from the popular Commune to oligarchic rule in the republican states of northern Italy, in the period covered by this review. Additional material is contained in Gene Brucker, "The Florentine Populo Minuto," 155–83.

25. See, for example, contemporary accounts: Matteo Villani, I, 4; Marchionne, 232; and Pagolo di Binghieri Rucellai, in F.W. Kent, "The Black Death of 1348 in Florence," 118. For a recent interpretation of these events, see Maria Serena Mazzi, "La peste a Firenze nel Quattrocento," in *Strutture familiari epidemie migrazioni nell'Italia medievale* (Naples: Edizioni scientifiche italiane, 1984), 109.

26. See Martines, *Power and Imagination*, Chap. V; and Lauro Martines ed., *Violence and Disorder in Italian Cities, 1200–1500* (Berkeley: University of California Press, 1972), which includes some of the papers delivered at a symposium on the theme of violence and civil disorder in Italian cities in the period 1200–1500.

27. Cited by D. Herlihy, "Some Psychlogical and Social Roots of Violence in Tuscan Cities," in *Violence and Disorder in Italian Cities, 1200–1500,* ed. Lauro Martines (Berkeley: University of California Press, 1972), 138–39.

28. Lorenzo Strozzi, "Descrizione della peste di Firenze dell'anno 1527," 33. This description was once attributed to Machiavelli.

29. Lorenzo Strozzi, 36.

30. Brian Pullan, "Plague and Perceptions of the Poor in Early Modern Italy," in *Epidemics and Ideas,* eds. Terence Ranger and Paul Slack (Cambridge: Cambridge University Press, 1992), 117.

31. Matteo Villani, Book I, Chapter 4; and Agnolo di Tura del Grasso, 556.

32. Marchionne, 232; Varchi, 223–24.

33. Cohn, 137.

34. Cohn, 169; Brucker, "Popolo minuto," 175.

35. Cohn, 84.

36. Cohn, 89.

37. See Morelli, 369–77; and Buonaccorso Pitti, in Brucker, *Two Memoirs*, 64.

38. Cohn, 111–12.

39. In a letter from Florence to her son, Alessandra Strozzi noted that in that year (1465) famine had struck at the same time as the plague. It was a very bad time for the poor, she added, since a great many died. See C. Guasti ed., *Lettere di una gentildonna fiorentina* (Florence: Sansoni, 1877, rpt. 1972), 507.

40. Anyone organizing a protest was harshly treated. In 1345, a man described in court documents as "of low condition and evil reputation" attempted to organize some fellow workers in the wool industry. He was tried for this activity, and hanged on the gallows. Cited in Brucker, *The Society of Renaissance Florence,* 235–36.

41. Brucker, "Florence and the Black Death," 23, notes that the communal authorities "made a special effort to import food into the city to reduce discontent among the poor." See also Brucker, "Popolo minuto," 171, for the increased surveillance involved.

42. Brucker, "Popolo Minuto," 163.

43. Cohn, 169.

44. *Archivio storico fiorentino*, Provisioni; Consulte e Pratiche (see n. 23), in Brucker, *The Society of Renaissance Florence,* 230–31.

45. *ASF*, Provisioni, 109, fols. 160v–61v, in Brucker, *The Society of Renaissance Florence,* 84.

46. Brucker, "The Florentine Populo Minuto," 174.

47. Casagrande, "The Protected Woman," 87.

48. Herlihy, "Some Psychological and Social Roots of Violence," 149.

49. Thomasset, "The Nature of Woman," 65–66.

50. Frugoni, 384, and in general, Dalarun, 15–42.

51. Cohn, 166–67.

52. Sherrill Cohen, *The Evolution of Women's Asylums since 1500: From Refuges for Ex-prostitutes to Shelters for Battered Women* (New York: Oxford University Press, 1992). Cohen asserts that this system of institutionalization for women preceded the systems which Foucault argued were models for later penitentiary practice. Cohen considered that Italy, France, and England viewed the rehabilitation of prostitutes and criminals as intrinsically linked.

53. Alberto Chiappelli, "Gli ordinamenti sanitari del Comune di Pistoia contro la pestilenzia del 1348," *Archivio storico italiano,* Ser. IV, Vol. XX (Florence: Vieusseux, 1887), 3–7.

54. Carlo M. Cipolla, *Public Health and the Medical Profession in the Renaissance* (Cambridge: Cambridge University Press, 1976), 13–14; Biraben, Vol. II, 138–43.

55. Cipolla, 13.

56. Lauro Martines, *Power and Imagination,* 204. See also Cohn, 183–84.

57. Carmichael, *Plague and the Poor,* 101.

58. The need for continuity in this area had been recognized earlier in other cities. Milan established such a commission in 1448, Pavia in 1485, Venice and Siena in 1486, with Florence following in 1527 (Carmichael, 122). See also Cipolla, 12, 21; and Ann Carmichael, "Contagion Theory and Contagion Practice in Fifteenth-Century Milan," *Renaissance Quarterly,* XLIV, no. 2 (1991): 216–17.

59. Cipolla, 13–14.

60. Varchi, 464–67, 470.

61. See Carmichael, *Plague and the Poor,* 100, 103–107, for a discussion of the way in which many of these controls were progressively introduced and then institutionalized.

62. The term "confinement" is used to highlight the fact that the poor districts where plague was present were physically isolated with barriers, and guards were positioned to ensure that the inhabitants of such districts did not move to other parts of the city. In the main, those from the upper levels of society who had been in contact with the disease were isolated in their own homes, and were required only to display a white ribbon at the entrance. These requirements are discussed in the main text.

63. Varchi, 465.

64. Varchi, 467.

65. Varchi, 470.

66. Varchi, 467.

67. Carmichael, *Plague and the Poor,* 4.

68. Carmichael, 4, believed that Florence was the only city in northern Italy to require evidence of cause of death before 1450.

69. Cipolla, 29–30.

70. Foucault, *Discipline and Punish*, 195–200. For an expansion of Foucault's concepts of the carceral state evolving from leprosy and plague control measures, see Stanley Cohen, *Visions of Social Control* (Cambridge: Polity Press, 1985), 26.

71. Foucault, 195.

72. Foucault, 136–38.

73. Ludovico Muratori, "Del governo della peste e delle maniere di guardarsene," in *Opere di Ludovico Antonio Muratori*, eds. Di Giorgi Falco and Fiorenzo Forti (Milan-Naples: Ricciardi, n.d.), 777.

74. This was the motivation for a great increase in charitable bequests during plague epidemics. Donors sought to gain divine favor through their actions, and so ward off plague infection.

75. Giordano da Rivalto-Moreni, from a sermon delivered in Florence in 1304.

76. Carmichael, *Plague and the Poor*, 121.

77. See Carmichael, chaps. 4 and 5; and J. N. Biraben, "Les pauvres et la peste," in *Études sur l'histoire de la pauvreté*, ed. Michel Mollat (Paris: La Sorbonne, 1974), 505–18.

78. Morelli, 294.

79. Guasti, 274.

80. Guasti, 281.

81. Boccaccio, 13–14. See also, Carlo Cipolla and Dante E. Zanetti, "Peste et Mortalité Differéntielle," in *Annales de Démographie Historique* (Paris: Mouton, 1972), 197–202, for an account of the proportionately higher death toll among the poor.

82. See, for example, Buonaccorso Pitti [Brucker, *Two Memoirs,* 22, 64, 87–88]; Dati, 96, 106; Giovanni Rucellai [Perosa, ed. *Giovanni Rucellai ed il suo Zibaldone I* (London: Warburg Institute, 1960), Introduction]; Alessandra Strozzi [Guasti, ed. 56, 82, 85]; Varchi, 12; Landucci, 23–27, 123, 125, 127.

83. Carmichael, *Plague and the Poor*, 102–103.

84. Carmichael, 103. For the establishment of plague hospitals in Milan, see Frederico Borromeo, *La peste di Milano,* ed. Armando Torno (Milan: Rusconi, 1987).

85. Landucci, 175.

86. See details of regulations in Luciano Banchi, "Provvisioni della repubblica di Siena contro la peste degli anni 1411 e 1463," already cited.

87. Landucci, 69–70; Carmichael, 105.

88. Extract from a letter dated April 12, 1493, sent by the *Otto di Guardia* to the captains supervising the approaches to Florence, cited in Carmichael, 103.

89. Carmichael, 159, n. 40.

90. Banchi, 331.

91. Cited in Iris Origo, *The Merchant of Prato* (London: Cape, 1957), 131.

92. Carmichael, 117–18.

93. See James A. Brundage, "Prostitution in the Medieval Canon Law," *Signs: Journal of Women in Culture and Society,* 1, no. 4 (1976): 824–45; and Bullough and Brundage, chapters 4 and 16, regarding the definitions of prostitution that applied in the Middle Ages.

94. *ASF,* Guidice degli Appelli, 66, no pagination, 67, fols. 14r–18v, cited in Brucker, *The Society of Renaissance Florence*, 192. See also Brucker, "The Florentine Populo Minuto," 167.

95. Cited by Vern L. Bullough, "Prostitution in the Later Middle Ages," in Vern L. Bullough and James Brundage, eds., *Sexual Practices and the Medieval Church,* 176.

96. Richard Trexler, "La prostitution florentine au XVe siècle: patronages et clientèles," *Annales Économies, Sociétés, Civilisations,* no. 36 (1981): 983.

97. *ASF,* Provisioni, 105, fols. 248r–248v, cited in Brucker, *Society of Renaissance Florence*, 190.

98. A detailed account of prostitution and homosexual activity in Venice can be found in Elisabeth Pavan, "Police des moeurs, société et politique à Venise à la fin du Moyen Age," *Revue historique,* CCLXIV, no. 2 (1980): 241–88.

99. Carmichael, *Plague and the Poor*, 123–24. The passage cited also notes that many limitations on their movements were applied to prostitutes "for fear of plague" in Spoleto in 1484, and in Perugia, Siena, and Mantua around 1485.

100. Denys Hay and John Law, *Italy in the Age of the Renaissance 1380–1530* (London: Longman, 1989), 83.

101. See Pullan, "Plague and Perceptions of the Poor in Early Modern Italy," 101–23.

102. Roberto Ridolfi, *Vita di Girolamo Savonarola,* 7th edn. (Florence: Sansoni, 1981), 35–36; Herlihy and Klapisch-Zuber, 251–52.

103. Cited in John T. Noonan, *Contraception: A History of its Treatment by the Catholic Theologians and Canonists* (Cambridge, Mass.: Harvard University Press, 1965), 260.

104. By the end of the fifteenth century, the term "sodomy" was used almost exclusively to refer to male homosexual activity. Before that, any non-procreative sexual activity, male or female, could be labelled "sodomy," so confusing many accounts of the extent of homosexuality. Accusations of sodomy were frequently levelled at persons deemed to be heretical, and also those who were political opponents. This was common throughout Europe, hence the propensity to label various cities as centers of homosexuality.

105. See Richard E. Trexler, "Ritual in Florence: Adolescence and Salvation in The Renaissance," 236–37, which supports the view that homosexuality was prevalent in Florence; and William J. Bousma, "Interventions on 'Rituals in Florence'," in the same publication, which questions the reliability of what he calls "an old stereotype," repeated from Dante into the seventeenth century.

106. Michael Rocke, *Forbidden Friendships: Homosexuality and Male Culture in Renaissance Florence* (New York: Oxford University Press, 1996).

107. See Guido Ruggiero, *The Boundaries of Eros: Sex Crime and Sexuality in Renaissance Venice* (New York: Oxford University Press, 1985), Chapter VI, for a detailed account of Venetian responses to homosexuality.

108. Peter Burke, "Homosexuality," in *A Concise Encyclopaedia of the Italian Renaissance*, ed. J. R. Hale (London: Thames and Hudson, 1981), 170. See Varchi, 224, for the renewal of penalties for the offense in 1527.

109. Michael J. Rocke, "Il controllo dell'omosessualità a Firenze nel XV secolo: Gli Ufficiali di Notte," *Quaderni storici,* no. 66 (1987): 704–705.

109. Origo, *The World of San Bernardino*, 146.

110. Rocke, "Il controllo," 718, notes that, although the term "sodomy" could include any form of same-sex activity, there are no cases of lesbianism to be found in the records of the Officers of the night. A similar magistracy was established in Lucca, another Tuscan city, in 1448.

111. Carmichael, *Plague and the Poor*, 98.

112. Nel Noddings, 43.

113. Origo, *The World of San Bernardino*, 146.

114. Cited in Maclean, 25.

115. Rocke, "Il controllo," 708.

116. Katherine Park, *Doctors and Medicine in Early Renaissance Florence* (Princeton: Princeton University Press, 1985), 4; Carmichael, *Plague and the Poor*, 88–89.

117. Carmichael, 123–25, notes that these two groups, as well as the itinerant poor, were marginalized even further in other cities of northern Italy. Apart from banishment from cities, or strict limitations on their activities, they were sometimes required to wear distinctive yellow clothing. See also Paolo Preto, *Peste e società a Venezia nel 1576* (Vicenza: Possa, 1978), 57, 84–85, for the continued application in Venice in 1576 of moral sanctions during plague epidemics, and of controls for "dangerous others," who were accused of spreading plague infection.

118. Gottfried, 52–53; Biraben, Vol. I, 57–65; Muratori, 781–82.

119. Bernardino of Siena, *Prediche,* Vol. II, 95.

120. Brucker, *The Society of Renaissance Florence,* 180–81, citing from original documents of the Commune.

121. Diane Owen Hughes, "Regulating Women's Fashions," in *A History of Women in the West: Silences of the Middle Ages,* ed. Christiane Klapisch-Zuber (Cambridge, Mass.: Belknap Press of Harvard University Press, 1992), 136–58.

122. Hughes, "Regulating Women's Fashions," 143.

123. See Cipolla, 29; Carmichael, 104–105, for examples of the impact on the community of this exercise of power by the Plague Officers.

124. Trexler, *Public Life*, 363–64.

125. Becker, "Aspects of Lay Piety in Early Renaissance Florence," 178.

126. Landucci, 148, and footnote 1.

127. Pullan, 113.

128. Marvin B. Becker, "Church and State in Florence on the Eve of the Renaissance (1343–82)," *Speculum,* XXXVII, no. 4 (1962): 533, records that from 1375, the state began to take over many areas previously the province of the church. There were some functions which the church was always happy to hand over to the state—to carry out sentences which involved executions. See Mundy, 320.

129. Brucker, "Florence and the Black Death," 25.

130. Becker, "Aspects of Lay Piety in Early Renaissance Florence," 177.

Chapter 7. The Diseased Body Confronts Medicine

1. Marsilio Ficino, *Opera omnia,* Vol. I (Turin: Bottega d'Erasmo, 1962), 607. Ficino, a prominent Florentine philosopher, was also trained in medicine.

2. Matteo Villani, Book I, 2.

3. This prophylactic advice was issued by the Venetian Council of Ten in 1576. It is recorded in the State Archives of Venice, and was cited by Paolo Preto, 214–15.

4. We use the term "medical practitioner" to cover the diverse range of people offering medical treatment and entitled to be members of the medical guild which issued a license to practice. In the late Middle Ages, the medical guild of Florence, and of many other northern Italian cities, included practitioners who gained their knowledge through practical experience (the "empirics"), and those who had graduated from a university medical school. University educated physicians and surgeons were in the minority. We have avoided the use of the word "doctor" since that suggests a university trained practitioner as we know it today. Graduates of any faculty at medieval universities could be addressed as "doctor."

5. Herzlich and Pierret, 86.

6. See, for example, Corinthians 6: 15, 19 and 20.

7. The Book of Leviticus focuses repeatedly on the polluting influence of the body.

8. Marie-Christine Pouchelle, *The Body and Surgery in the Middle Ages,* trans. Rosemary Morris (Cambridge: Polity Press, 1990), 53–54.

9. Cartwright, 42–43. There are many accounts of the foundation of this school, some suggesting its inception early in the next century. The discrepancy does not affect the general thrust of the argument.

10. Vern L. Bullough, "Training of the Nonuniversity-Educated Medical Practitioners in the Later Middle Ages," *Journal of the History of Medicine,* no. 14 (1959): 446–58; Cartwright, 40; Raffaele Ciasca, *L'arte dei medici e speziali nella storia e nel commercio fiorentino dal secolo XII al XV* (Florence: Olschki, 1927), 285; Park, 12.

11. See Siraisi, 13–16 for a general account of the evolution of the new medical culture.

12. Galenic theories have been commented upon by many writers. Two which might be consulted are Winslow, 56–74; and Vivian Nutton, "The Seeds of Disease: An Explanation of Contagion and Infection from the Greeks to the Renaissance," *Medical History,* no. 27 (1983): 1–34.

13. See Arturo Castiglioni, *A History of Medicine,* 2nd edn., trans. E. B. Krumbhaar (New York: Knopf, 1941), 325–33; and Brian Inglis, *A History of Medicine* (London: Weidenfield and Nicolson, 1965), 66–67 for an overview of the conflicting viewpoints of the church and the proponents of secular medicine.

14. Zaner, 116.

15. See Turner, *Medical Power and Social Knowledge,* 20–28 for a more extended treatment of this theme.

16. Kee, 44.

17. Pouchelle, 74–75.

18. See the relevant quotation at the beginning of this chapter.

19. Kee, 5.

20. Siraisi, 23–24.

21. Cartwright, 16–17; Pouchelle, 20.

22. Ciasca, 75. In this period the guild was known as *L'arte dei medici, speziali e merciai.* While the *speziali* (apothecaries) and *merciai* (merchants) included many subgroups, the *medici* (medical practitioners) were limited to medical practitioners with a wide range of backgrounds, and barbers (Ciasca, 60–61).

23. Ciasca, 304. See also Pouchelle, 45–46.

24. Ciasca, 305.

25. Cartwright, *A Social History of Medicine,* 16.

26. Pouchelle, 151.

27. This distinction could not be applied without some qualification. In northern Italian cities, for example, some surgeons received their training at universities as did some physicians. As already noted, however, university educated practitioners were in the minority during the fourteenth and fifteenth centuries.

28. See for example, Haskins, *The Renaissance of the Twelfth Century,* for a broad-ranging discussion of this period.

29. Ynez Viole O'Neill, "Innocent III and the Evolution of Anatomy," *Medical History,* no. 20 (1976): 429–33.

30. Baird, 621.

31. Castiglioni, 336.

32. See Castiglioni, 341–45; Siraisi, 78–86; and Jacquart and Thomasset, 41.

33. Mary Niven Alston, "The Attitude of the Church Towards Dissection before 1500," *Bulletin of the History of Medicine,* no. 16 (1944): 221–38.

34. Castiglioni, 344, notes that where discrepancies were found between Galen's treatises and the evidence offered by dissection, the lecturer would declare that the original text must have been changed by the Arabs or become corrupt in the various translations.

35. See Cartwright, 16. This declaration was made as late as the 1530s. The lecturer was Jacques Dubois under whom Vesalius studied in Paris.

36. Ronald Hare, *Pomp and Pestilence* (London: Gollancz, 1954), 72.

37. Boccaccio, 10, claimed that sometimes they could be the size of an apple, at other times that of an egg.

38. For further information on plague variants and their methods of transmission see McNeill, *Plagues and Peoples,* 123–25; Gottfried, *The Black Death,* xiii; É. Carpentier, "Autor de la peste noire: Famines et épidémie dans l'histoire du XIV siècle," *Annales: Economies, Sociétés, Civilisations,* no. 17 (1962): 1081.

39. See Frederick Cartwright, *Disease and History* (New York: Thomas Y. Crowell, 1972), 52. The identification of *Pasteurella pestis* was made almost simultaneously by a Japanese and a Swiss during an outbreak of plague at Hong Kong in 1884.

40. Refer to the two citations at the beginning of this chapter that show the part played by the theory of astral causation in medical discourse.

41. For a more detailed account of the many treatises on disease causation that appeared in the fourteenth and fifteenth centuries see, for example, Campbell, Chapter III; and Lynn Thorndike, *A History of Magic and Experimental Science* (New York: Columbia University Press, 1934), Vol. III.

42. John M. Riddle, "Theory and Practice in Medieval Medicine," *Viator,* no. 5 (1974): 158–61.

43. Muratori, 783.

44. This information was included in a chronicle written in Pistoia. See "Storie Pistoresi," *Rerum italicarum scriptores,* Vol. 11, pt. 5, ed. Silvio Barbi (Città di Castello: Lapi, 1907), 236–38.

45. Marsilio Ficino, *Opera omnia,* Vol. I (Turin: Bottega d'Erasmo, 1962), 610.

46. An extensive treatment of contemporary writing on astrological medicine can be found in several chapters of Thorndike, Vols. III and IV.

47. Marchionne, 230.

48. Matteo Villani, Book I, 2; Francesco Petrarca, *Invective contra medicum,* ed., Pier Giorgio Ricci (Rome: Edizioni di storia e letteratura, 1978).

49. Morelli, 292–98. This also included advice to refrain from sexual intercourse, and to generally avoid contact with women.

50. Marchionne, 230, 232.

51. Varchi, 466.

52. Pietro Aretino, *Lettere,* ed. Sergio Ortolani (Turin: Einaudi, 1945), "Medici," 82–83 and "Salute e Medicina," 99–101.

53. Quoted in Park, 36.

54. Enea Silvio Piccolomini, *I commentari,* 2 vols., trans.(from the Latin), Guiseppe Bernetti (Milan: Longanesi, 1981), Vol. I, 27.

55. Piccolomini, Vol. II, 784, recorded that many people believed that the benefits of one particular wild herb had been revealed to Carlo Magno by an angel.

56. Biraben, *Les hommes et la peste,* Vol. II, 56–62, reviews the extent to which Europeans turned to magic rituals during the plague epidemics. See also Muratori, 782–84.

57. Carlo M. Cipolla, "A Plague Doctor," in *The Medieval City,* eds. H. Miskimin, et al. (New Haven: Yale University Press, 1977), 65–72 refers to this situation within a broad discussion of problems faced by medical practitioners during plague periods.

58. Ciasca, 289, citing medical guild records of 1348.

59. Park, 31–34.

60. Michel Foucault, *Power/Knowledge,* ed. C. Gordon (Brighton, UK: Harvester Press, 1980).

61. Generally, the universities of northern Italy were in advance of other centers in providing education for physicians and surgeons. For this reason, university trained surgeons were more common in Italy than elsewhere.

62. Cartwright, *A Social History of Medicine*, 16.

63. Ciasca, 278, footnote 4, citing records of the resolutions, "per potere più chiaramente conosciere le malattie dei corpi."

64. Campbell, 111.

65. Ciasca, 278, footnote 4.

66. Ciasca, 277–78.

67. Ciasca, 281, cites this statute and notes that medical guilds in many other northern Italian cities were adopting similar programs at about the same time. They also called for regular dissections for educational purposes.

68. Herzlich and Pierret, 75.

69. Michel Foucault, *The Birth of the Clinic,* trans. A. M. Sheridan-Smith (New York: Vintage Books, 1975), chapter 8.

70. The extent to which dissection influenced the practice of medicine, and informed Renaissance and Enlightenment art and culture, can be seen, for example, in the following works: Jonathon Sawday, *The Body Emblazoned: Dissection and the Human Body in Renaissance Culture* (New York: Routledge, 1997; Carla Mazzio and David Hillman, eds. *The Body in Parts: Fantasies of Corporeality in Early Modern Europe* (New York: Routledge, 1997); and B. Stafford, *Body Criticism: Imaging the Unseen in Enlightenment Art and Medicine* (Cambridge, Mass.: MIT Press, 1993).

71. Bryan Turner, *Regulating Bodies: Essays in Medical Sociology* (London: Routledge, 1992), chapter 7, "The Anatomy Lesson."

72. Castiglioni, 413.

73. Castiglioni, 419.

74. Jacquart and Thomasset, 171; Ehrenreich and English, 13–16.

75. See Margaret A. Murray, *The God of the Witches* (London: Oxford University Press, 1970), 145–46; Noddings, 45; and Carol F. Karlsen, *The Devil in the Shape of Woman* (New York: Vintage Books, 1989), 142.

76. John Henderson, "The Hospitals of Late-Medieval and Renaissance Florence: A Preliminary Survey," in Lindsay Grimshaw and Roy Porter, eds., *The Hospital in History* (London: Routledge, 1989), 63–92.

77. Park, 106.

78. Turner, *Medical Power,* 157.

79. Turner, 162–63.

Part III. Fin-de-siècle Forebodings

1. Jean Baudrillard, *CTheory*, Article 34, March 8, 1995, available electronically from http://www.ctheory.com/ INTERNET. Originally published as part of Jean Baudrillard, *L'Illusion de la fin: ou La greve des even-emnets,* trans. Charles Dudas (Paris: Galilee, 1992).

Chapter 8. The Danger of Touch:
The Body and Social Distance

1. Landucci, 131–41, These extracts from the diary of Luca Landucci, a Florentine apothecary, are based on our translation. Landucci compared the physical manifestation of the disease with that of variola, more generally known as smallpox, which had been known in Europe for some centuries. The common term is derived from the old English word "pock" (plural pocks, now "pox") used to describe a pustule. From the early sixteenth century, two separate diseases were recognized—"small-pox," and the "great pox," the latter being the common name in English for the new scourge, syphilis.

2. Plague did largely disappear from Europe by the latter part of the seventeenth century. However, it continues to survive in rodent populations in many parts of the world, even in developed countries such as the USA. For instance, the squirrels and chipmunks in some wooded areas of California still harbour plague, and under favorable circumstances, the disease can be transmitted to domestic animals. Even more rarely, it is transmitted to humans. In other parts of the world, recent outbreaks have been more serious, notably in the Kazakhstan region of the former Soviet Union in 1993; and, more spectacularly, in India in 1994. Each year there are cases in Burma, Vietnam, Sudan, sub-Saharan Africa, and the Americas although the death toll is fairly low. Plague still appears to respond to treatment with modern drugs if used at an early stage.

3. Syphilis continues to be a "social disease" which is again causing community concern. It has reappeared on an epidemic scale in many areas in the latter part of the twentieth century. In its present form it is resistant to the drug treatments previously effective in the first half of the century We will take up this issue in the next chapter.

4. Francesco Guicciardini, *Storia d'Italia,* 4 vols., ed. Costantino Panigada (Bari: Laterza, 1967), 205.

5. The end of the fifteenth century and the early sixteenth century gave strong evidence of this expansion of intellectual horizons influencing medical theory. It paralleled expanding geographical, philosophical, and religious worlds.

6. Guicciardini, 204.

7. Girolamo Fracastoro, *Fracastoro's Syphilis,* trans. and ed. Geoffrey Eatough (Liverpool: Cairns, 1984). 97.

8. In a similar vein, Sander Gilman posits an association between the color black, particularly people with black skins, and the diseases of syphilis and AIDS, in the iconographic representations of disease. See his

"Touch, sexuality and disease," in *Medicine and the Five Senses,* eds. W. F. Bynum and Roy Porter (Cambridge: Cambridge University Press, 1993), 198–224.

9. Amerigo Vespucci was a Florentine explorer who took part in the Columbus expeditions, and later, undertook other voyages of discovery to the Americas. His name was given to the whole of the New World area.

10. Cited by Anna Foa, "The New and the Old: The Spread of Syphilis (1494–1530)," in *Sex and Gender in Historical Perspective,* eds. Edward Muir and Guido Ruggiero (Baltimore: Johns Hopkins University Press, 1990), 31–32.

11. Claude Quétel, *History of Syphilis,* trans. Judith Braddock and Brian Pike (Baltimore: Johns Hopkins University Press, 1990), 37–40.

12. See for example, Jacquard and Thomasset, 177–83; Quétel, 37–42.

13. Cartwright, *Disease and History* 60–62, states that it is a similar organism which produces yaws and syphilis. He explores the possibility of syphilis being a mutant of yaws introduced to Europe from Africa. See also Megan Vaughan, "Syphilis in Colonial East and Central Africa: The Social Construction of an Epidemic," in *Epidemics and Ideas,* eds. Terence Ranger and Paul Slack (Cambridge: Cambridge University Press, 1992), 269–302, for reference to the difficulties encountered even in the twentieth century in accounting for the differences between endemic syphilis, venereally transmitted syphilis, and yaws in Africa.

14. Castiglioni, *A History of Medicine,* 453–54. See also Alfred W. Crosby, Jr., *The Columbian Exchange* (Westport, Conn.: Greenwood, 1972), 141–48.

15. Guicciardini, 204.

16. Italy, with political power fragmented by rivalry between city-states and the Papal territories, became a battleground on which France and Spain fought for territorial supremacy from the late fifteenth century onward. The southern part of the Italian pensinsular was already dominated by Spain, while the French exercised great influence in certain areas of the north. Caught between these major powers, the states and the territories often aligned themselves first with one and then the other foreign power. This allowed invaders to rampage about Italy without meeting well-coordinated resistance.

17. See Guicciardini, 204–205, for contemporary use of these descriptions. This writer also advanced a theory which became more popular later, that it was the Spanish who had brought the disease to Naples in the first place.

18. See Quétel, 11–15; Crosby, 124–25; and Foa, 26.

19. Despite the variety of names given to the disease as it appeared in different countries, its most enduring label was the "French disease." Almost from its first appearance in Europe, it became known as *morbus gallicus* (the French disease) in medical circles, so perpetuating the attribution of blame for its spread to the French. It was only in the nineteenth century that the term "syphilis" was adopted, drawing on the title of the late Renaissance poem by Girolamo Fracastoro, a well-established figure in medicine, on the disease and its treatment. See note 7 above.

20. This argument is elaborated in Susan Sontag, "Illness as a Metaphor," in *Illness as a Metaphor and AIDS and its Metaphors* (New York: Anchor-Doubleday, 1990).

21. Quétel, 23–24.

22. Venus, the goddess of love (including sexual love); Bacchus, the god of wine; and Ceres, the goddess of corn and the harvest, were well known to educated men of the medieval and early modern periods, and their names were frequently invoked in circumlocutory accounts of everyday events.

23. An extract from Grunpeck's account of his illness, cited by Quétel, 17.

24. This is a well-known representation of a syphilitic. See, for example, Sander L. Gilman, *Disease and Representation* (Ithaca: Cornell University Press, 1988), 248–50.

25. A copy of the sketch and some comments on its iconographic significance are to be found in Gilman, 52–57. See also Quétel, 30

26. Quoted in Gilman, 56 [our translation].

27. Benvenuto Cellini, *The Autobiography of Benvenuto Cellini,* trans. George Bull (Harmondsworth: Penguin, 1981), 152–59.

28. Some examples of the use of the syphilitic in literature are referred to in Quétel, 67–72; 123–30. For similar attitudes to the responsibility for sexually transmitted disease, in this instance gonorrhea, see also James Boswell, *Boswell's London Journal 1762–1763,* ed. Frederick A. Pottle (Melbourne: Heinemann, 1951), 39–153. Boswell described his pursuit and seduction of women and the unpleasant consequences. He railed at the perfidy of the woman who caused his predicament.

29. Marbode of Rennes, cited by Jacques Dalarun, "The Clerical Gaze," 21.

30. Robert Graves, *The Greek Myths,* 2 vols. (Harmondsworth: Penguin, 1981), Vol. 1, 145. See also Thomas Bullfinch, *Bullfinch's Mythology* (New York: Avenal Books, 1979), 13–14, for two slightly different versions of the myth.

31. Penzer, 18; and 24–25. The *motif* has enjoyed a long life. Fatal poisoning by intercourse provides the basis for Machiavelli's play *La Mandragola,* written in 1518. (See Niccolò Macchiavelli, "The Mandragola," in *Five Italian Renaissance Comedies,* trans. and ed. Bruce Penman (Harmondsworth: Penguin, 1978), 11–58. The same theme is central to the drama *The Council of Love,* written by Oscar Panizza in 1895, and based on the arrival of syphilis in 1495. (See Quétel, 45–49).

32. Brunetto Latini, whose inspiration for Dante was mentioned in the *Divina Commedia,* lived in exile in France for several years, and this work was originally published as *Li livres dou Tesor.* We refer to the Italian version entitled *Il Tesoro di Brunetto Latini versificato.*

33. Haskins, 117; Penzer, 27–28.

34. Machiavelli's choice of title offers a rich field of semantic interpretations. The "mandragola," also known as a mandragora, is a member of the mandrake family, well known for its poisonous characteristics. The source of its many miraculous properties, including an ability to restore a woman's fertility, is the root of the plant. This is said to be shaped like the lower limbs of a man. See Martin Kemp, "'The Mark of Truth': looking and learning in some anatomical illustrations from the Renaissance and eighteenth century," in *Medicine and the Five Senses,* eds. W.F.Bynum and Roy Porter (Cambridge: Cambridge University Press, 1993), 86–87.

35. See chapter 7 for a more detailed discussion of the debate on menstrual blood.

36. Jacquart and Thomasset, 191.

37. See Ottavia Niccoli, "'Menstruum Quasi Monstruum': Monstrous Births and Menstrual Taboos in the Sixteenth Century," in *Sex and Gender in Historical Perspective,* eds. Edward Muir and Guido Ruggiero (Baltimore: Johns Hopkins University Press, 1990), 1–25, for a detailed account of discourses on monstrous births and on leprosy as an outcome of intercourse during menstruation.

38. Quétel, 25.

39. Cited by Winslow, 125.

40. Cited by Quétel, 25–26, from the treatise of the medical writer Cataneous (Jacobi Catanei de Lucamarino, *De Morbo Gallico Tractatus,* 1504).

41. Fracastoro, 67.

42. Quétel, 69.

43. Winslow, 125.

44. Although Italy had been the most important publishing country in Europe during the incunabular period (from the introduction of the printed

book until 1499), and it continued to be prominent in this field into the sixteenth century, book publishing also expanded rapidly in other countries as well. The outcome was a much greater dissemination of information on a wide range of subjects. New ideas and developments began to emerge from many other centers in Europe. For this reason, we will cite from relevant source material from various parts of Europe from this point on.

45. Some examples of medical practitioners reporting on their own problems with syphilis can be found in Quétel, 16–19 and 27–30.

46. Diaz de Isla, cited by Quétel, 35–36.

47. Fracastoro, 22, 67, 71, and 75.

48. The importance of these concepts for medicine were discussed in chapter 7.

49. In the early speculation about the origins of syphilis, medical experts canvassed the possibility that it was a form of leprosy. This hypothesis was quickly discarded.

50. Fracastoro, 55–57. In the original Latin, the term *caries* expresses the notion of rot and decay, singularly appropriate for the effects of syphilis on the body.

51. Guicciardini, 205.

52. Cited by Quétel, 10.

53. Desiderius Erasmus, *The Collected Works of Erasmus,* vol. 29, eds. Elaine Fantham and Erika Rummel (Toronto: University of Toronto Press, 1989), 259, in the dedicatory letter to *Lingua* (The Tongue).

54. See Cartwright, *Disease and History*, 62–65, and Quétel, 50–52.

55. For example, Guicciardini, 205, Crosby, 151–52 and Cartwright, 65.

56. Sontag, 133.

57. Amboise Paré, *Oeuvres,* "Le seizième livre traitant de la grosse vérole," cited by Quétel, 33.

58. Some disorders of the body are still characterized by attributions of moral deficiency, and regarded as posing threats to society. See Simon Williams, "Goffman, interactionism, and the management of stigma in everyday life," in *Sociological Theory and Medical Sociology,* ed. Graham Scambler (London: Tavistock, 1989), 150.

59. Herzlich and Pierret, 161, review the way in which the medical profession seized on the concept of the "social scourge" as an instrument for consolidating the physician's social status.

60. The medicalization of illness and disorders, and the social control such a process delivered to the medical profession, is an area that has been explored by an increasing number of writers over the last couple of decades. Peter Conrad, "Medicalization and Social Control," *Annual Review of Sociology*, no. 18 (1992): 209–32, examined the major conceptual issues involved and reviewed the literature published on this topic since 1980. Others have also made major contributions to the discussion, for example, Malcolm Bull, "Secularization and Medicalization," *The British Journal of Sociology* 41, no. 2 (1990): 245–61; and Turner, *Medical Power and Social Knowledge*. Among the early papers focusing on this issue is that of Irving Kenneth Zola, "Medicine as an Institution of Social Control," *Sociological Review* 20 (Nov. 1972): 487–504. In that paper, Zola noted a proliferation of social control mechanisms in the twentieth century, and concluded that medicine was "nudging aside, if not incorporating, the more traditional institutions of religion and law," in the field of social control.

The subheading for this section, "The Fine Seeds of the Invisible Contagion," is a phrase already cited from Fracastoro's poem *Syphilis,* 71.

61. Castiglioni, 466.

62. Girolamo Fracastoro, *Il contagio: Le malattie contagiose e la loro cura,* trans. (from the Latin), Busacchi (Florence: Olschki, 1950). This relatively small volume, whose title translates as "Contagion: The Contagious Diseases and their Cure," was arguably the most important of Fracastoro's many scientific works.

63. Fracastoro used the Latin *semen* (seed), but there is also another word *germen* whose principal meanings are bud, sprout, or sprig, but which also can be translated as seed. It is from *germen* that the Italian *germe,* the French *germe,* and the English "germ," are derived to convey the sense of an agent of infection

64. See Nutton, "The Seeds of Disease: An Explanation of Contagion and Infection from the Greeks to the Renaissance": 1–34.

65. Charles and Dorothea Singer, "The Scientific Position of Girolamo Fracastoro," *Annals of Medical History* 1, no. 1 (1971): 5. See also Castiglioni, 457.

66. The advice of Coridano Gilino, a medical practitioner of Ferrara in 1497, cited by Quétel, 22.

67. This hazard was referred to in a satirical poem written by Galileo in the late sixteenth century. He declared that if a man were naked, it would be obvious if he suffered from "some malady" [syphilis], but a woman would need "but three or four chestnut leaves" to hide any "blemish." See Galileo Galilei, "Capitolo contro il portar la toga" ["Satirical verse against the wearing of gowns"], in Lucio Felici, ed. *Poesia italiana del Seicento* (Milan: Garzanti, 1978), 479–80. Galileo is, of course, better known for his scientific works.

68. Observations made by Ulrich von Hutten, a devout Lutheran whose womanizing during the early sixteenth century introduced him to the pains as well as the pleasures of women. Cited by Quétel, 28.

69. Fracastoro, *Contagion,* 59.

70. Quétel, 23.

71. Fracastoro, *Contagion,* 7.

72. Marsilio Ficino, *Commentary on Plato's Symposium on Love,* trans. Sears Jayne (Dallas, Texas: Spring Publications, 1985), in general, but in particular, passages in Speeches VI and VII. To men of the Middle Ages and the Renaissance, earthly love was a form of folly or madness. This type of love was the antithesis of the spiritual love to which all humans should aspire.

73. Ficino, 162. It was common in early medical treatises to include a section on "the disease of love" (see p. 29, note 14). Love as a disease was a frequently used *motif* in Italian Renaissance poetry.

74. Roy Porter, "The Rise of the Physical Examination," in *Medicine and the Five Senses,* eds. W.F. Bynum and Roy Porter (Cambridge: Cambridge University Press, 1993), 190–91.

75. Porter, 179, observes that a doctor who omits a thorough "hands-on" examination of a patient nowadays would be considered negligent.

76. Vivian Nutton, "Galen at the Bedside: The Methods of a Medical Detective," in *Medicine and the Five Senses,* eds. W.F. Bynum and Roy Porter (Cambridge: Cambridge University Press, 1993), 11–13.

77. Chapter 7 contained an overview of the circumstances that led to the emergence of a medical profession based on university-trained practitioners, rather than those who had gained their knowledge by practice only. The same conditions resulted in a sharper definition of the roles of physicians and surgeons. Before the advent of syphilis, the physician considered it unnecessary, and undesirable, to touch the bodies of patients except for very limited diagnostic procedures. It was the surgeon, on the other hand, who carried responsibility for the manual manipulation of the body during treatment regimes.

78. Synnott, 19, saw these developments as part of the process that began to "privatize" the body in the sixteenth century.

79. Porter, 179–80, discusses these issues in relation to present day practice.

80. Jerome Bylebyl, "The Manifest and the Hidden in the Renaissance Clinic," in *Medicine and the Five Senses,* eds. W.F. Bynum and Roy Porter (Cambridge: Cambridge University Press, 1993), 40–60. Bylebyl

notes that da Monte's reputation faded after the end of the sixteenth century and his methods of hospital teaching had to be rediscovered in the early nineteenth century.

81. Bylebyl, 42.

82. David Armstrong, "Bodies of Knowledge: Foucault and the Problem of Human Anatomy," in *Medicine and the Five Senses,* eds. W.F. Bynum and Roy Porter (Cambridge: Cambridge University Press, 1993), 71, draws attention to these parallels in twentieth century medical practice.

83. Quétel, 6.

84. Fracastoro, *Contagion*, 60–61.

85. Varchi, vol. 2, 284.

86. Quétel, 65, refers to the decision of French authorities to opt to follow the Italian pattern and establish separate hospitals for syphilitics.

87. Varchi, vol. 2, 100–101, described the establishment of such a hospital in Florence in the mid-1500s. Other such hospitals were established in Italy, for example, in Genoa and in Rome. See Partner, 108, for an account of the way in which the hospital in Rome functioned.

88. As with plague, those who could afford to engage their own medical practitioners were treated for syphilis at home, unless they suffered major physical disabilities. Cellini, in his autobiography, described the treatment prescribed, and administered to him, by a number of visiting medical practitioners. (See note 27 of this chapter).

89. Bad odors had been blamed for disease transmission from the ancient past, and still feature in some community discourse. See Richard Palmer, "In bad odor: smell and its significance," in *Medicine and the Five Senses,* eds. W.F. Bynum and Roy Porter (Cambridge: Cambridge University Press, 1993), 65.

90. Castiglioni, 465; Palmer, 65; and Quétel, 65.

91. Syphilis may lie dormant, apparently arrested, only to reappear in its tertiary stage during which the disease attacks the central nervous system. A patient may then exhibit signs of syphilitic paralysis and mental derangement. See Quétel, 160–64.

92. It was common practice throughout Europe in the sixteenth century to house the "incurables" (syphilitics) and those afflicted by "madness" in the same hospitals. See Michel Foucault, *Madness and Civilization,* trans. Richard Howard (New York: Pantheon/Random House, 1965), 6 and 35 for passing references to disused lazar-houses being employed in France to house "incurables and madmen." However, Foucault did not identify the

nature of the apparently incurable disease, nor comment on whether the two categories of inmate he described might have had something in common.

93. For the upsurge in interest in "madness" in the sixteenth century see, for example, Foucault, 13–17, and Gilman, *Disease and Representaion*, 20–24

94. Because it takes from ten to twenty years for the tertiary stage of syphilis to develop, it is not surprising that the connection between syphilis and "madness" was not recognized early in the sixteenth century.

95. Quétel, 162–64.

96. Uta Gerhardt, "Parsons, role theory and Health Interaction," in *Sociological Theory and Medical Sociology,* ed. Graham Scambler (London: Tavistock, 1987), 121.

97. According to Richard E. Trexler, "La prostitution florentine," 1005, Florentine authorities perceived this as a crisis within the community.

98. Partner, 98. The courtesan operated from a salon rather that the streets, and served a higher class clientele. The first pornographic work of modern Europe, the *Ragionamenti* (1534–39) of Pietro Aretino had a courtesan as its central character.

99. Crosby, 156, and Castiglioni, 464.

100. See Partner, 97–99; and Kathryn Norberg, "Prostitutes," in *A History of Women in the West: Renaissance and Enlightenment Paradoxes,* eds. Natalie Zemon and Arlette Farge (Cambridge, Mass.: Belknap Press/ Harvard University Press, 1993), 458.

101. The role of prostitution in European cities is discussed in more detail in chapter 6 in the section headed "Managing Polluted Bodies."

102. The expansion of prostitution is seen as linked to the higher number of unmarried women in communities such as Florence. It would appear that many of these women, unable to fund the inflated cost of dowries then being demanded, turned to prostitution as a means of financial support. Contemporary documents show that even girls from the more affluent families frequently found the cost of a dowry a barrier to marriage, although a more modest amount of money could constitute a dowry suitable for their entry into a convent. At other levels of society, prostitution was one of very few avenues of escape from destitution. See, Trexler, "La prostitution florentine," 1005; and generally, Gene A. Brucker, "The Florentine *Popolo Minuto*," 155–83.

103. See Ruggiero, *The Boundaries of Eros*, 14–15, for links between unemployment and prostitution in Venice, a city typical of the larger urban centres of Europe in the early Modern period.

104. Trexler, "La prositution florentine," 1104–106.

105. Desiderius Erasmus, *The Colloquies of Erasmus,* trans. Craig R. Thompson (Chicago: University of Chicago Press, 1965), 156.

106. See chapter 6, where this material has been cited.

107. Cited by Crosby, 158–59.

108. Castiglioni, 465, and Quétel, 66.

109. Cited by Castiglioni, 465.

110. Castiglioni, 465.

111. Norberg, 460–61.

112. Vaughan, 272, provides an interesting twentieth century parallel with the early modern European construction of "woman." Vaughan cites the opinion of an African Prime Minister than an epidemic outbreak of syphilis was caused by the "emancipation of Baganda women from the surveillance to which they have hitherto been subjected."

113. The origins of institutions for women have been explored in detail in the work of Sherrill Cohen (cited above). See also Lucia Ferrante, "Honor Regained: Women in the Casa del Soccorso di San Paolo in Sixteenth-century Bologna," in *Sex and Gender in Historical Perspective,* eds. Edward Muir and Guido Ruggiero (Baltimore: Johns Hopkins University Press, 1990), 46–72, for an account of several such institutions in the Bologna region.

114. Michel Foucault, *Discipline and Punish,* 195 ff.

115. See chapter 5.

116. Fracastoro, *Syphilis,* 55.

117. Fracastoro, *Contagion,* 59.

118. Sara F. Matthews Grieco, "The Body, Appearance and Sexuality," in *A History of Women in the West: Renaissance and Enlightment Paradoxes,* eds. Natalie Zemon Davis and Arlette Farge (Cambridge, Mass.: Belknap Press of Harvard University Press, 1993), 65, reports the case of eight young men imprisoned for one month on bread and water in Frankfurt in 1541, for swimming naked in the river.

119. This opinion was expressed frequently. See, for example, reference to the 1564 treatise of Andrea Gilio da Fabriano, *Dialogo degli errori della pittura* ["An Account of the Errors in Painting"], in J.H. Elliott, *Europe Divided 1559–1598* (Glascow: Fontana/Collins, 1968), 153.

120. Desiderius Erasmus, "On Good Manners for Boys," in *Collected Works of Erasmus,* vol. 25, ed. J.K. Sowards, trans. Brian McGregor (Toronto: University of Toronto Press, 1985), 274–89. This passage appears on p. 279.

121. Erasmus, "Good Manners," 289.

122. Erasmus, "Good Manners," 277.

123. Synnott, 19.

124. Margaret Miles, *Carnal Knowing: Female Nakedness and Religious Meaning in the Christian West* (New York: Vintage Books, 1991), 135–36.

125. Grieco, 65.

126. Shilling, 55–58, discusses this issue and suggests further that the male sense of weakness was also directed toward people of "non-white" background, by Western society.

127. See Joan Scott, "Gender: A Useful Category of Historical Analysis," *American Historical Review,* no. 91 (1986): 1053–75, for a detailed discussion on the issues of gender and power relationships in history. Scott, 1069, concluded that: "Gender is not the only field, but it seems to have been a persistent and recurrent way of enabling signification of power in the West. . . ."

128. Miles, 162.

129. Castiglione, *The Book of the Courtier.*

130. Castiglione, 211.

131. Castiglione, 212.

132. Castiglione, 215.

133. This issue is discussed in more detail in chapter 6.

134. Some of the women who broke through the barriers are discussed in chapter 5.

135. We refer to this in chapter 6.

136. E.R. Chamberlin, *The World of the Italian Renaissance* (London: George Allen and Unwin, 1982), 193–94. The deliberations of the Council of Trent established much of the framework for the Counter-Reformation.

137. Olwen Hufton, "Women, Work, and Family," in *A History of Women in the West: Renaissance and Enlightenment Paradoxes,* eds. Natalie Zemon Davis and Arlette Farge (Cambridge, Mass.: The Belknap Press of Harvard University Press, 1993), 40.

138. Cited by Crosby, 159. The incident is also referred to by Cartwright, 64.

139. Erasmus, *Colloquies,* 150.

140. Erasmus argued that a marriage between a healthy person and one carrying syphilis was immoral and should be annulled. See Erasmus, "A Marriage in Name Only," *Colloquies,* 401–12.

141. Crosby, 159.

142. Erasmus, *Colloquies*, 150 and 402.

143. Erasmus, *Colloquies*, 150.

144. Grieco, 47–50.

145. Fracastoro, *Contagion*, 61.

146. Quétel, 57.

147. Fracastoro, *Syphilis*, 14, and 32 note 91.

148. See note 120.

149. Available in an English translation as Baldesar Castiglione, *The Book of the Courtier,* trans. George Bull (London: Penguin, 1976). The work was written between 1508 and 1518, but not finally published until 1528.

150. For some two centuries the treatise of Erasmus was being issued in an almost continuous stream of new editions and translations. See Elias, *The Civilizing Process*, 140, who cites Huizinga on this matter.

151. Erasmus, "On Good Manners," 273.

152. An expression that implies a degree of nonchalance, of presenting your abilities and attributes as of little concern to yourself, of acting in a manner which shows effortless ease and grace.

153. See note 150 above.

154. Elias, 56.

155. Elias, xii.

156. Synnott, 18.

157. Elias, 66.

Chapter 9. Corporeal Catastrophe: Bodies "Crash" and Disappear

1. Susan Sontag, *Illness as Metaphor and AIDS and its Metaphors* (New York: Doubleday, 1989), 175.

2. Andrew McMurry, "The Slow Apocalypse: A Gradualistic Theory of the World's Demise," *Postmodern Culture*, 6, no. 3 (May 1996), 15. Pub-

lished electronically by the Oxford University Press, and available at http://jefferson.village.virginia.edu/pmc/contents.all.html, INTERNET.

3. See, for example, Anna Briggs and Daniel Snowman, *Fin de Siécle: How Centuries End, 1400–2000* (New Haven: Yale University Press, 1996).

4. See James Berger, "Ends and Means: Theorizing the Apocalypse in the 1990s," *Postmodern Culture*,6, no. 3 (May 1996), previously cited; and references to the Book of Revelations.

5. McMurry, 2.

6. Center for Millennial Studies, published electronically on the INTERNET and available at http://www.mille.org/index.html.

7. See, for example, Manuel Castells, *End of Millennium* (London: Blackwell Publishers, 1998); Mark Kingwell, *Dreams of Millennium: Reports from a Culture on the Brink* (London: Faber and Faber, 1997); Joseph Margolis, *Historied Thought, Constructed World: A Conceptual Primer for the Turn of the Millennium* (San Francisco: University of California Press, 1995); and Avital Ronell, *Finitude's Score: Essays for the End of the Millennium* (Lincoln: University of Nebraska, 1998).

8. John Leslie, *The End of the World* (London: Routledge, 1996).

9. See Jean Baudrillard, *Simulacra and Simulations: The Selected Writings of Jean Baudrillard*, ed. Mark Poster (New York: Polity Press, 1988).

10. Sontag, 176.

11. Joe Sartelle, "Introduction to 'Apocalypse'," *Bad Subjects*, 15, no. 1 (1994), published electronicaly on the INTERNET and available at: http://english.cmu.edu/BS/default.html.

12. Adam Parfrey, *Apocalypse Culture* (Los Angeles: Feral House, 1990).

13. See Elaine Showalter, *Sexual Anarchy: Gender and Culture at the Fin de Siécle* (London: Virago,1992).

14. The fifteenth century epidemic of syphilis, which we examined in chapter 8, first established the image of the prostitute as the vector of contagion associated with sexually transmitted disease. Luther declared prostitutes to be "syphilitic whores" who did great harm "to young men." For Erasmus, they were as "public sewers" through which syphilis was transmitted. (See "Dangerous Bodies" in chapter 8.)

15. Showalter, 189.

16. Sontag, 158. See also Paula A. Treichler, "AIDS, Gender, and Biomedical Discourse: Current Contests for Meaning," in *AIDS: The Burden of History*, eds. Elizabeth Fee and Daniel M. Fox (Berkeley: University of California Press, 1990), 190–266.

17. Showalter, 190.

18. Singer, *Erotic Welfare*, previously cited.

19. Singer, 28.

20. Singer, 29.

21. Carolyn Rebecca Block and Richard L. Block, "Questions and Answers in Lethal and Non-Lethal Violence 1993," in *Proceedings of the Second Annual Workshop of the Homicide Research Working Group* (Washington: National Institute of Justice,1993), 190. See also Teri Randall, "Coping With the Violence Epidemic," *Journal of the American Medical Association*, 263, no. 19 (1990): 2612–14.

22. Aaron Lynch, *Thought Contagion, How Belief Spreads Through Society: The New Science of Memes* (New York: Basic Books, 1996).

23. Aaron Lynch, *Thought Contagion, How Belief Spreads Through Society: The New Science of Memes* (1996), chapter 1: "Self-Sent Messages and Mass Belief," 3. Available electronically on the INTERNET at: http: //www.ncs.net/~aaron/thoughtcontagion.html.

24. See Suzanne E. Hatty and Stuart Burke, "The Vermin and the Virus: AIDS in Australian Prisons," *Social and Legal Studies*, 1, no. 1 (1992):85–106.

25. Singer, 31.

26. Singer, 27.

27. See Jennifer Terry, "The Body Invaded: Medical Surveillance of Women as Reproducers," *Socialist Review*, 19, no. 3 (1989): 13–43; and Lisa Maher, "Punishment and Welfare: Crack Cocaine and the Regulation of Mothering," in *The Criminalization of a Woman's Body*, ed. Clarice Feinman (New York: Harrington Park, 1993), 168–82.

28. Anne Balsamo, *Technologies of the Gendered Body* (Durham: Duke University Press, 1996), 80.

29. Elaine Showalter, *Hystories: Hysterical Epidemics and Modern Culture* (New York: Columbia University Press, 1997).

30. Hysteria was a popular and much-discussed medico-psychiatric construct in the nineteenth century. Described initially by Charcot, and further developed by Freud, this construct became a highly visible phenomenon and a frequent condition, especially among female patients. Hysteria, according to Freud, involved a "conversion reaction": the presentation of symptoms that appear to have no physical or medical basis. It is regarded as a psychiatric condition, a disabling psychological illness with a tangible manifestation.

31. Elaine Showalter, Interview published on the Columbia University Press website at http://www.columbia.edu/cu/cup/feature/hystories/hystinterview.html.

32. Ibid.

33. Showalter, 1997, 2.

34. Albert Camus, *The Plague*, trans. Stuart Gilbert (Harmondsworth: Penguin, 1960).

35. *The Weekend Australian* (Sydney), March 6–7, 1996.

36. Richard Preston, *The Hot Zone* (New York: Doubleday,1994).

37. Preston, 81.

38. Preston, 189.

39. Preston, 18, 52, 54, and 56.

40. Preston, 29 and 106.

41. Preston, 30 and 96.

42. David Black draws a metaphorical link between the HIV/AIDS virus and femaleness.

> The disease, like a vampire, could manifest itself in many forms; and, like a vampire, it seems impossible to track down. It was out at night, stalking the backrooms of bars and lonely docks, its power lying in its attraction, its seductiveness, in the prey's willingness to surrender. Most of its victims were relatively young; it seemed to draw strength from the strong.

See David Black, *The Plague Years: A Chronicle of AIDS, the Epidemic of Our Times* (London: Picador, 1986), 40. The word "vampire" according to the Oxford English Dictionary and other authorities, appears to have been derived from the Turkish word for "witch." A common contraction of the word is "vamp," invariably linked to notions of the predatory female.

43. Preston, 91.

44. Preston, 153.

45. Preston, 320.

46. *Not of This Earth*, 1995, directed by Terence K. Winkler, Libra Pictures.

47. Laurie Garrett, *The Coming Plague* (New York: Farrer, Straus and Giroux, 1994).

48. Garrett, xi.

49. We might also view Stephen King's drama *The Stand* as representative of "the viral condition" in popular entertainment. In this drama, a "superflu" virus leaks out of a biological warfare laboratory maintained by the U.S. government. This virus kills a large proportion of the population.

50. *Outbreak*, directed by Wolfgang Peterson, Warner Brothers.

51. Garrett, 29.

52. Richard Preston, *The Cobra Event* (New York: Random House, 1997).

53. Jeffrey D. Simon, "Biological Terrorism," *The Journal of the American Medical Association*, no. 278 (1997):428. See also Leonard A. Cole, *The Eleventh Plague: The Politics of Biological and Chemical Warfare* (New York: Freeman and Co., 1998); Michael Oldstone, *Viruses, Plagues, and History* (New York: Oxford University Press, 1998); C. J. Peters and M. Olshaker, *Virus Hunter: Thirty Years of Battling Hot Viruses Around the World* (New York: Anchor Books, 1997); Richard Rhodes, *Deadly Feasts: Tracking the Secrets of a Terrifying New Plague* (New York: Simon and Schuster, 1997); and Frank Ryan, *Virus X: Tracking the New Killer Plagues Out of the Present and into the Future* (Boston: Little, Brown and Co., 1997).

54. President Clinton, "Meeting the Terrorist Threat of the 21st Century," White House Press Release, May 22, 1998.

55. See David Satcher, "Emerging Infections: Getting Ahead of the Curve," *Emerging Infectious Diseases*, 1, no. 1 (Jan-Mar, 1995). Published electronically on the INTERNET and available at http://www.cdc.gov/nicad/EID/Vol1no1/eid.html. Infectious diseases can be transmitted via a number of microbial pathways: bacteria; fungi; parasites; and viruses. The first two are independent life-forms. Parasites rely on the resources of a host to survive. (Strictly speaking, a virus is a kind of parasite. However, biomedical classification systems usually distinguish between the two major groups of parasites and viruses).

56. World Health Organization (WHO), *The World Health Report* 1996. The pre-release, published electronically on the INTERNET, is available at: http://www.who.ch/whr/1996/press1.html.

57. WHO, 1996.

58. WHO, 1996, 4.

59. See Alison Jacobson, "Emerging and Re-emerging Viruses: An Essay," 1995, published electronically on the INTERNET, and available at: http://www.outbreak.org/cgi-unreg/dynaserve.exe/index.html.

60. See Satcher, 1995; and WHO, 1996.

61. "Emerging" diseases are defined as those which have just been discovered, as well as those which are already known but are increasing in incidence or geographical spread; see Stephen S. Morse, "Factors in the Emergence of Infectious Diseases," *Emerging Infectious Diseases*, 1, no. 1 (Jan–Mar, 1995). Published electronically on the INTERNET and available at: http://www.cdc.gov/ncidad/EID/vol1.no1/eid/html.

62. See Jacobson, 1995; Morse, 1995; and Mary E. Wilson, "Travel and the Emergence of Infectious Diseases," *Emerging Infectious Diseases*, 1, no. 1 (Jan–Mar, 1995). Published electronically on the INTERNET and available at: http://www.cdc.gov/ncidad/EID/vol1.no1/eid.html.

63. Morse, 10.

64. Jacobson, 1.

65. WHO, 1996, 1.

66. Allison Fraiberg, "Of AIDS, Cyborgs and Other Indiscretions," in *Essays in Postmodern Culture*, eds. Eyal Admiran and John Unsworth (New York: Oxford University Press, 1993), 37–55.

67. Adrian Mackenzie, "'God has No Allergies': Immanent Ethics and the Simulacra of the Immune System," *Postmodern Culture*, 6, no. 2 (1996):2. Published electronically on the INTERNET (already cited).

68. Sontag, 1989.

69. John Dwyer, *The Body at War: The Story of Our Immune System*, 2nd edn. (St. Leonards, Sydney: Allen and Unwin,1993), 34–35.

70. Dwyer, 69.

71. Dwyer, 6.

72. Dwyer, 6.

73. Donna Haraway, *Simians, Cyborgs and Women: The Reinvention of Nature* (New York: Routledge, 1991).

74. Mackenzie, 4.

75. See Francisco Valera and Mark Anspach, "The Body Thinks: The Immune System in the Process of Somatic Individuation," in *Materialities of Communication*, eds. H. U. Gumbrecht and K. L. Pfeiffer, trans. W. Whobrey (Stanford: Stanford University Press, 1994), 270–88.

76. Haraway, 223, citing Klein.

77. Haraway, 221 and Mackenzie, 4.

78. Haraway, 212.

79. Arthur Kroker, Marilouise Kroker, and David Cook, *Panic Encyclopedia: The Definitive Guide to the Postmodern Scene* (London: Macmillan, 1989), 232.

80. U.S. National Library of Medicine, "The Visible Human Project, 1996," 6. Published electronically on the INTERNET and available at: http://www.nlm.nih.gov/research/visible/.

81. See U.S. National Library of Medicine, "Visible Human Project, 1996."

82. Multimedia Medical Systems, "Digital Human CD-ROM Homepage" 1996, published electronically on the INTERNET at http://www.mms.com/dighuman.htm.

83. See Bill Lorensen, "Marching Through the Visible Man,1996," published electronically on the INTERNET and available at http://www.nlm.nih.gov/research/visible/ . See also Bill Lorensen, "Marching Through the Visible Woman 1996," available at the same address.

84. Balsamo, 123.

85. Shannon McRae, "Coming Apart at the Seams: Sex, Text, and the Virtual Body," 1994. Published electronically on the INTERNET and available at: http://humanitas.ucsb.edu/shuttle/gender.html.

86. See Elizabeth Reid, "Cultural Formations in Text-Based Virtual Realities," Master of Arts Thesis, University of Melbourne, 1994. Published electronically on the INTERNET and available at http://www. Mcs.net/~zupko/popcult.htm.

87. N. K. Hayles, "Virtual Bodies and Flickering Signifiers," *October*, 66 (1993): 69–91.

88. See Julian Dibbell, "A Rape in Cyberspace," *The Village Voice* (New York), December 21, 1993: 36–42; and Reid, 1994.

89. See Thomas Mazur, "Working Out the Cyberbody: Sex and Gender Constructions in Text-Based Virtual Space," 1994, citing Bruckman, 1993. Published electronically on the INTERNET and available at http://www.ucet.efl.edu/~tmazur/projects/sgv/SEXGender.htm. See also Sherry Turkle, *Life on the Screen: Identity in the Age of the Internet* (New York: Simon and Schuster, 1995); and Judith Donath, "Identity and Deception in the Virtual Community," 1996. Published electronically on the INTERNET and available at: ftp.media.mit.edu/pub/donath.

90. Stelarc, *Archival Space*, 1996. Published electronically on the INTERNET and available at http://www.merlin.com.au/stelarc.

91. J. Deleuze and F. Guattari, *A Thousand Plateaux* (London: Athlone,1988).

92. Brian Massumi, "The Evolutionary Alchemy of Reason," published electronically on the INTERNET and available at: http://www.anu.edu.au/HRC/first_and_last/links.massumi_works.htm.

93. Stelarc, cited above.

94. Balsamo, 2.

95. Vicky Kirby, "Corporeal Habits: Addressing Essentialism Differently," *Hypatia* 6, 3 (1991): 4–24.

96. Bordo, *The Flight to Objectivity* (already cited).

97. Bordo, 5.

Works Cited

Primary Sources

Agnolo di Tura del Grasso, "Cronaca Senese di Agnolo di Tura del Grasso." In *Rerum italicarum scriptores,* Vol. XV, Pt. 6, eds. A. Lisini and F. Iacometti. Bologna: Zanichelli, 1931.

Aretino, Pietro. *Lettere,* ed. Sergio Ortolani. Turin: Einaudi, 1945.

Augustine, Saint. *The City of God.* 2 vols., trans. John Healey, ed. R.V.G. Tasker. London: J.M. Dent, 1945.

Augustine, Saint. *The City of God,* trans. G. Walsh, ed. V. J. Bourke. Garden City, NY: Doubleday-Image Books, 1958.

Baird, Joseph L., trans. and ed. *The Chronicles of Salimbene de Adam.* Binghamton, NY: Center for Medieval and Early Renaissance Studies, 1986.

Bernardino da Siena, *Le prediche volgari,* 5 vols., ed. Ciro Cannarozzi. Florence: Rinaldi, 1958.

Boccaccio, Giovanni. "Il Corbaccio." In *Letteratura italiana: Storia e testi,* Vol. 9, ed. Pier Giorgio Ricci. Milan: Riccardo Ricciardi, n.d.

Boccaccio, Giovanni. *Decameron.* 2 vols. 3rd edn., ed. Mario Marti. Milan: Rizzoli, 1979.

Borromeo, Frederico. *La peste di Milano,* ed. Armando Torno. Milan: Rusconi, 1987.

Castiglione, Baldesar. *The Book of the Courtier,* trans., George Bull. London: Penguin, 1976

Catherine of Siena, *The Letters of St. Catherine of Siena.* Vol. I, trans. Suzanne Noffke. Binghamton, NY: Center for Medieval and Early Renaissance Studies, 1988.

Cellini, Benvenuto. *The Autobiography of Benvenuto Cellini,* trans. George Bull. Harmondsworth: Penguin, 1981.

Compagni, Dino. "La cronica di Dino Compagni," in *Classici italiani,* Series II, Vol. XXIX. Milan: Istituto editoriale italiana, 1913.

"Cronaca Senese." In *Rerum italicarum scriptores,* Vol. XX, Pt. 6, eds. A. Lisini and F. Iacometti. Bologna: Zanchelli, 1931.

"Cronica volgare di un Anonimo Fiorentino." In *Rerum italicarum scriptores,* Vol. XXVII, pt.1, ed. Ellina Bellondi. Città di Castello: Lapi, 1915.

Dante Alighieri. *La Divina Commedia,* 3 vols., ed., Natalino Sapegno. Florence: La Nuova Italia, 1982.

Dati, Gregorio. "Il libro segreto di Gregorio Dati." In *Scelta di curiosità letterarie dal secolo XIII al XIX,* Vol. XXII, Disp. CII. Bologna: Commissione per i testi di lingua, 1968.

de Pizan, Christine. *The Book of the City of Ladies,* trans., Earl Jeffrey Richards. London: Pan Books, 1983.

"Diario d'Anonimo Fiorentino." In *Documenti di storia italiana,* Vol. VI. Florence: Deputazione sugli studi di storia patria, 1876.

Erasmus, Desiderius. *The Colloquies of Erasmus,* trans., Craig R. Thompson. Chicago: University of Chicago Press, 1965.

Erasmus, Desiderius. "On Good Manners for Boys." In *Collected Works of Erasmus,* vol. 25, ed., J.K. Sowards, trans., Brian McGregor. Toronto: University of Toronto Press, 1985.

Erasmus, Desiderius. *The Collected Works of Erasmus,* vol. 29, eds. Elaine Fantham and Erika Rummel. Toronto: University of Toronto Press, 1989.

Felici, Lucio, ed. *Poesia italiana del Seicento.* Milan: Garzanti, 1978.

Ficino, Marsilio. *Opera omnia,* Vol. I. Turin: Bottega d'Erasmo, 1962.

Ficino, Marsilio. *Commentary on Plato's Symposium on Love,* trans., Sears Jayne. Dallas, Texas: Spring Publications, 1985.

Fracastoro, Girolamo. *Il contagio: Le malattie contagiose e la loro cura,* trans. (from the Latin), Busacchi. Florence: Olschki, 1950.

Fracastoro, Girolamo. *Fracastoro's Syphilis,* trans. and ed. Geoffrey Eatough. Liverpool: Cairns, 1984.

Giordano da Rivalto-Moreni. *Prediche.* Florence: Pietro Gaetano Viviani, 1738.

Gregory of Tours. *The History of the Franks*, trans. Lewis Thorpe. Harmondsworth: Penguin, 1982.

Griffoni, Matteo. [Mathhhaeus de Griffonibus] "Memoriale historicum de rebus Bononiensium." In *Rerum italicarum scriptores,* Vol. 18, Pt. 2, eds, L.Frati and A. Sorbelli. Città di Castello: Lapi, 1902.

Guasti, C., ed. *Lettere di una gentildonna fiorentina.* Florence: Sansoni, 1877, rpt. 1972.

Guicciardini, Francesco. *Storia d'Italia,* 4 vols., ed. Costantino Panigada. Bari: Laterza, 1967.

Jacopone da Todi. In *Poesia italiana del Duecento,* ed. Pietro Cudini. Milan: Garzanti, 1978.

Kramer, H. and J. Sprenger. *The Malleus Maleficarum of Heinrich Kramer and James Sprenger*, trans. Montague Summers. New York: Dover, 1971.

Landucci, Lucca. *Diario Fioremtino dal1450 al 1516 di Luca Landucci,* ed. I. del Badia. Florence: Studio Biblos, 1969.

Lanza, Antonio ed. *Lirici Toscani del '400.* Rome: Bulzoni, 1973.

Macchiavelli, Niccolò. *La mandragola.* (Turin: Einaudi, 1980).

Marchionne di Coppo Stefani. "Cronaca fiorentina di Marchionne di Coppo Stefani." In *Rerum italicarum scriptores,* Vol. XXX, pt.1, ed. Niccolò Rodolico. Città di Castello: Lapi, 1903.

Michelangelo Buonarrotti. *Rime.* Milan: Rizzoli, 1954.

Morelli, Giovanni di Pagallo. *Ricordi,* 2nd edn., ed. V. Branca. Florence: Le Monnier, 1969.

Muratori, Ludovico. "Del governo della peste e delle maniere di guardarsene." In *Opere di Ludovico Antonio Muratori*, eds. Di Giorgi Falco and Fiorenzo Forti. Milan-Naples: Ricciardi, n.d.

Palmieri, Matteo. "Historia fiorentina." In *Rerum italicarum scriptores,* Vol. XXVI, Pt. 1. Città di Castello: Lapi, 1906.

Palmieri, Matteo. *La vita civile,* ed. Gino Belloni. Florence: Sansoni, 1982.

Passavanti, Jacopo. *Lo specchio della vera penitenza.* Milan: Silvestri, 1825.

Petrarca, Francesco. *Rerum familiarium libri I–VIII*, trans. Aldo S. Bernardo. Albany: State University of New York Press, 1975.

Petrarca, Francesco. *Le senili,* trans. G. Fracasetti, ed. Guido Martelloti. Turin: Einaudi, 1976.

Petrarca, Francesco. *Invective contra medicum,* ed. Pier Giorgio Ricci. Rome: Edizioni di storia e letteratura, 1978.

Petrarca, Francesco. *Rerum familiarium libri IX–XVI,* trans. Aldo S. Bernardo. Baltimore: Johns Hopkins University Press, 1982.

Piccolomini, Enea Silvio. *I commentari,* 2 vols., trans.(from the Latin) Guiseppe Bernetti. Milan: Longanesi, 1981.

Pitti, Buonaccorso. "The Diary of Buonaccorso Pitti." In *Two Memoirs of Renaissance Florence,* trans. Julia Martines., ed. Gene Brucker. New York: Harper and Row, 1967.

Plato. *The Last Days of Socrates,* trans. Hugh Tredennick. Harmondsworth: Penguin, 1982.

Savonarola, Girolamo. *Prediche sopra Giobbe,* ed. Roberto Ridolfi. Rome Belardetti, 1957.

Savonarola, Girolamo. *Prediche sopra Amos e Zaccaria,* ed. Paolo Ghiglieri. Rome: Belardetti, 1972.

Savonarola, Girolamo. *Operette spirituali,* Vol. II. ed. Mario Ferrara. Rome: Belardetti, 1976.

Sercambi, Giovanni. *Le croniche di Giovanni Sercambi,* ed. Salvatore Bongi. Lucca: Giusti, 1892.

"Storie Pistoresi." In *Rerum italicarum scriptores,* Vol. 11, pt. 5, ed. Silvio Barbi. Città di Castello: Lapi, 1907.

Strozzi, Lorenzo. "Descrizione della peste di Firenze dell'anno 1527." In *Opere di Niccolò Macchiavelli* Vol. VII. Italia [Firenze]: 1826.

Varchi, Benedetto. *Storia fiorentina,* 3 vols., ed. Lelio Arbib. Florence: Editrice del Nardi e del Varchi, 1828–41.

Vasari, Giorgio. *The Lives of the Artists,* trans. George Bull. Harmondsworth: Penguin, 1988.

Velluti, Donato. *La cronica domestica di Messer Doanato Velluti.* Eds. Isidoro del Lungo and Guglielmo Vopli. Florence: Sansoni, 1914.

Villani, Giovanni. *Cronaca,* 4 vols., ed. F.G. Dragomani. Frankfurt: Minerva, 1969.

Villani, Matteo. "Cronica di Matteo Villani." In *Chroniche di Giovanni, Matteo e Filippo Villani.* Trieste: Lloyd Austriaco, 1858.

Secondary Sources

Alston, Mary Niven. "The Attitude of the Church Towards Dissection before 1500," *Bulletin of the History of Medicine,* no. 16 (1944): 221–38.

Antonopoulos, Anna. "Writing the Mystic Body: Sexuality and Textuality in the *écriture-fémine* of Saint Catherine of Genoa," *Hypatia,* 6, no. 3 (1991):185–205.

Ariès, Philippe. *Centuries of Childhood,* ed. Robert Baldick. New York: Random House [Vintage], 1962.

Ariès, Philippe. *Western Attitudes to Death: From the Middle Ages to the Present,* trans. Patricia Ranum. Baltimore: Johns Hopkins University Press, 1985.

Armstrong, David. "Bodies of Knowledge: Foucault and the Problem of Human Anatomy." In *Medicine and the Five Senses,* eds. W.F. Bynum and Roy Porter. Cambridge: Cambridge University Press, 1993.

Ash, Jennifer. "The discursive construction of Christ's body in the late Middle Ages: resistance and autonomy." In *Feminine, Masculine and Representation*, eds. Terry Threadgold and Anne Cranny-Francis. Sydney: Allen and Unwin, 1990.

Bakhtin, Mikhail. *Rabelais and His World*, trans. Helene Iswolsky. Bloomington: Indiana University Press, 1984.

Balsamo, Anne. *Technologies of the Gendered Body.* Durham: Duke University Press, 1996.

Barker, Francis. *The Tremulous Private Body: Essays on Subjection.* London: Methuen, 1984.

Baudrillard, Jean. *America,* trans. Chris Turner. London: Verso, 1988.

Baudrillard, Jean. *Simulacra and Simulations: The Selected Writings of Jean Baudrillard,* ed. Mark Poster. New York: Polity Press, 1988.

Becker, Marvin B. "Church and State in Florence on the Eve of the Renaissance (1343–82)," *Speculum*, XXXVII, no. 4 (1962): 533.

Becker, Marvin B. "Aspects of Lay Piety in Early Renaissance Florence." In *The Pursuit of Holiness in Late Medieval and Renaissance Religion,* eds. Charles Trinkaus and Heiko A. Oberman. Leiden: Brill, 1974.

Ben-Yehuda, Nachman. "The European Witch Craze of the 14th to 17th centuries: A Sociologists's Perspective," *American Journal of Sociology*, 86, no. 1 (1980): 1–31.

Berger, James. "Ends and Means: Theorizing the Apocalypse in the 1990s," *Post Modern Culture,* 6, no. 3 (May 1996).

Biraben, Jean-Noël. "La médicin et l'enfant au Moyen Age," in *Annales de Démographie Historique.* Paris: Mouton, 1973: 73–75.

Biraben, Jean-Noël. "Les pauvres et la peste." In *Études sur l'histoire de la pauvreté,* ed. Michel Mollat. Paris: La Sorbonne, 1974.

Biraben, Jean-Noël. *Les hommes et la peste en France et dans le pays européens et méditerréens.* 2 vols. Paris: Mouton, 1975–76.

Black, David. *The Plague Years: A Chronicle of AIDS, the Epidemic of Our Times.* London: Picador, 1986.

Block, Carolyn Rebecca and Richard L. Block. "Questions and Answers in Lethal and Non-Lethal Violence 1993." In *Proceedings of the Second Annual Workshop of the Homicide Research Working Group.* Washington: National Institute of Justice,1993.

Bloomfield, Morton W. *The Seven Deadly Sins.* Michigan: Michigan State University Press, 1967.

Bonney, F. "Jean Gerson: Un nouveau regard sur l'enfance," in *Annales de Démographie Historique.* Paris: Mouton, 1973.

Bordo, Susan. *The Flight to Objectivity.* Albany: State University of New York Press, 1987.

Bordo, Susan. "Eating Disorders: The Feminist Challenge to the Concept of Pathology." In *The Body in Medical Thought and Practice,* ed. Drew Leder. Dordecht: Kluwer, 1992.

Boswell, James. *Boswell's London Journal 1762–1763,* ed., Frederick A Pottle. Melbourne: Heinemann, 1951.

Boswell, John. *Christianity, Social Tolerance, and Homosexuality.* Chicago: Chicago University Press, 1980.

Boswell, John. "Towards the Long View: Revolutions, Universals and Sexual Categories," *Salamagundi,* nos. 58–59 (1982–83): 103.

Boswell, John. *The Kindness of Strangers.* New York: Pantheon, 1988.

Bousma, William J. "Interventions on 'Rituals in Florence'." In *Pursuit of Holiness in Late Medieval and Renaissance Religion,* eds. C. Trinkaus and H. Oberman. Leiden: Brill, 1974.

Bowsky, William M. "Siena: Stability and Dislocation," *Speculum,* XXXIX, no. 1 (1964): 114–21.

Bowsky, William M. "The Impact of the Black Death upon Sienese Government and Society," *Speculum,* XXXIX, no. 1 (1964): 1–34.

Bowsky, William, ed. *The Black Death: A Turning Point in History?* New York: Holt, Rinehart and Winston, 1971.

Briggs, Anna and Daniel Snowman. *Fin de Siécle: How Centuries End, 1400–2000.* New Haven: Yale University Press, 1996.

Brody, Saul Nathaniel. *The Disease of the Soul: Leprosy in Medieval Literature*. Ithaca: Cornell University Press, 1974.

Brown, Peter. *The Cult of the Saints*. Chicago: Chicago University Press, 1981.

Brown, Peter. *The Body and Society: Men, Women and Sexual Renunciation in Early Christianity*. New York: Columbia University Press, 1988.

Brucker, Gene, ed. *The Society of Renaissance Florence*. New York: Harper and Row, 1971.

Brucker, Gene. "The Florentine Popolo Minuto and its Political Role." In *Violence and Disorder in Italian Cities, 1200–1500*, ed. Lauro Martines. Berkeley: University of California, 1972.

Brucker, Gene A. "Florence and the Black Death." In *Boccaccio: Secoli di vita*. Ravenna: Longo, 1977.

Brundage, James A. "Prostitution in the Medieval Canon Law," *Signs: Journal of Women in Culture and Society*, 1, no. 4 (1976): 824–45.

Brundage, James A. *Law, Sex, and Christian Society in Medieval Europe*. Chicago: Chicago University Press, 1987.

Bull, Malcolm. "Secularization and Medicalization," *The British Journal of Sociology* 41, no. 2 (1990): 245–61.

Bullfinch, Thomas. *Bullfinch's Mythology*. New York: Avenal Books, 1979.

Bullough, Vern L. "Training of the Nonuniversity-Educated Medical Practitioners in the Later Middle Ages," *Journal of the History of Medicine*, no. 14 (1959): 446–58.

Bullough, Vern L. "Heresy, Witchcraft, and Sexuality," *Journal of Homosexuality* 1, no. 2 (1974): 185.

Bullough, Vern L. "The Sin against Nature and Homosexuality." In *Sexual Practices and the Medieval Church*, eds. Vern L. Bullough and James Brundage. Buffalo, NY: Prometheus Books, 1982.

Bullough, Vern L. "Prostitution in the Later Middle Ages." In *Sexual Practices and the Medieval Church*, eds. Vern L. Bullough and James Brundage. Buffalo, NY: Prometheus Books, 1982.

Bullough, Vern L. and James Brundage, eds. *Sexual Practices and the Medieval Church*. Buffalo, NY: Prometheus Books, 1982.

Burke, Peter. "Homosexuality." In *A Concise Encyclopaedia of the Italian Renaissance*, ed. J. R. Hale. London: Thames and Hudson, 1981.

Bylebyl, Jerome. "The Manifest and the Hidden in the Renaissance Clinic." In *Medicine and the Five Senses,* eds. W.F. Bynum and Roy Porter. Cambridge: Cambridge University Press, 1993.

Bynum, Caroline Walker. "The Female Body and Religious Practice in the later Middle Ages." In *Fragments for a History of the Human Body,* 3 vols., eds. Michel Feher, et al. New York: Zone, 1989.

Calvi, Giulia, "The Florentine Plague of 1630–33: Social Behaviour and Symbolic Action." In *Maladie et Société (XIIe–XVIIe siècles),* eds. N. Bulst and R. Delort. Paris: Editions du CNRS, 1989.

Campbell, Anna Montgomery. *The Black Death and Men of Learning.* New York: AMS Press, 1966.

Camporesi, Piero. "The Consecrated Host: A Wondrous Excess." In *Fragments for a History of the Human Body,* 3 vols., eds, Michel Feher, et al. New York: Zone, 1989.

Camus, Albert. *The Plague,* trans. Stuart Gilbert. Harmondsworth: Penguin, 1960.

Carmichael, Ann G. *Plague and the Poor in Renaissance Florence.* Cambridge: Cambridge University Press, 1986.

Carmichael, Ann. "Contagion Theory and Contagion Practice in Fifteenth-Century Milan," *Renaissance Quarterly,* XLIV, no. 2 (1991): 216–17.

Carpentier, Élisabeth. "Autor de la peste noire: Famines et épidémie dans l'histoire du XIV siècle," *Annales: Economies, Sociétés, Civilisations,* no. 17 (1962): 1081.

Carpentier, Élisabeth. "Autor de la peste noire: famines et épidémie dans l'histoire du XIVe siècle," *Annales E.S.C.,* no. 17 (1962): 1062–92.

Carpentier, Élisabeth. "Orvieto: Institutional Stability and Moral Change," *Speculum,* XXXIX, no. 1 (1964): 108–13.

Cartwright, Frederick. *A Social History of Medicine.* London: Longman, 1977.

Cartwright, Frederick. *Disease and History.* New York: Thomas Y. Crowell, 1972.

Casagrande, Carla. "The Protected Woman." In *A History of Women in the West: Silences of the Middle Ages,* ed. Christiane Klapisch-Zuber. Cambridge, Mass.: Belknap Press of Harvard University Press, 1992.

Castells, Manuel. *End of Millennium.* London: Blackwell Publishers, 1998.

Castiglioni, Arturo. *A History of Medicine,* 2nd edn., trans. E. B. Krumbhaar. New York: Knopf, 1941.

Center for Millennial Studies, published electronically on the INTERNET and available at http://www.mille.org/index.html.

Chamberlin, E. R. *The World of the Italian Renaissance.* London: George Allen and Unwin, 1982.

Chaney, Edward F., ed. *La Danse Macabré des Charniers ds Saints Innocents à Paris.* Manchester: Manchester University Press, 1945.

Chiappelli, Alberto. "Gli ordinamenti sanitari del Comune di Pistoia contro la pestilenzia del 1348," *Archivio storico italiano,* Ser. IV, Vol. XX (Florence: Vieusseux, 1887): 3–7.

Ciasca, Raffaele. *L'arte dei medici e speziali nella storia e nel commercio fiorentino dal secolo XII al XV.* Florence: Olschki, 1927.

Cipolla, Carlo and Dante E. Zanetti. "Peste et Mortalité Differéntielle." In *Annales de Démographie Historique.* Paris: Mouton, 1972.

Cipolla, Carlo M. *Public Health and the Medical Profession in the Renaissance.* Cambridge: Cambridge University Press, 1976.

Cipolla, Carlo M. "A Plague Doctor." In *The Medieval City,* eds. H. Miskimin et al. New Haven: Yale University Press, 1977.

Clinton, W. J. "Meeting the Terrorist Threat of the 21st Century," White House Press Release, May 22, 1998.

Clark, Kenneth. *The Nude: A Study in Ideal Art.* London: John Murray, 1956.

Cohen, Sherrill. *The Evolution of Women's Asylums since 1500: From Refuges for Ex-prostitutes to Shelters for Battered Women.* New York: Oxford University Press, 1992.

Cohen, Stanley. *Visions of Social Control.* Cambridge: Polity Press, 1985.

Cohn, Norman. *The Pursuit of the Millennium.* Fairlawn, NJ: Essential Books, 1957.

Cohn, Samuel Kline, Jr. *The Laboring Classes in Renaissance Florence.* New York: Academic Press, 1980.

Cole, Leonard A. *The Eleventh Plague: The Politics of Biological and Chemical Warfare.* New York: Freeman and Co., 1998.

Comaroff, John and Jean Comaroff. *Ethnography and the Historical Imagination.* Boulder: Westview Press, 1992.

Conrad, Peter. "Medicalization and Social Control," *Annual Review of Sociology,* no. 18 (1992): 209–32.

Crosby, Alfred W., Jr. *The Columbian Exchange*. Westport, Conn.: Greenwood, 1972.

D'Irsay, Stephen. "Notes on the origin of the expression 'Atra Mors'," *Isis*, no. 8 (1926): 328–32.

Dalarun, Jacques. "The Clerical Gaze." In *A History of Women in the West: Silences of the Middle Ages*, ed. Christiane Klapisch-Zuber. Baltimore: Belknap Press of Harvard University Press, 1992.

Davis, Kathy. *Reshaping the Female Body*. London: Routledge, 1996.

Deleuze, J. and F. Guattari, *A Thousand Plateaux*. London: Athlone,1988.

Dellamora, Richard. *Apocalyptic Overtures: Sexual Politics and the Sense of Ending*. New Brunswick: Rutgers University Press, 1994.

De Sanctis, Francesco. *Storia della letteratura italiana*. 2 vols. 7th edn. Milan: Feltrinelli, 1978.

Descartes, Rene. *Discourse on Method and The Meditations*. Harmondsworth: Penguin, 1982.

Dibbell, Julian. "A Rape in Cyberspace," *The Village Voice* (New York), December 21, 1993: 36–42.

Diefendorf, Barbara. "Family Culture, Renaissance Culture," *Renaissance Quarterly*, no. 40 (1987):660–81.

Dols, Michael W. "The Comparative Communal Responses to the Black Death in Muslim and Christian Societies," *Viator*, no. 5 (1974): 269–87.

Dols, Michael W. *The Black Death in the Middle East*. Princeton, NJ: Princeton University Press, 1977.

Donath, Judith. "Identity and Deception in the Virtual Community," 1996. Published electronically on the INTERNET and available at: ftp.media.mit.edu/pub/donath.

Douglas, Mary. *Purity and Danger: An Analysis of the Concepts of Pollution and Taboo*. London: Routledge and Kegan Paul, 1984.

Douglas, Mary. *Risk and Blame*. London: Routledge, 1992.

Duncan, Nancy, ed. *Body Space*. London: Routledge, 1996.

Dutton, K. R. *The Perfectible Body*. London: Cassell, 1995.

Dwyer, John. *The Body at War: The Story of Our Immune System* 2nd edn. St. Leonards, Sydney: Allen and Unwin, 1993.

Ehenreich, Barbara and Deidre English. *Witches, Midwives, and Nurses: A History of Women Healers*. 2nd edn. New York: Feminist Press, SUNY: 1973.

Ekins, Richard and David King, eds. *Blending Genders: Social Aspects of Cross-Dressing and Sex Changing*. London: Routledge, 1996.

Elias, Norbet. *The Civilizing Process*, trans., Edmund Jephcott. Oxford: Blackwell, 1994.

Elliott, J. H. *Europe Divided 1559–1598*. Glascow: Fontana/Collins, 1968.

Erlanger, Rachel. *The Unarmed Prophet: Savonarola in Florence*. New York: McGraw Hill, 1988.

Falsini, Aliberto B. "Firenze dopo il 1348. Le conseguenze della peste nera," *Archivio storico italiano*, no. 129 (1971): 437–49.

Featherstone, Mike, Mike Hepworth and Bryan S. Turner, eds. *The Body: Social Process and Cultural Theory*. London: Sage, 1991.

Featherstone, Mike. "The Body in Consumer Culture." In *The Body: Social Process and Cultural Theory*. London: Sage, 1991.

Feher, Michel, Ramona Naddaff and Nadia Tazi, eds. *Fragments for A History of the Human Body*, 3 vols. (New York: Zone, 1989).

Ferrante, Lucia. "Honor Regained: Women in the Casa del Soccorso di San Paolo in Sixteenth-century Bologna." In *Sex and Gender in Historical Perspective,* eds. Edward Muir and Guido Ruggiero. Baltimore: Johns Hopkins University Press, 1990.

Fiorenza, Elisabeth Schüssler. *In Her Memory: A Feminist Theological Reconstruction of Christian Origins*. New York: Crossroad Publishing, 1989.

Flandrin, Jean-Louis. "Sex in Married Life in the Early Middle Ages: The Church's Teaching and Behavioural Reality." In *Western Sexuality: Practice and Precept in Past and Present Times,* eds. Philippe Ariès and André Béjin., trans. Anthony Forster. Oxford: Basil Blackwood, 1985.

Flandrin, Jean-Louis. *Sex in the Western World: The Development of Attitudes and Behaviour,* trans. Sue Collins. Chur, Switzerland: Harwood Academic, 1991.

Foa, Anna. "The New and the Old: The Spread of Syphilis (1494–1530)." In *Sex and Gender in Historical Perspective,* eds. Edward Muir and Guido Ruggiero. Baltimore: Johns Hopkins University Press, 1990.

Foucault, Michel. *Madness and Civilization,* trans., Richard Howard. New York: Pantheon/Random House, 1965.

Foucault, Michel. *The Birth of the Clinic,* trans. A. M. Sheridan-Smith. New York: Vintage Books, 1975.

Foucault, Michel. *Discipline and Punish: The Birth of the Prison.* Harmondsworth: Penguin, 1979.

Foucault, Michel. *Power/Knowledge,* ed. C. Gordon. Brighton, UK: Harvester Press, 1980.

Foucault, Michel. "The Battle for Chastity." In *Western Sexuality: Practice and Precept in Past and Present Times,* eds. Philippe Ariès and André Béjin, trans. Anthony Forster. Oxford: Basil Blackwood, 1985.

Fraiberg, Allison. "Of AIDS, Cyborgs and Other Indiscretions." In *Essays in Postmodern Culture,* eds. Eyal Admiran and John Unsworth. New York: Oxford University Press, 1993.

Frank, Arthur, W. "Bringing Bodies Back In: A Decade Review," *Theory, Culture and Society,* 7, no. 1 (1990): 131–62.

Frank, Arthur W. "For a Sociology of the Body: An Analytical Review." In *The Body: Social Process and Cultural Theory,* eds. Mike Featherstone, Mike Hepworth, and Bryan S. Turner. London: Sage, 1991.

Frank, Arthur W. *The Wounded Storyteller.* Chicago: Chicago University Press, 1995.

Friedman, John B. "He hath a thousand slayn this pestilence: The Iconography of the Plague in the Late Middle Ages." In *Social Unrest in the Late Middle Ages,* ed. Francis Newman. Binghamton, NY: Center for Medieval and Early Renaissance Texts, 1986.

Frugoni, Chiara. "The Imagined Woman." In *A History of Women in the West: Silences of the Middle Ages,* ed. Christiane Klapisch-Zuber. Cambridge, Mass.: Belknap Press of Harvard University Press, 1992.

Garin, Eugenio. *Lo zodiaco della vita.* Rome-Bari: Laterza, 1976.

Garrett, Laurie. *The Coming Plague.* New York: Farrer, Straus and Giroux, 1994.

Garrett, Stephanie. *Gender.* London: Tavistock, 1987.

Garrison, F. H. *An Introduction to the History of Medicine.* 4th edn. Philadelphia: Saunders, 1929.

Gatens, Moira. *Imaginary Bodies: Ethics, Power, and Corporeality.* London: Routledge, 1996.

Gellner, Ernest. *Reason and Culture: The Historic Role of Rationality and Rationalism.* Oxford: Blackwell, 1992.

Gerhardt, Uta. "Parsons, role theory and Health Interaction." In *Sociological Theory and Medical Sociology,* ed. Graham Scambler. London: Tavistock, 1987.

Gies, Frances and Joseph Gies. *Marriage and the Family in the Middle Ages.* New York: Harper and Row, 1989.

Gilman, Sander L. *Disease and Representation.* Ithaca: Cornell University Press, 1988.

Gilman, Sander. "Touch, sexuality and disease." In *Medicine and the Five Senses,* eds. W. F. Bynum and Roy Porter. Cambridge: Cambridge University Press, 1993.

Ginsburg, Carlo. "Folklore, magia, religione." In *Storia d'Italia* Vol. I. Turin: Einaudi, 1974.

Ginsburg, Carlo. *Ecstacies: Deciphering the Witches' Sabbath,* trans. Raymond Rosenthal, ed. Gregory Elliot. London: Hutchinson Radius, 1990.

Goffman, Erving. *Stigma.* Englewood Cliffs, NJ; Prentice-Hall, 1965.

Goodich, Michael. "Sodomy in Ecclesiastical Law and Theory," *Journal of Homosexuality,* 1, no. 4 (1976): 427–34.

Goodich, Michael. "Sodomy in Medieval Secular Law," *Journal of Homosexuality,* 1, no. 3 (1976): 299–300.

Gottfried, R. S. *The Black Death—Natural and Human Disasters in Medieval Europe.* London: Robert Hale, 1983.

Graves, Robert. *The Greek Myths.* 2 vols. Harmondsworth: Penguin, 1981.

Grieco, Sara F. Matthews. "The Body, Appearance and Sexuality." In *A History of Women in the West: Renaissance and Enlightment Paradoxes,* eds. Natalie Zemon Davis and Arlette Farge. Cambridge, Mass.: Belknap Press of Harvard University Press, 1993.

Grosz, Elizabeth. *Volatile Bodies.* Sydney: Allen and Unwin, 1994.

Grosz, Elizabeth and Elspeth Probyn, eds. *Sexy Bodies: The Strange Carnalities of Feminism.* London: Routledge, 1996.

Guidi, Guidobaldo. "I sistemi elettorali agli uffici della città-repubblica di Firenze nell prima metà del Trecento (1329–49)," *Archivio storico italiano,* no. 135 (1977): 414.

Haraway, Donna. *Simians, Cyborgs and Women: The Reinvention of Nature.* New York: Routledge, 1991.

Hare, Ronald. *Pomp and Pestilence.* London: Gollancz, 1954.

Haskins, Charles Homer. *The Renaissance of the Twelfth Century*. Cambridge, Mass.: Harvard University Press, 1982.

Hatty, James. "Coping with Disaster: Florence After the Black Death." In *Disasters: Image and Context*, ed. Peter Hinton. Sydney, NSW: Sydney Association for Studies in Society and Culture, 1992.

Hatty, Suzanne E. and Stuart Burke, "The Vermin and the Virus: AIDS in Australian Prisons," *Social and Legal Studies*, 1, no. 1 (1992):85–106.

Hay, Denys. *The Church in Italy in the Fifteenth Century*. Cambridge: Cambridge University Press, 1977.

Hay, Denys and John Law. *Italy in the Age of the Renaissance 1380–1530*. London: Longman, 1989.

Hayles, N. K. "Virtual Bodies and Flickering Signifiers," *October*, 66 (1993): 69–91.

Hays, H. R. *The Dangerous Sex*. London: Methuen, 1966.

Hecker, J. F. C. *The Epidemics of the Middle Ages,* trans., B.G. Babington. London,1859.

Henderson, John. "Confraternities and the Church in late Medieval Florence." In *Voluntary Religion: Papers at the 1985 Summer Meeting and the 1986 Winter Meeting of the Ecclesiastical Society*, eds. W.J. Shiels and Diana Wood. Oxford: Ecclesiastical History Society and Basil Blackwell, 1986.

Henderson, John. "The Hospitals of Late-Medieval and Renaissance Florence: A Preliminary Survey." In Lindsay Grimshaw and Roy Porter, eds. *The Hospital in History*. London: Routledge, 1989.

Henderson, John. "Penitence and the Laity." In *Christianity and the Renaissance,* eds. Timothy Verdon and John Henderson. Syracuse, NY: Syracuse University Press, 1990.

Herlihy, D. "Some Psychological and Social Roots of Violence in Tuscan Cities." In *Violence and Disorder in Italian Cities, 1200–1500,* ed. Lauro Martines. Berkeley: University of California Press, 1972.

Herlihy, D. "Did Women have a Renaissance?: A Reconsideration," *Medievalia et Humanistica*, no. 13 (1985): 2–22.

Herlihy, D. and C. Klapisch-Zuber. *Tuscans and Their Families*. New Haven, NY: Yale University Press, 1985.

Herzlich, Claudine and Janine Pierret. *Illness and Self in Society,* trans. Elborg Forster. Baltimore: Johns Hopkins University Press, 1987.

Hewitt, Martin. "Bio-Politics and Social Policy: Foucault's Account of Welfare." In *The Body: Social Process and Cultural Theory*, eds. Mike Featherstone, Mike Hepworth, and Bryan S. Turner. London: Sage, 1991.

Hufton, Olwen. "Women, Work, and Family." In *A History of Women in the West: Renaissance and Enlightenment Paradoxes*, eds. Natalie Zemon Davis and Arlette Farge. Cambridge, Mass.: The Belknap Press of Harvard University Press, 1993.

Hughes, Diane Owen. "Regulating Women's Fashions." In *A History of Women in the West: Silences of the Middle Ages*, ed. Christiane Klapisch-Zuber. Cambridge, Mass.: Belknap Press of Harvard University Press, 1992.

Hyde, J. K. *Society and Politics in Medieval Italy*. London: Macmillan,1982.

Illich, Ivan. *Medical Nemesis: The Expropriation of Health*. London: Calder and Boyars, 1975.

Inglis, Brian. *A History of Medicine*. London: Weidenfield and Nicolson, 1965.

Jacobson, Alison. "Emerging and Re-emerging Viruses: An Essay," 1995, published electronically on the INTERNET, and available at: http://www.outbreak.org/cgiunreg/dynaserve.exe/index.html.

Jacquart, Danielle and Claude Thomasset. *Sexuality and Medicine in the Middle Ages*, trans. Matthew Adamson. Princeton: Princeton University Press, 1988.

Karlsen, Carol F. *The Devil in the Shape of Woman*. New York: Vintage Books, 1989.

Kay, Sara and Miri Rubin eds. *Framing Medieval Bodies*. Manchester: Manchester University Press, 1994.

Kee, Howard Clark. *Medicine, Miracle and Magic in New Testament Times*. New York: Cambridge University Press, 1986.

Kelly-Gadol, Joan. "Did Women have a Renaissance?" In *Becoming Visible: Women in European History*, eds. Renate Bridenthal and Claudia Koonz. Boston: Houghton-Mifflin, 1977.

Kemp, Martin. "'The Mark of Truth': looking and learning in some anatomical illustrations from the Renaissance and eighteenth century." In *Medicine and the Five Senses*, eds. W.F. Bynum and Roy Porter. Cambridge: Cambridge University Press, 1993.

Kent, F. W. "The Black Death of 1348 in Florence: A New Contemporary Account?" In *Renaissance Studies in Honor of Craig Hugh Smyth*, Vol. I. Florence: Giunti Barbèra, 1988.

Kingwell, Mark. *Dreams of Millennium: Reports from a Culture on the Brink.* London: Faber and Faber, 1997.

Kirby, Vicki. "Corporeal Habits: Addressing Essentialism Differently," *Hypatia*, 6, no. 3 (1991): 4–24.

Klapisch-Zuber, Christiane. "L'enfance en Toscane début XVe siècle." In *Annales de Démographie Historique.* Paris: Mouton, 1973.

Klapish-Zuber, Christiane. "Attitudes devant l'enfant." In *Annales de Démographie Historique.* Paris: Mouton, 1973.

Krautheimer, R. *Rome: Profile of a City 312–1308.* Princeton: Princeton University Press, 1980.

Kroker, Arthur, Marilouise Kroker and David Cook. *Panic Encylopedia: The Definitive Guide to the Postmodern Scene.* London: Macmillan, 1989.

Lappe, Marc. *The Body's Edge: Our Cultural Obsession with Skin.* New York: Henry Holt and Company, 1996.

Laqueur, Thomas. *Making Sex.* Cambridge, Mass.: Harvard University Press, 1990.

Le Goff, Jacques. *The Medieval Imagination,* trans. Arthur Goldhammer. Chicago: Chicago University Press, 1988.

Leary, Stephen D. *Arguing the Apocalypse: A Theory of Millennial Rhetoric.* New York: Oxford University Press, 1994.

Leder, Drew, ed. *The Body in Medical Thought and Practice.* Dordecht: Kluwer Academic Publishers, 1992.

Lerner, Robert E. "Medieval Prophecy and Religious Dissent," *Past and Present,* no. 72 (1976): 3–24.

Lerner, Robert E. "The Black Death and Western Eschatological Mentalities." In *The Black Death: The Impact of the Fourteenth-Century Plague,* ed. Daniel Williman Binghamton, NY: Center for Medieval and Early Renaissance Studies, 1982.

Leslie, John. *The End of the World.* London: Routledge, 1996.

Lorensen, Bill. "Marching Through the Visible Man, 1996," published electronically on the INTERNET and available at http://www.nlm.nih. gov/research/visible/.

Lupton, Deborah. *Food, the Body and the Self.* London: Sage, 1996.

Lynch, Aaron. *Thought Contagion, How Belief Spreads Through Society: The New Science of Memes.* New York: Basic Books, 1996.

Macchiavelli, Niccolò. "The Mandragola." In *Five Italian Renaissance Comedies*, trans. and ed. Bruce Penman. Harmondsworth, Penguin, 1978.

Mackenzie, Adrian. "'God has No Allergies': Immanent Ethics and the Simulacra of the Immune System," *Postmodern Culture*, 6, no. 2 (1996):2.

Maclean, Ian. *The Renaissance Notion of Women*. Cambridge: Cambridge University Press, 1980.

MacSween, Morag. *Anorexic Bodies*. London: Routledge, 1996.

Maffesoli, Michel. *The Time of the Tribes: The Decline of Individualism in Mass Society*, trans. Don Smith. London: Routledge, 1996.

Maher, Lisa. "Punishment and Welfare: Crack Cocaine and the Regulation of Mothering." In *The Criminalization of a Woman's Body*, ed. Clarice Feinman. New York: Harrington Park, 1993.

Margolis, Joseph. *Historied Thought, Constructed World: A Conceptual Primer for the Turn of the Millennium*. San Francisco: University of California Press, 1995.

Martines, Lauro, ed. *Violence and Disorder in Italian Cities, 1200–1500*. Berkeley: University of California Press, 1972.

Martines, Lauro. "A Way of Looking at Women in Renaissance Florence," *Journal of Medieval and Renaissance Studies,* no. 4 (1974): 15–28.

Martines, Lauro. *Power and Imagination: City-States in Renaissance Italy*. Harmondsworth: Penguin, 1983.

Massumi, Brian. "The Evolutionary Alchemy of Reason," published electronically on the INTERNET and available at: http://www.anu.edu.au/HRC/first_and_last/links.massumi_works.htm.

Mazzi, Maria Serena. "La peste a Firenze nel Quattrocento." In *Strutture familiari epidemie migrazioni nell'Italia medieval*. Naples: Edizioni scientifiche italiane, 1984.

Mazzio, Carla and David Hillman, eds. *The Body in Parts: Fantasies of Corporeality in Early Modern Europe*. New York: Routledge, 1997.

McLaughlin, Eleanor Commo. "Equality of Souls, Inequality of Sexes: Women in Medieval Theology." In *Religion and Sexism, Images of Woman in the Jewish and Christian Traditions,* ed. Rosemary Radford Reuter. New York: Simon and Schuster, 1974.

McMurray, Andrew. "The Slow Apocalypse: A Gradualistic Theory of the World's Demise," *Postmodern Culture*, 6, no. 3 (May 1996).

McNay, Lois. "The Foucauldian Body and the Exclusion of Experience," *Hypatia*, 6, no. 3 (1991): 135.

McNeill, William. *Plagues and Peoples*. New York: Anchor/Doubleday, 1976.

McRae, Shannon. "Coming Apart at the Seams: Sex, Text, and the Virtual Body," 1994. Published electronically on the INTERNET and available at: http://humanitas.ucsb.edu/shuttle/gender.html.

Meiss, Millard. *Painting in Florence and Siena after the Black Death*. Princeton, NJ: Princeton University Press, 1978.

Mellor, Philip and Chris Shilling. *Re-forming the Body: Religion, Community and Modernity*. London: Sage, 1997.

Miles, Margaret. *Carnal Knowing: Female Nakedness and Religious Meaning in the Christian West*. New York: Vintage Books, 1991.

Miller, William Ian. *The Anatomy of Disgust*. Cambridge, Mass.: Harvard University Press, 1997.

Mollat, Michel. *The Poor in the Middle Ages: An Essay in Social History*, trans. Arthur Goldhammer. New Haven: Yale University Press, 1986.

Morse, Stephen S. "Factors in the Emergence of Infectious Diseases," *Emerging Infectious Diseases*, 1, no. 1 (Jan–Mar, 1995). Published electronically on the INTERNET and available at: http://www.cdc.gov/ncidad/EID/vol1.no1/eid/html.

Multimedia Medical Systems, "Digital Human CD-ROM Homepage" 1996, published electronically on the INTERNET at http://www.mms.com/dighuman.htm.

Mundy, John H. *Europe in the High Middle Ages 1150/1309*. London: Longman, 1980.

Murray, Margaret A. *The God of the Witches*. London: Oxford University Press, 1970.

Niccoli, Ottavia. "'Menstruum Quasi Monstruum': Monstrous Births and Menstrual Taboos in the Sixteenth Century." In *Sex and Gender in Historical Perspective,* eds. Edward Muir and Guido Ruggiero. Baltimore: Johns Hopkins University Press, 1990.

Noddings, Nel. *Women and Evil*. Berkeley: University of California Press, 1989.

Noonan, John T. *Contraception: A History of its Treatment by the Catholic Theologians and Canonists*. Cambridge, Mass.: Harvard University Press, 1965.

Norberg, Kathryn. "Prostitutes." In *A History of Women in the West: Renaissance and Enlightenment Paradoxes,* eds. Natalie Zemon and Arlette Farge. Cambridge, Mass.: Belknap Press/ Harvard University Press, 1993.

Nutton, Vivian. "The Seeds of Disease: An Explanation of Contagion and Infection from the Greeks to the Renaissance," *Medical History,* no. 27 (1983): 1–34.

Nutton, Vivian. "Galen at the Bedside: The Methods of a Medical Detective." In *Medicine and the Five Senses,* eds. W.F. Bynum and Roy Porter. Cambridge: Cambridge University Press, 1993.

Oldstone, Michael. *Viruses, Plagues, and History.* New York: Oxford University Press, 1998.

O'Neill, John. *Five Bodies.* Ithaca: Cornell University Press, 1985.

O'Neill, Ynez Viole. "Innocent III and the Evolution of Anatomy," *Medical History,* no. 20 (1976): 429–33.

Opitz, Claudia. "Life in the Middle Ages." In *A History of Women in the West: Silences of the Middle Ages,* ed. Christiane Klapisch-Zuber. Cambridge, Mass.: Belknap Press of Harvard University Press, 1992.

Origo, Iris. *The Merchant of Prato.* London: Cape, 1957.

Origo, Iris. *The World of San Bernardino.* New York: Harcourt, Brace and World, 1962.

Orioli, Luciano. *Le confraternite medievali e il problema della povertà.* Rome: Edizioni di storia e letteratura, 1984.

Palmer, Richard. "In bad odor: smell and its significance." In *Medicine and the Five Senses,* eds. W.F. Bynum and Roy Porter. Cambridge: Cambridge University Press, 1993.

Park, Katherine. *Doctors and Medicine in Early Renaissance Florence.* Princeton: Princeton University Press, 1985.

Partner, Peter. *Renaissance Rome 1500–1559.* Berkeley: University of California Press, 1979.

Pavan, Elisabeth. "Police des moeurs, société et politique à Venise à la fin du Moyen Age," *Revue historique,* CCLXIV, no. 2 (1980): 241–88.

Pels, Dick and Aya Crébas. "Carmen—Or the Invention of a New Feminine Myth." In *The Body: Social Process and Cultural Theory,* eds. Mike Featherstone, Mike Hepburn, and Bryan S. Turner. London: Sage, 1991.

Penzer, N. M. *Poison-Damsels.* London: C.J. Sawyer, 1952.

Perosa, A. ed. *Giovanni Rucellai ed il suo Zibaldone I.* London: Warburg Institute, 1960.

Peters, C. J. and M. Olshaker. *Virus Hunter: Thirty Years of Battling Hot Virues Around the World.* New York: Anchor Books, 1997.

Plumwood, Val. *Feminism and the Mastery of Nature.* London: Routledge, 1993.

Porter, Roy. "The Patient's View: Doing History from Below," *Theory and Society,* 14 (1985).

Porter, Roy. "The Rise of the Physical Examination." In *Medicine and the Five Senses,* eds. W.F. Bynum and Roy Porter. Cambridge: Cambridge University Press, 1993.

Pouchelle, Marie-Christine. *The Body and Surgery in the Middle Ages,* trans. Rosemary Morris. Cambridge: Polity Press, 1990.

Preston, Richard. *The Hot Zone.* New York: Doubleday, 1994.

Preston, Richard. *The Cobra Event.* New York: Random House, 1997.

Preto, Paolo. *Peste e società a Venezia nel 1576.* Vicenza: Possa, 1978.

Prusak, Bernard S. "Woman: Seductive Siren or Source of Sin?" In *Religion and Sexism: Images of Woman in the Jewish and Christian Traditions,* ed. Rosemary Radford Reuther. New York: Simon and Schuster, 1974.

Pullan, Brian. "Plague and Perceptions of the Poor in Early Modern Italy." In *Epidemics and Ideas,* eds. Terence Ranger and Paul Slack. Cambridge: Cambridge University Press, 1992.

Quétel, Claude. *History of Syphilis,* trans. Judith Braddock and Brian Pike. Baltimore: Johns Hopkins University Press, 1990.

Quimby, Lee. *Anti-Apocalypse: Exercises in Genealogical Criticism.* Minneapolis: University of Minnesota Press, 1994.

Randall, Teri. "Coping With the Violence Epidemic," *Journal of the American Medical Association,* 263, no. 19 (1990): 2612–14.

Régnier-Bohler, Danielle. "Literary and Mystical Voices." *A History of Women in the West: Silences of the Middle Ages,* ed. Christiane Klapisch-Zuber. Cambridge, Mass.: Belknap Press of Harvard University Press, 1992.

Reid, Elizabeth. "Cultural Formations in Text-Based Virtual Realities," Master of Arts Thesis, University of Melbourne, 1994. Published electronically on the INTERNET and available at http://www. Mcs.net/~zupko/popcult.htm.

Reuther, Rosemary Radford. "Misogynism and Virginal Feminism in The Fathers of the Church." In *Religion and Sexism: Images of Woman in the Jewish and Christian Traditions*, ed. Rosemary Radford Reuther. New York: Simon and Schuster, 1974.

Rhodes, Richard. *Deadly Feasts: Tracking the Secrets of a Terrifying New Plague*. New York: Simon and Schuster, 1997.

Riddle, John M. "Theory and Practice in Medieval Medicine," *Viator*, no. 5 (1974): 158–61.

Ridolfi, Roberto. *Vita di Girolamo Savonarola*, 7th edn. Florence: Sansoni, 1981.

Rocke, Michael J. "Il controllo dell'omosessualità a Firenze nel XV secolo: Gli Ufficiali di Notte," *Quaderni storici*, no. 66 (1987): 704–23.

Rocke, Michael J. "Sodomites in Fifteenth Century Tuscany: The Views of Bernardino of Siena," *Journal of Homosexuality*, 15 (1988).

Rocke, Michael J. *Forbidden Friendships: Homosexuality and Male Culture in Renaissance Florence*. New York: Oxford University Press, 1996.

Ronell, Avital. *Finitude's Score: Essays for the End of the Millennium*. Lincoln: University of Nebraska, 1998.

Ruggiero, Guido. *The Boundaries of Eros: Sex Crime and Sexuality in Renaissance Venice*. New York: Oxford University Press, 1985.

Runciman, Steven. *Byzantine Style and Civilization*. Harmondsworth: Penguin, 1975.

Russo, Mary. "Female Grotesques: Carnival and Theory." In *Feminist Studies / Critical Studies*, ed. Teresa de Laurentis. Wisconsin: Indiana University Press, 1986.

Russo, Mary. *The Female Grotesque: Risk, Excess and Modernity*. London: Routledge, 1995.

Ryan, Frank. *Virus X: Tracking the New Killer Plagues Out of the Present and into the Future*. Boston: Little, Brown and Co., 1997.

Sartelle, Joe. "Introduction to 'Apocalypse'," *Bad Subjects*, 15, no. 1 (1994), published electronicaly on the INTERNET and available at: http://english.cmu.edu/BS/default.html.

Sartre, Jean-Paul. *Being and Nothingness*, trans. Hazel Barnes. New York: Washington Square Press, 1966.

Satcher, David. "Emerging Infections: Getting Ahead of the Curve," *Emerging Infectious Diseases*, 1, 1 (Jan–Mar, 1995). Published electronically on the INTERNET and available at http://www.cdc.gov/nicad/EID/Vol1no1/eid.html.

Sawday, Jonathon. *The Body Emblazoned: Dissection and the Human Body in Renaissance Culture*. New York: Routledge, 1997.

Schullian, Dorothy M. "A Manuscript of Dominici in the Army Medical Library," *Journal of the History of Medicine*, III, no. 3 (1948): 395–99.

Scott, Joan. "Gender: A Useful Category of Historical Analysis," *American Historical Review,* no. 91 (1986): 1053–75.

Shilling, Chris. *The Body and Social Theory*. London: Sage, 1993.

Showalter, Elaine. *Sexual Anarchy: Gender and Culture at the Fin de Siécle*. London: Virago, 1992.

Showalter, Elaine. *Hystories: Hysterical Epidemics and Modern Culture*. New York: Columbia University Press, 1997.

Showalter, Elaine. Interview published on the Columbia University Press website at http://www.columbia.edu/cu/cup/feature/hystories/hystinterview.html

Simon, Jeffrey D. "Biological Terrorism," *The Journal of the American Medical Association*, no. 278 (1997):428.

Simon, William. *Postmodern Sexualities*. London: Routledge, 1996.

Singer, Charles and Dorothea Singer, "The Scientific Position of Girolamo Fracastoro," *Annals of Medical History* 1, no. 1 (1971): 5

Singer, Linda. *Erotic Welfare: Sexual Theory and Politics in the Age of the Epidemic*, eds. Judith Butler and Maureen MacGrogan. New York: Routledge, 1993.

Siraisi, Nancy G. *Medieval and Early Renaissance Medicine*. Chicago: University of Chicago Press, 1990.

Sontag, Susan. *Illness as Metaphor and AIDS and its Metaphors*. New York: Doubleday, 1990.

Southern, W. *Western Society and the Church in the Middle Ages*. Harmondsworth: Penguin, 1979.

Stafford, B. *Body Criticism: Imaging the Unseen in Enlightenment Art and Medicine*. Cambridge, Mass.: MIT Press, 1993.

Starkie, Walter. *Raggle Taggle*. London: John Murray, 1949.

Stelarc, *Archival Space*, 1996. Published electronically on the INTERNET and available at http://www.merlin.com.au/stelarc.

Synnott, Anthony. *The Body Social: Symbolism, Self and Society*. London: Routledge, 1993.

Tenenti, Alberto. "Témoignages Toscans sur la mort des enfants autor de 1400." In *Annales de Démographie Historique*. Paris: Mouton, 1973.

Tenenti, Alberto. *Il senso della morte e l'amore della vita nel Rinascimento*. Turin: Einaudi, 1989.

Terry, Jennifer. "The Body Invaded: Medical Surveillance of Women as Reproducers," *Socialist Review*, 19, no. 3 (1989): 13–43.

Thomasset, Claude. "The Nature of Woman." In *A History of Women in the West: Silences of the Middle Ages*, ed. Christiane Klapisch-Zuber. Cambridge, Mass.: Belknap Press of Harvard University Press, 1992.

Thorndike, Lyn. *A History of Magic and Experimental Science*. New York: Columbia University Press, 1934.

Thrupp, Sylvia L., ed. *Millennial Dreams in Action*. The Hague: Mouton, 1962.

Treichler, Paula A. "AIDS, Gender, and Biomedical Discourse: Current Contests for Meaning." In *AIDS: The Burden of History*, eds. Elizabeth Fee and Daniel M. Fox. Berkeley: University of California Press, 1990.

Trevor-Roper, Hugh. *The European Witch Craze of the Sixteenth and Seventeenth Centuries*. London: Penguin, 1978.

Trexler, Richard C. "The Foundlings of Florence, 1395–1455," *History of Childhood Quarterly*, I (1973): 259–84.

Trexler, Richard C. "Ritual in Florence: Adolescence and Salvation in the Renaissance." In *The Pursuit of Holiness in Late Medieval and Renaissance Religion*, eds. C. Trinkaus and H. Oberman. Leiden: Brill, 1974

Trexler, Richard C. *Public Life in Renaissance Florence*. New York: Academic Press, 1980.

Trexler, Richard C. "La prostitution florentine au XVe siècle: patronages et clientèles," *Annales Économies, Sociétés, Civilisations*, no. 36 (1981): 983.

Turkle, Sherry. *Life on the Screen: Identity in the Age of the Internet*. New York: Simon and Schuster, 1995.

Turner, Bryan S. *Religion and Social Theory*. London: Heinemann Educational, 1983.

Turner, Bryan S. *The Body and Society*. London: Sage, 1984.

Turner, Bryan S. *Medical Power and Social Knowledge*. London: Sage, 1987.

Turner, Bryan S. "Recent Developments in the Theory of the Body." In *The Body: Social Process and Cultural Theory*, eds. Mike Featherstone, Mike Hepworth, and Bryan S. Turner. London: Sage, 1991.

Turner, Bryan S. *Regulating Bodies: Essays in Medical Sociology*. London: Routledge, 1992.

Turner, Bryan S. "Theoretical Developments in the Sociology of the Body," *Australian Cultural History*, no. 13 (1994): 22.

U.S. National Library of Medicine, "The Visible Human Project, 1996," p. 6. Published electronically on the INTERNET and available at: http: //www.nlm.nih.gov/research/visible.

Valera, Francisco and Mark Anspach, "The Body Thinks: The Immune System in the Process of Somatic Individuation." In *Materialities of Communication*, eds. H. U. Gumbrecht and K. L. Pfeiffer, trans. W. Whobrey. Stanford: Stanford University Press, 1994.

Vaughan, Megan. "Syphilis in Colonial East and Central Africa: The Social Construction of an Epidemic." In *Epidemics and Ideas*, eds. Terence Ranger and Paul Slack. Cambridge: Cambridge University Press, 1992.

Vecchio, Silvana. "The Good Wife." In *A History of Women in the West: Silences of the Middle Ages*, ed. Christiane Klapisch-Zuber. Cambridge, Mass.: Belknap Press of Harvard University Press, 1992.

Vernadasky, G. *The Mongols and Russia*. New Haven:Yale University Press, 1959.

Watts, Sheldon. *Epidemics and History: Disease, Power and Imperialism*. New Haven: Yale University Press, 1998.

Weissman, Ronald E. *Ritual Brotherhood in Renaissance Florence*. New York: Academic Press, 1982.

Weissman, Ronald E. "Sacred Eloquence: Humanist Preaching and Lay Piety in Renaissance Florence." In *Christianity and the Renaissance,* eds. Timothy Verdon and John Henderson. Syracuse, NY: Syracuse University Press, 1990.

Williams, Simon. "Goffman, interactionism, and the management of stigma in everyday life." In *Sociological Theory and Medical Sociology,* ed. Graham Scambler. London: Tavistock, 1989.

Wilson, Mary E. "Travel and the Emergence of Infectious Diseases," *Emerging Infectious Diseases*, 1, no. 1 (Jan–Mar, 1995). Published electronically on the INTERNET and available at: http://www.cdc.gov/ncidad/EID/vol1.no.1/eid.html.

Winslow, Charles-Edward Amory. *The Conquest of Epidemic Disease.* Madison: University of Wisconsin Press, 1980.

Wolff, Janet. *Feminine Sentences: Essays on Women and Culture.* Cambridge: Polity Press, 1990.

World Health Organization (WHO). *The World Health Report* 1996. The pre-release, published electronically on the INTERNET, is available at: http://www.who.ch/whr/1996/press1.html.

Zaner, Richard M. "Parted Bodies, Departed Souls: The Body in Ancient Medicine and Anatomy." In *The Body in Medical Thought and Practice*, ed. Drew Leder. Dordecht: Klumer, 1992.

Ziegler, Philip. *The Black Death.* London: Collins, 1972.

Zola, Irving Kenneth. "Medicine as an Institution of Social Control," *Sociological Review,* 20 (Nov. 1972): 487–504.

Index

Agnolo di Tura del Grasso: caring for his dying children, 86; difficulties in burying the dead, 86, 93; the horror of the Black Death, 84

AIDS: 5, 15, 28; and intensification of surveillance and regulation, 238; HIV/AIDS as both invasive and polluting, 237; ideological similarities between HIV/AIDS and syphilis, 237; syphilis and HIV/AIDS provoking apocalyptic anxieties, 236–237

Albertus Magnus, 140; on menopausal women, 39; on the dangers from old women, 39

alternative medicine, 164, 179–180; and belief in miraculous cures, 180; and perceived incompetence of the medical profession, 179; chosen by Enea Silvio Piccolomini (later Pope Pius II) for plague treatment, 180; plague cures, 164; as opportunity for many with no background in medicine, 164, 180

amulets and charms: offered as cures for plague by many newcomers to medicine, 180; to combat disease, 42; to ward off the plague, 164, 180

Apocalypse, the, 25, 28, 99; pestilence and the Four Horsemen of, 57; threats of a nuclear disaster as a contemporary equivalent, 236

apocalyptic anxieties, 25; produced by fears of HIV/AIDS, 237; soothsayers of doom, 234; twentieth century societal concerns, 28

apocalyptic signs: Black Death as warning, 110; natural disasters heralding the dawn of the millennium, 107

apocalyptic tradition, 28; its re-interpretation in the postmodern era, 235–236; its secularization in the twentieth century, 235; signs of societal collapse and contemporary sub-cultures, 236

Aristotle: and the medieval church, 8; and the Poison-Damsel, 38–39; the female as representing "body," 37

astral influences: on disease causation, 43–44

atmosphere: corruption of the air and disease, 94; pestilential "miasmas," 43; pestilential nature of swamps and stagnant water, 167; polluted by poisonous breath, 38; sodomy causing both corruption of the air and plague, 121

Aretino, Pietro, 179

Augustine, Saint, 61, 71; on bodily disorders, 47

Bacon, Francis, 209

Balsamo, Anne: on fears of death and annihilation, 253

Baudrillard, Jean, 191; and contemporary hedonism, 22; on the modern body, 22

Beguines, 104–105; dissent stifled by Church, 105

Bernardino of Siena, Saint, 121–122, 124; attributing female characteristics to homosexuals, 156;

Bernardino of Siena, Saint *(continued)*
denouncing sexuality, 153; on
women's vanity and deportment, 157
parents fostering homosexuality in
their sons, 121–122; plague caused by
sodomy within the community, 121
Bianchi, the, 118
Black Death, 79; a challenge to the
medical profession, 163, 175–176;
and a crisis around the body, 125;
and new perceptions of the body,
183, 188–189; and the relationship
between priest and medical
practitioner, 170–171; and autopsies
for medical purposes, 183; and
worker unrest, 134; as an
apocalyptic sign, 110; deaths of
entire families, 86; desertion of
victims by relatives and friends, 85;
estimated death toll in Europe, 83;
families torn asunder, 85; headlong
flight from danger, 85, 88; homes
and cities abandoned, 88; no
apparent defence against the
disease, 84; undermining the status
of medical practitioners, 164,
181–182; views on the origins of the
calamity, 82, 86
blood: as a bodily humour, 167; as vital
life force, 171; medicinal value of,
168; polluting effects of, 168; spilling
of blood during surgery as
problematic, 170, Western European
abhorrence of, 168
blood letting, 167–169; and the Church,
170; as treatment, 45, 167, 177
Boccaccio, Giovanni, 120, 127;
abandonment of family member, 85;
advice on preserving good health
given by the city, 90; description of
symptoms, 96; description of the
Black Death in Florence, 85–86;
dislocation of civic affairs 133;
lawlessness in the community, 135;
multitude of bodies, 94; on
gravediggers for plague victims, 135;
recourse to religious rituals, 87;
sanitary measures adopted in
Florence, 132; uneven incidence of
death, 88–89, 96

bodily perceptions: genitalia as
shameful, 220; natural functions
abhorrent and offensive, 219, 221,
228; the creation of the modern
body, 218–231; nudity as vulgar, 220
bodily practices: advice from medical
practitioners on moderation to avoid
plague, 167, 178; bodily functions as
coarse, 221, 219; current focus on, 5,
7; "safe," 5; socially acceptable, 7, 21
body and soul: as inextricably linked, 3,
188; Cartesian view of, 3–4
body as project, the, 5, 18; pursuit of
bodily health and beauty, 18, 23
body fluids and discharges, 168–169; for
diagnosis, 169
body in social theory, the, 4–7
body in society, the, 6–7 ; and the
consumer culture, 23; as a sociocultural construct, 7, 15, 28, 31;
considerations of class, culture, and
gender, 6; regulated by the State
and the medical profession, 14, 24,
29; shifts in perception caused by
syphilis, 194, 207; the body as vile
and disgusting, 206–207, 219–220
body, the disordered, 40–41; as
challenge to social order and control,
31–32; and gender differences, 32;
and the healing arts, 41; epidemic
disease and changing perceptions of,
255; from disease or illness, 40; of
dangerous others, 41; of lepers,
50–53; of women, 31–32, 36–37, 40;
postmodern images shaped by
responses to major epidemics, 234
body, the female, 33–34; as an
"incomplete" male body, 32, 34; as
"defective," 35; as "disordered," 110,
125; as polluting, 125; as source of
pollution during male rituals of
flagellation, 111; as threat to male
power, 32; and its excess of
openings, 172; contaminating
effects, 37; efforts to control,
102–103; literary metaphors of a
woman's sealed body, 172; not for
women's pleasure, 104; perpetual
target of the male gaze, 21; target
for investigation by the medical

profession, 16; the disruptive influence of the "impure" body, 111, 116; the height of abomination,100; threat to men's spiritual and physical health, 125

body, the human, 32–33; abhorrence of any sensory pleasure, 125; and medicine, 16–17; and self-identity, 22; and the deconstruction of the corporeal in postmodernity, 234; as a cyborg, 248; as a focus of attention, 88, 98; as a machine, 3–4; as a metaphor for social equilibrium and order, 34; as an enclosed system, 165, 171; as an object, 4, 22, 164, 188; as a project, 5; as a weapon of destruction, 92; bodies of plague victims exposed to public gaze everywhere, 95; body as prison of the soul, 100; computerized representation of, 250–251; dangers of indulgence, 102; de-personalized and institutionalized through the hospital system, 187–188; early perceptions, 35, 32; emergence of the nude in Renaissance art, 99; horror of the body, 37; medieval concepts of, 164–166; medieval rejection of the body versus humanist ideals, 98–99; outer beauty as sign of inner goodness, 99; plague and the fragility of life, 94, 97; primacy of the mind over, 4; progressively privatized, 21; reconfigured in postmodern biomedical discourse, 249; re-discovery of Greek appreciation of the body, 98; replacement parts for, 249, 251; repressed and marginalized since the seventeenth century, 19; sacred versus vile and polluting, 165; still an abomination to many, 100; the body beautiful versus the body vile, 98–100; the inevitability of decay and dissolution after death, 95, 97. See also denial of the body; and disembodiment

body, the "impure," 116–117, 159–60; as defined by the State, 159; of the poor, 144; of the sick, 166

body, the male, 33–34; and nocturnal pollution, 124; as "ordered," 110; as prototype for human beings, 34; defended in response to the plague, 125; in religious and public events, 125

body, the "pure," 116, 159; as defined by the State, 159; paramount examples in Mary and Christ, 116; relics of saints and martyrs, 117; young boys as asexual, 119

Bono Giamboni, 61, 73

Bordo, Susan, 21, 24–25, 254

Boswell, John: on changing attitudes to homosexuality, 69

Botero, Giovanni, 135

brothels: closed to minimize the spread of syphilis, 217; public brothels established by Florence in the early fifteenth century, 151–152, 217

burial of plague victims, 135, dumped into pits without traditional rites, 93; recourse to mass burials, 93, 95; special regulations for, 142; with financial benefits to some groups, 135

Bynum, Caroline, 117

Cadigan, Pat: and disembodiment, 252

Calvi, Guilia, 95

Camus, Albert, 241

Carmichael, Ann G., 147

Cartesian body, 6, 17–19

Cartesianism: and changing perceptions of the body, 24; concepts challenged, 18; dominant influence in bio-medicine, 17; in twentieth century science, 255: reinforcing gender differences, 255

Cassian, 70, 71

Castiglione, Baldesar, 99; on desirable feminine attributes, 223–224

Catherine of Genoa, Saint, 126

Catherine of Siena, Saint, 105, 126

Cellini, Benvenuto: his encounter with syphilis, 200

chastity: as ideal way of life for laity, 103; advisable for men, 103; recommended for men, 36; required

chastity *(continued)*
of women, 103, 122; superior virtues
of virginity, 122
children: abandoned by parents, 85, 91;
begging in the streets, 91; buried by
their father, 86; many parents
unable to feed families, 91; male
children preferred, 90; more girls
than boys abandoned, 91; orphaned
by the plague, 91
Christianity: as State religion of the
Roman Empire, 36, 46; new
perceptions of the body, 44
Christ's suffering. *See Imitatio Christi*
Chrysostom, Saint John, 40
Church and medicine, 47–50; attitudes
to disease shaped by Church
doctrine, 47; Church claims
authority in medical matters, 48;
illness and disease as punishment,
47; monastic medicine, 47, 49;
perceived nexus between sin and
illness, 47, 52; priority given to
curing the soul, 48; reliance on
divine intervention, 43, 47–48
Church and society: sexually repressive
views, 62; shaping community
perceptions, 62; sins against nature
and crimes against nature, 68, 76
Church and State: contrast between
ecclesiastical and secular laws, 66,
70; perceptions of sodomy, 68; State
and Church courts, 66
city-state. *See* commune, the
class relations: class boundaries and
dress codes, 136, 158; destitution of
the underclass after plague
epidemics, 91; discontent at scarcity
of food and lack of work, 136;
discontent with the social structure,
135; disproportionate death toll
amongst the poor, 89; distribution of
food to the poor, 91; emerging
middle class, 64–65, 130; inferior
status of the unwashed, 227; large
section of Florentine under-class
disenfranchised, 131; no work and
no income for the underclass after
the Black Death, 91; patterns of
violence and civil disorder, 134–145;

plague and class bias in control
regulations, 134; poorer classes
hardest hit by plague, 89; targeting
disadvantaged and marginalized
groups, 130; temporary inversion of
the social order, 136; the underclass
of Florence (*popolo minuto*), 131
clergy: and canon law, 66; controlling
dissemination of information, 103;
credibility and authority challenged,
119–120; defining roles of men and
women, 102; defining sodomy, 68;
denunciation of sinful behavior, 69;
deviant behavior amongst the
Church hierarchy and the
priesthood, 106–107, 108; loss of
community respect, 120, 136; many
secular clergy lacking education, 74;
parish clergy, 75; preoccupation with
sexuality and sexual sins, 71, 102;
responses to the plague, 119; the
avarice of some priests and friars,
120, 135
clerical gaze: defining "woman" and the
"body," 103
Cohn, Samuel, 141
Colonna, Vittoria, 126
commune, the, 130–134; and potentially
dissident groups, 138–139; control
by a conservative ruling elite, 134;
delegation of powers during the
Black Death, 133; distribution of
grain and bread to the poor, 138;
emergence of, 130; harsh penalties
to deter dissidents, 139–140; new
apparatus of State control followed
outbreaks of plague, 137, 144–145;
perceived challenge from the
disaffected poor, 137; plague
disrupted administrative functions,
132–133; power structure, 133–134;
watchful for signs of conspiracy, 137
community discourse: and changing
attitudes to the body, 185; Church
indifference to plight of the poor,
107; competence and ethics of
medical practitioners questioned,
178; homosexuals viewed as
aberrant females, 155, 160;
influenced by forthright preachers,

124; misogynist views more entrenched after the plague, 127; moral condemnation and syphilis, 198–199; nexus between sinfulness and divine retribution, 79; natural events as signs of God's displeasure, 77; on plague cures, 180; on sin and the body, 70; perceptions of the female body, 172; plague epidemics as punishment, 101; recognition of connection between syphilis and sexual activities, 195, 209, 219; reflecting Church dogma, 72; rejection of calls for sexual restraint, 106; women's sexuality blamed for transmission of syphilis, 199

community healers, 46, 49; and advice on the plague, 164, 180; treated most common ailments for the community, 178. *See also* "wise women"

community responses: changes in patterns of marriage, 90; grief and anguish, 84, 86; increased birth rate following plague outbreaks, 91;many children abandoned by parents, 85, 91; marked increase in the size of families, 91; overwhelming fear of the plague, 84; workers reluctant to perform usual tasks, 136

Constantine, Emperor, 36

confinement: and the carceral state, 146; of plague victims as primary control measure, 144; of the poor, 147

confraternities: as corporate bodies, 66; devoted to private religious rituals of repentance, 112; growth during the plague epidemics, 114; focus of flagellants on rejection of the body, 114; for young boys, 119; groups focusing on charitable works, 112; *laudesi*, groups glorifying the Virgin Mary, 113; participation of boys' groups in processions, 119; origins, 112, 114; the *flagellanti*, groups involved in ritual self-flagellation, 113–115

consumer culture: and bodily images, 23; idealized images of youth, fitness, and beauty, 23

contagion, 209–211; and avoidance of direct bodily contact, 209; and extension of regulatory apparatus of society, 237; and public health discourse, 180; fears shaping social interaction, 28; first official use of term by *Signoria* in fifteenth century, 143; medical profession slow to accept concept, 143; reconfigured perceptions and social relationships at the close of the twentieth century, 237; reconfigured within postmodern lexicon, 234; social problems and "contagion," 237–238

contraries: as cures, 177

crisis of confidence: in the medical profession after the plague epidemics, 178–179

cyber age: a tour of the digitized body, 250–251; and deconstruction of the corporeal, 234; and the bionic body, 249; cyborgs, 248–249

da Monte, Giovanni: and the teaching of clinical methods, 212

dangerous Other: and sexually irresponsible men, 197–109; foreigners as, 149–150; lepers as, 55–56; prostitutes and homosexuals, 156; syphilis introduced by outsiders, 196–197

Dalarun, Jacques: on hostility towards voices of women, 105

Dante Alighieri, 59; *The Divine Comedy*, 73

Dawkins, Richard, 238

d'Este, Isabella, 126

de Pizan, Christine, 126

death: as physical decay, 95; bodies exposed everywhere, 95; by intercourse as variation of Poison-Damsel theme, 202; challenges to traditional attitudes to death, 95, 97; changing perceptions, 96–97; corpses in large numbers, 94; disproportionate number of plague deaths among the poor, 148; dead bodies and pestilential atmospheres,

death *(continued)*
167; fear of contact with bodies of
plague victims, 94; followed by
bodily decay, 96–98; from plague as
a form of disgrace, 85; new
awareness of its unpredictability, 96
Defending the Male Body, 125–127
Deleuze, J. and Guattari, F., 253
denial of the body: a conspiracy of
silence and invisibility, 221; and
physical immortality, 253; implicit
in the concept of the technologized
body, 253; in the name of modesty,
221. *See also* renunciation of the
body
denunciation of the body: a constant
theme of the clergy, 102; and its
sexuality, 102
Descartes, René, 3, 18, 209; the body as
a machine, 3
deviance: conflating deviance and sin,
102; deviant behavior as defined by
religious reformers, 102,124;
dissenting voices as deviant, 111;
groups with views differing from
Church and State as deviant, 147;
mendicant friars' declaration of
some sexual behavior as deviant,
121; prostitutes and homosexuals as
deviants, 156; sexually irresponsible
men as deviant, 198; the behavior of
some women, 218
diagnostic procedures: and computer
technology, 250; examining body
fluids, 169; in the late Middle Ages,
176; reading the external body signs,
165, 173
disadvantaged groups: increased
surveillance and constraint
following plague, 160; stigmatization
of, 172
discourses on the body: reshaped by
repressive attitudes of sixteenth
century, 219, 227
disease and illness: bodies of the sick as
"impure," 166; in the medieval
period, 40–41; long succession of
plague epidemics in Florence, 87–88;
plague and the disintegration of the
body assailed by disease, 91, 97;

reconfiguration in terms of the
medical model, 189
diseased body, the, 26, 28; confined or
banished, 160; dealing with, 142–146;
due to bodily imbalances, 167; late
medieval treatment of, 165; of plague
victims, 181; of the syphilitic as
deformed and repugnant, 206; risk of
contamination from, 142; treatment
by physicians and surgeons, 173, 178,
186
disembodiment: a concept of
postmodern culture, 249
disordered body, the: and new levels of
medical surveillance, 214; as
subordinated to the medical
practitioner, 212, 229–230
dissection: autopsies to advance
knowledge of plague, 183; concerns
about reunion of body and soul at
Judgement Day, 174; first recorded
instance for medical purposes in the
West, 174, 183; first recorded instance
of officially sanctioned, in Florence,
183; for forensic purposes, 174; never
formally prohibited by the Church,
175; plague autopsies in various
Italian cities, 183–184; publication of
Anatomia, to accompany practical
exercises in, 174–175; re-introduction
of the knife in surgery in thirteenth
century Bologna, 174; using a
computerized representation of the
human body, 250–251
divine retribution: Black Death as
punishment for human
transgressions, 86–87, 101; need to
placate God to avoid punishment for
sins, 77–79; nexus between sin and,
73–74
Dominican Order: friars denouncing
sinful behavior, 69; its role, 74–76
Douglas, Mary, 55–56
dualism, 8, 11, 19; and Aristotle, 8;
stereotypes of "good" and "bad"
women, 11
Dürer, Albrecht: representation of a
syphilitic, 198–199
Dwyer, John: on the immune system of
the body, 247–248

ecosystems: and emerging infectious diseases, 245–246; their destruction and the spread of pathogenic microbes, 243

Elias, Norbert: and the civilizing process, 12, 19, 228, 230–231

empirics: 176; qualified by experience only, 183

epidemic diseases: and socio-cultural changes, 26; and the extension of medical authority, 214; drug resistant strains of old diseases, 245–246; infectious diseases as leading cause of death, 245; many social ills now categorized as epidemics, 238; shaping societal perceptions of the body, 25

Erasmus, Desiderius: and rendering the body asexual, 220; on men as vectors of transmission, 216; on presentation of the body, 227; on the prostitute as a public sewer, 216; on safe distances, 225; on standards of behavior, 220–221; on syphilis as the worst disease known to the world, 206

exclusion and inclusion, 141–144

fear: of bathing, 210, 226; of calamitous events, 28; of contagion, 28; of feminization, 242, 254–255; of infection in crowded places, 225; of sharing eating utensils, 210; of the female body, 20; of the dissolution of bodily boundaries, 255; of the loss of individuality, 255; of touch and proximity, 255

Fraiberg, Allison: on body fluids, 246

Feher, Michel et al., 5

feminism: and theories of the body, 6; 11–12

Ficino, Marsilio, 156, 163, 178, 211

flagellants, 108–111, 113; acting to save the community from disasters, 109; bodily deprivation during rituals, 111; public processions of flagellants banned by the Pope in 1349, 110; public rituals widespread during the Black Death, 110

flagellation: as way of expiating sins, 72; by religious ascetics, 72; collective exercises inspired by itinerant preachers in late Middle Ages, 108; extended to lay groups, 72; imitating the suffering of Christ, 72; rituals described, 108. See also Imitatio Christi

flight from danger: as primary response to the Black Death, 88; many priests deserted their parishioners, 119; many too poor to flee from the plague, 88, 148; medical practitioners and the plague, 179; no abandonment of families during outbreaks after the Black Death, 88

Florence: and social changes, 26; as a sinful city, 67, 77; as an important international center, 63; calls for displays of community contrition to end plague, 87; community life, 63–64; population in the fourteenth century, 63; death toll during the Black Death, 83; distribution of grain and bread, 91; entry denied to travellers from plague areas, 142, 149–150; growing enthusiasm for gathering statistics, 145; lawlessness in, 133, 135; legislation aimed at control of plague, 90; perceived challenges to male power and supremacy, 129; perceived connection between homosexuality and low population growth, 154; plague and new opportunities to control disordered bodies, 160; plague and the increased masculinization of society, 127; plague remained endemic after the Black Death, 87–88; power structures, 64–66; regulating the bodies of citizens of, 130; regulations for conduct of public brothels, 151–152; restrictions imposed during times of crisis to limit divine retribution, 79; sense of community identity and cohesion, 63; the middle classes in fourteenth century, 135; threats of disorder, 136–137; under-class as threat to civic stability, 132;

Florence *(continued)*
upheavals in the social and power structures following the Black Death, 89–91
Foucault, Michel, 6, 146, 182, 184, 188; "Man-as Machine,"17; power and sexuality,13; "women's diseases" and hysterization of the female body, 11
Fracastoro, Girolamo: and contagion, 209–210; and the serpent metaphor, 205; as the father of modern pathology, 209; new theories on disease causation, 208, 209, 218; on connection between syphilis and sexual intercourse, 203, 210; on shameful parts of the body, 220
Franciscan Order: denunciation of sinful behavior, 69–70; its role, 74–76
Frank, Arthur, 6
French disease, the, 196–197

Galen, 33–34, 166–167; as interpreter of Greek medicine, 33; on diagnosis and treatment, 45–46; on human anatomy, 33–34, 172, 175; on surgery, 183
Galenic theories: of disease and illness causation, 166–167; of disease transmission by pestilential atmospheres (miasmas), 180; on anatomy, 172, 175; on diagnosis and treatment, 45–46
Garrett, Laurie: on emerging epidemic diseases, 243
Geoffroy of Vendôme, 38, 101
gender: binary oppositions, 7; evidence of gender bias in Florentine legislation, 155, 158; identity established at birth, 7; inequality socially constructed, 12; legitimating male dominance, 8; shaped by social and biological factors, 9–10; sixteenth century images of masculinity and femininity, 223; viruses and the collapse of gender identity, 242
gendered body, the, 7–12, 222–225; epidemic disease and changing perceptions of, 255; sixteenth

century concepts and twentieth century attitudes, 224–225
germ theory, 208; and infection by indirect means, 210
Giles of Rome: women readily surrender to their passions, 102
Ginsburg, Carlo, 56
Giordano da Rivalto-Moreni: on the moral failures of Florentines, 67–68; 78
Goffman, E., 56
Gonzaga, Elisabetta, 126
Greek Herbal, 45, and contraries, 177; and medicinal value of blood, 168
Greek medicine: adopted in Roman Empire, 44–47; decline after fall of Roman Empire, 46; early concepts, 44–45; animal and human dissections, 45; disease and the supernatural, 44; re-introduced to the West, 44
Gregory of Tours, 48–49
grotesque body, the, 19–21; and the female body, 20, 223; characteristics of, 20
Guicciardini, Francesco, 196, 206
guilds, 63, 65–66; manipulation of the electoral system by major guilds, 133–134, membership of, required of all practicing medicine, 170. *See also* medical guild

Haraway, Donna: the immune system as an internal military machine, 248
health boards: formed to implement government measures on disease control, 187; medical practitioners never appointed to, 187
health officers, 143, 145. *See also* plague officers
Herlihy, David, 127
Herzlich, Claudine and Pierret, Janine, 184
Hippocrates, 32–33, 44
holistic medicine: and preventative treatments, 5; "listening" to the body, 5
homosexuality: claimed to be encouraged by parents, 121

definitions of sodomy, 68; efforts to discourage, 151; evidence of, in many European cities, 153; illegal but not prosecuted vigorously in Florence until fifteenth century, 154; in Florence, 153–155 of great concern to Church and State, 68

homosexuals, 153–155; as deviants, 156; ejected from the city during times of crisis, 79, 132, 156; gathering evidence on offenders, 64; new magistracy to prosecute, 154; penalties imposed in Florence, 69; seen as an aberration of the female sex, 155, 160

hospitals: as agencies for the depersonalization and institutionalization of the body, 188; and the new medical bureaucracy, 188; expansion and consolidation of hospital system during plague epidemics, 187; filled with plague victims, 144; for syphilitics, under the control of medical practitioners, 214; hospices of the late Middle Ages, 187; new opportunities for physicians and surgeons, 187–188; separate plague hospitals established, 148; special hospitals for syphilitics, 213; staffing, 188; temporary accommodation for large numbers of plague cases, 148

Hughes, Diane, 157–158

human anatomy: and the Church, 171, 173; continued reliance on Galenic concepts through late Middle Ages, 175; contributions of Michelangelo and Leonardo da Vinci to study of, 185; early perceptions, 33–35, 45, 173–175, 185–186; essential element of medical education after early dissections,184; Galen's view, 33–34; in late medieval concepts, 165, 171–172; influence of Vesalius, 186; one-sex model, 34–35

human sexuality: and gender, 9; as a barrier to moral purity, 118; as target for State intervention, 14; as threat to social stability, 13–14; constrained by societal pressures,

13; emphasis on heterosexual and domesticated sexuality, 239; fear and repugnance of, 68, 70; increasing focus on, 76–77; marriage as second-best solution to demands of, 103; repressive attitude of the Church, 73; restrictions on most forms of sensory pleasure, 130; separation of men and women at public baths to curb expressions of, 155; sins against nature, 68, 76; viewed as grotesque, 100

identity: and gender, 12; and sexuality, 14; and the medieval community, 63; fears about loss of individuality, 255; perceived loss of, with mass burials, 95; relationship with the body, 4; the concept of individuality, 248, 254–255

Imitatio Christi: divine patronage through self-inflicted bodily pain, 72; imitating the suffering of Christ, 105. *See* flagellation

institutions: for reformed prostitutes, 141, 218; girls without dowries sent to convents, 141; of authority, and their perceived ineffectiveness, 233; refuges for women with marital difficulties, 141; women under control of, 141

itinerant preachers: and apocalyptic prophesies, 108; return to basic Christian moral values, 108

Jacobson, Alison: on microbial and viral predators, 246

Jacopone da Todi, 70

Jacquart, D. and Thomasset, C., 35, 38–39

Johnson, Karl: and the Ebola virus, 242

Jung, Carl, 11

Kelly-Gadol, Joan, 127

Kirby Vicki, 253

Kroker, Arthur, 249

Landucci, Luca, 149, 159, 193–194
Laqueur, Thomas, 9–10, 34
Leder, Drew, 17
Lederburg, Joshua, 245
legislation, social: against those perceived as deviants, 147, 156; directed against women, 130; enforcing dress codes to define social class boundaries, 136; limiting wage rises during plague epidemics, 136; new systems of surveillance and control, 137, 143–146; Officers for Decency, 151; Officers of the Night, 154
Le Goff, Jacques, 36, 100
Leonardo da Vinci, 100, 185, 199
lepers: and sexual desire, 51–52; banished from the community, 54–55; bodily signs, 53; burnt at the stake, 56; control and surveillance, 54, 56–57; loss of legal and civil rights, 55; persecuted throughout Europe, 56; rituals of segregation, 54–55; their isolation in leprosaria as model for plague hospitals, 148
leprosy: and medieval medical practitioners, 175; and bodily excesses, 171; as punishment for sexual excesses, 50–51; as sexualized disease, 52; associated with biblical accounts of the disease, 51; as vile and shameful, 166; final diagnosis by priest, 53; new regulatory apparatus for State control, 57; parallels with dangers of the Poison-Damsel, 51; theories of disease causation, 51; visible indications of, 173; women as vectors of transmission, 50–51
Leslie, John, 235
lived body, the: central to contemporary social theories of the body, 18; its importance, 4; should be "listened" to, 5; should displace the Cartesian body, 18
Luther, Martin: on venomous syphilitic whores, 217
Lynch, Aaron, 238

Machiavelli, Niccolò, 120; *La Mandragola* and death by intercourse, 202
Mackenzie, Adrian, 246, 248
Maclean, Ian, 127
Madonna of Impruneta, 117
Maffesoli, Michel, 23
mal francese. See French disease, the
Man: as symbolic of a higher order, 37
Marbode of Rennes, 38
Marchionne di Coppo Stefani, 94, 96, on the ignorance of medical practitioners, 179
marriage: age at first marriage, 90; as preventative medicine, 77; as second-best solution, 103; limits on displays of affection, 77; plague hastening marriages, 90; sixteenth century accent on sanctity of, 224; threatened by sodomy, 154
Massumi, Brian, 252–253
McLaughlin, E. C.: "demonizing" sex, 36
McMurry, Andrew, 233–234
medical discourse: and the biological weaknesses of women, 9; and the concept of contagion, 143; attitudes toward sexuality, 220; fears of contamination from disordered bodies, 165; gradual acceptance of the concept of contagion, 189; nineteenth century stereotypical "women's complaints," 16; on bathing the body, 210; on leprosy shaped by Church doctrine, 52–53; perceived nexus between sexuality and disease, 219; progress of leprosy, 53; reconciling Galenic principles and Church dogma, 167–168; suspected connection between syphilis and madness, 214; underpinned by moral condemnation, 207
medical education: clinical training within hospitals, 212; involvement of some women during the late Middle Ages, 186; requirement that dissections be included, 184–185; women barred from studying at new universities, 186

medical gaze, 15, 177; and the intimate parts of the body, 211–212, 230

medical guild, 164, 176; efforts to marginalize the empirics, 183; efforts to restore confidence, 182; membership, 170; hallmarks of professional organization, 181

medical practitioners: and twentieth century diseases, 5, 16; challenges to competence, 163, 175, 178; claimed privileged role in diagnosis and treatment of disease, 178, 182, 186; diagnosis by observing the outside of the body, 165, 173, 177; drive to regain their privileged position, 182–183; guild membership, 170, 182; little involvement in State management of plague epidemics, 180; loss of prestige and loss of political influence, 179, 182; no treatment of seriously ill patients before confession of sins, 170–171; perceived limitations of, 5; profiting from the plague, 135; re-defining syphilis as a "social scourge," 208, 218; regained authority with new knowledge of anatomy, 186; relationship with the priest, 171; tension between physicians and surgeons, 183; the power/knowledge factor, 15

medical profession: and psychosocial factors, 18; and repression of sexuality, 207; and stigmatization and exclusion, 16; as privy to the secrets of medicine, 178; debate on novelty or otherwise of syphilis, 195; diagnosis and control of new disorder of "madness," 214; emerged as a major influence in social control, 208; gradually displaced women in midwifery, 187; not gender-neutral, 16; shaping the socially constructed body, 15; specialized knowledge and great influence, 15; strong efforts to marginalize women practitioners, 186–187; subordination of the patient to the practitioner, 212–213

medical science: disentangled from teleological associations, 209; new reproductive technologies, 239; public confidence shaken, 4; the use of military metaphors, 247

medical theory and practice: advanced by the new universities of Europe, 166–167; and medicalization of the body, 189; and secularization of medicine, 189; and women's reproductive cycles, 202; changes due to the syphilis epidemic, 194; consensus view that syphilis was a new disease, 195; diagnosis by external observation, 165; distinction between physicians and surgeons, 172–173; exercising control over body openings, 171; fifteenth century connection between menstrual blood and syphilis, 203–204; "medical dehumanization," 17; medicalization of bodily disorders, 164, 189; of the Middle Ages, 164–166; medicalization of the illness experience, 15; new protocols for touching a patient's body, 212; sexual relations with women and plague infection, 178; shaped by moral precepts of the Church, 164; use of blood letting, purging, and diets, 168; women's disorders in the twentieth century, 16

medicalized body, the, 15–17, 164, 189; an outcome of medicalization

monastic medicine: practitioners of, 47, 49

Mellor, Philip, 24

men: age at marriage, 90; and chastity, 37; and perceptions of inherent superiority, 222; at center of religious and secular rituals, 125; dominant position supported by dualism of gender, 8; led into sexual temptation by women, 79; occupied public space, 125; temptations of novices, 70; shaping societal behavioral norms, 218, 223

mendicant friars: creation of Orders, 74–76; denouncing sinful behavior, 69; Dominican and Franciscan

mendicant friars *(continued)*
Orders, 69, 77; and heretics, 112; and lay participation in religious rituals, 75; and penitential processions, 115; reputations as preachers, 69; preaching against the temptations of sex, 67–69; strident denunciation of deviant sexual behavior, 121; strong links with local communities, 69, 75

menstrual blood: affecting offspring, 39; and defilement, 36; and syphilis, 203; and taboos, 35; ambivalent attitudes to, 168; as a danger to men, 35–36; as a plague precaution, 163, 168; as containing a poison, 202–203

menstruation: and sexual intercourse, 35, 39; as defilement, 36; medieval Church and menstruating women, 36; monstrous births from sexual relations during, 202; post menopausal women most dangerous, 140

miasmas: causing humoural imbalance, 167, 180. *See also* atmosphere, pestilential

Michelangelo, 99–100, 185

millennial concerns: at the turn of the century, 233

millennial dreams: inspiring popular religious demonstrations, 107

modern body, the, 21–25; emergence of, 4; preoccupation with self-realization and self-identity, 21

modernism: and the body, 6–7

monastic medicine: challenged, 166; fees for service banned, 169; practitioners of, 47, 49; surgery banned by the Church, 170

Monastic Orders, 47

Mondino de' Luzzi, 174

morality: sixteenth century attitudes, 219–221; sixteenth century standards of modesty, 221

Morelli, Giovanni di Pagolo, 147–148, 179

Morgagni, Giovanni, 184

Morse, Stephen S., 246

Muratori, Ludovico, 146–147, 177

natural events: as portents of disaster, 79

Odo of Cluny, 61

old women: as highly dangerous to the community, 140; their destructive powers, 140

O'Neill, John, 6, 14–15

one-sex model, the, 9, 33–34: and disordered bodies, 36; displaced after the Enlightenment, 10; legitimating male supremacy, 34; women's bodies as "defective," 35; of illness, 15; and high technology developments, 17; important construct of theories of the body, 15

origins of syphilis: associated with New World explorations, 195; counter-arguments against the Columbian connection, 196; the Unitarian theory, 196

orphans: charity and begging, 91

Original Sin: Eve's actions visited on all women, 37–38

Otherness: and biomedical discourse, 248–249; and changing socio-cultural values, 7, 28; and differences between male and female bodies, 20, 25; and epidemic diseases, 25; a term now including viruses, 234; bans on travellers from centers affected by plague, 93; boundaries between self and the Other, 248; concepts of "inclusion" and "exclusion, 29; foreigners as a suspect group, 150; of lepers, 55; of the poor, 147; medieval walls and inclusion/exclusion, 63; strangers blamed for spreading plague in Asia Minor, 82, 92; syphilis infection from a far-off land, 196; syphilis infection from outside the community, 196–197

outsiders: as dangerous others, 149–150; controls not applied consistently, 150; evidence of class bias in classifying as, 150; those beyond the city walls, 159; travellers from plague areas as vectors of disease, 149

Palmieri, Matteo, 127
Parfrey, Adam, 236
Partner, Peter, 215
Passavanti, Jacopo: on vileness of the
    body, 101
penitential exercises, 108–110;
    flagellation as most frequent
    practice, 114; public displays
    inspired by itinerant preachers, 108;
    public processions a regular feature
    of Florentine life, 113, 115–116
penitentials, 71; on pre-Christian
    practices, 106
persecution: Mendicant Orders
    pursuing heretics, 112; of deviants
    and heretics, 111; of subversive
    voices by the Church, 111; of women
    as witches, 111
pestilence, 57; arrival at Genoa, 87;
    travelling from China to Europe
    with trail of death, 81
Petrarch, Francesco, 179; Black Death
    as God's punishment, 86; description
    of plague's effects, 84; on the
    fragility of the body, 91; sudden
    deaths of some plague vitims, 85–86;
    victims not always deserted, 85
physicians: and the definition of illness,
    230; College of Physicians, 186;
    correcting imbalance of humours,
    172; differentiated from surgeons,
    172–173; status and power enhanced
    within expanded hospital system,
    187
Pitti, Buonaccorso, 120
plague: and increased masculinization
    of Florentine society, 127; appeared
    in three forms, 176; did not
    disappear after the Black Death,
    87–88; enforcing plague control
    measures, 139, 158; entrenched
    male supremacy in the community,
    125; family and community
    responses, 84; horrendous death
    toll, 84; of major concern to
    Florentine authorities, 132;
    overwhelming number of bodies for
    burial, 93; perceived as a disease of
    the poor, 147; profiting from the
    epidemics, 135–136; provided

challenges to the credibility of the
    clergy, 119–120; restrictive
    measures directed against women,
    130; roving bands of parentless
    children, 91; the epidemic moving
    from Asia to Europe, 92–93
plague officers, 143–144; and
    prohibition of traditional assemblies,
    158–159; established precedent for
    permanent health boards, 143; first
    permanent group appointed in the
    sixteenth century, 143; initially *ad
    hoc* groups only, 142; punitive
    powers of, 149
plague regulations: as social controls
    also, 145; confinement of victims of
    plague, 144–145; harsh penalties for
    the poor, 149; initially enforced by
    an existing magistracy, 142; many
    public gatherings prohibited, 158;
    prohibitions in force in Florence,142,
    158–159; targeted at specific groups,
    146–147; victims to display
    distinguishing signs, 144
plague symptoms: contemporary
    accounts of signs, 95; described, 176;
    terror felt when signs of disease
    appeared, 95; three forms of plague,
    96
Plumwood, Val, 8
Poison-Damsel, 38–39, 201–202, 218;
    and leprosy, 51; popularity of legend
    in the Middle Ages, 39
polluted bodies: regulating, 151–156
poor, the: near destitution during
    plague epidemics, 135; perceived as
    principal vectors of plague
    transmission, 146–149; perceived
    threat to stability of Florence, 135;
    principal targets of surveillance and
    constraint, 139; State management
    of, during plague epidemics,
    138–140; temporary dependence on,
    during plague epidemics, 136; their
    "impure" bodies to be segregated,
    144, 147, 158–160; their perceived
    Otherness, 147
popolo minuto, 131, 139. *See* class
    relations
postmodernism: and the body, 7

poverty: bearing the "stain of sin," 107; high level in Florence, 131; near destitution of many during the Middle Ages, 107

presentation of the body: definitions of seemly attire and decorous conduct, 220–221; the wearing of wigs by men and women, 227; women to be feminine, not provocative, 223–224; women to exercise restraint and decorum, 104

Preston, Richard, 242–243

privatization of the body, 21; as part of the sixteenth century civilizing of the body, 221; maintaining appropriate social distance, 209, 226

processions, religious: boys dressed in white as sign of their bodily purity, 119; carried images of the Virgin and sacred relics, 117; in Florence, 87; public penitential processions to placate God, 108, 115–116; segregation of sexes to avoid perceptions of sexual laxness, 116; to show community solidarity, 116

prostitutes, 151–153,156; and health checks for syphilis, 217; as challenge to social order, 216; as main danger to men at the close of the nineteenth century, 236; as worst example of uncontrolled female sexuality, 215; banished from Florence during crises, 79; fear that their "unclean" bodies might transmit plague, 153; large increase in numbers in the sixteenth century, 215–216; linked to spread of syphilis, 216; penitent prostitutes, 218; refuges for the reformed, 141; required to wear distinguishing clothing, 130, 151; their sexualized bodies, 160

prostitution: and the discourse of pollution, 236; as a necessary evil, 151; as a social problem for State and Church, 218; evidence for prosecution, 64; increased concern in the sixteenth century, 215–216; made illegal by many European governments during the sixteenth century, 217; not illegal in medieval Florence, 151

public health discourse: at variance with fifteenth century medical discourse, 158; closure of public bath-houses to limit the spread of syphilis, 217, 226; contagion as means of disease transmission, 143, 180

punishment: disproportionate levels inflicted on women, 141; enforcing plague regulations with harsh punishment, 149

quarantine: arresting the spread of plague, 146

Reformation and Counter Reformation, 120; repressive attitude toward the body and sexuality, 13, 219; the sanctity of marriage and the virtues of motherhood, 224

Régnier-Bohler, Danielle, 126

Regulating the Sexualized Body, 121–125

religious discourse: and astral influences, 43–44; body openings as entry points for sin, 171; conflicting discourses on religious issues, 105; contaminating effects of the female body, 36; continued to shape perceptions of the body, 100; "demonizing" sex, 36; denunciations of all non-procreative sex, 77; divine punishment discourse, 42–43; incorporation within the Church of some groups with a dissenting discourse, 112; increased prominence given to repentance, 75–76; legitimating control of women's sexuality, 37; Man as representing "mind" and "soul," 37; new avenues for salvation, 72; on public displays of the female body, 104; perceptions of the body and its sexuality, 36; shaping medieval medical theory and practice, 165; the body as God's sacred handiwork, 164–165; the one-sex model, 36, 37; trend to sexualization of sin, 76; virginity as the ideal, 36; Woman as helpmate of Man, 102; Woman as symbol of "body," 37

religious rituals: for repentance, 72; frequent recourse to, 87; lacking at mass burials, 93; seemingly ineffective against the plague, 87

renunciation of the body: recommended by the Church, 36; secularization of moral laws, 130; suppressing desires of the flesh, 123; to constrain passion and reduce temptation, 122; the superiority of virginity, 122

repentance: individual and collective rituals, 87; public rituals of, 107–111, 132

Rocke, Michael: on homosexuality in Florence, 154

Russo, Mary, 20

Salimbene de Adam, 64, 76–77, 108, 174

Sartelle, Joe, 235

Sartre, Jean-Paul: the body and identity, 1; obscenity of the female body, 20

Savonarola, Girolamo, 121–125 153, 159; bands of boys as reformers, 124–125; morals campaign against lust and sodomy, 123

"sealed" body, the, 171; and virginity, 172; concept challenged by syphilis, 205; literary metaphors for, 172; little interest in exploring its contents before the late Middle Ages, 173 ; no intrusion by human agencies, 173

Secretum Secretorum, 38

secular medicine: and monastic medical practice, 169; based on Galenic concepts, 166; its revival in the ninth century, 166

sexual activities: constrained by religion, law, and medical injunctions, 13; early recognition of role in syphilis transmission, 195; of

prostitutes and homosexuals as a threat to the community, 151, 153, 160

sexual intercourse: and leprosy, 51; abstinence advised, 163, 178; as ritual defilement, 36; debilitating effects, 37, 178; denunciations of all but procreative sex, 77; generally deemed shameful, 122; harmful to body and soul, 102; perceived debilitating effects, 102; to be avoided to escape syphilis, 209; to be free of affection, 77

sexual practices: involvement of governments in regulation of, 13–14

sexual restraint: by fasting and denial of the body, 122; calls for, 103; general population rejected calls for, 106

sexuality of men: blamed initially for the spread of syphilis, 198

sexuality of women: and blame for the spread of syphilis, 199–200; and leprosy, 50; as a danger to men, 37; as factor in persecution of witches, 105; as an abomination, 100; led by their passions, 102, 127; sumptuary laws to curb, 157–158; the virgin saint and the evil whore, 73; to be denied, 103; women as poisoners, 38; women as sexually voracious, 35

sexualized body, the, 12–15; a postmodern lethal object, 15; and State intervention, 14; of prostitutes and homosexuals, 156; twentieth century debate on conceptual basis of, 14, 29

shame, sense of: at deaths from plague, 95; at loss of hair from syphilis, 227; at the transformed body of the syphilitic, 207; the body's shameful parts, 35, 220; the Church and nudity, 220

Shilling, Chris, 13, 22, 24

Showalter, Elaine, 236–237, 239–240

Signoria: administrative role of, 286, n.14; paid for autopsies of plague victims, 183. *See also* commune

sinful behavior: changing concepts of sin in the Middle Ages, 67; late

sinful behavior *(continued)*
medieval focus on carnal sins, 67,
69–70; new ways of purging sins,
72–73; sins of the flesh, 77
Singer, Linda, 28–29, 237–238; and the
"age of the epidemic," 237
sins of the flesh, 102; high price to be
paid, 102
social diseases: and the sexualized
body, 27; syphilis as the first in
modern times, 194
social practices: and socially acceptable
behavior, 223–228; and State
intervention, 230; bathing the body
abandoned, 210, 227; decline in
intimate gestures of affection, 226;
maintaining a safe distance to avoid
syphilis, 226; no sharing of drinking
vessels, 226; powders and perfumes
as substitutes for bathing, 226;
preservation of personal space, 226;
recommendations of Erasmus,
227–228; wearing of wigs, 227
social structures, Florence, 13–14;
discontent within, 135; family
remained a patriarchal and patrilineal
institution, 90; the heterosexual
couple as "legitimate norm," 14; the
remasculinization of society, 255
sociology of the body: influence of
modernism, and postmodernism,
6–7; and feminism, 6
Sontag, Susan, 206, 233, 235, 247
Soranus: and the benefits of male
chastity, 37
State, the: and the medical profession
as a powerful duopoly, 230; avenues
for intervention expanded when
social problems are defined as
"epidemics," 237–238; convergence of
penal and public health systems,
143; emergence of new bureaucratic
control systems following epidemics,
137, 160; increased intervention in
community and Church affairs after
the plague, 160; increased
intervention following the syphilis
epidemic, 229
Stelarc: on repudiation of corporeality,
252–253

Strozzi, Alessandra, 148
Strozzi, Lorenzo, 135
supernatural, the: in agrarian religious
beliefs and Christian doctrine, 105
surgeons: and manipulation of the body,
172; computer technology and the
"digital surgeon," 249–250;
differentiated from physicians,
172–173; in the hospital system, 188
surveillance and constraint: of
confraternities, 139; of the poor, 139;
of those infected by plague, 144–146,
149; of women defying male
authority, 218
symptoms of syphilis: obvious to the
casual observer, 194–195; signs of
mental deterioration in tertiary
stage, 214
syphilis: acquired a variety of names,
193, 197; and its serpent metaphor,
204–205; and long-term medical
surveillance and intervention, 213;
and loss of hair, 227; as divine
punishment, 198, 207; a disfigured
and odorous body, 205–206; a
significant social issue at the close of
the nineteenth century, 236;
culpability shifted from men to
women, 199–200; development of
mutant strains, 194, 206; extensive
early documentation of the disease,
204; first appeared in Italy, 193;
first associated with small pox, 194;
gradually became less severe and
contagious, 206; high death toll in
early years of epidemic, 206; initially
viewed as a just punishment, 198;
more persistent than plague, 194;
progress of the disease, 205–206;
widespread incidence throughout
community, 199
Synnott, Anthony, 8, 16, 17

taboos, 35–36, 41
taverns: as meeting places for working
people, 136–137; closed during times
of crisis, 79, 132, 137; closed to limit
opportunities for prostitutes to meet
clients, 217

theories of disease causation, 32, 39,
    41–44, 50, 52; astral configuarions,
    166, 177; common theory prevailing
    in fourteenth century, 176;
    Fracastoro's germ theory, 208–210;
    gradual acceptance of concept of
    contagion by medical profession, 189;
    imbalance of bodily humours, 167
theory of the body. See body in social
    theory, the
Thomas Aquinas, Saint, 71, 151; and
    late medieval Church doctrine, 77;
    on prositution, 216; sexual relations
    harmful to body and soul, 102
touch: as a sensual act, 211; as an act of
    healing, 211; as an erotic act, 211,
    218; as dangerous, 211
transmission of syphilis: by prostitutes,
    216; perceived threat from outsiders,
    197
treatments: by removing pestilential
    atmospheres (miasmas), 167, 177; by
    restoration of humoural balances,
    167; improving lifestyles, 177;
    medical practitioners guided by
    astrological predictions, 177; no
    "magic bullet" cures, 5; use of
    arsenic as a contrary to ward off
    plague, 177; use of blood-letting,
    177; use of contraries, 177; using
    diets and drug therapies, 177; using
    pills, potions, and charms, 164, 180
Turner, Bryan S., 5–6, 13, 16, 34, 184,
    188; on control of the body by
    religion, 105, 122
two-sex model, the, 10, 254; defining
    gender roles in nineteenth century,
    11

vagrants and beggars: as dangerous
    others, 150; excluded from the city,
    150; with syphilis, compulsorily
    confined to hospitals, 213–214
Varchi, Benedetto, 96, 143–144, 148;
    flight of medical practitioners from
    the plague, 179
Vecchio, Silvana, 127
Vesalius: as founder of modern science
    of anatomy, 186

Villani, Giovanni: death from plague in
    1348, 85; enormous death foretold in
    the stars, 82; news of a great
    outbreak of pestilence in China,
    81–83; sinful behavior among
    Florentines responsible for various
    calamities, 78–79; views on
    Florence, 62
Villani, Matteo, 163, 179; brother of
    Giovanni, took over writing the
    Chronicles, 85; not all deserted sick
    relatives, 85; on bodily signs of
    plague, 96; on haste to marry after
    the Black Death, 90
Virgin Mary: and confraternities,
    112–113; and processions of
    repentance, 117; appeals to, seeking
    cures for disease or illness, 47; as
    example of ideal womanhood, 72;
    Cult of the Virgin Mary, 72;
    proliferation of images of the
    Madonna, 72; worshipped for her
    virginal state, 116
viruses: and apocalyptic messages in
    popular culture, 243; and
    catastrophic new plagues, 241;
    metaphorical relationship to
    femaleness, 242; and Otherness,
    234, 248
Visible Human Project, 250–251
voices of dissent: against deviant
    behavior of clergy, 106, 112; against
    efforts by the Church to control
    bodies, 105; deemed heretical by the
    Church, 111–112; imposing controls
    on women's voices, 105; itinerant
    preachers, 108; secular women of
    letters, 126; the Beguines, 104;
    women of the late Middle Ages, 104
vulnerability of the body, 5; to disease
    from sexual intercourse, 209–210

"wise women": and midwifery services,
    105; as community healers, 105;
    offering traditional treatments, 46,
    178–179; virulent attacks on, by
    male medical practitioners, 187. See
    also community healers
Wolff, Janet, 20

Woman: as an imperfect male, 34; as a
symbol of body, 37; as Other, and
syphilis, 200–202; as the archetypal
"disordered body," 37; as the
helpmmate of Man, 102; inherently
inferior to Man, 103

women: age at marriage, 90; and
leprosy, 50; and medical
surveillance, 239; and the serpent
methaphor, 38; as a danger to men,
73; as disordered and dangerous, 40,
57; as "failed" men, 34; as fragile and
without intellectual ability, 223; as
threat to men's spiritual condition,
102; confined to the private space of
home, 224; counselled to renounce
sex, 73; increasing focus on women's
bodies, 36–37; constantly under
surveillance of law makers, 140;
inherently inferior to men, 102;
institutions for those sexually
deviant or defying male authority,
218; loss of status and power after
plague, 127; marginalized in medical
practice, 186–187; men's efforts to
control women's bodies, 32;
punishment for sexual offenses, 141;
relegated to inferior positions, 37;
segregated in, or excluded from
public events, 126; should be in the
custody of a male relative, 140–141;
some as "pure" and "virginal," 116; to
deny their sexuality, 103; unattached
women viewed with suspicion, 140;
"wise women," 46; women's bodies,
32; women's bodies as signifiers of
difference, 36

women's demeanor: criticism of dress
and appearance during plague
epidemics, 156–158; modesty to be
highlight of, 104; to be restrained
when in public, 104, 124

women's role: contribution to the
Florentine economy, 131;
importance of reproductive processes
established by pre-Christian
religions, 105; procreation, 9, 14–15;
primarily as child bearers, 103; to
produce male heirs, 127

World Health Organization: and the
impact of infectious diseases,
245–246